SOCCER
SKILLS & TACTICS

by Ken Jones and Pat Welton
Introduction by Bill Nicholson
Foreword by Paul LeSueur

CROWN PUBLISHERS, INC. NEW YORK

INTRODUCTION

I have always felt that football is a game which repays the amount of work that an individual puts into it. If you are a young player, your performance will improve the more you endeavour to better your own skills and your understanding of the game. If you are one of football's millions of spectators, your enjoyment will increase the more you can comprehend what happens on the pitch in front of your eyes.

This book sets out to illustrate facets of the game which the professionals regard as important. It combines an outline of each aspect—from the offside trap to the overhead kick—with a coaching commentary. Colorful stories about the major exponents of each skill or tactic are backed up by expert articles showing how you and your team can reap the benefit.

As any manager will tell you, theory is only valuable when it can be put into practice on the field. Therefore, this is no text-book, more a practical manual which will enable you to get the best, at any level, out of your favorite game.

W Nicholson

OF TOTTENHAM HOTSPUR AND ENGLAND

Edited by Martin Tyler

First published in the United States
by Crown Publishers, Inc 1976
Second U.S. printing 1977

© Marshall Cavendish Limited
1971, 1972, 1973, 1974, 1975, 1976, 1977

Printed in Great Britain

This edition is not to be sold outside the United
States of America, Canada and the Philippines

Library of Congress Cataloging in Publication Data

Jones, Ken
Soccer Skills and Tactics

   1. Soccer. I. Welton, Pat., joint author.
II. Title.
GV943. J54 1976 796.33'42 75–44289

ISBN 0-517-52594-1 (cloth)
ISBN 0-517-529149 (paper)

Foreword by Paul LeSueur

Football is recognized as the national game in approximately 80 countries. Usually called soccer in the United States, it now the fastest growing American sport. Both amateur and semi-professional soccer began expanding here slowly in the early 1900s. However, at the professional level, the game failed to take hold until the 1970s. Prior to this time the 'foreign game' of soccer attracted only small numbers of spectators, mostly immigrants from the countries in which the sport was so popular.

Growth at the professional level has been accompanied by a rapid expansion of high school and college play. Two professional leagues were founded and are still operating: the American Soccer League (ASL) dating back to the 1930s and the more successful North American Soccer League (NASL) presently consisting of twenty full-time professional teams.

This book, probably one of the most comprehensive ever prepared for any sport, was written for the British soccer market—coach, player and fan. Upon careful examination the decision was made to publish it in the USA without change because the values of the book are universal, and its principles can be applied to soccer wherever it is played.

The coach is given the most complete and scientific analysis of the game, ranging from the skill of dribbling to the more complex tactical aspects. The player will benefit from an increased depth of understanding in both skills and strategy. The fan can add to his enjoyment by becoming familiar with the very matters affecting coach and players.

Soccer Skills and Tactics, which might be considered a completely up-to-date coaching manual, is valuable and adaptable for both the soccer beginner and the more seasoned professional. It treats six areas of skills and tactics, drawing from the experience of the world's top soccer professionals. Each section is introduced with a piece of relevant soccer history, providing the reader with some behind-the-scenes insight, the atmosphere of excitement and color that can be found only in the art of soccer. The reader will be able to relive some of the great moments including the feats of such soccer giants as Pele, Banks, Best, Law, Puskas and Beckenbauer.

As a proper analysis should, the book not only explains the players' strengths but also exposes their limitations. Each section is supplemented with full-color, self explanatory diagrams which allow the reader to visualize actual game situations. Finally, a coaching inset concludes each section, providing important information about the improvement of training techniques to increase player performance, especially under game situations. These insets also present modern drills and exercises, adding variation and fun to training routines as opposed to the stale, traditional approach.

It is most important at this stage of our soccer development to increase our knowledge and experience of soccer skills and tactics, especially if the United States is to be able to compete on the same level with the rest of the footballing world. This book is one step toward that goal.

Surely, other American sport texts could learn from this educational soccer bible—a must for the library of any soccer enthusiast.

CONTENTS

Set-piece play

Striking at goal

Team tactics

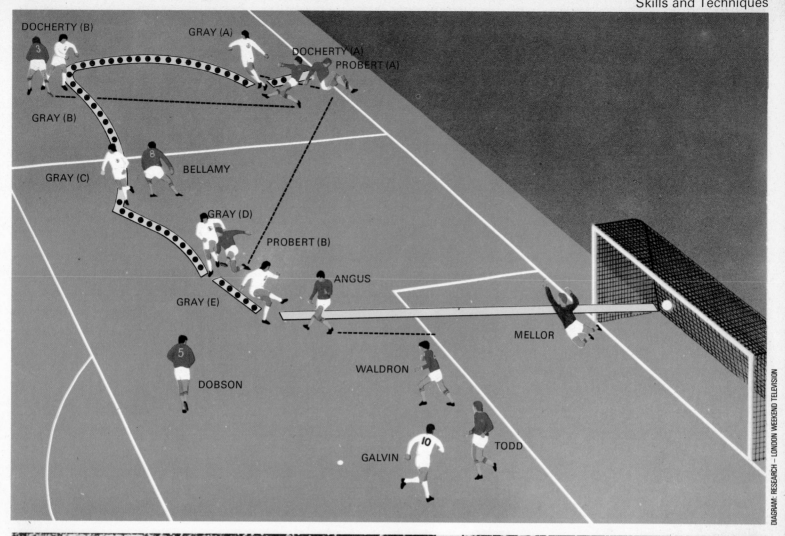

Labels in diagram: DOCHERTY (B), GRAY (A), DOCHERTY (A), PROBERT (A), GRAY (B), BELLAMY, GRAY (C), GRAY (D), PROBERT (B), ANGUS, GRAY (E), MELLOR, DOBSON, WALDRON, GALVIN, TODD

DIAGRAM: RESEARCH – LONDON WEEKEND TELEVISION

THE YORKSHIRE POST

Running with the ball — the dribble

Top Diagram of a superb solo goal by Eddie Gray for Leeds United against Burnley in 1970.
Above Gray (hidden behind No 4, Waldron) cracks his final shot past Burnley keeper Mellor.

As Leeds fidgeted through the dressing-room build-up to the 1970 FA Cup Final against Chelsea, their manager Don Revie issued precise instructions to left-winger Eddie Gray.

The order was shatteringly simple: 'You have got the skill to take them on and tear them apart. Go out there and do it.'

Gray was a Scottish international. Tall for a winger, he was beautifully balanced and he had a magical touch on the ball. Only his temperament had prevented him from emerging as one of the outstanding artists in British football—an artist in what had seemed a dying art, the skill of dribbling.

That Cup Final was to confirm that Gray had conquered self-doubt. Had there been any justice Leeds would have won the Cup, and Gray would have been seen to have done more than any other player to achieve that end. Chelsea were more than aware of what Gray could do. His talent was clear enough, and it had been presented in spectacular fashion a few weeks earlier.

Playing against Burnley at Elland Road he suddenly produced an astonishing dribble which brought him a goal and the crowd to their feet in thunderous acclaim. Gray had already scored what Revie regards as one of the finest goals he has seen—a thirty-yard chip which carried just beneath Burnley's crossbar with the goalkeeper caught off his line.

Revie recalled: 'Eddie looked up and saw that a chip was on. Its execution was perfect and only a player with such great skill and confidence would have attempted it.'

Gray was quickly to prove again that he had an abundance of both these qualities. Burnley were in no great danger when Gray collected the ball close to their right corner-flag. They were back in strength, and it looked as though a burst of machine-gun fire would be needed to clear their penalty area. Gray had other ideas.

He began by rolling the ball beneath his left foot. As he did so, his shoulders swayed. He was on his toes, inviting challenge. Had the young Burnley defenders simply stood still they would have survived.

7

DIAGRAM

Above *Diagram of George Best's magnificent individual goal that ended Sheffield United's unbeaten run at the start of the 1971-72 season.*
Right *The Best run that destroyed Sheffield United.*

COLORSPORT

But they were betrayed by their eagerness. Probert, Docherty, Bellamy, Probert again and then Angus hurled themselves in to try and win the ball, and one by one they were dismissed by Gray's skills. A smooth drag back with the sole of the foot left two of them flailing at a ball that was no longer there. Gray was now in full bloom. There was nothing hurried or untidy about it. In fact Burnley were almost destroyed in slow motion, as the Leeds winger picked his way through them.

When he finished with a scoring shot the crowd were for a second stunned. Then, as Gray loped away, one hand raised in self-salute, they roared their appreciation. Revie said: 'It was magic. In those few seconds Eddie confirmed all the things we knew about him.'

The Cup Final was to underline Gray's talent. His immediate opponent was David Webb, a burly, aggressive defender whose style was essentially intimidating. Webb set out to stifle Gray's dribbles at birth. He committed himself to early tackles, but the Leeds man was in no mood to be put off. Webb was to spend much of the match floundering on his backside.

But for all Gray's magic Chelsea survived and went on to win the replay at Old Trafford. It was significant that they chose to rearrange their defenders for the second match. Webb became one of the central defenders, and Ron Harris was brought in to do a more physical job of marking Gray.

Dribbling had become something of a luxury skill in England. It was seen by many managers as an unnecessary interruption of team play, and few of them were willing to license this form of individual expression. Football, they argued, was a team game, and accurate passing was the most essential feature of the game. The argument was supported by the common character of great dribblers. Aware of their skill on the ball, the majority of them were self-indulgent.

Many coaches dismissed them as players who could charm crowds out of their seats, but who made little definite contribution to the cause. It was even argued that Stanley Matthews, immortalized by the description 'Wizard of the Dribble', would have struggled in the modern game. Matthews was still mesmerizing defences when in his forties. An unlikely looking athlete, he shuffled clear of tackles, and great speed from a standing start took him in behind defences. Subsequently knighted, Matthews disappeared in the mid-sixties and, although others imitated him, dribbling soon became an unfamiliar problem for British defenders.

Elsewhere the skill was still looked upon as a valued asset. In Scotland, a succession of pattern-weaving wingers from Alan Morton to Jimmy Johnstone were given rein to develop their individual talents. The Brazilians also used the skill well, and in Garrincha, an illiterate Indian, they had one of the great dribblers of all time.

However extravagant their individual tech-nique, the Brazilians gave their collective game much thought. They saw that Garrincha, with his curiously deformed physique, had the ability to tear the guts out of opposing defences. They simply gave him the ball, and let him play.

Feola, a portly, unlikely looking team manager, who was to be deposed following Brazil's miserable displays during the 1966 World Cup in England, said: 'We don't attempt to support Garrincha. He attracts defenders to him, and we make sure that he has space in which to try and destroy them.' Destroy them he did until domestic upheaval undermined his talent.

It was probably the arrival of George Best which led to a revival of the dribbler's art in the Football League. Best could not have gone to a more productive environment when he left Belfast to join Manchester United. Within a few months Best had given notice of an exceptional talent. Five-a-side training games developed into a contest of who could take the ball from him, and United's management did nothing to stifle his skills.

They gave him his head, and he was to come through as a player worthy of world stature. Best could be irritatingly selfish. Pat Crerand, a talented, thinking midfield player said of him: 'There are times when you want to wring his neck. He hangs on to the ball when other players have found better positions, and you know that these players will not keep running into space if they aren't going to get the ball. Then out of the blue he does something which wins the match. It's then that you know you are in the presence of something exceptional.'

Best's ability to win a game out of nothing was never more vividly demonstrated than when Manchester United beat Sheffield United at Old Trafford in the autumn of 1971. Sheffield had made a remarkable start to the season. Newly promoted, they were top of the First Division and unbeaten when they took on a Manchester United side that had been revitalized by a new manager, Frank O'Farrell, and a new coach, Malcolm Musgrove.

It was stalemate when Best received the ball just inside the Sheffield half of the field. Sheffield had just replaced injured left-back Ted Hemsley with a substitute forward, Gil Reece. Best was to benefit from it, but not before he had confirmed the murderous extent of his individuality. Where other players might have elected to pass, Best simply ran on, first past Geoff Salmons. His marvellous balance enabled him to survive as Hockey and Colquhoun moved across to cover.

George Best inspired coaches to rediscover a forgotten art

Sheffield United were suddenly in confusion, and Best, although gradually pushed wide to his right, was still running within range of goal. Had Hemsley still been on the field he might have picked off Best's dribble with an instinctive covering position. But Reece was not in tune with a situation foreign to him, and Best was left with an angle for a shot. Goalkeeper Hope plunged out at Best's feet, but he drove the ball into the net off the inside of the far post. The little Irishman had been consistently involved in such moments, and other clubs had begun to look for players who could make the running on their own.

Best's self-indulgent nature was more than balanced by his effectiveness as a goalscorer. It was an unusual combination. Arsenal paid £100,000 to Hibernian for Peter Marinello, a fine dribbler, but he could not settle down to play consistently in English football.

Chelsea had Charlie Cooke, whose superb close control and body balance was a decisive factor when they beat Real Madrid in the final of the European Cup Winners Cup in the summer of 1971. Cooke was infuriatingly inconsistent. On his day he could run through a team, but there were too many days when he was lost on the fringe of the contest.

Cooke had a curious problem. He recognized the need to blend his talent into team play. But it became an obsession with him. An articulate man, he could find no real justification for his rare skills. He looked too hard for an answer, and in looking he fell short of being the player he could have been.

But the need to find a way through astutely organized defences breathed new life into the dribblers' skills. Men like Matthews, Tom Finney, Len Shackleton and David Jack had made an indelible impression in their day. Jimmy Greaves had scored great goals without assistance, and Best and Cooke had been able to emphasize their value.

Leeds, a team steeped in system football and team-work, found a place for a dribbler, and Don Revie indicated the thoroughness with which he approached the game when he said: 'Dribbling has become a lost art because we have tended to discourage it. But players who can make themselves something out of nothing close to goal must be influential and must be given licence.' The public at large, bored by the unsmiling nature of the game, were in no way put out by the prospect.

Coaching: Learn how to carry the ball and attack defenders

One of the most thrilling sights in football is that of a Charlton, a Gray or a Chivers in full flight with the ball under total control, twisting by a string of opponents and unleashing an unstoppable shot at goal.

Looking at these players you will note they always know where they are going, and they have the ability to work the ball fluently. The important quality to cultivate is of manipulating the ball whilst moving at speed.

Whenever you possibly can, work with a ball. This will help cultivate its feel, and help you to learn to lift your head from time to time whilst you play the ball so that you can look around. Practise with both feet—using both the inside and outside as well as the full instep, pushing the ball directly in front of your movement. Begin by walking with it, then go on to jogging, then to running fast. The position of your upper body is important; it must be inclining slightly forward. A basic point you will be learning here is that it is much harder to run with the ball than without it, so in a game only run with the ball when you have something definite in mind, and you think something positive can be accomplished.

In dribbling you must concentrate on keeping the ball close to you, away from opponents. Keep your eyes on the ball when you are making contact, but in between two touches look up for a split second to see what is going on around you. Not looking up is a basic fault amongst many young players. Remember not to hold your ankle too stiff on contact or your touch will be too firm, and you will push the ball too far in front of you.

Having worked at keeping the ball under control without breaking the rhythm and swing of your stride, work with a dozen team-mates in the centre-circle. Everyone has a ball, and the idea is to move about without running into each other or losing your ball. Try to develop a change of pace. On a given signal every player must turn and sprint for a few yards, again without body contact. You can play a game where the idea is to kick everybody else's ball out of the circle whilst keeping control of your own. After a specified period, ten or fifteen minutes perhaps, the player who has lost his ball the least number of times is the winner. The centre-circle is an ideal area to use for all sorts of dribbling activities.

You should now be ready to face an opponent. This is where your unpredictable change of pace is of the utmost importance, and you will need to cultivate a body swerve to wrongfoot an opponent.

Speed of running is mainly natural, but speed off the mark can be improved with quicker speed of thought and constant practice. There are numerous small games that will help and be interesting. Draw a circle about five or six feet in radius on the ground. A stick is planted in the middle of a smaller circle within the big circle. Two players face one another on each side of the stick, and the idea is for one player to try to catch the other player without knocking the stick over or putting a foot in the smaller circle.

One player approaches another who is retreating in a channel about four or five yards wide. The idea is to go past the retreating player without being caught. To be successful you will have to feint to go down one side, then quickly change direction to dart down the other side.

Now practise sending an opponent the wrong way whilst manipulating a ball. Draw a line on the ground about ten yards long. The bye-line between the goal and penalty area can be used. You stand one side of the line with a ball whilst your pal stands the other side. The idea is for you to get the ball to the end of the line before your pal. Now, your pal does not know which way you are going, so you must work the ball making your pal think you are going one way then go quickly the other. No tackling is allowed unless the ball crosses the line. There are many ways to wrongfoot your pal. Go to your local professional club the next time they are playing at home, and watch very closely. You will pick up lots of ideas, and practice will soon make you aware of the best methods for you. A word of warning—the effectiveness of your feints will not always be determined by their quality. The results they produce will depend to a great extent on the reactions of the opposition. It is not a simple matter of the better the opponent, the better the feint required to beat him. Good feints will often fail to take you past inferior players.

You should now be ready for the real thing, to take on an opponent and get a shot in at goal. Stand on the half-way line whilst your partner stands just outside the penalty area with a ball. He plays the ball to you, then acts as a defender. You should have enough confidence to move on to the ball, control it in your stride, go at speed at the defender just at the right moment, change direction with a sudden burst of speed past him and hit the ball hard at goal. Retrieve the ball and change functions.

Move on to playing a six-a-side game in which each player must take on an opponent before passing or else his side forfeits possession. One final practice is to play a game where no passing is allowed, and you must dribble the ball until you lose it. These games will bring out the qualities you need—balance, control, acceleration.

Practise on these lines and, when in a game you have a definite purpose in mind, you will be able to run full tilt at a defence and set up the chance for a spectacular goal.

Below Diagram showing a training routine for practising dribbling. A dozen players, each with a ball, move about in the centre-circle avoiding each other, each keeping their own ball under tight control.

Labels on diagram: GRAY, NEWTON, GILZEAN, LABONE (5), PETERS (11), MOORE (6), BANKS, STEIN (9), COOPER (3)

Heading for goal

Sir Alf Ramsey had been England's team manager for six years and had won the World Cup before he saw the Scots put to flight at Wembley.

Beating them had by then become something of an obsession with him. The Scots, failures in the wider field of international football, had still been able to raise their game when confronted with their oldest enemy.

England had only beaten them once during Ramsey's reign, but never at Wembley. The sequence of disappointment ended on a May evening in 1969, when Scotland were finally overwhelmed by the certainty of England's shooting.

Yet even as they stumbled towards a humiliating defeat, which was to undermine their attempt to qualify for the World Cup the following year, they managed to score one memorable goal—from a classic header at the far post.

The scorer was Colin Stein, a tall, industrious attacker who had cost his club, Rangers, the first six-figure fee ever to be paid between two Scottish clubs.

Stein looked the type of player who would have done well in the English game. He was a good runner whose willingness to hunt out space made him difficult to contain. He was immensely strong in the air. And it was this particular talent which was to temporarily disrupt the flow of England's football, and, for a few minutes, threaten Ramsey's

coveted win.

England had already scored twice when Stein suddenly set off on a run that was to provide Eddie Gray with the opportunity to display his remarkable accuracy. An articulate left winger who had made his mark with Leeds, Gray had been brought in to bring balance and discipline to Scotland's midfield play.

But Gray was essentially an attacker, a man who could destroy the most certain defenders with a silky swerve and definitive dribbling. He could also cross a good ball. The one he crossed into Stein's path from way out by the left corner-flag threw England into confusion.

He aimed the ball into a space deep by the far post, far enough from goal to stop Gordon Banks from moving out to make a catch.

It was then that Stein pounced, shrugging off the challenge of left-back Terry Cooper. He soared upwards to direct the ball back beyond Banks' right hand into the far side of the goal with a thrust of his blond head.

There have been few better examples of a player making full use of opportunity when blessed with the equipment to do the job. It proved, too, that while centres to the far post might have fallen from fashion in the late sixties they were still deadly when there were players capable of dealing with them.

After the 1966 World Cup a more subtle note had been injected into attacks aimed in from the flanks. Keen observers had noted that the legendary Hungarians picked up goals by attacking the near post. They were simply capitalizing on habit. When the ball was out wide on the touchlines, defenders automatically positioned themselves to deal with the centre lofted to the far side of the penalty area.

By sending men in to attack the ball driven at the nearer post the Hungarians added a new dimension to angled assaults.

English teams picked it up quickly. But the best of them did not ignore the more traditional alternative. West Ham, for instance, registered many vital goals out of Geoff Hurst's brave keenness to move in on to passes which the astute Martin Peters dropped short at the near post in front of defenders.

But they varied their attacks, and opponents suddenly found themselves being outjumped and outheaded at the far post in an area they had temporarily forsaken.

Ron Greenwood, West Ham's manager, said at the time: 'We had gained a big reputation for scoring goals at the near post. Teams were waiting for us to drop the ball short. So we simply attacked the far side of the goal. It was all a question of common sense.'

An equally perceptive comment was made by Bill Nicholson, whose record of achievement as Spurs' manager made him one of the most important figures in the game. Nicholson's teams were not only successful, they were also appealing. Spurs assembled their attacks with silky smooth passing movements that depended upon accuracy, mobility and confidence.

But they never ignored the fundamental

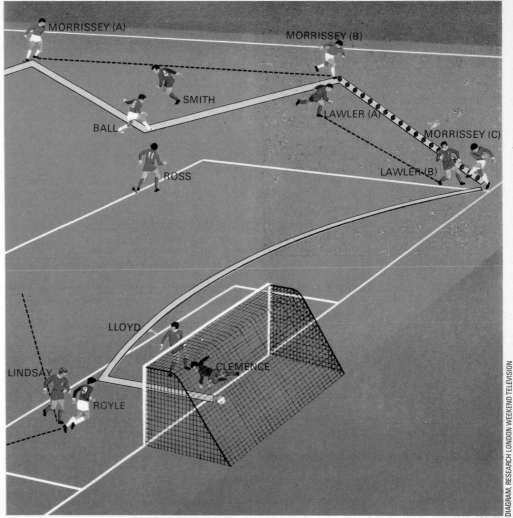

Diagram labels: MORRISSEY (A), MORRISSEY (B), SMITH, BALL, LAWLER (A), MORRISSEY (C), LAWLER (B), ROSS, LLOYD, LINDSAY, CLEMENCE, ROYLE

GARY TALBOT

DIAGRAM, RESEARCH LONDON WEEKEND TELEVISION

PRESS ASSOCIATION

Above left Joe Royle, at Liverpool's far post, heads Everton into a 2-0 lead at Anfield in 1970.
Above Diagram of the move that led up to Royle's goal. Johnny Morrissey got to the bye-line, and his deep cross gave Royle the chance.

principles of play. Many of their goals were scored on the far post and, in a Nicholson side, there was always at least one player capable of delivering powerful headers.

Nicholson said: 'No matter how the game evolves tactically the fundamental principles will always apply. There will always be a need for defenders who are capable of dealing with attacks through the air and for forwards who can make those kind of attacks pay off.'

Spurs were never short of those kind of players and, in Welsh international Cliff Jones, at first sight an unlikely looking danger in the air, they had one who was outstanding.

Devastating pace helped to make Jones a world class player, but it was his courage and athleticism which made him a great goalscorer.

Although he was only five feet seven inches tall, Jones could outjump almost anyone. He was a constant danger when coming in at the far post

and his fearless nature took him into scoring positions that were continually scorned by others less brave.

Spurs capitalized on this talent splendidly. They had a brilliant, creative forward in John White, who was to be tragically struck down by lightning in the prime of his career. They also had an intimidating attacker in Bobby Smith, whose muscular aggression could unsettle the most composed defences. Indeed there was almost a note of predictability about many of Tottenham's attacks. White, who had a talent for freeing himself from marking, would drift clear to the flanks where he could receive the ball and make an angle for a centre.

Smith's belligerent challenge would cause panic beneath the ball as it came in, and then Jones would suddenly arrive above the confusion to flash his forehead at the ball—even if it meant, as it invariably did, diving forward over the backs

and shoulders of defenders.

Jimmy Murphy, for many years the Welsh team manager, said of Jones:

'He got goals out of nothing because he was always looking to make things happen. He was the classic example of what a player can achieve if he can marry courage to skill. There have been few better in the air. Considering his lack of inches he was phenomenal.'

Murphy did not have to look far to find another in the same mould. As assistant to Matt Busby at Manchester United he had much to do with the deal which brought Denis Law back from Turin to play with sustained authority at Old Trafford. Law, like Jones, was not particularly tall. Indeed, he had not been outstanding in the air when he left Manchester City for Turin. But hours of practice and his fearless approach led to him becoming as respected as any of the great far post forwards.

Whereas Jones seemed to swim through the air Law fought his way upwards. In a crowded goalmouth his blond head would suddenly wriggle free to get the vital touch into goal. These two fine players were exceptional because of their prodigous leaping power.

But it was inevitable that the tall and the powerful should emerge as great players when their heading ability was included in a comprehensive range of talent.

In the nineteen thirties, Everton were fortunate in being able to span a decade with two of the most devastating far post attackers the game has ever seen.

Billy 'Dixie' Dean was not as tall as most people supposed. But it was when he rose to meet the ball that he stood head and shoulders above everyone. Dean played many times for England

11

Coaching: Learn to use your head and increase your power in the air

Above Peter Osgood of Chelsea climbs high to send in a characteristic far post header.

as did his successor, Tommy Lawton. As a youngster who arrived from Burnley he studied every aspect of Dean's talent and power. He knew that Dean did not get into the air by accident. He worked at it. Dean could jump off two feet onto a billiard table. Lawton tried it too.

Both of them seemed to hang in the air. It was an illusion created by the excellence of their timing. It has been said that they were on the way up to the ball while defenders were already on their way down. A more accurate point is that they got to the ball first.

Everton supporters who had lived through the days of Dean and Lawton could have been forgiven a sudden spasm of excitement and expectation when Joe Royle was introduced to their team in the sixties.

If he never really matched up to his illustrious predecessors, he still scored many fine goals, and he reserved a splendid effort for a local derby against Liverpool in 1970.

These games are always very special affairs, completely dividing a city. This one was to be even more special than the rest.

It was played at Anfield and by half way through the second half Everton, the visitors, were in front by two goals.

The second of these goals came from Royle's head. John Morrissey a combative and skilful little winger who had been signed from Liverpool some years previously played a wall pass with Alan Ball. The return pass got him in behind the Liverpool defence. He raced to the bye-line.

His centre was lofted to the far post, and, as the Liverpool defenders twisted beneath it, Royle rose high and confidently to head a marvellous goal.

Liverpool recovered to take the match by 3-2, but Royle had a permanent place in the memory of a wonderfully competitive game.

A place in Brazil's repertoire of exciting and convincing skills was reserved for the far post header. A superb effort at Italy's far post by Pele put Brazil on the way to triumph in the 1970 World Cup final in Mexico City, and players with the ability to outjump defenders in this fashion continued to play an influential part in the game at such exalted levels.

Derek Dougan scored such goals for Wolves, and it was significant that there was a player who could provide him with the ammunition. Left-winger, David Wagstaffe crossed a fine ball, and he was encouraged to persist with the skill. Ron Davies, served at Southampton by wingers like Terry Paine, John Sydenham and Tom Jenkins, was similarly successful.

No matter how ruggedly astute defenders became, brave forwards like Stein, Jones and Royle profited from accurate crosses to their dangerous heads at the far post. . . . And when Scotland's Eddie Gray slung over his dangerous cross to Colin Stein's head on that May evening in 1969 Sir Alf Ramsey, above all other spectators, must have appreciated the value of the move.

No matter how the tactics of football change, the cross to the far post will always be an effective way to goal. Invariably, centres crossed to the far post will call for a header, either directly at goal or down for another player to finish with a shot. The skill of jumping and heading under pressure takes courage and is a complex movement.

Begin by suspending a softish ball from a cross-bar so that your forehead can make contact with it when you are standing. Only go on to practices with a fully inflated ball when your confidence has been gained. A laceless ball can have a piece of leather stitched on to the outer case for rope attachment. This piece of apparatus is essential for every club because it forms the basis of all heading techniques.

You should make contact with the ball square on so that the forehead can strike it. Keep your eye on the ball all the time. In fact, you should cultivate the habit of 'throwing the eyes' at the ball.

To transfer power to the ball you must also get power from your body. This is best done by swaying the upper part of your trunk backwards and forwards from the hips with one foot in front of the other. If you can strengthen your neck muscles this will obviously help, so work on these during your weight-training sessions (again only under qualified supervision).

Once you have gained confidence about striking the ball you must concentrate on timing. As the ball is swinging, the body movement must coincide with the head making contact. Really try to punch the ball with your head, using your body to gain extra power.

Now increase the height of the suspended ball by about eight inches. You will now have to jump to make contact, and you must jump early enough to get your body in a position to add the power. Jump from both feet, hollow your back slightly then thrust forward from the hips at the right time with your body and head. Throw the eyes at the ball, and head it with a jack-knife action. As you thrust forward you will notice that your feet move forwards as well. There are two movements here, one of jumping as high as you can and the other in the heading movements. The two must be moulded together.

Put the ball a few inches higher still and take a few paces back. With a couple of springy strides

take off from one foot, and head the ball powerfully downwards.

It is very good sense to start all heading sessions on the suspended ball before going out on to the practice pitch for more serious work. A heading practice session needs good service—either chipping or throwing. An excellent game to start with is a game across half a pitch—played like basketball in which you play the ball alternately with head and hands. A goal can only be scored by heading the ball in.

The ideal final pass to the far post is to a point just outside the corner of the goal area, just out of the goalkeeper's reach. Leave space in front of you so that you can move forward at the right time, jump high and head at the goal. The best place to put your header is back across the goal, because the keeper will move across to cover the post nearest to you.

You can put your heading skills to the test in several team routines.

The keeper can start the first routine by throwing or kicking a longish ball to a player around the half-way line who can either kick it or head it first time to a wing player. He dribbles round an imaginary opponent before crossing the ball to the far post. Strikers line up at the far post to head the crosses at goal.

For a second exercise split the players into groups of three—one of whom acts as a winger. Two players interpass towards goal from the half-way line, before one hits a firm ball down towards the far corner flag where the winger—the third player—will race to meet the pass. The other two players will then move in on the goal, one towards the near post, the other to the far post. The ball is then crossed to the far post where the player who has run there can either head for goal or head down for the near post player to finish off.

Make sure that you do not move in too early and have to wait for the ball. Check your judgement so that you do not jump too late.

Bring opponents into the picture in all practices when you feel confident enough to cope. This will add to your sense of timing, not only when you jump to head the ball but when you arrive into space—because the only way to get away from the harrassing attentions of the opposition is to keep on the move.

Go hard for the ball. Want to win it, and you will get far more goals than headaches.

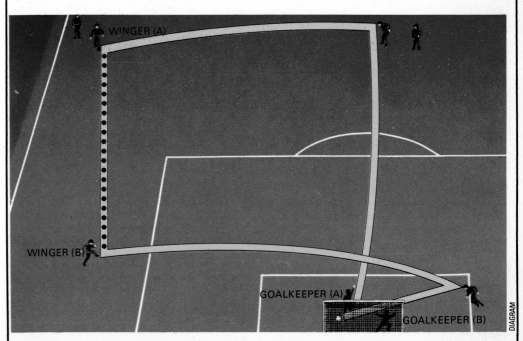

Above Far post header practice. The keeper throws out to a defender, who plays it for a winger to centre.

Ball control – trapping with the feet

Geoff Hurst's second goal in the 1966 World Cup final will always hold a place in the memory for the controversy that surrounded it. But for Hurst, the fact that his thunderous shot was only adjudged to have rebounded from the cross-bar over the line on the decision of a linesman was almost irrelevant; the critical moment had occurred seconds earlier. For the control he had shown in manoeuvring the ball into a shooting position had dissolved a doubt about his ability that had persisted since he had been given his first England shirt to wear.

England had suffered the awful possibility of ultimate failure when the Germans equalized in the dying minutes of the match to stretch it into a further 30 minutes of play. Alf Ramsey, angered by the wastefulness which had prevented his team from taking the goals which would have consolidated victory, strode out and told them: 'You have won it once. Now get out there and win it again.' The words were to become as historic as the goals which Hurst was now to score.

In the tenth minute of extra time, Alan Ball propelled himself into another major assault at the left flank of the German defence. His personal prize that day was the overall destruction of Karl Schnellinger. The tall, blond German defender, wearied by Ball's persistent dribbling, allowed him room to centre but the ball flew slightly behind Hurst as he moved in at the near post. There was no chance for a first time shot. The ball had to be controlled instantly—and with feet tired from approaching two hours running Hurst did just that, killing it in full flight he worked it to his right foot and drove a fearsome shot against the underside of the crossbar. When it bounced down, England appealed immediately for a goal.

Referee Gottfried Dienst consulted the Russian linesman and after an agony of waiting pointed towards the centre. England were ahead.

Hurst was to score again to give England a convincing victory, but it was in that moment of controversy that he had proved the value of working hard at a skill which was to serve him well over the years.

And yet little over a month before Hurst scored his historic hat-trick even his keenest admirers were struggling to present a case for his inclusion in the England team.

In the four-game tour which preceded the finals that year, Ramsey had thoroughly examined his players, working steadily towards the formation which would have to carry England through some of the sternest defences in the business. It was the last match against Poland which revealed his hand. Martin Peters was brought in to play on the left side in midfield and Jimmy Greaves seemed to be permanently re-instated as the most likely of England's goalscorers.

There was no room for Hurst and doubt had gathered around him during the previous match against Denmark in Copenhagen when a dry, rutted pitch had exposed glaring inadequacies in his control. This was the sort of surface on which Hurst was to suffer most during his entire career. A powerful, muscular player, he had begun his professional career as a willowy half-back with a desire to go forward. Then after he had almost been sold to Crystal Palace as a makeweight in West Ham's purchase of the highly skilled but wayward Johnny Byrne, he was given the chance to form a devastating partnership.

A willingness to work hard at his game enabled Hurst to convince West Ham's manager Ron Greenwood that there was a latent talent which would blossom with encouragement. Byrne's immaculate control when receiving the ball under pressure set him apart from most of his contemporaries. It was a skill which Hurst envied and which he was to work hard at improving.

Byrne's lack of discipline was to cost him a place in the 1966 World Cup squad, whilst Hurst's diligent application was to bring him immortality. The clumsiness that was evident in Copenhagen disappeared when Ramsey called upon him to play in the quarter-final against Argentina as a replacement for the injured Greaves. Wembley was smooth and well grassed. There were no ruts to disturb Hurst's confidence.

Hurst was not blessed with a delicate touch.

Left Geoff Hurst's shot rebounds down from West Germany's crossbar to put England 3-2 ahead in the 1966 World Cup final at Wembley Stadium.
Below left But as the diagram shows, the critical point in the build-up to the goal occurred when Hurst had to control a fast, low centre from Alan Ball to set up the opening for the shot.
Below For Hurst it was a special triumph as he had had to work hard at his control when making the switch from wing-half to front player. This crucial goal was fair reward for his diligent application in correcting a weakness in his game.

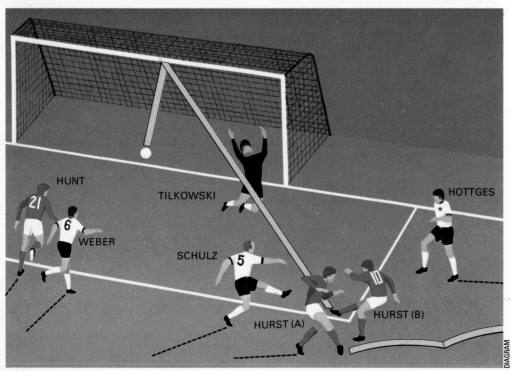

GERRY CRANHAM

HUNT
21
6
WEBER
TILKOWSKI
SCHULZ
5
HOTTGES
10
HURST (A)
HURST (B)

DIAGRAM

FOX PHOTOS

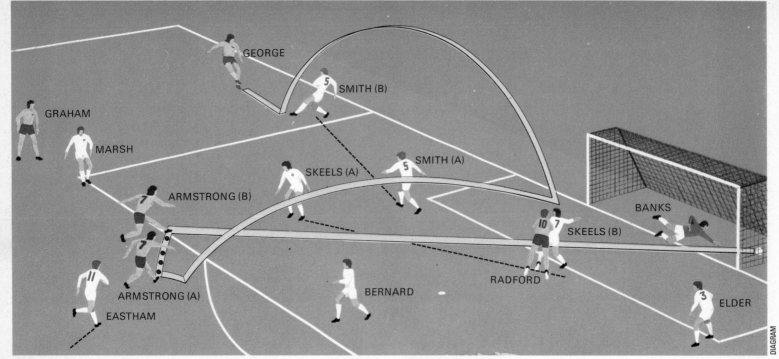

Labels on diagram: GEORGE, GRAHAM, SMITH (B), MARSH, SMITH (A), ARMSTRONG (B), SKEELS (A), BANKS, SKEELS (B), ARMSTRONG (A), BERNARD, RADFORD, EASTHAM, ELDER, DIAGRAM

SYNDICATION INTERNATIONAL

PRESS ASSOCIATION

He was not among the most fearless. But his intelligence and willingness helped to make him an outstanding target man when his partner Byrne departed sadly from Upton Park. He was to say: 'There was no better example of a man who could take any kind of pass than Johnny. His feet seemed to be like cushions and the ball never ran away from him. I envied him this. He was a fabulous player and he should have had a much more convincing career.'

Byrne had a brief resurrection the year following the World Cup when Ramsey took him to Canada for an international tournament in which England played under the banner of an FA XI. England arrived to discover that their matches would be played on a surface that had been savaged by a travelling circus. Elephants had stomped over a pitch on which valuable players would now be asked to risk their limbs and few relished the prospect.

The ebullient Byrne found it no problem at all. His mastery of the ball stood him out among talented opponents and he gave sparkling proof of his touch while waiting to take part in a training session.

A colleague recalled: '"Budgie" was just standing there when someone drove a ball at him from the other side of the arena. He was talking at the time—as usual. He hardly seemed to notice the ball. But when it came to him he killed it dead, like it was a lump of cotton wool, juggled with it briefly and then volleyed it away. Then he called for the ball and did it again. Then again. And again. There were a lot of good players around at that moment, the Russian Olympic team, and club sides from West Germany, Belgium and Mexico. Most of them stood open-mouthed. That's how good a player this feller was.'

Absolute certainty when receiving the ball with the feet became a vital skill for any forward who hoped to be effective against modern defences.

Half-chances were a luxury and two touches at the ball was the most that players could expect in moments of crisis at top level.

The ability to eliminate the need for time helped to establish Peter Osgood of Chelsea as an outstanding attacker. Tall but blessed with a low centre of gravity because of short legs, he quickly showed that he was something special and only lacked a willingness to apply himself to the game. A fine dribbler, good in the air and a splendid shot, he was to score many fine goals out of a talent for pulling the most difficult passes clear of lunging defenders before striking at the target almost in one movement.

Mike England, a big Welshman who with Spurs proved to be one of the best centre-halves of his day, fought many belligerent battles with Osgood but found time to credit him with great skill. He said: '"Ossie" is at his most dangerous when you think you have got everything in your favour. He has the confidence to settle for two touches in front of goal and the skill to make it pay off. You think you have got to him. Then he has pulled the ball clear with one foot and hit it with the other.'

George Best, Denis Law, Allan Clarke, Jimmy Greaves, Rodney Marsh, Alan Gilzean, Colin Bell and Francis Lee all had this talent going for them and it put them all into the category of outstanding finishers. And little George Armstrong of Arsenal struck a special goal against Stoke in the 1972 FA Cup semi-final in a sure two-touch movement.

But instant control with the feet was not the prerogative of goalscorers. It became a necessary facility for defenders and midfield men.

There were few better at it than Dave Mackay who was able to use his nimble skills to marvellous effect after leaving Spurs to play his part in the building of a fine Derby County team. Mackay had a reputation for committed effort,

Top It took Arsenal's George Armstrong just two touches of the ball—one to control, one to shoot— to score Arsenal's goal in the 1972 FA Cup semi-final against Stoke City at Villa Park.
Above left Stoke keeper Gordon Banks dives too late to stop Armstrong's strong, left-footed drive.
Above The Arsenal players rush to congratulate Armstrong on his goal, which was a testimony to the winger's ability to control the ball.

for football which seemed to carry the echo of bagpipes. But above all else he was immensely skilful, a marvellous striker of the ball whose immaculate talent was not lost on the young Derby centre-half Roy McFarland.

McFarland was to emerge as the best of England's young centre-halves; and it was from Mackay that he learned the value of instant control. He said: 'When Dave came to us he was no longer as mobile as he had been. He sat in at the back, providing us with cover as well as giving us encouragement. The fact that he was into the veteran stage led to the belief that he could be put under pressure. It meant that teams pushed players up on Dave. But he was much too cute for them and they never really caught him out. I've seen Dave pull balls out of the air and whip them away to me before anyone could get near to him. It was tremendous stuff and only a truly top-class player would have attempted the things he did.'

Controlling the ball with the feet was a fundamental skill, but some did it better than others and even internationals such as Hurst had to work hard at it.

Hurst's patient preparation was to pay off on an historic occasion. He was not one of the great instinctive players. But sheer hard work helped to make him an immortal figure in the history of the game. A hat-trick in a World Cup final was reward enough for his application.

Coaching: Learn how to kill the ball with your feet

To be in command of the ball is of paramount importance to every player irrespective of the role he plays in the game. The ability to control an awkward bouncing ball quickly and efficiently gives great personal satisfaction, is a delight to watch and can be the difference between success and failure in any particular situation in the course of play.

As football demands more speed, there is a greater need for first-time passing. This, however, cannot always be put into practice. The ball has to be trapped or stopped, or the player may have to dribble with it, because no teammate is in a position to receive a first-time pass. Time and space are allied in football. The less time a player takes to do something, the more time he will have to take advantage of it, because when controlling a ball a player will do one of three things after taking control: he will screen the ball by interposing his body between the ball and his immediate opponent; he will pass the ball or shoot; or he will dribble the ball. The space and time he has to do these things will depend on how good he is at receiving the ball.

Try to cultivate a feel for the ball. Feel means touch, and a fine touch requires tenderness. Interpass a ball with a friend or find a wall so that the ball rebounds. The object here is to control the ball before making a pass. The inside of the foot is best for this particular exercise, and the position to be taken is almost the same as the one required when kicking with the inside of the foot. The standing leg should be slightly bent at the knee and ankle. The other leg should be turned outwards from the hip so that the kicking foot is at right angles to the line of flight. As the ball is coming to you make sure your body is in the line of flight, and as it arrives the controlling foot should be slightly in front of the standing foot; at the moment contact is made the controlling leg should immediately start moving backwards from the hip. The controlling surface should relax and the movement should be gauged to be almost as fast as the speed of the ball, thus allowing the contact with the inside of the foot to last as long as possible. In this way the foot can take the pace off the ball so that it comes to a stop at a point just in front of the foot.

This movement which reduces the speed of the ball cannot always be so exaggerated. Only when the ball is moving at a reasonable pace is it possible to move the foot at the same speed as the ball. When the ball is arriving fast, it is impossible to move the foot backwards at anywhere near the same speed. The idea, then, is 'to tame' the ball through a shorter and quicker backward movement of a relaxed ankle. The ball comes in contact with a swinging surface which can considerably reduce the pace, and eventually the ball will stop, again just in front of the foot.

Stand about 10 yards from your friend and push the ball to him with the inside of the foot. Gradually increase the distance as you increase the pace, until you are eventually playing the ball really firmly from about 20 yards apart. Help cultivate the feel by controlling the ball and turning, so that you immediately move off without changing the direction of the ball; you are reducing the pace of the ball to the speed of your movement so that you run along with it for a few yards before turning and playing it back to your friend.

Almost the same technique is required if the ball is coming directly to you at knee height, or slightly higher, and to one side of you. The foot has to be lifted to correspond with the level of the approaching ball.

Now get your friend to play the ball at you whilst another player is marking you. Not only must you concentrate on taking the ball cleanly but you must make sure you move to meet it, otherwise the marking player will get in first. Having taken possession, screen it for a few seconds before playing it back to your friend. After a little practice, try taking the ball to one side either by using the inside or outside of your foot. The object here, is to move on to the ball played by your friend and, as the ball arrives, to take it quickly to the left or right. Again, touch is vital. If you do not play the ball hard enough, you are likely to fall over it; if you play it too hard, you lose control.

When this type of control has improved, try coming on to a ball whilst running quickly, and without checking your stride, control it and get a shot in at goal. This means relaxing the foot as contact is made, sufficiently not only to absorb the pace of the ball, but also to reduce the pace of your own body movement. The ball should run in front so that you strike it after only a couple of strides. Remember to get over the ball so that it does not leave the ground, otherwise your shot will be delayed.

Balls coming out of the air can be controlled by using a part of the foot as a wedge so that the ball is gently squeezed against the ground. The inside or outside of the instep are best suited for this control. If you have put in sufficient work on the previous exercises this should be quite easy, as long as the area selected for control makes contact above the ball, just as it strikes the ground. It is identical to the trap pass in execution but is only played a short distance, enough for you to keep control without over-stretching.

Try this first by throwing a ball up about 10 feet high; then, as it reaches the ground, control it by taking it on one side of the foot, and shoot at a target on a wall so that the ball comes back easily. When confident ask your friend to throw the ball to you, from about 10 yards, so that it reaches the ground just in front of you. He then moves in quickly to harass you. The object here, is for you to control the ball by using either the inside or outside of your instep to take the ball to one side to create a shooting or passing angle.

Other methods of control with the feet will come to you when you have cultivated a feel for the ball. The full instep can be used for catching balls before they bounce or the sole of the foot when you want to push the ball in front of you. The same principles will apply: get into the line of flight of the ball and make an early choice of control; relax and withdraw the controlling surface.

Finally put your control to the test in a five or six-a-side game of two-touch, one to control the ball, the second to pass or shoot. Remember, that good control is the ability to take the ball with one touch in such a way that you can play the ball with your next movement without having to chase to reach it.

The ability to control the ball with the feet is basic to football. It is a skill that is totally instinctive to some, but that is harder for others. But at whatever level you play your control can always benefit from practice.

Below left Diagram showing a simple practice for increasing ball control. One player, under pressure from a defender, has two touches to control a pass and play the ball back to the feeder.
Below Leeds United and England striker Allan Clarke has cultivated a fine touch and a talent for controlling the ball even in the most crowded goalmouths. Here he outwits the Liverpool defence to score in an FA Cup tie at Elland Road.

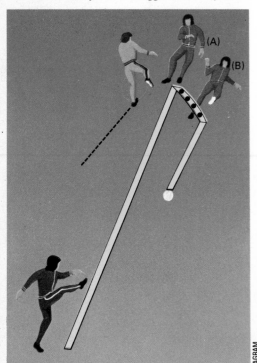

DIAGRAM

SYNDICATION INTERNATIONAL

The diagram labels: HEALEY, CARR, 10, BOOTH, STEIN (B), 9, STEIN (A), DONACHIE, DIAGRAM

Quickness on the turn

'We're robbing Peter to pay Paul,' said Coventry manager Joe Mercer after selling centre-half Jeff Blockley to Arsenal for over £200,000 in October 1972.

Within a week, Blockley, tall, aggressive and already an Under-23 international, was to win his first full cap for England when he was recruited to play against Yugoslavia at Wembley.

Blockley was well fancied. Discarded by Arsenal when with them as an apprentice, he had established himself as a First Division centre-half. Arsenal, Leeds and Crystal Palace were among the clubs who had looked hard at his talents. And it was Arsenal, looking to the future, who made the most positive move.

'It was a problem,' said Mercer. 'We knew that Jeff was among the best young defenders in the business. But our forwards weren't getting goals. We needed to put that right. To put it right we needed money. The only way we could get money was to sell one of our outstanding young players.'

With money in the bank, Mercer and Milne were able to move. They had already lined up their targets. Colin Stein, an energetic Scottish international who had been made available by Glasgow Rangers and Tommy Hutchison, a tall, swift, skilful left-winger who had grown increasingly unsettled at Blackpool. In both players Mercer was looking to sharpen his attack, to provide the thrust that would turn defences.

The players were bought within ten days. But it was Stein, gathering his skill together to produce a definitive performance on his first home appearance, who was to make the most obvious impression.

'Forwards who can do their stuff early on are halfway there,' said Mercer. 'The crowd are looking for something special. It's easier for a forward if he can turn it on. The professional will recognize the qualities in a defender. But a player who makes goals or who can knock one in doesn't need a lot of public understanding.'

Stein's home debut emphasized that. It emphasized too that he was a much more skilful player than he had appeared to English eyes on his occasional appearances for Scotland. After making his debut in an away match at Crystal Palace he was presented at Coventry against Manchester City.

The confrontation was in every way poignant. Mercer and Malcolm Allison facing each other for the first time since they had parted company the previous summer at Manchester City.

Allison had his problems. City had made a poor start, unable to re-fashion the thoughtful, definitive football which had made them one of the most attractive teams in the country. They were floundering near the foot of the First Division. Mercer's purchase of Stein was to present his former partner with immediate problems.

Top *Diagram showing how Colin Stein, on his first home appearance for Coventry City, made a goal for Willie Carr in the 3-2 win over Manchester City. Left free by Booth, Stein wriggled clear of Donachie's challenge with a sharp turn and played the ball into Carr's path.*
Above *Carr slides the ball home for a goal that owed much to Stein's speed on the turn.*

CHANNON (C)

CHANNON (B)

CHANNON (A)

ROYLE

MARIC

BALL

DIAGRAM

COVENTRY EVENING TELEGRAPH

SYNDICATION INTERNATIONAL

SYNDICATION INTERNATIONAL

Top *The goal that gave England their share of a 1-1 draw with Yugoslavia at Wembley in October 1972. Mick Channon, the Southampton striker, played a vital part in his first international.*
Right *He carried Colin Bell's pass towards the left touchline before turning elastically past the nearest defender and crossing the ball.*
Above right *Alan Ball lays on the goal for Royle.*

Much of Allison's discomfort stemmed from the loss of form in his defence and in particular the inability of centre-half Tommy Booth to come to terms with a variety of critical situations. Uncertainty was a clear symptom of Booth's lack of confidence. Stein, wily and surprisingly thoughtful in his application, was to take immediate advantage.

Allison had always impressed the value of closing down in the area of the ball. But an obsession with this tended to leave his defence without width and it gave Stein the opportunity to display the value of being able to turn with the ball under pressure.

Hutchison's mazy dribble led to a pass which found Stein with his back to goal some five yards outside City's penalty area and almost in line with the penalty spot. Booth, uncertain, hung off. Willie Donachie, a tenacious, but still inexperienced, Scottish international left-back was lured across, committing himself to challenge. Stein reacted splendidly, holding off the tackle and whipping his body into a sharp turn to slip past Donachie on the young full-back's right side. City's now unguarded left flank was exposed.

With Booth still rooted in space, the Scot simply slid the ball square and Willie Carr, advancing rapidly from midfield, came through to shoot a fine goal.

There was considerable irony in the moment. Allison had always insisted that this ability to turn, especially under pressure, was an essential feature in the make up of great attackers. He regarded this as the most specialized skill in the game, and recognized that it called for great courage as well as skill.

He saw both these qualities in the play of Jimmy Logie whose generalship had done much to keep Arsenal in the forefront of England's teams during the years immediately following the Second World War.

Logie had gone to Arsenal as a junior, a teenager plucked from the prolific breeding grounds of Scottish football. The war robbed him of good years. But Logie, curiously shaped, with long arms

17

and a peculiar shoulder-shaking style, was to prove a great brain and the architect of many Arsenal successes.

Bill Dodgin who went to Arsenal from Fulham had a deep visionary appreciation of what was good in the game. He said of Logie: 'The great thing was the man's ability to find space. John White had it too. But Jimmy always seemed to be free.

'In some ways it was an illusion. The secret was that you could play balls up to Jimmy and know that he could cope with them even when he was marked tight. He had this trick of swaying as he came off to collect a pass. He could kid an opponent that he was going one way and then at the last second he would sway back across the line of flight and drag the ball clear in the opposite direction.

'You can't really coach people to do that. It's something that they are born with. Johnny Haynes had it too. John always wanted the ball and there were times when it looked as though he wasn't really in a position to receive it. You know, with a man beating down his back. But that's the way John liked it. He was confident that he could cope. He liked being tightly marked because he could destroy people that way. Now you couldn't do that unless you could turn and, more important, turn when the pressure was on.'

In a forward the gift of turning quickly was the quality which separated the ordinary from the outstanding. It brought England a fine goal in October 1972 as Alf Ramsey's young side met Yugoslavia at Wembley. One of four new caps, instilled in the team because an aggravating glut of League Cup replays had robbed Ramsey of his regulars, was the Southampton forward, Mick Channon. A player of almost over-enthusiastic running and blessed with exceptional skill on the ground, Channon played a major part in England's share of the 1-1 scoreline. Breaking from the right-back position, he embarked on a gigantic run off the ball down the right touchline.

As England built on the opposite flank through Marsh and Bell, Channon cut in sprinting across the front of the area to receive Bell's pass. He was forced out left and tightly watched by a Yugoslavian defender. But his quickness on the turn extracted him from these attentions and more-over made space for a cross. Although the final centre lacked accuracy, the speed of its execution panicked the Yugoslavs and Ball laid on the goal for Joe Royle.

Among the outstanding turners was Johnny Giles of Leeds, an Eire international whose talent was not fully appreciated by Manchester United when they sold him for a paltry £35,000. Leeds bought Giles to eventually replace Bobby

Collins as the guiding influence in their team play. Manager Don Revie saw things which Manchester United did not and his judgement was fully borne out.

Giles had two great feet. Combative, even mean, he was a difficult proposition in midfield and it was his talent for turning which set him apart from most of his contemporaries.

Like Jimmy Logie he perfected the trick of deceiving tight markers with a body sway as he shaped up to collect a pass driven to him out of defence. He had remarkable strength for a small man and the courage to dismiss belligerent tackles from behind. His passing, once free of pressure, was invariably devastating.

Turning was not a comfortable exercise in English football until a clamp down on delinquent tackles in the 1971-72 season. But the willingness to attempt it despite the threat of butchering tackles from behind was one of the reasons why Geoff Hurst was able to establish himself as a £200,000 attacker long before a fee of that size became commonplace. Hurst was slipping downhill when a charter of firmer refereeing began to make life easier for forwards.

And yet the skill which helped to make him famous had not lost its value when Joe Mercer was able to satisfy himself that he had done good business in the autumn of 1972.

Coaching : Improve your speed on the turn and sharpen your game

Speed in football is much more than just the ability to sprint. The simple talent to run quickly is an excellent weapon to have, but it is not sufficient in itself. There are players who can cover ground very rapidly but who have great difficulty in starting, stopping and, most important, in changing direction. Good situations are often lost through the inability to turn quickly and, of course, the slow-turning defender can be exploited by the ball played into the area behind him.

Strength in the legs will certainly make you quicker on the turn, but you can also be improved by constant practice. Begin by standing with your back to a line some 6 to 8 yards behind you. On a signal turn and get to the line as quickly as possible. Practise turning both ways because you never know in a game which way you will have to turn.

Now enlist the aid of a friend. He trots towards you and when he is about two yards away from you he makes a break; the object here is for you to turn to whichever side he has gone past you and try to catch him. Change roles after every sprint. You will quickly learn that by approaching the oncoming player at an angle you can be on the half-turn before he makes his break. This way, you encourage the attacking player into the area you want him to go, making it easier for you to deal with him.

This type of work will stand you in good stead when, during a game, you are approached by an attacker in possession of the ball; you can shepherd him into an area away from the goal so that you are on the half-turn ready to pounce in on the tackle, if he makes an error, or to turn quickly to challenge should he go by. Ask your friend to come at you with a ball; it will be good experience of containing and then turning to challenge. You must be very careful here not to commit yourself unnecessarily and make it easy for him to go past. Also make sure that you approach from a definite angle and do not turn your side to the opponent allowing him to turn you completely round.

This principle must also apply when marking players off the ball. Two players can practise this in a small area five yards wide and thirty yards long. One player approaches while the other one tries to keep track of him when he makes a sudden dash to go by within the limited area.

These are excellent practices to quicken players for defensive duties, but attackers, too, must be quick to turn.

As a forward you are always attempting to lose your marker. This is a vital part of offensive play, to turn defenders; they do not like to be turned round and made to run back towards their own goal. Speed and surprise are the elements of success.

Decoy movements make this a lot easier. A

Below Francis Lee prepares to use his power of rapid change of direction to attack the West Bromwich Albion defenders. To repel forwards of Lee's speed and balance, defenders have to be equally nimble when turning under pressure.
Bottom West Ham's England captain Bobby Moore faces the twin challenge of Willie Morgan and George Best, both deft at twisting past tackles.

midfield player has the ball, for example. The wing player moves back along his line to support, luring the opposing full-back with him. When he has got the full-back moving with him he turns and looks for the ball either inside the defender or over the top.

The technique of turning is important here. Many players turn away from the opponent taking the long way round. This is vital time wasted. Try to cultivate the turn into the defender; this means that you are really attacking him and also that you are not turning your back on the opponent or the ball. Working on the left side of the pitch, the defender marking you will be on your left shoulder as you turn to support your midfield player, you should be on the half-turn ready to receive the ball on your right foot. The sudden turn must be to your left; all you have to do is place your left foot back and you are away like lightning, forcing the defender to turn.

Try this as a practice. One player stands on the halfway line with a ball. Another player, who is marked by a third member, stands on the edge of the penalty area out towards one of the wings. The player who is marked tries to pull away from the defender by moving wide and towards the player on the ball. This movement creates space because the opponent either stays where he is, allowing the attacker to move away from him and collect a pass in space, or he moves with him, leaving space at the back of him. For this first practice, ask the defender to follow him and when sufficient space has been created, the attacker suddenly turns and gets on the back side of the defender as the ball is delivered into the same space. If the attacker pulls away so that he is already on the half-turn, he will invariably beat the defender to a ball played through.

A lot of defenders are not easily deceived in this way; so in order to get them in close with you, the ball can be played up as you are pulling away from the defender. As you receive the ball, the defender will be more inclined to come in close. This gives you the opportunity to lay the ball back and turn suddenly, looking for a return ball behind your opponent. Alternatively, you can swivel quickly on the ball beating your opponent by feinting to play the return pass and by turning quickly.

Variation in play is essential in top football. If you lay the ball back every time you get it, your play will become predictable. Learn to vary your play so that you keep opponents guessing. Turning on the ball means often taking a chance of losing it. Make sure of your techniques and that the odds favour you. Be quick and you may well take your opponent by surprise.

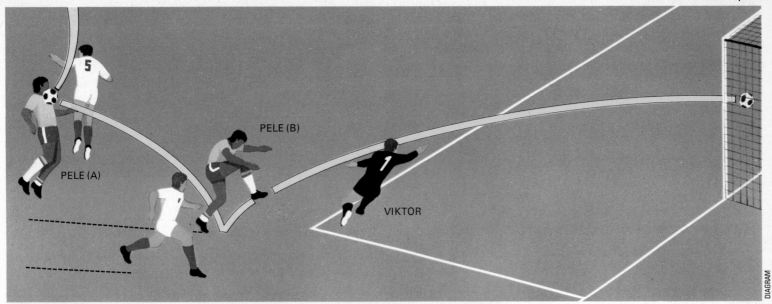

PELE (A)

PELE (B)

VIKTOR

DIAGRAM

UNITED PRESS INTERNATIONAL

Ball control – trapping on the body

Above *Diagram illustrating Pele's masterful control of the ball on his body. Against Czechoslovakia in the 1970 World Cup, he leapt to take a pass from Gerson. In mid-air he cushioned the swerving ball on his chest, dropped it to his feet and crashed it past the goalkeeper.*

Left *Keeper Viktor is helpless as Pele scores a goal totally fashioned by his superb control.*

Adamec wasted a chance gifted to him by Carlos Alberto. But having survived that anxiety they took a cunning equalizer when Pele, Gerson and Jairzinho decoyed an opening for Rivelino's murderous free-kick.

But it was in the second half that the world was to witness again the remarkable range of Pele's talents and the near perfection of his ball control.

Pele, it seemed, had devised more ways of dropping the ball dead at his feet than any other man in the business. That he could do this when running at top speed made even great players bow in deference.

Now his speed and control blended beautifully to bring Brazil another goal. As Pele drifted temptingly across the Czech defence, the educated midfield player Gerson curled a 40-yard pass into the great man's path.

Pele, bouncing upwards, took the pass on his chest while a foot off the floor and then as the ball angled down he drove it right-footed beyond goalkeeper Viktor's right hand.

The execution of that goal was Pele at his best. There was no way that any other player in the world could have matched him at that moment.

It seemed at times that his body was coated with adhesive. No pass was too difficult for him to control and no movement seemed to be beyond the contortion of his muscles.

All the Brazilians revealed great joy in their ability to make the ball do their bidding. It was part of their heritage, a product of their environment and the ethnic combination which compounds the Brazilian character.

Helmut Schoen, the West German team manager, was to say: 'It would be pointless trying to play like these people. They have their own special way. It is the football of the sun. It is not that they have devised a new way of playing the game. The basic techniques are common to all footballers. But that does not mean to say that we cannot improve these techniques.'

England's manager Sir Alf Ramsey was to be criticized for suggesting that the Brazilians had taught him nothing. In saying that Ramsey suffered once more from his inarticulateness. He had not learned anything he did not know before, he had learned nothing he could hope to copy: but there was a better way of saying so.

Indeed Ramsey four years earlier had introduced a note of caution to the wild enthusiasm for England's victory in the 1966 World Cup.

He said: 'If we are going to keep the World Cup

An American watching soccer for the first time during the 1970 World Cup in Mexico failed to recognize that Pele's standards were as unique as Babe Ruth's had been in baseball, as Joe Namath's were in grid-iron football.

Consumed by Pele's virtuosity and on his feet in excitement, the American exclaimed: 'This game is beautiful and that black man is the most beautiful thing in it.'

Football, of course, was not always beautiful. At its best it could be appealing and emotive. But it could also be hard, dull, mean, sly and cruel. Pele had been forced to accept that, even to acquire a degree of cynicism himself.

But there was no doubt that he brought beauty to the game, that he blessed it with a very special

talent, a complete mastery of the ball. In a complete repertoire of skills, his ability to control the ball on all parts of his body was exceptional. The devastation of this type of control was exhibited before the world in 1970 playing against Czechoslovakia in Guadalajara.

As Brazil prepared for that opening match Pele had claimed that he was better equipped for a World Cup than at any time since an astonishingly adult debut as a seventeen-year-old in Sweden twelve years earlier.

But Brazil were not to start without aggravation. Petras, an alert blond who proved to be the best Czech forward, shot a splendid goal. It was merely the prelude to destruction.

Brazil could have lost a second goal when

19

BERGMARK PELE (B)

PELE (A)

GUSTAVSSON AXBOM

SVENSON

DIAGRAM

in Mexico we must improve our technique. We must learn to kill the ball more cleanly. There is a need for players who can do this quickly. We are short of this type of player.'

Economy had long been an outstanding feature of English play. There had been little encouragement for techniques which seemed to do no more than dress the game up, and ball control was rarely seen to stray beyond an area of fundamental principle.

Even outstanding individuals such as Stan Matthews and Tom Finney concentrated on perfecting simple, well-adjusted techniques and there were only a few who had the independence to dabble in experiments.

When England beat Italy at White Hart Lane, Tottenham, in 1949 they owed their victory to the alert goalkeeping of Bert Williams. But much was made of the ease with which the Italians killed passes with their thighs, and suddenly there was a new mood.

Nevertheless British managers were still emphasizing the principles which went with heavy, ankle-high boots and extravagantly padded legs. 'Don't show off. What's the point of catching the ball on your instep when it's more simple to use the sole of the foot?'

The argument was damaging because it held players back from a whole new concept of play.

A famous Hungarian victory at Wembley in 1953 gave greater emphasis to coaching. The Hungarians, when receiving a pass, turned with the ball in one movement, taking the pace off it and easing through into their stride.

British players were still doubling the effort. They stopped. They turned. Time was becoming more valuable and tighter, and much more varied.

Coaches grew to recognize that there was no need for standard procedure. It did not matter how the ball was killed as long as it was killed quickly and fluently.

Pele's chest trap in Guadalajara was in no way unique. It was the fact that he had been airborne at the moment of contact and the speed with which he used the skill which made the moment exceptional.

Johnny Byrne, when dovetailing with the young Geoff Hurst in the West Ham team of the mid-sixties, had a wide and expressive range of control

COLORSPORT

COLORSPORT

COLORSPORT

Above *Even at 17 Pele exhibited extravagant control. Amidst the tensions of his first World Cup final—in Sweden in 1958—he caught a cross on his thigh, whipped the ball over his head and volleyed it past the Swedish goalkeeper.*
Left *A feature of the play of Ajax, European Cup winners in 1971 and 1972, is the instinctive control shown by their players. Such skill is particularly effective in front of goal as Swart illustrates in the 1972 European Cup quarter-final against Arsenal. He uses his thigh to take the pace out of the ball, setting himself up for a volley that brought a fine save from Wilson.*

skills. He could be hit confidently with passes out of defence because he could take the ball with his chest or his thigh without suffering any discomfort.

Spurs in their push-and-run era under Arthur Rowe made good use of Len Duquemin's ability to cushion long passes with his chest.

Rowe recalls: 'Although the basis of our game was quick, accurate short passes and continuous movement, we needed variety. Len was the perfect target man. Alf Ramsey, for instance, could drive long balls at his chest and we could then build up from an advanced position.'

Geoff Hurst, encouraged by Byrne's excellence, was to perfect chest control himself, and it was to become an outstanding feature of his play, especially when meeting long clearances under pressure from opposing defenders.

Defenders too had to be confident of dealing with chest-high balls. Bobby Moore developed the technique to the point where he could turn back to face his own goal with the ball under perfect control.

No one demonstrated this better than the Russian Voronin in the third place play-off match during the 1966 World Cup.

Voronin's football contradicted the uncluttered, stolid style which the Russians presented to the world. The team played by the book. Voronin, often to the disgust of his coaches, played with his heart.

When he was confronted by two Portuguese forwards challenging beneath a high ball on the edge of the penalty area, Voronin might have taken the obvious way out by attempting to head clear. Instead he took a step back, caught the ball on his chest and turned elegantly away towards the touchline.

By 1972 Johann Cruyff, a lean superbly athletic Dutchman, had begun to qualify as one of the game's great players. A supreme individual, he had Pele's facility for instant control and it was to bring him many memorable goals.

Playing against Arsenal in the European Cup quarter-finals, he was to win a volume of praise from Alan Ball, a player whose own techniques were widely admired.

Ball, ineligible for the match because he had been signed too late from Everton, said: 'Cruyff showed us everything last night. This feller can do the lot and he's brave with it.'

One of the things Cruyff had done was to take a driven pass on the top of his right thigh as the preface to a fierce volley which was only a few inches off target.

Few English players could match this sort of control, but those who could made their mark. Peter Osgood, a tall, powerful but deft Chelsea forward, had the ability to make chances out of nothing, and he showed it no better than when scoring a fine goal against Arsenal during the 1971-72 League season.

It was pure skill which gave him the edge over the Arsenal defence. The skilled Charlie Cooke knifed his way to the bye-line on the Chelsea left and crossed. In the midst of desperate opponents, Osgood pulled down the waist-high centre and with elegance and deceptive casualness volleyed the ball past Bob Wilson.

Pele would undoubtedly have stood and applauded, but these moments were still all too rare in English football.

Coaching: Develop the ability to kill the ball on your body

It is not always possible to pass the ball along the ground. Long clearances and chipped passes over opponents are often the only way out of some situations, and in order to be in a position to engineer further situations, the player receiving is often forced to control the ball instead of passing it on directly.

Lack of knowledge and practice are major reasons for the shortcomings of some players who experience difficulties in control. They have to touch the ball three or four times before it is placed sufficiently to use accurately. Ideally a player, on receiving the ball, should be capable of using the ball positively with his second touch.

Many parts of the body can be used to make a control but the principles are the same. No matter whether the thigh, the lower and upper chest or the head are used it is important to get into the line of flight, to make an early choice of what part of the body you are going to use and to present a controlling surface to the ball which must relax and give on contact.

Many factors will determine which part of the body is to be used and how the technique is going to be performed. The angle at which the ball approaches, what you intend doing with the ball after control, the position of defenders, whether you are stationary or on the move at the moment of contact and the speed of the ball are just a few of the considerations.

If the ball is dropping just in front of the body and you do not want it to make contact with the ground or the ball is approaching just above knee height, then the thigh is an excellent method of control.

You should position yourself facing exactly the direction from which the ball is coming. Stand on one leg, and present the other thigh to the ball in such a way that the ball, after coming in contact with the thigh, drops to the ground under control. This means that if the ball is coming down steeply the knee must be bent and raised so that the thigh is horizontal to the ground. Should the ball be travelling horizontally, then the knee should be bent with the foot raised behind you. This allows the thigh to withdraw from the ball on contact.

Try this for yourself. Throw a ball into the air and position yourself so that as the ball comes down you bend your knee and the ball is allowed to make contact on your thigh which should be horizontal to the ground. On contact, the leg relaxes allowing the ball to drop to the ground; then you must either dribble the ball for a few yards or half-volley it at a target on a wall. Because of the speed of the ball it is almost impossible for the ball to drop straight to the floor from the thigh. The ball must be allowed to bounce slightly from the thigh and the angle of this bounce will determine how close the ball is going to bounce away from you and in what direction you want the ball to go.

Working with a team-mate, ask him to throw the ball to you from about ten yards. Control it with the thigh and half-volley the ball back along the ground with the inside of the foot. Then move off to receive a return pass which you pick up. You now throw the ball to your friend who controls it with the thigh and half-volleys it back to you along the ground. He then moves away

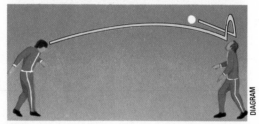

Top The thigh trap—exhibited by Charlie George for Arsenal against Leeds United.
Above Diagram of a practice for head control. The ball is interpassed between two players, each player in turn having one touch to control and a second touch to make the pass.

to receive a return pass from you.

The soft surface of the abdomen and lower chest is extremely suitable for absorbing the pace of a ball which bounces up at you from the ground. This method is useful when you are moving in to make an interception and you want to carry through the movement. Again it is essential to get into the line of flight, and as the ball makes contact with your stomach it can be directed by slightly twisting the body if necessary. Throw a ball up against a wall, move in on it just after it has bounced, bend well over the ball to present a surface so that the pace is absorbed and the ball drops to the feet for you to carry on through the interception.

If you are in a position to let the ball come to you, you can correct your balance by taking a pace back on contact. A team-mate can help by throwing or chipping the ball up on to a wall, then as you move in to make your control he comes in with you to act as an opponent. This will make a more realistic practice, forcing you to move off quickly to keep the ball away from him. You will find that when you have slightly misjudged your interception that either the thigh, if you have gone in too early, or the upper chest, if going in late, can be used instead. When using the chest make sure your hands are held wide of the body. Not only will it give you a wider area for control but it lessens the risk of handling the ball.

Because of this large surface, the chest trap is a very popular method of control. When you cannot, because of tactical considerations, make a pass with the head, the chest can be used to absorb the pace and to turn the ball in a new direction. This is done by twisting the trunk from the hips on contact towards the direction in which you wish to run or pass.

Two techniques must be mastered here, one for balls approaching along a horizontal plane and the other for balls coming down steeply. But if you remember that basically the ball must be stopped, or the pace absorbed, you cannot go far wrong.

The movement of the chest on contact is all important. One foot in front of the other is a good stance with the chest pushed out so that the upper part of the body resembles an arc with a slightly backward inclination. If the ball is approaching horizontally, the knees are straightened as the ball strikes the chest following a sudden backward movement of the hips, and the front foot moves back closer to the rear one. As the hips move back, the chest should give and be arched inwards on contact so that now the upper part of the body resembles an arc pointing forward to direct the ball towards the ground.

When the ball is coming down steeply, the ball can be stopped by the chest so that it bounces up slightly after contact.

Both these techniques must be developed to cultivate the feel for the ball. Get your team-mate to serve balls up to you, and take one technique at a time. Then ask him to vary the service so that you get used to dealing with the situation as it occurs. Remember to keep varying your movement by turning the ball sideways— before moving off. This saves a lot of time in the game. Feint movements before contact can help wrong-foot an opponent, making it easier for you to get away.

Now move on to a practice involving four or five players and two footballs in an area about 50 yards square. One player is put under slight pressure by three other players, two of whom have a ball each. The third member is spare. One player with a ball chips up to the performer who, with one touch, has to bring the ball down under control. His next touch should send the ball accurately to the spare man. The other ball is then served in and again the idea is to control and find the spare man who is now the player who served in the first ball. Change frequently because of the physical demands. More pressure can be applied by bringing in a fifth member to act as opposition to the player who is performing. This will make him move quickly to meet the ball and if the spare man is on the move you will have a very realistic situation.

Control with the head is a very difficult skill. Practise on a suspended ball by heading it so that it swings, then watching the ball very carefully on to the forehead. Try to absorb the swing by relaxing the neck muscles and tucking in your chin on contact. Once you have got the feel, build up this technique in much the same way but do not be disappointed if your progress is not so fast as with the other techniques. Practise in 'twos heading the ball to one another first of all, then using one header to control and a second to pass the ball back.

Control is what the game is all about. The more parts of the body you can use to master the ball, the better you are as a player. For once you have the ball under control you are ready to contribute positively to a game.

Speed off the mark

no obvious muscular power and his shuffling run made him look harmless. But once Matthews had wrong-footed a full-back with a swerve, his acceleration was devastating.

Pace from a standing start helped to make Matthews one of the great players of his time, although many good judges felt that he always was second to Preston's Tom Finney. Unlike Matthews, who was essentially a creator of openings, Finney got great joy from scoring goals. He was quicker over longer distances, and it is reasonable to suppose that he was the better all-round player.

But he would have been only half the performer

Manchester City could find some consolation in Rodney Marsh's exhilarating form when they completed their 1971-72 League programme just short of winning the Championship. After faltering in the last lap of a dramatic struggle with Derby, Leeds and Liverpool they recovered their poise to overwhelm Derby before a 55,000 crowd at Maine Road.

Marsh's contribution to that victory was in every way significant. Signed from Queen's Park Rangers for £200,000 on the eve of the transfer deadline a month earlier, he had failed to provide the inspiration which City manager Malcolm Allison had been looking for.

The outcome was criticism. Much of it directed at Marsh because of the extravagance of his style, some of it at Allison for introducing a new face at a crucial stage of the conflict.

All the criticism was to be dispersed in that one match against Derby when Marsh, fined down by sterner training than he had known before, produced memorable football at great speed. Marsh had become an almost magical figure in the game, renowned for the insolent skill that had prompted comparison with the Brazilians. But he had never been famed for his swiftness.

But a goal, taken in the first half against one of the surest defences in the First Division, not only convinced a critical assembly that they were in the presence of genius, but emphasized the value of speed when applied to a definitive skill. Collecting a slanted pass wide on Derby's left flank, midway in their half of the field, Marsh swayed clear of England centre-half Roy McFarland's challenge and then destroyed full-back John Robson with a devastating burst of acceleration.

Pushing the ball past Robson's left side, Marsh dropped his left shoulder before squeezing past, and a shot, struck in full flight, flew across goalkeeper Colin Boulton to find the net on the far side of the goal. It was a superb example of what Marsh could achieve with his gifted touch, self-confidence and the speed which had increased as he shed surplus pounds.

Speed was nothing new to City's fans. They had seen it from Francis Lee, from Colin Bell and Mike Summerbee, and they had been fed the information that Allison was almost obsessed with the technique of running style.

Allison employed Derek Ibbotson, a former world record miler, and Joe Lancaster, an AAA coach, to introduce expertise into this aspect of his training sessions. He said: 'Unless you can run well and sustain that running, you cannot hope to make a lasting impression. Top-class football demands speed and stamina, as well as great skill. If you can put these things together, you are getting somewhere.'

Millwall, whose brave bid for First Division status just failed in 1972, built their attacks on the speed of two sprinting forwards, Barry Bridges and Derek Possee. They combined to score a memorable goal against Birmingham, who eventually foiled their run for promotion. Bridges turned on a long clearance and played the ball into space. Possee won a 40-yard dash to reach the ball first and score decisively.

Speed, in the outstanding player, was directly linked to reaction time. The quick thinker could gain a yard on an opponent and sprinting power did the rest. There were no physical yardsticks. Stanley Matthews was hardly a picture of athleticism. He hunched over the ball, he had

he was without the burning speed which left beaten defenders with no chance of recovery. Finney's England career ended during the 1958 World Cup in Sweden when Brazil informed football that they were about to play a dominating role in the game.

It was in Sweden that Brazil introduced Pele, a 17-year-old, whose powerful physique was to fully complement his remarkable skills and make him the greatest footballer the world had ever seen. But although Pele made a memorable contribution to the final against Sweden, there were other Brazilians to attract and charm football's gathering clans.

One of them was Garrincha, an almost illiterate South American Indian whose physique suggested gross deformity. Garrincha's legs were bowed as though he had been tortured at birth.

It was when he was given the ball wide on Brazil's right that this odd little man displayed the mark of genius. Devastating close control lured defenders in to be destroyed by a sudden release of energy which left them flat-footed and helpless. Others were able to sustain their speed over longer distances without losing control of the ball. When Burnley were trailing 3-1 to Spurs in the 1962 FA Cup Final they were denied the chance to recover when Danny Blanchflower

began to feed his passes to Cliff Jones.

Jones, a Welsh international, was astonishingly quick. Genetics were in his favour. His father Ivor had been an astute forward and his maternal grandfather, Bryn, a speedy Rugby League three-quarter. Jones in full-flight and at the zenith of his career looked as though he might be more likely to appear among fifteen players than eleven. His running was smooth and effortless, his hip sway and swerve a direct link with a different game.

When Blanchflower gave him the ball in that 1962 Final, it was with the rapped instruction to run and run. Jones ran, carrying play deep into

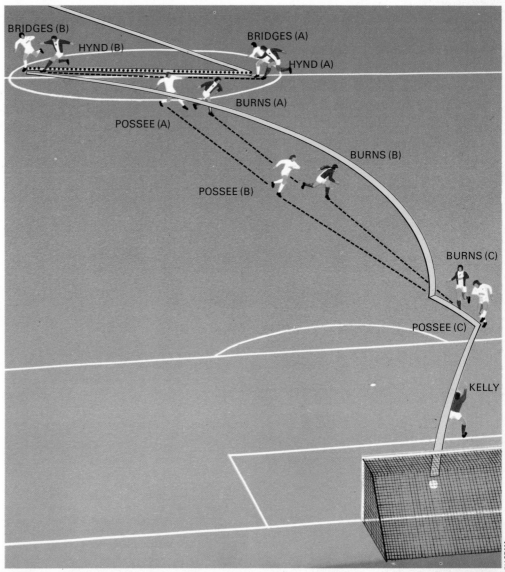

Left Diagram of a brilliant individual goal by Rodney Marsh for Manchester City against Derby County at Maine Road in April 1972.
Below Four shots of the Marsh magic. A player with a reputation for intricacy, Marsh surprised his critics. Never renowned for his speed, he raced inside McFarland and evaded the cover of Robson and Todd before scoring. The value of First Division training was starting to show.
Above Derek Possee of Millwall scores a goal against Birmingham City that was all about speed.
Right Diagram of Possee's goal. A long clearance found Bridges who played the ball into the space behind the Birmingham defence. Possee, starting behind Ken Burns, won the race and beat Mike Kelly to score a goal that won a television competition as the best of the 1971-72 season.

Burnley's half. Jimmy Adamson, Burnley's captain and later their manager, said: 'That was the end for us. We were trying to rebuild our spirit and we were very tired. Then all of a sudden this feller began to run the legs off us. How do you feel in the last twenty minutes of a Cup Final when there is someone with enough energy and pace to carry the ball 50 yards? When Cliff Jones started to do that it was all over.'

Speed helped to make Francisco Gento one of the most exciting players in a Real Madrid team which dominated the early years of the European Cup. When the others had gone Gento was still there. The kings had departed—di Stefano, Puskas, Kopa, Santamaria, Del Sol, Canario and the rest. But in Athens in the early summer of 1971, Gento still paraded himself in the glare of European competition.

It was the end for him when Real fell to Chelsea in a replay of the Cup Winners Cup. But there were memories. Gento was as quick as they came. He had lacked Jones' courage and scoring ability, but he might have been even quicker

when the mood took him.

Speed lifted Stan Mortensen from the ranks of ordinary footballers and helped to make him a famous England forward. Mortensen was an insignificant figure, an unknown on Blackpool's staff and in danger of being released, when he began to concentrate on speed.

He knew he was slow, painfully slow. So he set out to improve. In training he would get someone to push balls towards goal from the edge of the penalty area. Mortensen knew that if he could catch the ball before it crossed the goal-line he was getting somewhere—and he did. He was to emerge as a forward famous for his killing pace and enthusiasm, his willingness to pursue a seemingly lost cause. It was testimony to the punishing endeavour he put into his training.

Speed was not an obvious feature of Martin Chivers' play when he forced himself into the England team after recovering from a knee injury which had threatened to end his career. Chivers was impressively built, but his speed power was concealed by apparent indolence. It was deceptive,

and a Spurs player said at the time: 'When we sprint in training Martin is nowhere for the first ten yards. Then you sense that he is taking over. When you get to twenty yards, he's at your shoulder. At fifty, he's pulling away. That's when he frightens you.'

The speed was a product of Chivers' tremendous physique, and when he found himself in the mood to utilize both qualities he became virtually unstoppable.

'We try and play too quickly,' said Joe Mercer, Manchester City's general manager in the spring of 1972, in a discussion about the strengths and weaknesses of British football. He was referring to the dangers of hurried team play. This had little value. But speed of thought and movement, when built into the play of an individual and when used sensibly, separated the great from the merely good.

It was why Manchester City could manage a smile on 22 April 1972. There would be another year, and Rodney Marsh would have a big part to play in it.

Coaching: Improve your speed and quicken the pace of your play

The ability to run fast is a vital part of a player's make-up, but it is not sufficient in itself. Starting, stopping, twisting, turning, changing direction and jumping, as well as straightforward running, are all actions that must be performed with as much speed as possible.

Many regard speed of running as natural and not capable of being developed. In relation to the development of strength and endurance, this is to some extent true, but by working at good speed-training routines, reactions and the suitability of the muscles and joints for carrying out the commands of the nervous system may be improved.

Before embarking on training routines, obtain a stopwatch and ask a friend to take a few times for you. Measure out distances of approximately 60 yards and 12 yards according to the facilities you have. Cover the longer distance once and the shorter distance eight times as a shuttle run. Make three recordings for each distance and work out the average, then record your best and average times. This gives you a yard-stick from which you can measure your progress.

Now ask your friend to count the number of paces you take when sprinting hard over a distance of 20 yards. By trying to increase the length of your stride while you still maintain the speed of your legs, you can cover more ground faster.

Strength is an important attribute of speed. With the aid of a qualified person, work out a weight training schedule to develop your power in the muscle groups used for sprinting. The ability to move the legs quickly can also be

improved by running on the spot in short, sharp bursts with a jogging action in between. In this exercise try to get a higher knee lift without losing speed of movement.

Speed training should be done at the start of your training programme after a good warming-up period. It is inadvisable to work at speed development after a strenuous training session. The body must be thoroughly prepared and very willing for such dynamic action.

The first few yards in football are vital, so an explosive start can often give you the edge on your opponent. Work from the goal-line to the edge of the penalty area. Sprint as fast as you can across this area to the line, then come to a stop gradually over another 15 yards before walking back to the goal-line. Work from different starting positions, lying on your back, your front, legs in the air, sitting, squatting, and any position that requires quick body movement before getting under way. To condition your body for stopping and starting, turn sharply on the penalty area line and sprint back to the goal-line. With a number of players you can have a competition to see who is the first one back in the original starting position.

Shuttle sprints for four to eight players will help improve starting and turning. These players should stand in two groups 15 yards apart. One player starts by sprinting across to the other group and releasing a player by touching him, as for a simple relay, but immediately he has touched him he sprints back after him, so returning to his original group and waiting to be released and chased by a member from the other group. This is a continuous practice which

because of its physical demands cannot be sustained for long periods.

Move on to work with a friend over an area about 20 yards wide. He stands on a line holding his hand out in front of him. You stand close enough to him so that you can touch his hand with yours. The idea here is for you to touch his hand three times. On the third touch you must sprint to the line 20 yards away whilst your friend chases to try to catch you. If he touches you before you reach the line, you have to carry him back to the starting line. If he does not, then he has to carry you.

In a small group of players, pair off and stand or sit so that you are about one yard from your partner and so that the group is in two teams forming two straight lines. Each team is given a name or colour—cranes and crows or reds and blues etc. The idea is for the coach to call the name or colour and for each member of that team to sprint to a line about 20 yards away without being touched by his partner. Again, if you get caught you have to give him a lift back. You can make this even more difficult by giving each team not only a name, but also a colour, a letter and a number so that they have to be really alert.

These exercises are devised, along with many others, to improve your reactions and develop your speed of movement. This is important obviously, but it is more important to be able to perform skills whilst sprinting or after having moved quickly. Practising this with a ball can be made very interesting with a little thought.

Sit down, legs apart, with a ball in your hands. Bounce the ball between your legs, then jump up quickly to control the ball as it bounces again and move off about five to ten yards at speed with it. Do the same exercise from a prone position. This time, hollow the back and bounce the ball hard. This is a difficult exercise, and you will have to be really sharp.

Now place a skittle about five yards away from you. Throw the ball about ten feet in the air, and, before it bounces a second time, sprint round the skittle, control the ball and move off quickly.

In another exercise, two players stand ten yards apart, one with a ball. The object here is for the player with the ball to push a firmish pass to his partner who jumps up, feet together, allowing the ball to go underneath. Then as he lands, he turns to sprint after it. The player who made the pass follows up so that he is about ten yards from his partner when he gets to the ball. He then can take his turn of jumping, twisting and sprinting.

These are just a few of the exercises that one can work at to develop speed of thought and action. Talk and experiment to find others that will help you build a variation of exercises to keep the work interesting.

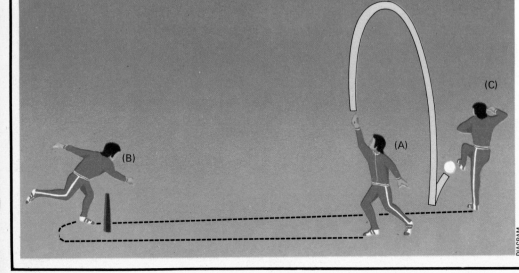

Left *A solo practice to develop speed. A ball is thrown in the air and the player races around the skittle to control it before it bounces twice.*

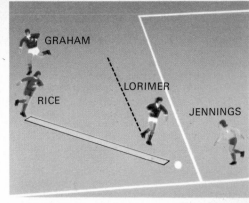

The backheel

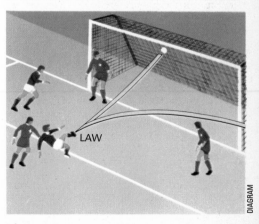

Jackie Milburn's two goals against Blackpool at Wembley in May 1951 not only won the FA Cup for Newcastle but registered him as one of football's genuine heroes.

Milburn was to play twice more on the winning side in a Wembley Final to contribute greatly to Newcastle's reputation as outstanding Cup fighters, but it was in 1951 that he became an everlasting symbol of Tyneside's marvellous association with the game's history.

Milburn had already made his mark on the match with the opening goal when he was proclaimed its hero; a rifling left-footed shot crashed past goalkeeper George Farm for the decisive second score. But whilst it was Milburn who was acclaimed, his shooting opportunity had been presented to him by inside-forward Ernie Taylor's imaginative backheel.

Taylor was one of the smallest forwards to appear regularly in League football and his one dubious claim to international distinction was to play for England against Hungary in the 6-3 defeat which ended an era of insular attitude.

In the 1953 Cup Final, he wore a Blackpool shirt and prompted his side and Stanley Matthews to success against Bolton at Wembley, using his nimble brain and visionary passing to devastating effect in the final 20 minutes of an historic drama.

In 1958 he was recruited by Manchester United to father a team hastily repaired following the awful tragedy of Munich, but although he schooled them to the Final, once more against Bolton, it ended there.

Those 20 minutes against Bolton in 1953 when he sensed the mesmeric effect of Matthews' dribbling on an injury-hit and panic-stricken defence will be remembered as Taylor's finest hour.

But his cunning and confidence were never more vividly demonstrated than when he set Milburn up for that spectacular and memorable goal in the same arena two years earlier. This time it was a goal which symbolized football's appeal. A goal of exciting suddenness. The sort of goal which suspends a vast crowd in awed silence.

Taylor's backheel brings Jackie Milburn Cup immortality

Tommy Walker, a winger who seemed to have no legitimate claim to play alongside such skilful and appealing forwards but who performed consistently well enough to keep his place, turned a pass inside to Taylor just outside the Blackpool penalty area.

Taylor's area of vision had taken in the fact that Milburn, slightly behind him, had launched forward. The little man simply and deliberately backheeled the ball into Milburn's path and the centre-forward joyfully struck a left-foot shot beyond goalkeeper George Farm's right shoulder. Taylor had changed the direction of the attack, and for a second Blackpool's defenders stood, wrong-footed. By the time they had recovered,

Above left Denis Law volleys home Peter Lorimer's cross for Scotland against Ireland in 1972.
Above The diagrams illustrate how Lorimer made the goal by his use of the backheel. Intercepting a back-pass, he beat goalkeeper Pat Jennings by backheeling the ball, turning and crossing first time. Law's agility did the rest.

Farm was collecting the ball from the back of his goal.

Newcastle had won the Cup. Milburn was immortal and Taylor had gained the total respect of professionals who immediately recognized his superb artfulness and confident application.

The skill of backheeling itself was not difficult. But knowing when to use it and having the confidence to use it was usually the prerogative of truly outstanding players.

Many managers discouraged it because it could be as disconcerting to colleagues as it could to opponents. The danger of using it in critical defensive situations was obvious.

The value of a backheel was that it could completely reverse the angle of attack bringing an element of surprise to a passing movement. It had clear limitations, not the least of them muscular. Unless the ball was backheeled on the volley or half-volley it was impossible to get loft, and any great range and accuracy in such cases was out of the question.

It was a close-range weapon when used deliberately and a spectacular addition to the repertoire of skills which outstanding players could call on in pressure moments. For instance, Peter Lorimer was to make a goal for Denis Law when playing for Scotland against Northern Ireland in the British Championship of 1972 because the backheel was part of his game.

Lorimer's imaginative backheel gives Scotland victory over Ireland

The game at Hampden Park was teetering towards a 0-0 draw, as the Irish showed the strength of their defensive formation, until right-back Pat Rice made a mistake. Drawn on the cover to the left side of the field, he was under pressure from George Graham as he tried to play the ball back to his goalkeeper, Pat Jennings.

Lorimer sensed his move. He dashed in to intercept as Jennings made to collect the ball. But pressed close to the bye-line, the Leeds United winger had little room to manoeuvre. An orthodox turn with the ball would have taken him either away from the goal or in where Jennings could take the ball off his toes. He solved the problem by backheeling it away from the bye-line and turning quickly. He was then perfectly positioned to cross left-footed.

Law, who had suffered a long exile from international football until Tommy Docherty brought him back to the Scottish team that season, turned the ball into the unguarded goal with a superb acrobatic volley.

George Graham, whose persistence had needled Rice into that mistake, included the backheel in his own range of subtle skills. It worked memorably in a match between the League Champions of 1971 and their successors, Derby County, at Highbury. Charlie George put Arsenal in front with a lunging header from Graham's cross, but an incident seconds earlier had unsettled the Derby defence.

Graham, dribbling across the penalty area, checked, backheeled the ball to George Armstrong and sprinted wide to the left. Armstrong fed the return and Graham was clear to send over a driving centre. For a second the rigid composure of the Derby defence was disturbed and it gave George the half-yard of room that he needed. He flung himself into the path of the powerful centre and diverted it past Colin Boulton who had been enjoying a memorable afternoon in the Derby goal. The goal tipped the scales in the match, and Arsenal at least had the satisfaction of a home League victory over their successors as League Champions.

Skilful, thinking players who were also blessed with great confidence used the backheel as a psychological weapon once they sensed that the opposition had been unnerved by successful attacking play.

Alan Ball, when playing for Everton, Arsenal and England developed a technique where he would set himself up to play a ball from outside

WALKER

TAYLOR

MILBURN

WALKER

FARM

TAYLOR

MILBURN

DIAGRAM: RESEARCH—PATHE NEWS

Coaching: Learn when and how to use the backheel

The secret of success in football is so often adaptation. It is not always possible to position one's body to perform an orthodox method of kicking, and time does not always allow a player to wait until he is positioned correctly before playing the ball.

Several parts of the body can be used to propel the ball forward, sideways or backwards, but, because the very nature of the movement and the size of the area with which contact is made makes the success of the pass very doubtful, they are used only as an emergency or as a method of deceiving an opponent.

Kicking with the heel has grown in football as the necessity for speed of thought and action has increased. Defenders too, have become harder to deceive and now wherever and whenever possible you must try to introduce imagination into your play.

There are three main varieties of backheel: when the ball is in the air, either when it has travelled over the player's head and fallen behind the body or when it is approaching from behind and falling short; when the ball is on the ground, the inside of the non-kicking foot is placed by the side of the ball and the heel of the kicking foot comes in contact with the ball; and when the feet are crossed so that the outside of the non-kicking foot is placed by the ball and the kicking foot comes forward and across so that the heel is in a position to play the ball backwards. All methods require accuracy of contact. The heel bone is very narrow, and unless contact is made exactly dead centre the pass will go astray.

Get the feel of the contact by using it as an emergency stop. In fact you will find as you cultivate this technique that it can be used very successfully in stopping quickly and moving off in the opposite direction.

Start with the ball stationary; place the inside of your non-kicking foot next to the ball, take your kicking foot over and in front of the ball so that the heel bone is in a line with the centre of the ball and the intended line of movement. The foot comes back so that the heel makes contact with the ball and follows through to make the first stride as the body turns to follow the ball. It is important during this action that the eyes are focused on the ball to ensure a clean and central contact.

Practise turning both ways because you may find that you turn quicker by turning the opposite way to the leg you are kicking with. Once you are confident about making contact and are comfortable in turning, try this technique on the move, walking at first.

Allow the ball to run slightly ahead as in dribbling, then suddenly place your non-kicking foot just ahead of the ball. Bring your kicking foot over and forward quickly, be sure to watch the ball, knock it backwards with the heel and turn to move in the opposite direction quickly. Gradually increase your speed of movement until you can do this at a reasonable running pace.

You may find this technique useful when used as a skill whilst working across the pitch. Test this by asking a friend to work with you. Run with the ball across the edge of the penalty area, with your friend concentrating on keeping his

Left Diagrams showing how Ernie Taylor of Newcastle United made a famous goal for Jackie Milburn in the 1951 FA Cup Final. Newcastle were leading Blackpool 1-0 when Taylor received the ball from his right-winger Tommy Walker. Sensing Milburn approaching from a deep position, he backheeled it into his path. For a second the Blackpool defenders stood wrong-footed, long enough for Milburn to crash home a left-footed shot.
Above Taylor, extreme right, watches Milburn's drive flash past Farm and into the Blackpool net. Newcastle won 2-0 and Stan Matthews had to wait another two years before earning a Cup winner's medal. On that day Matthews' inside-forward partner against Bolton Wanderers was Ernie Taylor.
Above right Liverpool's Peter Thompson rolls the ball back in an attempt to beat Peter Simpson.

his left foot with his right heel.

He would do this to emphasize his team's control of a game, just as Danny Blanchflower did when leading Spurs to great triumphs during the early sixties.

Blanchflower had an extravagant range of such skills and he used them repeatedly. He said: 'If I am playing against someone who is constantly coming through to pass the ball about with flicks and backheels I must start to think that this guy is right on top of his game.

'That's why I go out to do the things that might look flashy. But if I play a simple sidefoot pass, it doesn't make that much impression. It's what they expect, isn't it? But on the other hand, if I do something extravagant the other people are entitled to wonder what's going on. If they think

we are playing that well, then we are halfway there.'

Oddly it was the threat of a backheel which was never carried out that proved most valuable to some players. Alex James, when playing for Arsenal in the thirties, was adept at wrong-footing opponents by waving his right foot back over the ball while running at speed. James did not make contact with the ball but the movement confused and checked his opponent leaving James to run on with a vital yard in his favour. Charlie Cooke, of Chelsea, was another Scot who perfected this sort of deception, and he had the acceleration to leave the baffled defender standing.

A yard was all that top players needed as Taylor and Milburn proved on that day at Wembley in 1951.

Above George Best demonstrates how the back of the heel can be used to collect a pass. If the ball falls short and behind you, it can be flicked up and forward with the heel so that it falls conveniently into your stride—a difficult skill, but one that is useful in emergencies.

body between you and the goal. Suddenly backheel the ball, turn quickly and try to get a shot in after a couple of strides. Better still dribble past him and get closer to goal before trying your shot.

As a winger you may find this useful when you have had to turn away from your opposing full-back and now face a supporting team-mate. The ball is with the foot furthest away from the opponent so that you are screening it, not allowing the full-back to get in a tackle but inviting him to come in fairly close to challenge. In this situation you can use your supporting player as a decoy by pretending to pass the ball to him. As your foot comes forward to make contact, you allow it to move over and forward of the ball; you now backheel it and move off quickly down the line.

Try this first of all out on the touchline, on your own so that you can get the feel of the ball and the environment of the position. As a winger it would be good practice to do this when working on crossing for other players to head or shoot at goals. Ask one of your team-mates to come over and act as a full-back, just to make his presence felt. The fact that he knows what you are going to do should not put you off; he must allow you to continue the movement. The success of this movement will come in the game when you have deceived your opponent into thinking that you are going to pass the ball or into thinking that he can get the ball by moving in and tackling.

Once you have the feel of kicking with the heel for yourself, it is comparatively easy to use this for passing to a team-mate. Good scoring opportunities can come when you are dribbling across field and a team-mate crosses over the back of you. A sudden backheel movement could take the opponent following you by surprise, change the direction of the attack and leave your colleague clear.

As a centre-forward, you may be running forward when you find a through ball is dropping short of you. As the ball bounces behind you, you can use the heel to knock it over the top of you or allow your foot to come across the line and pass it with the heel to another player better positioned than you are.

Try this by throwing a ball in the air so that it is going to bounce just behind you. As it bounces up to about hip height bring your foot up at the back and knock it with the outside of the heel over the top of you and control it in front of you before shooting at a target. Then, play the ball up on to a wall so that it comes back and bounces just behind you. Again making good use of your judgement and keeping your eye on the ball, knock it over the top or have a target which you try to hit. When attempting to do this working with opposition, check your stride and deceive your opponent by leading him to believe you are going to stop and control the ball. Suddenly you make your second movement and you may well find yourself completely in the clear.

You must consider the risk you are taking with this method of kicking and realize that the chances of failure, unless you have cultivated a very good technique, are high. Generally this is an emergency movement or one used to deceive the opposition. But as with all difficult skills it is usually unexpected. If you perform the skill correctly, it is likely to confound your opponents.

Do not let your play become obsessed with frills and flicks; try to resist them until you are satisfied with your basic orthodox techniques. But when you have reached this standard you can embroider your game in this way. Remember, though, to treat the backheel as a serious, positive skill—something which will help your team and not just please spectators.

Stamina

If the Leeds United players had been feeling the strain of their long and cruelly exhausting season as they approached the 1970 Cup Final, they could have been excused slight thoughts of un-easiness at the prospect of meeting Chelsea at Wembley.

For while Leeds, hampered by fixture conges-tion and consequent injury, had been battling in vain for two other prizes, the Football League Championship and the European Cup, Chelsea had been winning games through the very quality the battle-scarred Leeds players might now lack: stamina.

In reaching the Final, Chelsea had scored 21 goals; more significantly, 15 of them had come in the second half. Of those, 14 had been netted after more than an hour's play, in the last third of matches where physical fitness and the willingness of players to push their bodies to the absolute limits were the qualities that mattered.

Ian Hutchinson, a brave, selfless runner whose emergence as a striker had coincided with Chelsea's push to Wembley, summed it up: 'Being fit is not enough, unless you are also willing to go on making runs again and again. There comes a period when players begin to tire and start to wonder whether it is worth going off on another big chase.' When other teams hesitate, Chelsea do not.

Chelsea's semi-final against Second Division Watford, who had themselves shown fitness above their station in deleting Liverpool and Stoke City from the competition, more than proved Hutchin-son's point. Although David Webb had given Chelsea an early lead, Terry Garbett equalized, and at half-time the match was evenly poised. But almost on cue, on the hour, Peter Osgood headed Chelsea back in front, and then, on the cloying mudheap of a White Hart Lane pitch, their stamina took over.

Three goals followed in a six-minute show of strength. Peter Houseman snatched one, Hutchin-son another and then Houseman again—all goals born out of durability as much as skill.

Chelsea were contravening a goalscoring pat-tern that emerged from a random study of the times goals are scored. 28 per cent of goals taken from a sample of Saturday games were scored in the first half-hour of the match, 40 per cent in the second, and 32 per cent in the last third. But in this last phase of the game, including extra time, Chelsea had scored two-thirds of their goals that

Below Diagram showing Peter Houseman scoring Chelsea's third goal in their 5-1 win over Watford in the 1970 FA Cup semi-final. Chelsea showed remarkable stamina in reaching Wembley that season, scoring 14 of their 21 Cup goals after more than an hour's play. Then in the Final they equalized against Leeds in the last few minutes of the first match, and finally Osgood and Webb scored late in the replay to win Chelsea the Cup.
Bottom Houseman drills in Chelsea's third goal.

had taken them to the Cup Final, a staggering proportion.

Dave Sexton, their manager, was not surprised: 'This is how we play—flat out. And then we suddenly play harder still. It's hunger for goals that does it.' A hunger that only the ability to keep on running could stimulate.

The way Chelsea won the Cup now became totally explicable. Hutchinson's equalizer only four minutes from the end of full-time at Wembley and winning goals from Osgood and Webb late into the replay hit Leeds where they might possibly have been at their weakest, in coping with the physical problem of surviving, right up to the final whistle, the demands of yet another crucial match.

What Chelsea possessed as a team, individuals, such as Alan Ball, had been able to use to turn the course of matches. At Wembley in 1966, Ball could see victory written into the agony on Karl Schnellinger's face. 'He'd gone,' said Ball during the ecstatic aftermath of England's World Cup triumph, 'he'd really gone. You could tell from his eyes. I'd run the legs off him.'

Ball had done just that, flogging himself unmercifully and sustaining his effort through a gruelling period of extra time.

With a few minutes left he raced to rob Schnellinger, when it seemed that no one on the field had that amount of energy left.

'I saw the ball run free and that Schnellinger was after it. I thought: "Not again. I'm done." I was looking for a breather and I'd already died twice. But I went and I got the ball.'

It was more than just running which had torn the heart out of the tall, blond German full-back. In that match, Ball finally emerged from an unruly apprenticeship to take his true station in football. But it was his phenomenal stamina, his astonishing physical output, which registered him as an exceptional performer at the highest level of the game.

His pal Nobby Stiles, whose boyishly joyful reaction to triumph was to make him the popular symbol of England's success, recalled:

'Ballie was unbelievable. He ran and he ran and when no one else had any running left he was still running. He never stopped.'

To do this, Ball not only needed exceptional fitness but the will to keep working. This had always been an outstanding feature of the British game. There were long, hard winters to contend with and teams needed more than just skill to survive them. England were undoubtedly the strongest and best prepared team in the 1966 competition.

It was not overlooked when a FIFA study group issued a report on the tournament the following autumn: 'Though skill and technique, individually and collectively, is important, greater emphasis is now being given to physical condition and team tactics.'

More and more clubs began to employ athletic

trainers to improve their level of stamina and speed. Manchester City, for instance, were to engage Derek Ibbotson, once a world-record miler, and Joe Lancaster, an athletics coach, to introduce expertise into their training sessions.

Malcolm Allison, City's coach and later their manager, made this point in an excellent book, 'Soccer for Thinkers'.

'First, a player's running must be increased. This is the easiest way of becoming almost overnight a better player. He does not necessarily have to use it all in a game, but he needs to be able to produce it when required. Old players fade out of the game because they cannot run far enough or fast enough.'

Allison went on: 'When di Stefano was seventeen, the Argentine coach, Rigomino, said he was the fastest thing on two legs he had ever seen. And whenever he played he continually popped up in every part of the field with seemingly inexhaustible energy. When he could no longer run enough

Below *Diagram illustrating the stamina of Colin Bell, regarded as Britain's fittest footballer, as he scores a late winner for Manchester City against Arsenal at Highbury in December 1971. Bell sprinted upfield from deep in his own half to touch on Donachie's cross, and then he moved forward to slide in Lee's low centre.*
Bottom *Wilson, Storey and Nelson look on helplessly as Bell turns Lee's cross over the line.*

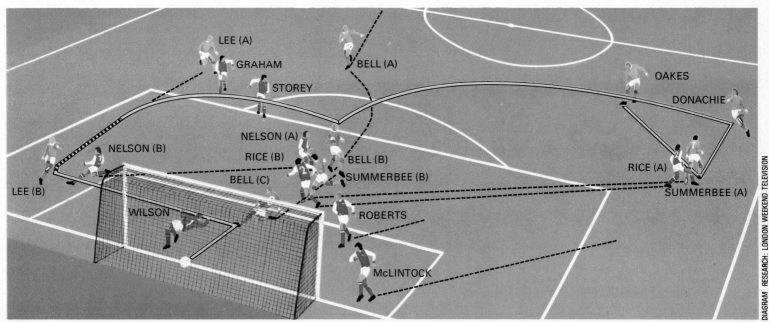

for the top level he was finished, although his skills and experience remained almost matchless. Without the ability to run he was nothing.'

There was nothing obsessional about Allison's thinking. His teams played attractive, skilful football. But he never overlooked the need for supreme fitness, and in Colin Bell he had probably the fittest man in the Football League and possibly in football history.

Bell was signed from Bury, while rival clubs were still expressing doubts about him. Bell looked to be one-paced, although brave and talented. It was why Leeds United, among others, fought shy of signing him.

A north-easterner, Bell was turned down as a boy by both Newcastle and Sunderland because of a slight physique. But by the time he had established himself as an outstanding midfield player and an international he had completely overcome all the conjecture about his ability to keep on running.

Allison said of him: 'He runs like a deer, has great stamina, is tremendous in the air, beats players as he likes, shoots with both feet, tackles, and plays the ball as accurately as anybody in the business. Without doubt he is the best player I have ever worked with or played with. He is the fittest man I have come across in all my time in the game. In fact I have never come across anybody who really approaches him.'

There were those who regarded this as an extravagant reference, especially as Bell had been unable to establish himself in the England team. It was argued that Bell playing for England had never taken a game over as Ball almost did in 1966 in the World Cup final at Wembley.

Joe Mercer, City's general manager and one of the great names of his day, countered this by saying: 'Colin has never been given the opportunity to take charge. You have to unleash Colin, let him go where he wants to. It's pointless restricting him to one side of the field. We give him his head because we know that he has the discipline to be where he is most wanted.'

It was clear that Bell was something of a physical freak. Part of it was that he had a very slow pulse rate and a big heart. Allison said: 'We have never been able to push him to his limit. We simply try to find out what his limit is. Colin does the same training as the other players but he does it faster and better.'

So naturally fit, Bell played though he had not trained for four months

'There was one occasion when he had been off with an injury and he hadn't trained for four months. We put him straight back into the team against Tottenham and he scored in three minutes. We didn't have to think about his match fitness.'

Bell's stamina and its effect on a game was never more evident than when City played at Arsenal in the autumn of 1971.

In the closing minutes of a hard-fought game, he challenged successfully for a ball in the air on the edge of Arsenal's penalty area.

As he hit the floor, he propelled himself forward as City built an attack, finally arriving in front of Arsenal's goal to touch in a low centre from Francis Lee. The goal won City the match. A few minutes earlier George Graham, Arsenal's elegant midfield player, had attempted a long crossfield pass which he instantly recognized as an error of judgement.

'I was whacked. I didn't really have the strength to drive the ball over a long distance. When I saw Colin Bell do what he did I was astonished. He was still going as strongly as he had been during the opening minutes of the match. When he scored that goal he was the fastest, strongest man on the pitch and the game was almost over.'

Natural fitness helped to make Ron Burgess one of the outstanding wing-half-backs of his day, and he used it to inspire the Spurs team of the fifties. A lean Welshman who went to White Hart Lane as a boy, Burgess could run all day. Spurs' style at that time was based on the simple principle of push-and-run play which had been encouraged by their manager, Arthur Rowe.

Burgess' ability to involve himself constantly in these passing movements and to be back in defence at crucial moments registered him as something of a physical freak too. Eddie Baily, later to become Spurs' assistant manager, was in that team and recalled:

'Ron suffered from stomach trouble and eventually had an operation for an ulcer. He smoked and he liked a beer. There were times when his stomach played him up so much before a match that he was physically ill. But he'd go out there and outrun everybody. He was astonishing in that respect. Over the years he amazed all of us at White Hart Lane.'

It was argued that the concentration on stamina interfered with the development of more certain individual technique and that the overall pattern of running and aggression tended to suppress skill in England.

But the success of teams like Chelsea who with players like Osgood, Hudson, Cooke and Hollins could never be accused of lacking in talent, argued against this. They simply showed that with stamina their skills could be sustained for much longer periods.

Coaching: Learn how to gain stamina and outlast your opponents

Stamina is one of the most important aspects of fitness. However skilful or quick a player may be, he will be of little value to his team during a hard match unless he has the endurance to do these capabilities justice.

And, apart from the effect on ability, the lack of stamina can cause cramp, when the blood circulation is incapable of coping with fatigue caused by stresses and strains brought about by the movements necessary in the game.

After a rest during the close season, most clubs concentrate on general stamina building at the commencement of the pre-season training. Almost any exercise is suitable when it is performed over a prolonged period. Walking and running, games like hand-ball or basketball are all ideal activities performed for about an hour or so. If you are lucky enough to have a forest or open country handy, this can be really useful for your long, slow distance work to help build general stamina.

From this you can graduate to quicker, interval work. You can begin by running 2,000 yards, broken down into ten 200-yard stints, resting for 3 minutes between each stint at first, then gradually increasing the distance and cutting down the rest time until you are covering about 4,000 yards in 400 yard stints with a two-minute rest period. During the rest periods, you can practise various skills with a ball, like continuous heading, keeping the ball up using the feet, or simple passing activities at a jogging pace.

This training will have built up general stamina, but for the special demands of football another type of stamina is also required. 'Doggies' or shuttle runs will condition you for the sort of sprints you must make in matches. From a starting line, objects are placed at intervals of 5 yards up to 25 yards. Players must sprint to each object in turn, returning to the starting line after each visit. 150 yards is covered on each stint. Start with six or eight stints, allowing 45 seconds for the running with a resting period of 45 seconds in between.

The number can be increased to a maximum of 14.

The human body can adapt itself quite quickly to rhythm running, but running in football is irregular so, although maintaining the same overall rest period, break up the actual times, 30 seconds for one, 60 seconds for another, and so on. This type of running can be the basis of your training during the season. It is economical both in the time it takes and the area you need to perform.

Variation in training routines helps to keep away staleness, so introduce variety where possible. One alternative method involves marking out a square of about 25 yards. A small group of players start at one corner, they sprint to the next flag 25 yards away, then jog to the next one, sprint to the next and jog to the next. Complete ten laps of the square this way. Then another variation. Sprint one side and jog three sides—sprint two sides and jog two—sprint three, jog one—sprint four, jog four—this should be performed twice. Then split the players into two groups; one group sprints round the square until they catch the other group up who are jogging round the square. Then this group sprints around to catch the first group who have continued jogging round. Repeat, then send each file in turn back in the opposite direction. This should be done twice.

Other routines can involve using a ball. A particularly effective one involves two players standing at markers, 25 yards apart. One dribbles the ball towards the other who runs in to meet him. As they come close, A passes to B and both continue on their way to the posts. There they turn and repeat the exercise. Do this eight times before resting.

Strength endurance can be built by weight training, but this must be done under strict supervision. General endurance and some strength can be developed by circuit training and the principle of this is to set out a series of exercises—press-ups, sit-ups, star-jumps etc. Repeat each exercise as often as you possibly can in 30 seconds. If you work with a partner he can count them and put them on a card, this way you can keep a record which you can try to beat each time you do the circuit. Your friend can then do his stint whilst you count and record his. This means that two players can perform on each exercise and each pair can move from one exercise to the next.

This is a very convenient way of keeping yourself fit during bad weather when you cannot get out. Remember the benefit from this is long term; do not go mad the day before a match, for instance. Perform these exercises regularly and you will have plenty of stamina to last the season through.

Below The 'shuttle run' is an ideal way to build up stamina. The player visits each object in turn, rests and then repeats the course. Each 'shuttle' should be completed within 45 seconds, and there must be 45 seconds rest before the next sprint. The number of repetitions can be increased to about 14 or 15. If a player can manage this number, no one should doubt his stamina.

Passing – the wall pass

Each of the 71 goals scored by Arsenal in winning the Football League championship in 1971 was important, most were deserved, a few were memorable. One, struck by George Graham against Liverpool at Highbury, was a classic.

It was an important goal for Arsenal because it swept away another prickly obstacle from their path to the title. It was a deeply satisfying goal for Graham, who had been dropped from the side and came seething off the substitutes' bench to reclaim his place. It was an exhilarating goal for the fans, who had seen drifting towards deadlock a match that needed to be won.

And the way that Graham scored it was a fine example of a skill of which most schoolboys possess the rudiments, yet which is seldom seen at football's higher levels: the wall pass.

The wall pass was a basic tactic in the alleys between the back-to-back houses where British football stars were traditionally bred. Every budding seven-year-old George Best learned early that the best way to beat an opponent was to push the ball around him against the playground wall or a high kerb, and then run on to collect the bounce.

At the higher levels of the game, however, most players use the wall pass rarely, or not at all. Defenders here are both too knowing and too numerous to be easily beaten. And the human 'wall'—the team mate who must flick the pass back—is a small target, fast-moving and unpredictable. Yet it can be a profitable manoeuvre if performed with absolute conviction, pinpoint accuracy—and cheek.

A playground skill that few stars have the cheek to use – but it still wins matches

It was this last quality, audacity, that George Graham brought into the match with Liverpool. Liverpool's defence, the most uncompromisingly successful in the League, had just dispossessed an Arsenal forward yet again. The counter-attack had begun to work its way clear—when crisis loomed. The captain, Tommy Smith, could not find a ready target for a forward pass from just outside his penalty area. He chose instead to play the ball slightly in front of square to Ian Ross, some twenty yards to his left.

By most judgements it was a risk but Smith knew that few forwards were willing to dispute possession at close quarters with his defence; he may have forgotten Arsenal's growing reputation for swift hustling at all points.

Ross was suddenly in trouble when Jon Sammels put him under pressure. Graham closed in quickly. Sammels nudged the ball free to Graham and darted forward into space. Smith's scurrying pursuit of Graham and despairing challenge emphasized the developing danger. Graham, avoiding the tackle, saw at

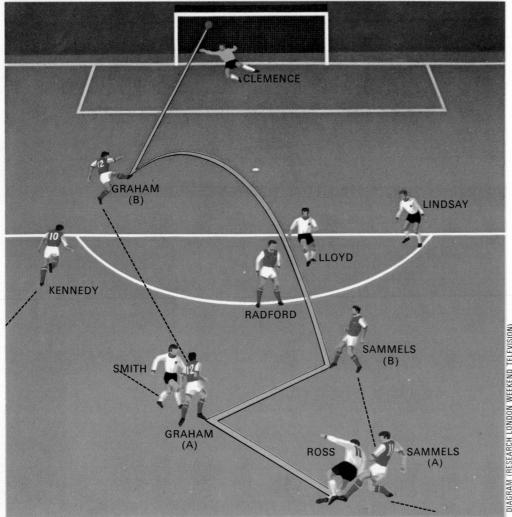

An outstanding wall pass won Arsenal a vital League match against Liverpool, at Highbury, in the 1970-71 season. George Graham, coming on as substitute, was both the instigator and the finisher of the move. Arsenal won the game 2-0.
Left *Diagram of the wall pass that finally broke down the Liverpool defence. Jon Sammels, who won the ball for Graham with a determined challenge on Ian Ross, acted as the 'wall' and played a perfect return chip into Graham's path.*
Above left *Graham's volley gave the move a perfect finish, utterly beating Ray Clemence, the Liverpool keeper. Just a few minutes later Graham made the second goal, for John Radford.*

PETERS

PERRYMAN
(A)

PERRYMAN
(B)

PEARCE

once that a wall pass was 'on'. He struck a crisp pass to Sammels' feet and then thrust himself through and into the space Liverpool could no longer cover.

Sammels knew his priorities. Speed was more important than accuracy. He flicked his return, first-time, over the head of the remaining Liverpool defender to drop into Graham's path. Unmarked—indeed, unmarkable—Graham sent a perfect instant volley past Ray Clemence. Arsenal 1, Liverpool 0.

What makes a successful wall pass? Perhaps the best illustration is to consider the ways in which Graham's move could have failed. It would have failed if the initial short pass to Sammels had not been perfectly directed. It would have failed if Sammels' reply had not been immediate. It would have failed had Graham not struck his volley irresistably. And above all, it would have failed had Graham not made his explosive run the moment he played the ball to Sammels.

It is this sudden change of tempo that catches defences napping, as Graham demonstrated in another match the same season, against Stoke City in an FA Cup semi-final replay at Villa Park. Again the ball was knocked almost haphazardly into his path, this time by Charlie George. Graham took it in full stride, hitting a superb half-volley that took goalkeeper Gordon Banks by surprise—so much so that he almost fumbled it over his line. Banks admitted later that he had expected Graham to run on into more obviously exploitable range.

In both cases, it was a sudden switch in rhythm which enabled Graham to pierce the defence. From a slow build-up, he suddenly rapped the ball to a team-mate and instantly wrong-footed his opponents.

Sammels' comment after the Liverpool match, 'George's run was so decisive, he made up my mind for me', points up another requirement of the successful wall pass: decisiveness. The attacker's run must be so positive that it leaves his team-mate in no doubt what is expected of him.

Bobby Charlton produced a classic example at Wembley in 1969. It was unusual for him, for, in spite of his quality, he rarely showed a willingness to play the ball off at close range, preferring to set himself up for hostile long-range shooting. But in this international against Wales he worked a perfect opening with Francis Lee when it seemed that the

Spurs won acclaim in the 1970-71 season by scoring against Burnley from a move of 11 passes without the intervention of a defender. The crucial tenth and eleventh passes were a wall pass manoeuvre, played by Steve Perryman and Jimmy Pearce. Demoralized Burnley lost 4-0.

Above *Diagram showing how penetrating the wall pass can be in a crowded penalty area.*
Below *Clear of the pursuing defenders, Perryman turns the ball towards the Burnley net.*
Right *The elation of a successful wall pass. Perryman celebrates with a jubilant headstand.*

Welsh would hold on to a one-goal lead. Lee's first-time return was chillingly accurate; Charlton's power did the rest.

As Lee said afterwards, 'When the ball was pushed up to me, my first thought was to turn with it and "take them on". But Bobby was so positive, it was obvious he wanted it back.'

Similar decisiveness was shown by Steve Perryman, an impressive recruit to the Tottenham Hotspur team which won the Football League Cup in 1971, in scoring in a League game against Burnley.

Spurs' traditional style—accurate linking play, often at high speed—had taught Perryman the possibilities of using a colleague as a 'wall'. Here again, the change in tempo was vital. Perryman was involved in the slow early stages of the move, then shot ahead to offer himself in support as the ball was worked forward.

Perryman's pass to Pearce was a long one, but his willingness to keep going took him to a shooting position unmarked. And his killing shot was the pay-off.

Goals like these illustrate how deadly a wall

pass can be. Yet many top teams in the 1960s and early 1970s, West Ham and Leeds among them, refrained from using this tactic for striking in the penalty area, though they used it in other areas of build-up play. They believed, apparently, that the odds were too heavily stacked against the move succeeding. They prefer other methods. But the tactic will work unless a team lacks players of sufficient skill—or if the skills are there, but courage is missing.

Playing Real Madrid in the final of the European Cup Winners Cup in Athens in May 1971, Chelsea found themselves embarrassed by a level of skill which threatened to 'take them apart'. But the Real Madrid of that season lacked the aggressive purpose which their earlier great teams had shown in winning a succession of European Cup finals. They opened up Chelsea in the same old extravagant style, but there was no longer a di Stefano or a Puskas to finish, once the ball had been put in the penalty area. Amancio continually laid the ball off into space that no colleague had the bravery to contest with the rugged Chelsea

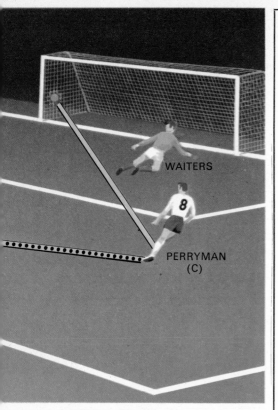

WAITERS

8

PERRYMAN
(C)

SYNDICATION INTERNATIONAL

Coaching: Learn how to deliver a pass crisply and accurately

It does not matter what kind of pass you use. What matters is that you deliver the ball in such a way that it does not present too great a problem to the man who has to receive it. This is particularly true of the wall pass.

If the pass is badly timed it will be difficult to control and the opportunity to return it accurately and at speed may be lost. To master the wall pass you must combine speed off the mark with this crisp accuracy of your passing.

Here are three ways to improve your skill in the wall pass.

1. *On your own*—Use a mark on a wall as a target. Continually play the ball at this target; even professional players can be found doing this. As you get more confidence you can increase the distance and vary the type of contact. For instance, you can try playing the ball on the half volley as it hits the ground, and then play it on the volley. A point to remember in all these exercises is movement. In games you rarely get the opportunity to receive the ball when standing still or without someone challenging you for it. So get into the habit of moving to meet the ball while at the same time having a quick look around so that you have an idea of where other players might be.

Next, start to play the ball at the target from an angle so that the ball will rebound some distance ahead of you. To reach the rebound you will have to sprint hard; speed off the mark, especially over the first five yards, is vital in all aspects of play. When you have controlled the angled rebound turn and repeat the movement, this time with the other foot. You can vary this by using the inside and outside of each foot for passing, and by controlling and shooting the rebound at another target when you collect it.

2. *In a group*—Start off by passing simply between each other and then slowly build up to more ambitious things. Begin to move about. Once you have given the ball, sprint forward into a new position where you can collect a return.

Now take things a stage further, as you did when playing the ball at a target. Start pushing it around first time, and slowly increase the range.

You might not find this easy at first because good timing is needed to move the ball over long distances. But if you practise hard and long enough the timing will come. Remember as you play the ball to move off and put in this five to ten yard sprint.

Next, split up into pairs and repeat the target move that you used against the wall with one of the pair becoming the target. You will

find this harder because the 'rebound' from a player or 'the return pass' is not so reliable as the direct rebound from a wall. Practising in this way will show you how important it is to be accurate with the first pass. If you do not hit your human 'target' you will not get the ball back again.

3. *In a 'game situation'*—However hard you practise your skills you will never be able to rely on them unless you practise them under conditions and pressures you are likely to meet in an actual match. Only when you have built up your confidence by practising on your own and with your team-mates should you move onto this exercise.

Turn the centre circle on your practice ground into a miniature pitch by making goals, about a yard wide, opposite each other on the edge of the circle. Divide the group into teams of two, and then play a two-a-side game within this area. The only way a goal can be scored is if it results directly from a wall pass move, with the player who receives the return pass scoring. Working in such a confined space you will learn not only the value of being accurate with your first pass, but also how important it is that you make your run off the ball into a space where your team-mate can find you with the return pass. Always remember to call to your colleague. If it was possible to silence the crowd noise at a League game you would hear the constant chatter that goes on between players.

You will find this exercise hard and you will score very few goals at first. Do not be discouraged, because by holding the ball and waiting for the right moment to spring the move you will realize when and how to use your new skills in a competitive match.

Below Playing two-a-side in the centre circle improves wall passing in a 'game situation'.
Bottom *Graham's goal from a wall pass against Crystal Palace was voted the best of the 1969-70 season in a television competition.*

DIAGRAM

TOPIX

defenders.

It takes courage to go in among belligerent defenders and hit the ball first-time; but if it is not struck instantly, the chance will be lost among urgent tackles and the wall pass ploy will have failed.

Perhaps the greatest exponents of the wall pass in the 1960s and 1970s were Brazil, the world champions. Their build-up was deceptively slow and lazy looking, a perfect springboard for quicksilver changes of pace. Pele, Tostao and Jairzinho, both as instigators and as the 'wall', showed impudent mastery of all the required skills.

From delicate flicks to the subtle stabs that impart backspin or send the ball into vertical take-off, these players had all the tricks needed to defeat the tightest marker. They also possessed the confidence and nerve to use these skills even in the most important of their matches.

Such skills helped Brazil win the Jules Rimet Trophy for the third time in 1970. Graham's goal, Charlton's goal and Perryman's goal, however, showed that the world champions hold no monopoly.

The overhead kick

The 1967 FA Charity Shield match between Manchester United and Spurs was the exception to the rule that stated that the match between the FA Cup winner and the League Champions was a mundane, disappointing affair.

It was a day when United introduced Brian Kidd, a tall, eager youngster to their team and when Spurs goalkeeper Pat Jennings entered himself in the record books by scoring a goal with a kick from his hands which was helped in at the other end by United's keeper Alex Stepney.

But the game's greatest souvenir, which would have earned its place in the museum of great goals, was erased by the decision of the referee. Denis Law had appeared to register what should and would have been one of his greatest goals—with the most marvellous overhead kick.

Spinning beneath a centre lofted in from Spurs' left flank, and with a wrench of his muscles, Law propelled himself upwards, his legs criss-crossing into a bicycle volley which drove the ball into the roof of the goal.

For a fraction of a second the whole ground was silent. It was the Stretford End which reacted first with an explosion of acclaim as Law, bounding up from the floor, turned to them, his right arm raised in a familiar, imperious Roman salute.

Then he disappeared beneath congratulating colleagues. They had grown used to great goals from the man. But this was something special. Suddenly there was silence as the crowd realized that the goal had been disallowed. No one knew for what. But the referee had killed it off, and it would have no place in the records, only in the memory.

Law threw his head back in disgust, and then turned to the crowd his arms out, the palms of his hands raised in a gesture of total disbelief. There has been no more effective protest. But the referee stood firm.

Law's instinct for the spectacular had not been overlooked by Italian clubs intent on plundering the best of British talent. Encouraged by the shameful restriction of a totally unrealistic maximum wage in the Football League, they came seeking the best and it was inevitable that Law should figure on the list. Excitingly quick and devastatingly sharp in front of goal, Law had been brought up by Huddersfield Town and then sold to Manchester City. But it was when he went to Italy with Torino that Law was to cultivate the theatrical style which helped to make him one of the world's most feared attackers.

He recalled: 'I never settled down in Italy. It was a different way of life and not my kind of life. But there was something about the football which appealed to my instincts. Italian footballers have great technique. If they were allowed to play as they would like to, they would probably be better to watch than the Brazilians. They used to excite me because they were never afraid to indulge in spectacular attempts at goal. I liked that.'

Law had already shown a talent for unorthodox skill. When he finally returned home to join Manchester United for a then record £115,000 in July 1962 he had harnessed that unorthodoxy to his courage and a refusal to conform. The combination proved deadly. They loved him at Old Trafford, and at the Stretford End they proclaimed him King. Whenever he launched himself into the extravagant horizontal position of the overhead kick, the Stretford Enders would hold their breath in amazement and then roar with delight at the audacity of it all.

It was a skill which appealed most out of its unfamiliarity. Few British players had the confidence to attempt the bicycle kick, and managers brought up with a belief in more orthodox principles rarely encouraged it.

In Europe and South America it was a consistent feature of play. Spectators warmed to the spectacular, and defenders as well as forwards indulged in it. The great Hungarian forward Sandor Koscis was not only an outstanding header of the ball, but a gymnastic finisher when meeting angled crosses.

Few British players achieved any great success with overhead kicks, and those who did found that referees consistently penalized them for

Left Denis Law launches himself into a characteristic overhead kick against West Ham. His willingness to attempt the spectacular has brought him many goals of breathtaking brilliance.

Right Tottenham's Martin Peters prises open the Manchester City defence with an overhead kick in a 1972 League match at White Hart Lane.

Below right Diagram of the move that led to the goal. From Chivers' long throw, Oakes could only half clear and Neighbour headed the ball back. Peters was facing away from the goal but saw his chance, and his overhead shot deceived Corrigan.

dangerous play. But there was a more subtle point which helped to stifle the skill in Britain while it was being nourished abroad.

Headwork has always been an outstanding feature of the British game, but for many years it was largely ignored in other countries. This helped to influence the kind of ball contacts which were made above shoulder height, and those made with a boot were unlikely to be encouraged.

But the gathering volume of international competition not only left its mark on tactical thinking but on individual approach. Within twenty-four hours of Hungary's triumph over England at Wembley in 1953, League professionals were experimenting with skills that had been spectacularly displayed by Puskas and his team. It was no longer enough to be good at the accepted and the orthodox. There was room for other things, and gradually there came players who were good at them.

When West Ham first introduced Martin Peters to their team in 1962, he looked to be a useful attacking wing-half who might eventually suffer from not having a change of pace when going forward. Four years later he was in the England team which won the World Cup at Wembley, and only seconds away from scoring the winning goal; Sir Alf Ramsey was to describe him as a player 'ten years ahead of his time'.

Martin Peters—never content to settle for the ordinary

Ramsey added at the time: 'Martin Peters is always going for a winner. The winning pass, the winning shot. He is not content to settle for the ordinary. Much of what he attempts goes unnoticed because he is working to such fine margins that he might not quite achieve what he is looking for.'

After being transferred to Spurs in exchange for Jimmy Greaves and a large fee, Peters found himself criticized for ignoring the obvious, but Spurs had no cause for complaint when he took a spectacular goal from Manchester City in January 1972.

City's inventive, ambitious football had made them outstanding challengers for the League Championship while Spurs were still working to establish some consistency in their play. But they were at their best against the best and this enabled them to create and take a fine goal. It began when Martin Chivers hurled a long throw from close to the corner flag on the Spurs left wing. Alan Gilzean jumped to meet it, hoping to use his delicate heading skills to deflect the ball back dangerously across the face of the goal. City had prepared for this by moving Alan Oakes, a burly, competent defender, to mark Gilzean.

Oakes could only do half the job. He got to the ball first but it glanced out at an angle, and another Spurs attacker, Jimmy Neighbour, helped it back into the goalmouth with a reflex header. Peters had sensed an opportunity, and as the ball came at him he fell backwards and kicked it over his head into goal.

City were shortly to score in similar fashion against Huddersfield when centre-half Tommy Booth finally finished off a corner-kick taken by their veteran midfield player, Freddie Hill.

Hill's kick was aimed at the dangerous head of Welsh striker Wyn Davies, but the centre-forward could not reach it as he went up with the Huddersfield defence. It sailed beyond the far post

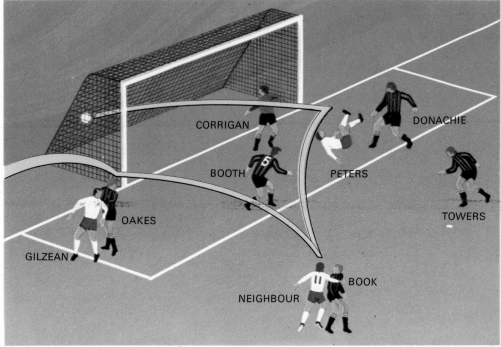

CORRIGAN · DONACHIE · BOOTH · PETERS · TOWERS · OAKES · GILZEAN · NEIGHBOUR · BOOK

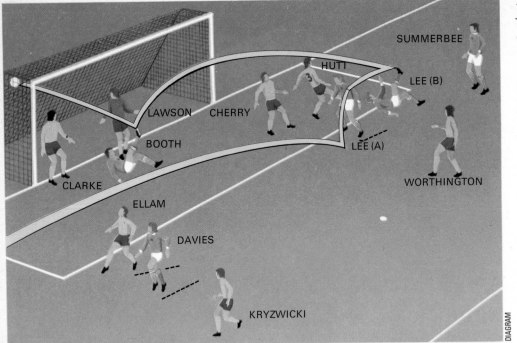

Left *Diagram showing how Manchester City fashioned a match-winning goal out of two overhead kicks against Huddersfield Town at Maine Road.*
Centre left *From Hill's corner the ball fell awkwardly to Lee. But with his back to the goal, he hooked it over his head towards the net.*
Bottom left *It fell to Tommy Booth, their centre-half, who was moving away from the goal-line where he had been positioned for the corner. Booth had to improvize and he showed all the skills of a ball player as he bicycle-kicked the ball past the surprised Huddersfield defenders to score.*

where Francis Lee made to control the ball with his body; it bounced away from him and from the goal.

But with the quickness of thought and movement that characterized his play, Lee flung himself to hook the ball over his head and back towards the other post. Booth, beginning his movement out from the goal-line, found the ball coming to him. With his back to the goal, there was little alternative for him if he wanted to try a shot. Another quick overhead flick, and City had pocketed the only goal of the match.

Lee, particularly, was always willing to try his luck with the spectacular, and was desperately unlucky not to score with a splendid scything overhead volley against West Ham earlier in the 1971-72 season.

He was to say: 'If you don't go for this kind of thing, then you are letting yourself down. Everybody likes to score goals. But there are goals and goals. These days the ball comes in early because this is what players are encouraged to do. It comes in early and at great speed. Often you know that you are only going to get a touch at it. That might be enough. But you have got to be in position to get that touch.

'You see chances being passed up simply because players want the ball to come in at a more exact angle. They can't expect this anymore. It's often the unexpected which kills a defence so why not try the unexpected.'

Lee's philosophy was once brilliantly supported by Dave Sexton in the days before he became manager of Chelsea. Sexton was a budding coach on a course at Lilleshall when students were set this problem: 'Try and break down a defence that has fallen back in force to reform on the edge of the penalty area.'

Dave Sexton's bicycle kick—a colourful way to break down defences

Some groups attempted to play themselves through with an interchange of passes. Others looked to get in from the touchlines. Sexton had a more colourful idea. Backing on to the defenders, he got the ball chipped up to him and then launched himself into a bicycle kick which lifted the ball into goal.

The move brought a smile from Walter Winterbottom, then the Director of Coaching. He was seeing an outstanding example of the originality which was to make Sexton an outstanding manager in years to come.

It was lack of originality and a natural caution which did most to stifle the development of spectacular skills like the bicycle kick, which involved such flamboyant movement.

Most managers preferred their players to go for the obvious . . . a powerful header, a lunge. They saw a greater percentage in more orthodox finishing and they continually said so. The game was hardly burdened with romantics.

But Matt Busby was a romantic, and when he bought Denis Law from Torino he bought a player who was to appeal to the senses of all who saw him. A great player. A showman. A brave player. But, above all, a player who refused to conform to the dull-eyed principles which had done more to make British football leaden-footed than any other factor.

Law, like Pele, like Puskas and other great finishers, thrived on the impossible. Football had much to thank them for.

Coaching: Develop the skill to score spectacular goals

Many moments in football require a player to adapt his play quickly. A situation that can require such improvization is when you are in the penalty area and the ball is in front of you about head height. If you are facing your own goal, you may have no choice but to kick it overhead. If you are close to your opponents' goal and unsupported, a hopeless situation can be turned to advantage by a well executed overhead shot.

Kicking high can be punished as dangerous play if opponents are close and in danger of being kicked. However, if you are careful, this can be an extremely effective skill when used in the right place at the right time.

Try the technique for yourself. Throw a ball in the air in front of you, let it bounce, then try to kick it over your head as it comes down, before it bounces again. You will quickly notice that the higher the ball is when contact is made the lower the flight of the ball off your foot. Make contact with the full instep and hold your ankle firm with the toes pointing away; you must end with a follow-through. When contact is made, the flight of the ball will depend on the position of the knee in relation to the ball. If in shooting you wish to keep the ball very low, throw both feet off the floor.

To get a better understanding of this technique, make marks on a wall behind you at varying heights. Put a landing mattress behind you, because to hit the lower targets you will have to be leaning so far back on contact that you will probably fall backwards. When it comes to finding

DIAGRAM

the really low target for shooting you will have to perform a scissors kick—that is to throw one leg in the air by thrusting upwards with the other foot, then quickly bringing that foot off the floor to actually kick the ball. This means you will fall on your back and shoulders, and your hands can be used to break your fall. Remember in doing this to make sure your fingers are pointing forward as your hands make contact with the ground, thus allowing your elbows to bend and not lock so that your fall can be absorbed by palms, arms and shoulders.

To get the idea of scissor kicking, practise it standing up, kicking the ball forward. A ball suspended about knee high is ideal. Put your left foot by the side of the ball, and with a hopping action thrust the body up with the right foot and kick the ball with the same foot. As the right foot goes forward to strike the ball, the other foot is withdrawn quickly to land on. Gradually increase the height of the ball.

Now suspend the ball at about shoulder height, and just in front of you. As you fall backwards, bring your left leg up to the ball, then quickly thrust the right leg off the floor to kick the ball over your head. If you have put the mattress in the right place, you should have a soft landing. Practise with a stationary ball to gain confidence, then allow it to swing. You can begin with the ball swinging towards you so that you help the ball on its way, always remembering to direct it down. Then you can allow the ball to swing across you, so that you have to change the direction of the ball. This is very difficult so watch the ball carefully.

These two simple practices will give you sufficient confidence to move on to the more difficult practices requiring a serving partner. Two players stand about 12 yards apart, with a third player half-way between them standing on a mat or softish ground. The player at one end throws a lob to the one in the middle, who passes with the full instep to the player behind him, either from a standing position or using a complete scissor kick. He then turns to do the same the other way round.

Move on to a practice specifically for a striker involving three servers and a goalkeeper. One player stands in the middle of the pitch about 25 yards from the striker who is standing about eight yards from goal; the other two act as wingers, one left, one right. The ball is first chipped in from the middle player, the idea being for the centre-forward to position himself to scissor-kick the ball as it comes to him. Having done that, one winger crosses the ball high so that it is just falling over the top of the centre-forward who has to turn and, with his back to goal, scissor-kick the ball past the goalkeeper. He then prepares himself for a ball coming from the other winger. This is a continuous practice. Much depends on the service and a quick return of the balls to the servers. The servers can throw the ball if the chipping is inaccurate. This is not meant to be a pressure practice, so do not have the balls coming in too quickly. When you feel tired swop with one of the servers.

Defenders should practise the overhead kick as well, with three players working together. They stand some 30 yards apart and in a triangle. One starts off by bouncing the ball then kicking it overhead to one of the others who in turn allows the ball to bounce before kicking overhead to the third member and so on. Full-backs often have to volley the ball over one shoulder facing their own goal. It is useful practice here to chip the ball high over the full-back who has to turn and chase back; when he reaches the ball he has to half turn and volley the ball back to the server over one shoulder.

COLORSPORT

Above *The overhead kick can be practised in threes; the player in the middle using the technique to direct the ball alternately to the other two.*
Left *For many years the bicycle-kick was regarded in England as extrovert, continental indulgence. A Greek defender shows Martin Chivers how effective it can be in a 1971 European Championship tie.*

DIAGRAM

Goalkeeping – cutting out the cross

When big Joe Corrigan was first seen in Manchester City's goal comparisons were inevitable. He was built like Frank Swift, and that was enough to excite the imagination of City's older followers.

Swift was a journalist when he died in the 1958 air crash which savaged Manchester United at Munich. But for years he had stood supreme among England's goalkeepers. For such a huge man he was marvellously agile, and many of his saves bordered on the miraculous. He had hands like shovels and he made good use of them. No one caught the ball more cleanly. But his catching alone would not have set him apart from a battalion of excellent British goalkeepers because the ability to come off their line to catch or punch the ball was a skill common to them all.

The skill was seen to be completely necessary, and yet a steady increase in the volume of international competition showed that it was almost peculiar to the Football League. There was a reason for this. Until soccer style and strategy became more integrated and international in concept, only the British placed any great value in aerial attacks.

They fitted an aggressive pattern of play, and outstanding headers of the ball such as Billy 'Dixie' Dean and Tommy Lawton had to be supplied with ammunition. The Deans, the Lawtons and the Drakes had to be repelled in mid-air, and the outcome was the perfection of a technique which helped to give British goalkeepers command of the world scene.

Bert Williams of Wolves, Ted Ditchburn of Spurs, Gil Merrick of Birmingham City and later Gordon Banks of Leicester and Stoke maintained England's supremacy, and there was a host of others only slightly less competent.

For instance, had Hungary been able to recruit any one of the three keepers chosen by England in the 1966 World Cup they might well have won the competition. Banks, Ron Springett and Peter Bonetti all caught the ball well, and it was a technique which had been drilled into them from their earliest years in the game.

Goalkeepers hampered— by 17 or 18 players milling around the area

Continentals preferred to punch, and it was a hazardous way of dealing with crosses unless the ball was got away with certainty. In the late sixties, penalty areas became increasingly crowded as corners and free-kicks grew in importance in attacking plans. Most teams sent forward big defenders to join their forwards, and often seventeen or eighteen players would mill around the goal area. In this climate goalkeepers did well to get a touch at the ball, but catching still remained of primary importance.

The best teams had tall, courageous keepers and Corrigan's emergence was no accident. Malcolm Allison, then Manchester City's coach, found him playing in a local park, and the boy's height and physique were instantly appealing to one of football's outstanding tutors.

Allison took Corrigan and made him into a First Division keeper, breathing belief and confidence into a player who began with almost nothing but his build. Corrigan punched almost as often as he caught, but only because it was becoming necessary. Bob Wilson, who played a memorable part in Arsenal's League and Cup

Top Diagram showing Joe Corrigan winning the ball from a left-wing cross. The red zone indicates the area which a keeper might be expected to command from these types of crosses.
Left Well outside the six-yard box, Corrigan leaps to win the ball against Chelsea in 1971.

COLORSPORT

1 Crawford; Colchester v
  Leeds—1971
2 Stein; Scotland v England—1969
3 Pele; Brazil v Italy—1970
4 Madeley; Leeds v Liverpool—1970
5 Graham; Arsenal v Derby—1971
6 Hutchinson; Chelsea v Leeds—1970
7 Hurst; England v Argentina—1966

DIAGRAM

KEYSTONE

Above *Ted Ditchburn of Spurs was one of England's outstanding keepers in post-War football. Here, he cuts out a West Ham cross in 1949.*
Above right *Diagram showing the positions from which seven famous goals were headed from left-wing crosses. Only in Crawford's goal did the keeper try to stop the cross before it reached the scorer.*
Right *Gordon Banks comes off his line to claim the ball. An important part of his skill is the way he controls events in his penalty area.*

triumph in 1971, said of this:

'When I began in the game I looked around and saw that people such as Gordon Banks and Peter Bonetti were always looking to cut out crosses cleanly. Their judgement was tremendous and they refused to be put off by opponents challenging them in the air. Banksie was outstanding in this respect. It convinced me that I had to perfect this particular aspect of my game. I was nothing unless I could deal with the ball in the air. I had to be good at it.'

Wilson confirmed that he was a good and quick learner with an almost unblemished season in 1970-71. But it was some months later, in a critical encounter against Spurs, that he was to truly justify his rating in the game.

Arsenal, who had suddenly lost their way, faced Spurs at White Hart Lane following four successive defeats. Wilson had conceded five goals at Wolves the previous week, and he had become the subject of doubt and criticism. He dithered through the opening phase of that game in November 1971, but brilliantly survived a stern examination of his skill and courage in the second half.

A goal down, Spurs sustained a startling level of combative, attacking play which included a stream of centres from both wings, aimed at dangerous aerial strikers, Alan Gilzean, Martin Peters and Martin Chivers. Wilson was inspired as he climbed beneath those centres to repel the Spurs attackers. He was eventually beaten when Martin Chivers swooped on to a back pass from Arsenal full-back Pat Rice, but Wilson had done more than enough to silence criticism.

Later that night, Pat Jennings, Spurs' Irish international goalkeeper, was to say: 'It was an astonishing performance. I think Bob would admit that everything went for him. But you had to admire the way he fought his way up to get those crosses.' Had Wilson elected to punch instead of catch Arsenal could well have been in trouble as Spurs zoned in on their penalty area.

Jennings, who admired it all at long range, was himself an outstanding catcher in the tradition of

GERRY CRANHAM

his illustrious predecessor, Ted Ditchburn. After Spurs had suffered a shock Cup defeat at Bournemouth in the fifties, Ditchburn had to suffer the jibe, 'Butterfingers', a cruel reference to the fact that he had a grocer's shop.

But few players handled the ball with more certainty or caught it in greater style. Arthur Rowe, one of Spurs' great managers, said of him: 'Ted was one of the greatest of goalkeepers. He was just unlucky to be around at a time when Bert Williams was in the England team.'

Jennings was to approach and indeed equal Ditchburn's quality, and he too was blessed with enormous hands. Signed from Watford when still a raw youngster, he reached a position of prominence in the game, and he was consistently brilliant when dealing with crosses.

Strong and agile, he disputed the theory that catching was no longer profitable in congested penalty areas, but he recognized that there were problems. He said: 'I cannot remember the last time I went out and caught a ball between the six-yard line and the edge of the penalty area. There are so many bodies about that you can never get that far out. But I always prefer to catch. It's safer because you are immediately cutting out an attack, whereas if you punch, the ball might come back before you have.'

Wilson analysed the situation intelligently and said: 'There are times when I must settle for getting a touch. I may not be able to do more than deflect the ball away. It really has got as bad as that.'

The problem of whether to catch or punch introduced a note of doubt into the potential of Peter Shilton who was seen to be Banks' natural successor in the England team. They had both played for Leicester, and Shilton as a teenager had learned much from the man who was acknowledged to be the world's best.

When Banks was committed to a League Cup replay for Stoke in November 1971, he was rested from the England team two days later and Shilton replaced him. It was not a happy night. England struggled to master Switzerland in a European Championship game, and Shilton struggled to master a succession of crosses early in the match.

Three times England were put in trouble by Shilton's punching

Three times he chose to punch when Sir Alf Ramsey was convinced that he should have caught the ball, and on each occasion England were put in trouble. Shilton had performed consistently for his club, but there seemed a flaw in this aspect of his technique and Ramsey could not overlook it.

Banks, despite a flutter of uncertainty when playing against the Swiss in Basle the previous month, remained almost unassailable in England's goal. No one could deny his excellence. Banks produced his best form when playing international football. He responded to the big event and there was a definitive quality about all his work.

The legendary Swift, the supremely athletic Bert Williams, Russia's brilliant Lev Yashin and Grosics of the Hungarian side of the fifties ranked alongside him in the history of the game. It was no accident that all of them rose splendidly to the occasion when the ball was lofted into their penalty areas. Their greatness was tied much more to their ability to command their goal area than to any talent for pulling off the occasional blinding, reflex save. And at the highest levels of international football, no defence survived without the authority of such goalkeeping giants.

Top right *Pat Jennings of Spurs punches the ball clear against Liverpool. Goalkeepers like Jennings prefer to catch the ball, but admit that there are times when it is safer to punch. Often this is because there are so many players in the penalty area that a keeper does well to even reach the ball at all.*

Right *England's Peter Bonetti takes the ball spectacularly from the head of Gerd Muller during the 1970 World Cup quarter-final in Leon.*

OWEN BARNES

FOTOSPORTS INTERNATIONAL

(A)

(B)

DIAGRAM

Left Diagram showing one way a goalkeeper can practise coming off the line to deal with crosses. The practice requires four other players, three of whom will cross the ball from varying angles; the fourth puts pressure on the keeper. The three outfield men have two balls between them. As one plays a cross the keeper must catch the ball and throw it out to the third player. Then the other ball is crossed, and the practice runs on continuously.

Coaching: Develop the technique to handle crosses confidently

Any team challenging for cup or league success is going to find it difficult without a good goalkeeper and an adequate reserve. It would be fair to say that the goalkeeper's knowledge and judgement as to when to leave his goal-line will have a large bearing on how successful your team is going to be. What he does when he leaves his line will have a greater bearing still.

The most controversial subject in goalkeeping is when to leave the line. This is possibly the big difference between the good and very good. Basically, there are two reasons for the goalkeeper to leave his goal. One is to narrow the angle when an opposing player has broken through, and is about to shoot; the other reason is to get the ball. The goalkeeper who hesitates in this situation will not get the ball nor will the other defenders know whether to cover him or go for the ball themselves. On the other hand, a goalkeeper who is positive in his approach to this problem will leave nobody in doubt as to what his movements or decisions are. He will call to let his team-mates know what he wants, either for them to clear the ball or clear the way and give him cover because he is leaving his line for the ball. Having made his decision he must go with determination to get to the ball, ready to make yet another decision, either to catch the ball, if he is reasonably clear and in no danger of dropping it when challenged, or to punch it wingwards, sufficiently far enough that it cannot be volleyed back. If there is any doubt as to whether or not you should catch the ball, get your fists to it and get it away towards the touchlines.

The first technique to master is that of catching the ball overhead. This is a difficult technique and special care must be taken when catching in this manner. Since the hands are not backed by a second barrier, you are in trouble if it slips through.

Practise whenever possible with another goalkeeper, either a friend or your club's second keeper. Throw the ball to one another so that the ball arrives overhead and has to be caught and brought to the chest before being thrown back in the same way. This is a very basic practice, but one that is necessary to simply get the feel of the ball. It can be made more interesting and more difficult when one of the goalkeepers is made to catch the ball whilst moving backwards, the ball now being thrown just that little bit harder and higher so that it is dropping to the back of him.

Now stand further apart, and throw the ball one-handed, overarm, so that you get plenty of height and distance. The receiving goalkeeper must catch the ball in as high a position as he possibly can by jumping off one foot, catching the ball at full stretch and then bringing it down safely to his chest. The main concern here is preparation for the jump. The feet must be in a position to give you the maximum power. A take-off from one foot will get you much higher because you can swing into the jump. Fix your eye firmly on the ball because the path of the ball is not always true. It dips, swerves and spins in the air, so to take your eye from the ball for a split-second will often prove fatal. Watch the ball right into the hands. The hands must be behind the ball, thumbs reasonably close together; take the ball into the base of the fingers making them close on the ball. Bend your arms slightly so that they can give on contact in order to take the pace from the ball, and relax the wrists for the same reason. Do not forget during this practice to cultivate the habit of bringing the ball down to the chest and holding it securely in the arms and hands in case you are fairly charged and have to take a tumble. It is worthwhile taking a roll now and again; bend your knees on landing, drop one shoulder, tuck your head in and roll on to your shoulder.

No practice really comes alive without opposition and the proof of your skill will be when under pressure, but make the opposition passive at first. Practise in the goalmouth to get the feel of the right environment, and have the keeper with an opponent, two wingers, one on each side, and a player about thirty yards away down the middle. Two balls are required. Two of the outfield players have a ball each, leaving one spare. The idea is that one ball is either thrown or kicked into the goal area. The goalkeeper, pressured only slightly by his opponent, must jump to catch the ball, then distribute it to the spare player. The other ball is then thrown or kicked into the goal area and again the goalkeeper must collect and distribute to the spare player who is now the player who played the first ball in. This is a con-tinuous practice, but be sure not to have the balls coming in too quickly at first. The goalkeeper must be allowed time to position himself for each ball coming in. The work should be done in short, sharp periods.

Before increasing the number of opponents and making them fully active, an alternative method of dealing with this type of ball must be worked at. Sometimes, when the goalmouth is crowded by attacking players who hamper the goalkeeper, it is dangerous for the goalkeeper to attempt to catch. In such cases, the goalkeeper will be well advised to clear the ball by punching with the fist. Punching has its disadvantages, because when a goalkeeper catches the ball he can determine the next movement of play. Despite this, the use of the fist is an important and indispensable weapon for a goalkeeper.

Practise this initially on a suspended ball. The ball need not be too hard, so that contact can be made without skinning your knuckles. Keep your eyes fixed on the ball and aim dead centre. When you move for the ball, take off from one foot, bending the other knee up in front for protection. Keep your arms bent so that your fists are ready for contact. The fists should be held close together presenting a broad area of contact. Practice should include the use of one fist because it is not always possible to get two fists to the ball when penalty areas are very crowded.

It is dangerous for defenders to tell the keeper to come out

You should now be ready for more active work. The previous practice can be stepped up to include three defenders marking three attackers who are backed up by two midfield players, two wingers, one on each side, and a target man around the half-way line for the defenders, including the goalkeeper, to find when they gain possession. The ball is played by a midfield player to a winger who works the ball and crosses into the goalmouth. Now the goalkeeper must control the action. First he must decide whether he is going to deal with it himself or instruct the other defenders to go for it. It is extremely dangerous for the defenders to call the keeper out. The goalkeeper must make his own decision or this will have him in two minds. Defenders are committed to play the ball unless the goalkeeper calls that it is his ball; this is why it is so important that the goalkeeper controls the action. If the ball falls to the midfield players, they can either shoot or play wingwards for another cross. The practice is restarted when the ball goes over the goal-line by a clearance to the target man who heads or passes to the midfield players who again pass to the winger.

From all that has been said it should be obvious that the goalkeeper of the seventies has to be much more than somebody who stands on the goal-line making desperate saves. He is a vital member of a defensive unit, moulding his play with the other defenders, keeping aware of everything they do and letting them know what he is doing all the time.

Defenders will respond to a positive goalkeeper. He can make them more efficient players, and indeed he must possess the confidence to inspire the men in front of him. If you are going to become a goalkeeper, these are the 'bread and butter' skills that you must develop. Master the techniques of cutting out crosses, and you are well on your way to success.

Goalkeeping – distribution

CUMBES

Top *Diagram showing the devastating distribution of Aston Villa goalkeeper Jim Cumbes. Using his ability to clear the ball well into the opposing half, Cumbes' target was striker Andy Lochhead. His task was to flick the ball on to sprinting colleagues. Against Bolton in 1971, Ray Graydon raced on to such a flick to score.*
Above left *Clear of the Bolton defence, Graydon finishes the move started by Cumbes.*
Above *Against Shrewsbury the same season, Cumbes aimed another clearance at Lochhead (fourth from the right). This time the centre-forward won the ball himself and ran on to shoot home.*
Above right *Cumbes joins in the celebrations.*

Halting a slide from First Division football that had been one of the saddest features of British football in the sixties, Aston Villa won the Third Division championship in 1972 with an impressive total of 70 points.

With the staggering support of a home gate that averaged around 35,000, Villa had the resources to boost their side from time to time with expensive signings. Ian Ross arrived from Liverpool for £60,000 and Chris Nicholl from Luton Town for £75,000, but perhaps the most significant newcomer was the goalkeeper Jimmy Cumbes, bought from neighbouring West Bromwich Albion for £35,000.

Not only did Cumbes bolster a defence that had been sagging in front of an out-of-form Tommy Hughes, but he added a new dimension to Villa's attack, proving the importance of a goalkeeper's distribution.

Once the ball is in the keeper's hands, his side is in possession. They should aim to keep it, even though it is a simple matter for the goalkeeper to clear his line by thumping the ball aimlessly downfield. If there is no plan, the odds are strongly in favour of the ball landing on an opponent's head and he is now in a position to start a counter-attack. An accurate kick or throw is as important as an accurate pass made by an outfield player.

Jim Cumbes, tall and strong with the physique of a fast bowler, his summer profession, could throw and kick the ball immense distances, and the Villa manager Vic Crowe quickly integrated his talents into the team's overall attacking plan. Cumbes' target, waiting on the halfway line and beyond, was the balding head of striker Andy Lochhead.

Lochhead had both the experience and the

physique to win the dropping ball; the other Villa players were responsible for giving him alternatives. Lochhead said: 'Mainly I'm trying to knock the ball into space behind the defence. We've got two fast wingers in Ray Graydon and Willie Anderson and as soon as I'm going up they're looking to race on to the deflection.'

Cumbes had only been at Villa a month when the plan worked perfectly against Bolton. He drove a clearance downfield, Lochhead made the deflection and Graydon raced clear to score. But the goalkeeper had to be prepared to alter his tactics. Cumbes admitted: 'If Andy is getting beaten in the air, I can still try to find him because he is a good target player and always available. But now I'll try to drop it short of him so that he can shield it with his body. I might kick the ball lower and flatter, but more probably I'll throw it. The low trajectory

GRAYDON (A)

GRAYDON (B)

LOCHHEAD

makes it very difficult for Andy's marker to reach the ball before him. Andy can then lay it back to our midfield players and we go on from there.'

Against Shrewsbury Town at Villa Park, another alternative emerged. Cumbes aimed another high clearance that landed deep in the Shrewsbury half. Lochhead and the centre-half both missed the ball, but the Villa striker recovered quicker. He turned and found himself clear to run through and score.

Spurs goalkeeper Pat Jennings went one better when he volleyed an enormous right-foot clearance deep into Manchester United's half during the 1967 Charity Shield match at Old Trafford.

For what looked at first to be a commonplace attempt at putting United's defenders under long-range pressure quickly developed into a wicked assault on Alex Stepney's goal. Stepney, stationed somewhere near the edge of his penalty area, seemed safe enough until Jennings' kick was seen to be of prodigious length.

As he began to back off, responding to the judgement which told him that he could be in trouble, the ball bounced, rose high and then dropped behind Stepney and into his goal as he twirled helplessly backwards.

A big, friendly Irishman who once he had rid himself of a natural shyness developed into one of the game's great keepers, Jennings said: 'I couldn't believe it. I wasn't even sure that it counted in the laws of the game. Then the lads ran back and congratulated me. It was a goal alright. But you had to feel sorry for poor Alex. We all get beaten by outfield players. But

how about being beaten by another goalkeeper? Takes a bit of living down that.'

It was a freak score but Jennings had deservedly earned himself the reputation for astute distribution. He could guarantee distance even when forced on to his less effective kicking foot by challenging forwards. He could consistently clear defenders who had pushed up to the halfway line who were then threatened with being turned and outpaced by speedy forwards.

Whether goalkeepers should kick or throw provided football with a wide area of debate. The answer lay with discretion and judgement. But kicking was certainly more popular and more widely used by the teams of the seventies.

A goalkeeper who could get great distance when kicking out of his hands was particularly effective against defences who elected to concede the centre of the field.

There was an outstanding example of this in November 1970 when Peter Shilton, Leicester's brilliant young goalkeeper, established himself as Banks' permanent deputy in the England team.

Shilton was brought in against East Germany at Wembley and saw the chance to use his great kicking strength to unsettle a defence which rarely ventured within range of the halfway line.

German attempts at clearing Shilton's kicks when under pressure from aggressive English forwards led to untidy defensive play and considerable confusion. In circumstances such as these Shilton's long-range bombardment was instantly destructive.

Real Madrid had recognized the value of such

tactics even though it seemed to contradict their reputation for fluent, appealing football. They told their goalkeepers to concentrate on trying to hit the opposing centre-half with high balls aimed down the middle. They used one attacker to hustle and challenge and the remainder zoned in to try and pick off half clearances.

It proved to be very effective, especially where there were forwards with the skill to take absolute advantage of a loose ball. Real certainly possessed forwards of the calibre to capitalize.

Good kicking by keepers could also help to overcome the problem of coping with teams who were particularly aggressive in the centre of the field. Against Leeds, for instance, it was almost fatal to try and compete there on equal terms. They had skill and aggression and the danger of losing possession to men who could turn defence into penetrating attack with one killing pass was a very real one.

Teams who tried to build up attacks from deep positions began to find that hard-working forwards hustled them into error and it diminished the value of short-range passing by the goalkeeper. For instance, it was significant that when England played West Germany in the second leg of a European Championship quarter-final in Berlin in May 1972, Banks invariably ignored Bobby Moore's requests for the ball to be rolled out to him on the edge of the area.

England trailed 3-1 from the first leg and the third German goal had stemmed from a Banks throw to left-back Emlyn Hughes. Hughes had been caught in possession and Gerd Muller scored after the Germans had snapped back into the attack.

Banks was clearly conscious of the sharpness which the Germans had revealed and settled for pumping the ball forward into the other half.

Banks had the vision to pick out players who would break forward for him and Manchester United were very aware of this when preparing to face Stoke City in a League Cup tie during the 1971-72 season.

Before a new manager, Frank O'Farrell, and a new coach, Malcolm Musgrove, arrived at the start of that season United, for all their greatness, had been relatively naive in their team play. Their forwards had been allowed to assume that they were there to score goals and little attention had been paid to such things as closing down on opposing defenders. Indeed it had rarely been necessary in United's early days because their attacking prowess had aroused caution.

Defenders were unwilling to desert their posts when a United forward was in the vicinity and long passes forward were easily picked off by United's under-rated defenders. But new techniques promoted unheard of problems for United. They now found that forwards were being left isolated upfield because defenders were eager to break away from defence into attack.

Musgrove said: 'It wasn't easy to make great players such as Denis Law and George Best see the need to guard against the possibility of quick counter-attacks. But it was important that we did this against Stoke because Banksie was so good at setting people free with long throws. He could see situations quickly and right-back Marsh was especially good at sprinting forward to take throws up near the halfway line.'

The best goalkeepers put a lot of thought into their play when delivering the ball. They had to know the various weaknesses of their team-mates to ensure that no one was put under unnecessary pressure. They had to be aware of the kind of service which would be most profitable and above all they had to be safe with their distribution. Many goals were given away because keepers cleared carelessly into areas where there was immediate pressure.

Standard practice when throwing was to put the ball out to the opposite flank from which it had been received. It was inevitable that there would be fewer players there. It was not only safer but there was a greater possibility of launching a significant counter-attack by stretching the opposing defence.

It was argued with some certainty that goalkeepers ought to be the best kickers of a ball in the team. They had to kick dead balls, they had to be able to volley and half-volley, often in pressure conditions. Good half-volleyers were rare. The technique was difficult but when used well it was a decisive weapon, because it allowed a low delivery.

Jim Standen proved this when keeping goal for West Ham during a successful period for that club in the mid-sixties. West Ham's play was built around swift, accurate passing and Standen played his part in this with superbly accurate low kicks which gave the receivers no problems.

When a goalkeeper had the ball he was an attacker as Arthur Rowe emphasized when encouraging the superb Ted Ditchburn to help promote the push-and-run technique which was to characterize Spurs' revival during his time as their manager. Spurs' play was all about possession and Rowe insisted that possession began when Ditchburn had the ball. Ditchburn invariably threw to players in the most comfortable positions.

It was ironic that Pat Jennings should be wearing a Spurs' jersey when he kicked himself into football history some fifteen years later.

It was not that the game had changed all that much. But it was quicker and more aggressive. Forwards worked harder and advantage had to be taken of everything. Jennings kicked because it was often more profitable to kick. He could have hardly expected such spectacular return.

Coaching: Learn to start attacks from your own goal

Once the goalkeeper has taken full possession of the ball, he must attempt to use it in such a way that an attack on the opponents' goal can be set up as soon as possible. He must give the pass the same tactical considerations as any outfield player. This means that the ball must be thrown or kicked so that it can be easily controlled when passed over short distances or so that it gives one's own players an advantage when played over long distances.

How the keeper distributes the ball will depend upon the ability of his own players and the tactics that are employed. It is a waste of time kicking long balls down the middle unless you have forwards capable of using such clearances and it is dangerous rolling short balls out to defenders who are not sharp enough to take advantage of such tactics.

There are three main methods to master when throwing the ball and two when passing with the feet. The goalkeeper who is limited in his methods of distribution is like the one-footed player who can only pass the ball over short distances. Opponents can position themselves to close down his passing possibilities.

When passing the ball over very short distances, possibly to a full-back just outside the box, the ball can be rolled along the ground. This technique is particularly useful in starting attacks quickly. It gives maximum speed and accuracy and it reaches the team-mate on the ground, making control that much easier. This action is very similar to tenpin bowling. The ball is held in both hands in front of the body at hip height. The palm of the throwing arm supports the ball from underneath, the other supports it from the top and inside. The fingers are well spread to give maximum control.

Start the movement by taking a pace forward with the leg opposite the hand which will roll the ball. As you take this step, move your arms slightly behind the body to the throwing side to gather swing. Take the top hand off the ball, straighten your elbow in the throwing arm, leaving your body well forward. As your throwing hand starts to swing forward, transfer your weight gradually on to the front leg. The swinging arm gathers speed quickly, the ball leaves the hand as it is at right angles to the ground, and the hand follows through giving a final thrust and direction.

Practise this on your own by rolling the ball against marks on a wall; then with the help of a

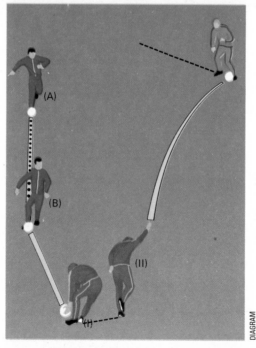

Top Tony Book of Manchester City dashes into space to receive the ball from Joe Corrigan. Book is then soundly placed to start an attack.
Above Throwing practice for a keeper. He receives the ball from one player, finds the other with a throw, receives it again and so on.

couple of team-mates practise finding a moving target. Get two friends, each with a ball, to dribble the ball towards you one at a time. When they get about 10 yards away, they pass the ball to you and move off quickly. Your job is to collect the ball and then return it so that they do not have to check their stride and so that the ball runs into space for them to receive and control easily.

The ball rolled along the ground loses its pace quickly, especially when the going is heavy. If you want to pass the ball over a slightly longer distance, it should be thrown from the shoulder.

The starting position is the same for rolling the ball. Instead the ball is taken back over the shoulder with a bent arm. The opposite leg and shoulder move forward in preparation for the throw. The throwing arm is brought forward from the shoulder simultaneously with the forearm being flung forwards and downwards.

Practise in the same way as for rolling the ball, except that now your team-mates will not have to come too close and when you throw the ball you must allow it to bounce a couple of times before reaching its target. Do not give the ball any unnecessary 'air'. Throw it direct from the shoulder to the target so that it reaches it in the least amount of time possible. For throwing further the ball will have to be thrown with a cricket overarm bowling action. The power will come from a straight arm used as a lever against the body.

A good functional practice for two goalkeepers involves the use of two strikers and two midfield players as well. Use one goal and make a second just over the halfway line with a goalkeeper in each. The strikers position themselves about 15 yards from each goal; the midfield players support them so that they make pairs. One goalkeeper throws a long ball to the striker furthest away who lays it back first time to his supporting midfield player. He passes first time to the other goalkeeper who fields it and immediately throws it to the striker furthest away so that there is a continuous practice.

Of course it is not always possible nor desirable to throw the ball every time. The very long clearance can be made very dangerous so goalkeepers should practise the volley and half volley from the hands as well as their dead-ball kicks. The half-volley or drop-kick is especially useful because the flight is much lower and the ball can be directed more accurately; it is also easier for the receiving player to control.

The goalkeeper must be brought into the general team tactics and must be encouraged to use the ball, not just kick it as far as he can.

Goalkeeping - the courageous dive

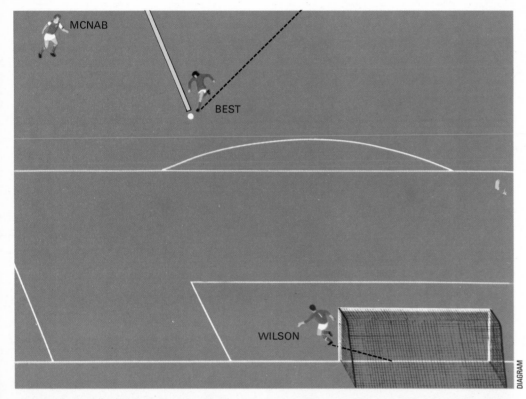

MCNAB

BEST

WILSON

DIAGRAM

As Arsenal edged towards the First Division Championship in the spring of 1971 with a string of narrow victories, it became patently clear that they were heavily in debt to their goalkeeper, Bob Wilson.

Wilson had begun that season among the herd—competent but rarely mentioned in discussions about outstanding players. Yet with a string of commanding and daring performances in League, Cup and European competition, he proved himself to be a goalkeeper of undoubted quality.

But amongst his all-round attributes one particular talent stood apart—his courageous and willing ability to fling himself at the feet of inrushing opponents, and emerge triumphantly with the ball.

As early as the second Saturday of a campaign which was to prove the most successful in Arsenal's history, he emphasized the increasing extents of his gifts.

Manchester United were the first visitors of the season to Highbury, and Arsenal gave notice of things to come with a thumping four-nil win. It was early in the second-half of that match, with Arsenal leading by two goals, that Wilson offered a broad hint of what he was to achieve in the months ahead.

United were then stumbling through, their reputation undermined by a persistent inability to align their magnificent skills to the way football was being played.

But they still had George Best, Denis Law and Bobby Charlton, and their appealing presence could still ensure a full house.

In this match all three were largely ineffective. But players of this calibre are capable of producing moments of magic even when they and the team are well below par.

Four minutes into the second half one such moment arrived. Arsenal had pushed forward to the half-way line behind a ball played out of their defence, when Denis Law was given possession in midfield about fifteen yards in from his right-hand touchline.

Instinct, reflex and vision were among the qualities which made Law a world-class player. They were put together in a flash as he sent an instant pass forward directly between Bob McNab and Peter Simpson. Best had already launched himself into space, and the pass and the run were perfectly in tune.

A classic confrontation —and a situation that George Best relished

Arsenal were caught square and without cover. Best was through into the classic confrontation between attacker and goalkeeper—a situation he relished as he had vividly proved when breaking through to score against Benfica in the 1968 European Cup final.

But this time he was dealing with a keeper who used courage and commonsense to take charge of the situation.

Unchallenged, Best struck straight at goal. Wilson came purposefully from his line. They met just inside the penalty area. Best flickered as though going left and brought the ball back to his right foot. But before he could shoot, Wilson had spread himself to take the ball in a flurry of arms and legs.

He said later: 'It was probably the most satisfying save I have ever made. Best is brilliant in those situations. He has such great control and confidence. He brings the ball right in close and there are a variety of things he can do. He has the skill to go round you, the skill to chip the ball over your head and if you watch his body you can be thrown right off balance by his feint.

'I had to work things out quickly. If I had committed myself too soon I would have given George the chance to chip the ball over the top of

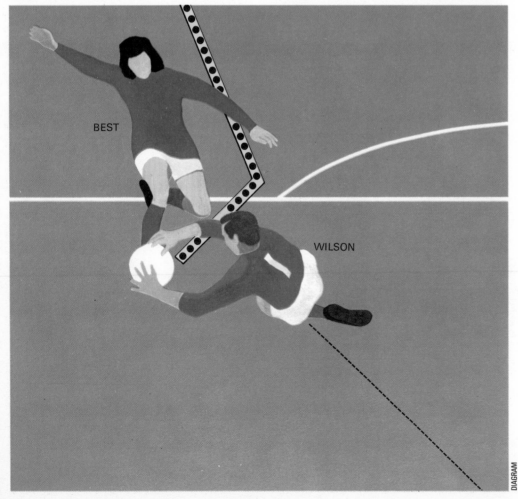

BEST

WILSON

DIAGRAM

Above left *On 22 August 1970 at Highbury George Best is through with only Bob Wilson to beat.*
Left *But with the odds against him Wilson races off his line with perfect timing to grab the ball.*

me. If I had left my move too late he could have taken his time choosing his angle. It had to be just right. What I was trying to do was put him in two minds. The vital thing, then, was to give him as big a problem as I possibly could. I kept my eyes on the ball, and when I decided to go for it I spread my body into as big a barrier as possible. I was thrilled when I got the ball in my arms.'

Wilson was to make many such saves during the season and many of them at Highbury where Arsenal were forced to take chances against opponents who settled for defence and only occasional counter-attacks.

Arsenal were always compressing the game into midfield by pushing their back men up quickly to the half-way line, and it meant that Wilson had to adopt the role of a cover man.

It was not a new technique. When Liverpool emerged among the six outstanding clubs in the Football League during the sixties they had a goalkeeper who looked as though he had stepped straight out of a comic charity match. Tommy Lawrence, a Scottish international, looked undertrained and untidy. He was too short to be truly efficient in the air, but it was when he came from his line to deal with forwards who had broken through the defence that Liverpool proved they had chosen wisely.

Like Arsenal, Liverpool, with a sound balance of strength and skill, put constant pressure on their opponents by compressing the game into midfield. In doing this they gambled on leaving space behind certain defenders who were notoriously slow on the turn. They could afford to take such risk only because of Lawrence's courage and willingness.

Centres were invariably dealt with by a giant centre-half, Ron Yeats. This was not Lawrence's job. He was chosen because of the speed and daring which he displayed when Liverpool were pierced by through balls.

Bob Wilson has said: 'This was the outstand-

British goalkeepers are the bravest in the world.
Left *Wilson's strong, positive dive thwarts Best.*
Below *Peter Bonetti saves from Liverpool's Graham.*
Left inset *John Hope dives to save Sheffield Utd.*
Right inset *Bobby Graham is foiled again—this time by the courage of Manchester Utd's Stepney.*

ing part of Tommy's game. He was the best in the business at coming out to deal with through balls, and he had an extremely high percentage of success. He knew when to come and how to come, and he was very brave.'

Wilson was fearless himself, and a succession of bruising injuries to his arms and shoulders were evidence of the fact.

During the late fifties England used two keepers who were similarly courageous and who used swift decision and judgements to balance their lack of inches.

Eddie Hopkinson of Bolton and Alan Hodgkinson of Sheffield United not only had similar names. They were amazingly sharp off their line and consistently brave. This willingness to accept physical contact marks all the outstanding keepers, all of whom are well aware that there is considerable danger involved.

One of the great tragedies of the game occurred when a fine young Celtic keeper, Johnny Thomson, died after making a save during a derby game against Rangers.

Thomson was only 21 years old and already established in Scotland's team when he attempted to take the ball from the feet of the Rangers forward, Sam English.

English was unable to pull up in time, and Thomson took a fearsome blow on the head. It was pure accident but Thomson died in hospital.

In the 1956 FA Cup Final, Bert Trautmann, a former German paratrooper who had been detained as a prisoner of war in England, came close to suffering similar tragedy when he hurled himself at the feet of Birmingham's forward Peter Murphy as they both raced to meet a cross from the Birmingham right flank.

Trautmann clutched the ball to his chest, but Murphy had no chance to avoid a juddering collision with the big German. His knee cracked violently but accidentally against Trautmann's neck. After treatment the keeper carried on although he could hardly stand up straight, and

Above right *David Lawson of Huddersfield Town goes down fearlessly at the feet of Martin Chivers.*
Right *Bert Trautmann and Peter Murphy collide in the 1956 FA Cup Final.*
Below *Diagram of the incident—from which Trautmann collected the ball and a broken neck.*

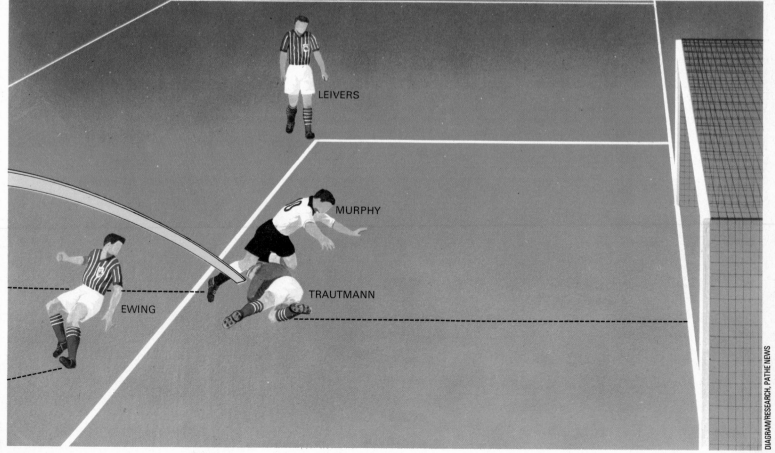

LEIVERS

MURPHY

TRAUTMANN

EWING

incredibly he plunged again at a Birmingham player's feet a few minutes later.

City won that Final, but in the dressing-room afterwards it was discovered that Trautmann had played through the final phase of the game with his neck broken.

Goalkeepers have always had to accept the perils of their profession, but even greater emphasis was put on the physical side of the game during the sixties. Moreover, goalkeepers in Britain enjoyed far less protection than their continental counterparts.

They had to contend with tactics designed to unsettle their confidence, and they were called upon to be even more decisive in the midst of a crowded goalmouth. And in Gordon Banks, Peter Shilton, Ray Clemence among many, many others, British football produced a succession of goalkeepers who could be numbered among the bravest in the world.

Recognizing this need for bravery, Don Howe, during his time as Arsenal's coach, worked hard at bringing Bob Wilson to a fever pitch of resolution. Wilson had never been a coward, but Howe showed that courage—often thought of as purely a natural quality—could be improved and

Above *Les Green of Derby County risks all as he plunges in where the boots are flying to save heroically from Manchester City's Glyn Pardoe.*

developed in coaching.

Wilson recalls: 'Don had a practice which he would put me through at least once a week. It was a fierce thing. It was all about getting in to take the ball away from him. He would try to stop me, and I had to get the ball ten times in succession. He kept me at it until I did.'

Howe recalls staging this practice when a leading German goalkeeper visited Arsenal to study training methods.

Howe says: 'He was a big blond lad who really looked the part. We were very busy at the time but he kept pestering me to take him on a training session.

'I put him through the sort of stuff I did with Bob Wilson. After five minutes he didn't want to know any more. Goalkeeping as far as this lad was concerned was all about agility and style. He just couldn't see the need to get involved in what we were demanding from our men.'

It was this sort of approach which set British goalkeeping standards—standards so high that Bob Wilson, who would have been welcomed by at least a dozen national teams, could not get near a place in the England team, and so was welcomed by Scotland under a parental qualification.

Coaching: How to get out and snatch the ball from an opponent's feet

'You don't have to be mad to be a good goalkeeper, but it helps.' The remark, repeated over many years, recognizes that to be a good goalkeeper a man must willingly risk injury by diving into a ruck of players, or dive at the feet of an incoming forward to keep his goal intact. The saying is not entirely true. Courage, rather than madness, is what is needed.

As a goalkeeper faced with an opponent about to shoot, what you must do is get as close to the forward as possible, giving him as little space as possible in which to score. This has got to be done in the most efficient manner with the least amount of injury risk.

Before going into any serious practice make sure you are properly clothed. Repeatedly diving down on your side on firm ground will certainly give you grass burns or grazes. A good track suit will help to prevent this or use some padding made up with cotton wool strapped to the hips. In the initial stages select softish ground until you get hardened.

Work with a partner and ask him to dribble at you from thirty yards, slowly. Advance to meet the ball in a crouched position to cut down his angle. When fifteen yards from the ball, prepare to go down by keeping the body as low as possible so that you do not have to swoop on the ball and so that the head can be kept steady. Throw your legs sideways and your body towards the ball so that the side of your calf, thigh and then hip come in contact with the ground

early enough not to allow the ball to slide under your body.

As you hit the ground the momentum of your body will still be moving forward (this is when you collect your burns) and the ball is gathered with your lower arms. Your knees will now come up quickly and head slightly forward so that you completely smother the ball. The best place to gather the ball is into the lower chest.

If the forward attempts to take the ball round you, your hands will help one way whilst your feet can be used if he goes the other way. By going down in this manner the injury risk is minimized. To go down head first is not only dangerous but your body covers only a fraction of what can be covered going down sideways.

Once you have gained confidence at going down, get your pal to dribble the ball towards you and to lose control slightly. Advance to meet him in a crouched stance and look for the mistake. When he loses control go down at the ball.

Now make it more realistic by asking him to take you on at speed and score if he can. Look for a slight error such as when he has played the ball too far in front of him.

A problem for goalkeepers is the ball pulled back from the goal line close to goal. The goalkeeper's position at this stage must be at the near post, but as the ball is pulled back, instead of moving backwards along the line to a more central position as a lot of goalkeepers do, move to the player who is coming on to the ball and

try to smother the shot. This will take courage, but if you stay on the line you will have little chance.

Get your friend to come along the bye-line, and to pull the ball back to a team-mate. If you hold your ground you will have no chance with the shot, but going down at his feet quickly will give you a chance. The closer you can get to him the less chance he has.

Your next problem is to judge when to leave your line to smother a through ball.

Incorporate the aid of two friends. One has a ball thirty yards out and plays it goalwards. The other player chases in after it to score. You have to judge now whether you can get to the ball either before or at the same time as the forward, or is the forward running in going to have full control of the ball. If you can arrive before or at the same time be sure to smother the ball correctly. If your opponent has the ball make sure that you are not caught out—that you are in a crouched position ready to pounce on a possible error or are prepared to dive either way for a shot.

A goalkeeper must be courageous especially in these dangerous situations. If he is afraid of diving at the feet of an advancing forward, he cannot be considered a 100% player.

At training sessions, make sure that you practise your goalkeeping skills to get this confidence. It is a great temptation to join in every five-a-side game and play out of goal. By all means do this occasionally, but never neglect your own position. With two or three team-mates practise the above routines as often as you can. This will instil the confidence you need to be a competent, courageous goalkeeper. Remember, work hard at your game—a mistake can mean a goal.

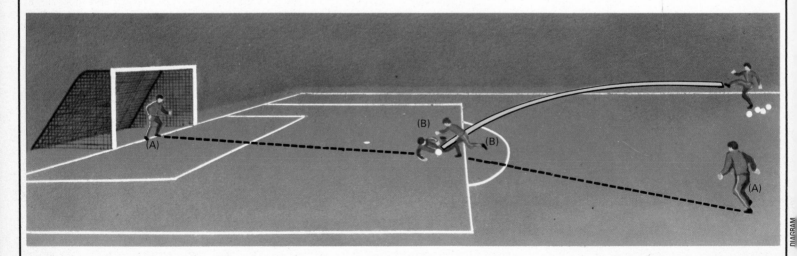

Above *Diagram of a training routine for goalkeepers. Balls are hit to the edge of the penalty area, and the keeper must get out to them before the inrushing forward.*

Goalkeeping – shot-stopping

In the spring of 1971 Tottenham fans forgot, for a few seconds, the pain of a home defeat in the FA Cup to salute the man who had done most to oust them from the competition.

Ray Clemence, the young Liverpool goalkeeper, had graced White Hart Lane with a display that had emphasized the very essence of what his job was all about. Goalkeeping had become a multi-sided art. Cutting out crosses, plunging recklessly at forwards' feet, positional astuteness and the skill to distribute the ball accurately—all these techniques had to fall within the compass of the First Division keeper.

But Clemence had reminded those assembled at White Hart Lane that evening of the skill—or instinct—that ultimately defines goalkeeping. Liverpool had lived because of the taut reflexes that had enabled Clemence to twist and tumble to stop every shot that the Spurs attack had driven at the Liverpool goal.

Liverpool had been held 0-0 at Anfield in the sixth-round tie and Spurs rejoiced in the prospect of reaching yet another semi-final. But they had not bargained for Clemence, and it was no surprise that he came through to challenge Peter Shilton of Leicester as Gordon Banks' most likely successor in the England goal.

Clemence stopped everything, displaying marvellous agility against some of the best finishers in the business. He kept out a murderous volley from Martin Chivers, a delicate curling chip from Martin Peters and somehow managed to get to a thundering drive from Alan Mullery.

Mullery said afterwards: 'As the game went on I began to realize that we weren't going to score. That this feller was going to get in the way a lot. Everything was going for him and on top of that he is a fine keeper. That's an unbeatable combination. You see it happen from time to time, and when it does you might as well pack up and go home.'

Bill Shankly, Liverpool's outrageously expressive manager, was surprisingly reluctant to publicize his team's hero. 'That's his job,' growled Shankly. 'That's what he is there for. That's what we pay him for. And don't forget there were ten others out there battling.' So there were. But it had been Clemence who had driven the Spurs players and fans to distraction.

But goalkeepers could be equally infuriating to their own supporters and sometimes their teammates. 'They should all be drowned at birth,' snarled a famous England player in the sorrowful, alcoholic aftermath of defeat in Mexico.

It was an understandable if cruel reaction to the errors which had cost England a two-goal lead and what had seemed to be a certain place in the semi-finals. Peter Bonetti of Chelsea had made those errors, and in the months which followed he was not allowed to forget it.

Banks—the one player to go sick on England's 1970 Mexican tour

An agile, confident keeper, he had only played in that fateful quarter-final because Gordon Banks was suddenly found to be unfit on the morning of the match. Banks' absence—he was the one England player to fall sick during two months in South America—merely amplified the tragedy of Bonetti's fumbling. The argument was clear and simple. Banks was the world's best. Had Banks played, England would have gone on unhindered. But it was Bonetti who played and England were beaten.

Bonetti, who left immediately after the game to spend a holiday in Acapulco with his wife, was to deny that the experience had any effect on his future form. But in the season that followed he began to falter. Under pressure from a young reserve, John Phillips, it was only his experience which won him a place in the European Cup Winners Cup final against Real Madrid.

And yet, just a short while before the Mexican disaster, Bonetti had played a game at Wembley which was to go a long way towards the winning of the FA Cup and to establish him as Banks'

outstanding deputy. In that Cup Final of 1970 Chelsea were totally outplayed by a Leeds team determined to remove for all time the charge that they were efficient but unattractive.

Although Wembley's famous turf had been abused beyond recognition, Leeds set out to achieve a colourful victory. They would have done so had not Bonetti played out of his skin throughout two hours of gruelling action.

Chelsea players had a name for him—'Catty'. It was a tribute to his gymnastic style, but on that day at Wembley it had something to do with nine lives. Jack Charlton, Leeds centre-half, recalled: 'Bonetti was brilliant. He got to shots he was never entitled to see. He caught balls he was only entitled to touch. If it hadn't been for him we would have had six goals, and it could have been all over at half-time.'

It was not all over at half-time, and Ian Hutchinson's late equalizer helped to set up a replay at Old Trafford, Manchester, which was to emphasize that Bonetti was brave as well as brilliant. Felled by Mick Jones' belligerent challenge, Bonetti was hard pushed to play on,

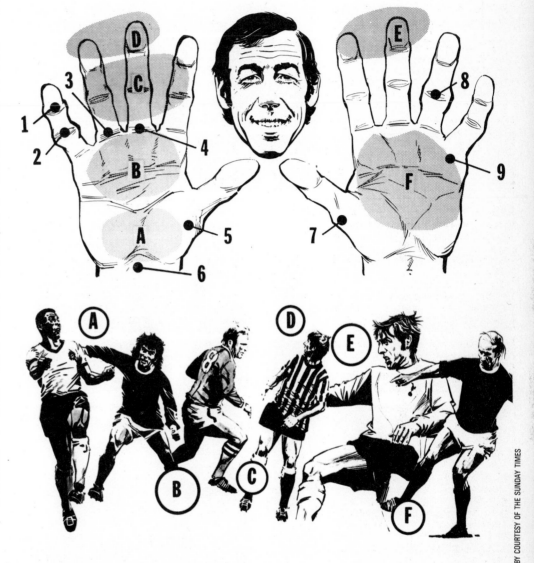

Above The two diagrams, reproduced with the kind permission of The Sunday Times, illustrate the pain and pleasure of shot-stopping through the eyes of the greatest exponent, Gordon Banks. Pain comes from a succession of throbbing injuries: the right little finger broken at the top, **1**, and middle joints, **2**; dislocations to the third, **3**, and middle, **4**, fingers on the same hand; a broken and dislocated right thumb, **5**, and wrist, **6**; a torn and dislocated left thumb, **7**; a break in the third finger of his left hand, **8**, and a mysterious knuckle injury, **9**, which has left him a knuckle short. But the battle-worn hands have given Banks the pleasure of making many world-class stops. In the 1970 World Cup, he amazingly lifted Pele's downward header over the bar with his right lower palm, **A**. The middle of the same palm, **B**, robbed George Best, clean through in a 1969 League game. The bridge of three fingers on his right hand, **C**, saved a Francis Lee free-kick in 1971, and the same finger tips, **D**, foiled Wyn Davies in 1968. In similar vein, the left-hand saved from Martin Peters, **E**, in 1970, and a Bobby Charlton rocket failed to beat the left palm, **F**, in 1969.

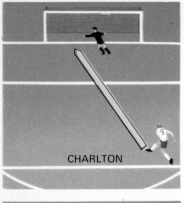

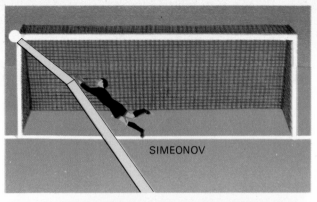

CHARLTON

SIMEONOV

CHARLTON

SIMEONOV

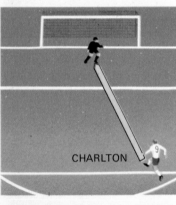

CHARLTON

SIMEONOV

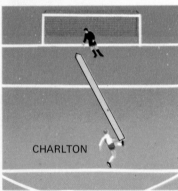

CHARLTON

SIMEONOV

and quickly lost a goal when Jones broke through to connect with Allan Clarke's pass.

Had Chelsea lost Bonetti at any time in that first half, they would have lost the Cup. But he chose to play on in pain and to play a convincing part in a triumph which was in the end all about spirit and durability.

Like all the outstanding goalkeepers, Bonetti was capable of making the miraculous save. He was not a Banks because Banks was exceptional, but there was enough in the play of the Chelsea man to put him apart from most of the others.

It was never an easy job and the popular assumption was that a man had to be crazy to attempt it. Some were good at dealing with crosses, others, were exceptional when coming from their line to deal with through passes. But the truly great ones—Banks, the Russian Yashin, Grosics of Hungary, Frank Swift, Bert Williams, Ted Ditchburn and Bert Trautmann—were all capable of pulling off the miraculous.

Even Pele admitted it was the greatest save he had ever seen

Banks in Mexico made a save from the Brazilian star, Pele, which was immediately entered in the folklore of the game. It was a centre from the right which gave Pele the chance to head powerfully from above Alan Mullery's attempted challenge, and the Brazilian admitted later that he had never felt more certain about scoring.

But Banks diving backwards scooped the ball over the bar with the inside of his right wrist, and Pele clutched his dark head in disbelief. He was to say: 'That was the greatest save I have ever seen by the greatest goalkeeper I have ever seen.'

A succession of great saves enabled England to avoid their first defeat at home when Italy came to play at Tottenham in 1949. Four years later Hungary were to expose England's belief in their invincibility by winning an historic match at Wembley. But they would have been denied the honour had Bert Williams not played the game of his life at White Hart Lane.

Billy Wright's international career was to span both matches, and Williams was his team-mate at Wolves. He recalls: 'Bert was fantastic. The Italians gave us a lesson in skill and running off the ball. There was only one reason why they didn't beat us and that was Bert Williams.'

The boot was on the other foot when England, and Bobby Charlton in particular, were thwarted by the magnificent reflexes of the Bulgarian goalkeeper, Simeonov, at Wembley in December 1968.

Charlton was in the shooting form which had made him feared throughout the world. He was almost always on target and his shots were struck with tremendous hostility. All of them were parried or turned away by a goalkeeper who was in no mood to be beaten. England had to be content with a one-all draw on a night that Charlton ought to have celebrated four goals.

Spectacular saves were always thrilling for the public, and Arsenal's crowd were treated to some outstanding ones when they beat Derby County to renew a challenge for the Championship in February 1972. The extravagant Charlie George scored twice for Arsenal that day, but might easily have doubled his tally had not young Colin Boulton been in outstanding form.

Goalkeeping of this calibre gave teams confidence as much as mistakes drove them to despair. Gary Sprake of Leeds was always capable of pulling off the near impossible, but was also prone to error and it was his errors which were remembered. Television seemed to follow his mistakes around and Sprake said: 'It's only the ricks they

Above left A series of diagrams showing how a marvellous exhibition of shot-stopping by Bulgaria's Simeonov frustrated England's Bobby Charlton at Wembley in 1968. Simeonov plunged to save four superbly hit shots which on many other nights would have brought Charlton four goals.

Left Charlton holds his head in despair as Simeonov turns away another shot to safety.

remember. The good saves they forget about.' It was not entirely true. Good goalkeeping was readily acclaimed and easily remembered.

But few ever came close to attaining Banks' level of consistency. Pat Jennings of Spurs and Northern Ireland could have walked into most of the world's teams, but Banks stood alone and Sir Alf Ramsey knew it.

When he chose him to play' for the Football League against the League of Ireland in September 1971, Banks, with his vast experience and rich memory, might have regarded the game as a low-level activity. England footballers had no reason to relish Dublin. The fixture had a tradition of personal disaster, and this one was no exception. Unable to get together against part-time players who had nothing to lose, England performed miserably until the ball reached Banks.

He made one astonishing save, clutching a deflected cross when most keepers would have been content to get a touch. Sir Alf Ramsey was moved to announce that the man was incredible.

He said: 'He has no challenger. If he goes on like this he will play until he is forty.'

Banks did go on like that, saving a penalty-kick from Geoff Hurst to keep Stoke City in the semi-finals of the 1972 League Cup and then making saves in the two replays which helped his team on towards Wembley. Had he not gone sick in Leon two years earlier, Bonetti would have been spared the one irretrievable blemish on an otherwise spectacular career. And England might have retained the World Cup.

Coaching: Sharpen your reflexes and improve your shot-stopping methods

In order to keep his goal intact from the threat of direct shots, a goalkeeper requires excellent reflexes and a supple body. With these attributes and a good handling technique, a keeper should be capable of stopping shots, although by careful positioning and anticipation he should be able to reduce the number of situations in which his reflexes are severely tested.

Before embarking on any practices check your basic position. This position will help cope with the unexpected and enable you to run out and jump for a ball or make a diving save in the quickest possible time. Stand with your feet about hip width apart, knees bent slightly and leaning your trunk forward from the hips. Bend your arms so that the forearms are almost parallel with the ground about hip height. Keep your eyes fixed on the ball, but watch for any indication as to which way the ball is going to go.

In training, goalkeepers should always have specialized coaching. Whilst their team-mates work at their outfield skills, you can work on your own if necessary. Lie on your back holding a ball on your chest. Push it hard into the air with both hands, then you must get to your feet as quickly as you can to catch it. You should be aiming to jump to make the catch. As you improve, use a medicine ball instead; it is a good exercise for sharpening your reaction.

Safety in handling the ball cannot be over-emphasized; however sharp your reflexes become they could let you down if you cannot hold the ball when you have reached it. The best method of increasing safety when catching the ball is to provide a second barrier whenever possible. When you take a low ball, the feet and legs should be close enough together not to allow the ball to go through should it slip through your hands, and the stomach or chest should be well behind the flight of the ball when possible. Special care must be taken when catching balls above head height because it is impossible to back the hands with a second barrier. In this situation you must make sure that the palms are right behind the ball and that the pace is absorbed by allowing the hands to give slightly on contact.

Either of two methods can be used when dealing with low shots. In the first method, keep your legs just a few inches apart and straight, bend your trunk well forward and take the ball in front of the legs with the fingers and palms of both hands which are held close together. As the ball makes contact with the fingers and palms, its speed will make it roll up the forearms on to your body. Straighten up, bending your elbows to bring the ball into your chest, clutching it firmly to prevent it bouncing off your body. Be sure to watch the ball right into the hands.

The second method is not so popular, but is safer because the whole body is behind the ball. This is performed by turning the hips slightly one way and kneeling on one knee; one knee should touch the ground just in front of the arch of the other foot so that there is no way for the ball to get through if you should mishandle it. The ball is taken in exactly the same way as the first method. Try both methods; you may find the second way better for bumpy or very wet slippery grounds when you feel it essential to take extra precautions.

Two keepers can often practise these techniques together. One volleys the ball from about ten yards into the other's chest—not too hard to start with. Concentrate on getting behind the ball and allowing the body to absorb some of the pace. The volley kick can be very accurate so vary the service aiming the ball low, high or into the chest. This is a continuous practice with each goalkeeper serving to the other alternately; it is also good basic training for handling and reflexes, and should only be worked at for short, sharp periods.

An outfield player can serve the ball in another routine. He should stand about five yards from the goalkeeper; you roll the ball to him or just drop it at his feet so that he can play it first time at you. The more experienced you become, the harder he can play the ball or the closer together the two of you can stand.

With a second keeper defend makeshift goals set about 15 to 20 yards apart in another routine. The object of the exercise is to drop-kick the ball and beat the other goalkeeper. In order not to violate your safety-first principles you will have to dive to get as much of your body as possible behind the ball. When diving, remember to take the ball with your hands in front of the body and try to dive slightly forward or directly along the line. This action takes courage and you might like to start diving practices from a kneeling position. If you feel confident enough to catch the ball whilst diving do so; if not remember that when you are diving out infield, get your fist to it so that the ball clears the area, or if you are diving along the line, get your palms to the ball and deflect it well past the post. The ball should never be palmed infield; this is only likely to set up close-range chances for forwards lurking in the goalmouth.

Remember in all your goalkeeping practices, only work until you become tired; if you continue to practise when you are exhausted, you will only develop bad habits.

Below left Sheffield United's Hope dives right to parry a close-range shot from Liverpool's Evans. Below Diagram of a reflex-sharpening practice. The keeper lies on the ground, pushes a ball high into the air, and then leaps up to catch it.

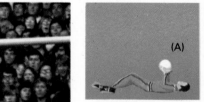

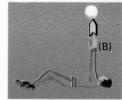

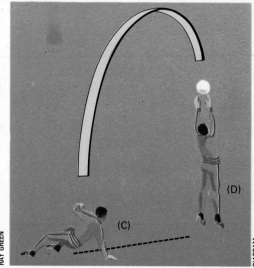

Goalkeeping — the four-step rule

Had Gordon Banks been able to receive Granada Television at his Staffordshire home he would probably have avoided the serious eye injury which threatened to end his illustrious career in October 1972.

Banks, the Stoke City and England goalkeeper, was still widely regarded as the world's best when he set out by car on a fateful Sunday afternoon to watch television at a friend's home.

It was an important mission for Banks. The previous day at Liverpool he had been penalized for allegedly infringing the law which restricted goalkeepers to four steps when they had possession of the ball.

Banks had disputed that decision with Leicester referee Roger Kirkpatrick and his anger multiplied when Liverpool scored from the indirect free-kick which they had been awarded.

No one was more annoyed than Banks who was still protesting vigorously as the teams left the field. Was Kirkpatrick right to penalize him? Banks knew that Granada were putting the match out and he intended to see it. He never made it.

His car was wrecked in a collision with a van and he had an emergency operation to remove glass splinters from his right eye. No one knew whether he would ever play again.

The irony was total. World football was stunned and for a week Banks lay in darkness able only to reflect on it all.

If the four-step amendment to the Laws had not been introduced during the sixties he would not have been involved in controversy. Had there not been any controversy he may not have bothered to try and see the match.

It was not the first time that Banks, in the latter part of his career, had run into trouble with the ruling. Indeed all goalkeepers saw it as an unnecessary restriction, denying them the opportunity of evading fierce physical challenge.

The amendment was introduced by FIFA to try and help speed up the game and in an attempt to end the practice of prolonged possession by goalkeepers in the penalty area.

Immediately controversial, it inspired a variety of minor tactical measures which forced the various Football Associations to clearly define the ruling. For instance, it was not enough to use the word possession. Coaches saw through that, or more importantly, saw a way around it.

The law seemed too specific. 'The goalkeeper is allowed no more than four steps while holding, bouncing or throwing the ball in the air before releasing it so that it can be played by another player.'

But was there any reason why the goalkeeper should not temporarily 'lose' possession by rolling the ball forward so that he could then reclaim his right to four steps after gathering it again?

Referees were not sure. Clever coaches had caught them out and steps had to be taken to clarify the point. 'A total of four steps,' said the Football Association. 'A total of four, no matter how they are made up or broken up.'

That much then was clear but it was only the beginning of the problems. Shrewd, cunning people saw quickly that goalkeepers now had a problem which ranged beyond the immediate nervous pressure of knowing that two of their four steps were invariably used up when fielding the ball. Forwards were detailed to move in quickly, ordered to post themselves in front of goalkeepers who, having used up the statutory number of steps, could not dodge clear.

The forwards could not make any direct physical challenge. On the other hand they could position themselves in such a way that it was almost impossible for the goalkeeper to kick a full distance or to select the most productive angle for his clearance.

In the beginning there was panic. Pat Jennings

Above Gary Sprake, the Leeds United goalkeeper, rolls the ball out towards the edge of his penalty area to avoid breaking the four-steps rule.
Below left The goalkeeper is allowed to carry the ball only four paces before releasing it. If he rolls the ball after taking two paces, he is temporarily 'losing' possession and he still has two paces in hand to make his clearance.

RAY GREEN

of Spurs and Northern Ireland, later to challenge for the supremacy of Banks' standing, suffered embarrassment in a game against Manchester United at Old Trafford.

The man who caused it was George Best. Best cunningly waited while his fellow Irishman used up the four steps. For a second he appeared to

Below The rule becomes an immediate problem to the keeper when an opponent blocks his movement. Gordon Banks is forced to kick left-footed in the 1971 Ireland–England match by the attentions of George Best, who had a goal disallowed after robbing Banks in a similar situation.
Below right As long as the attacker refrains from physical contact, he can harass the keeper.

show disinterest—a trick he was to use many times afterwards—then as Jennings prepared to kick clear, Best raised his right foot and blocked the ball. When it ran free he turned and scored. Spurs protested that Best had been guilty of an infringement but the goal was allowed to stand.

Some years later when England met Northern Ireland at Belfast in May 1971, Best almost brought off the same move. This time it was Gordon Banks, already showing some reaction to the pressure of having to captain his club Stoke, who almost found himself robbed in a moment of controversy.

Once again Best waited innocently. Once again he raised his right foot and as Banks kicked the ball was blocked. Best ran on to score but this time the referee ruled in the goalkeeper's favour.

Banks was to say: 'Life is becoming impossible for goalkeepers. If we are to be restricted to four steps then at least they should allow us the opportunity of making a clearance. The idea behind this ruling was a speeding up of the game. But I don't think goalkeepers in Britain were ever guilty of deliberately wasting time.

'It happened a lot in other countries but not here. The difference is the difference in attitudes. Goalkeepers never get touched abroad do they? They get complete protection. I'm not asking for that. But for goodness sake give us a chance.'

The plea was a common one but it aroused little sympathy. Goalkeepers had to get on with it and it was to their credit that they evolved new techniques.

Throwing, for instance, had been used almost exclusively as a means of starting attacks at short range. Now goalkeepers, invariably big, powerful men, began to throw to and even beyond the halfway line.

It was necessary for them to react sharply to possession. They had to assess a wider area of possibility for their clearances and to be more accurate and positive.

Although restricted to a total of four steps, they could, if they were sensible and perceptive, use the full extent of their penalty area, rolling the ball out and then collecting it for a clearance.

One major instruction was based on immobility. Panic in a crowded goalmouth could be fatal. 'Stand still,' said coaches, 'get the ball in tight to your chest and wait until the area has cleared. Defenders will have come up at corners and free-kicks. Once you have the ball they won't hang

around. They will be sprinting back to the halfway line. Wait until they have gone. Wait until you have time and space in your favour. There isn't anything which says you must get rid of the ball quickly.'

This became accepted practice, ironically defeating the original motive behind the decision to restrict keepers to four steps. Far from speeding the game up, it often served to slow it down. It was interesting that many Continental teams paid no account to putting keepers under the sort of pressure which had become commonplace in Britain.

When Chelsea reached the final of the European Cup Winners Cup in 1971 they needed two matches to beat the famed Real Madrid in Athens. The first game went into extra time and Chelsea won the replay 48 hours later, a game unseen by the majority of their supporters who had been unable to stay on in Greece because of Charter Aircraft restrictions.

During the three and a half hours of play which Chelsea needed to win a major European trophy, their goalkeeper Peter Bonetti was never challenged once he had collected the ball.

He said: 'It was an unusual experience. These people don't seem to bother about putting you under pressure. I think they are much more concerned with getting their players back into the middle of the field.'

There was some point in this. Certainly one or two English First Division clubs, whose confidence in their goalkeepers was complete, were often happy to see a prized attacker used to apply pressure if the ball had been pushed back into their own penalty area for the goalkeeper to gather.

'Let them go in there,' said one astute manager. 'We like them to go in there. Once our goalkeeper has cleared the ball upfield those attackers who have been trying to put him under pressure have got to run thirty or forty yards to get back into the game. A few runs like that and they aren't much use for anything.'

Nevertheless, British clubs still considered it valuable to close down on the opposing goalkeeper, denying him angle and the comfort of room in which to kick.

It was perhaps inevitable that goalkeepers should take aggressive steps to protect themselves and one First Division keeper gained a reputation as someone to keep away from.

COLORSPORT

DIAGRAM

His technique was simple enough. Confronted by a challenging attacker, he would set himself so that the follow through of his clearance often meant that the opponent suffered physical damage from a lunging boot.

Such things were barely, if ever, considered by the various refereeing organizations. A code of conduct was viable in council, but not always on the field of play.

The majority of professionals were not interested in morals. They were only interested in winning. They saw the four-step ruling as an unnecessary imposition. But having been stuck with it they made the best of it. That was life.

Gordon Banks had to live with that. His agility and reflexes, his courage and timing combined to establish him as probably the greatest of all goalkeepers. It was sad that he was seen to leave the stage, for the last time before a tragic accident interrupted his career, with violent protest written on his face.

Coaching: Improve your positional play as a goalkeeper

The goalkeeper's main function is to prevent the ball entering his team's goal. How he does it does not really matter as long as he succeeds; some favour the spectacular and acrobatic methods whilst others prefer to be less eye-catching. Nevertheless correct positioning and orientation by the goalkeeper will put him in the best area to deal with every situation.

Theoretically, the goalkeeper should take up a position on what is called the 'bisector'. Draw an imaginary line from the ball to both the posts, now another line from the ball to the centre of goal. This line, which equally divides the first two lines, is the 'bisector'. This puts the goalkeeper in a central position allowing equal space on both sides. If the goalkeeper positions himself on this line he is giving himself a chance to make a save on either side with a minimum amount of movement.

Although this principle should be applied when a direct shot is threatening his charge, he must deviate from it in certain situations. When the ball is out on the flanks the goalkeeper should position himself closer to the far post in readiness to collect balls crossed into that part of the goalmouth. He should also be prepared to move forward quickly to deal with balls played into the near post area. When the ball is moved from the flanks closer to the goal, the goalkeeper should gradually move forward towards the near post because the danger of a direct shot is gradually threatening.

As soon as a shot is on, the original principle must be applied. Groups of three players can help the goalkeeper with this technique. The first player with a ball runs at and commits the second player, who acts as a defender, some 25 yards out from goal. The goalkeeper's position must be on the 'bisector' in preparation to deal with a possible shot. As the attacking player commits the defender he passes the ball out to the third player on the wing. According to how the ball is played he can now do one of two things. If the ball is played short he can bear in at goal and shoot. If the pass is longer then he can cross for the attacking player to head at goal under pressure from the defender. The goalkeeper must be alive to this situation and react quickly. The coach should stop the play in order to check the keeper's position.

When play is deep in the opponents' half, the goalkeeper should be encouraged to be some 12 yards out from goal, prepared to move forward even more to intercept long through balls. As the play nears an area from which it is possible for a direct shot, then the goalkeeper must retreat closer to his line in order to reduce the danger of a ball chipped over his head. During this period his attention should be focused on the ball and the movement of opponents.

Once you have left your goal-line you may experience difficulty in orientating yourself. You may not be able to assess your own position in relation to the goal without looking back; obviously a dangerous thing to do. When standing on the goal-line between the posts you can see them peripherally whilst still concentrating on the ball and players. Once you move forward, this is no longer possible, so you must find other methods. Marking the pitch by using your studs is illegal, but there are enough legal marks around if you look for them. The corners of goal area, the penalty spot, the corners and arc of the penalty area are all useful visual aids to help you know where you are once you are out of goal.

You should spend a considerable amount of time on your own, taking up positions for imaginary shots. You can then look back to check for yourself. The best experience will be during practice matches when your coach can stop the game in order to discuss this point. Situations change very quickly in football, especially around the box, so you must get used to changing your position with the situations without taking your eyes off the ball and the general movement.

Goalkeeping is full of problems in positional play, but thought and practice, together with ever-increasing experience, will help you learn how to cope with them.

Below left Peter Thompson of Liverpool puts the pressure on Southampton's Eric Martin.
Below Diagram of the 'bisector', the line along which the keeper should come out to narrow the angle; here he can cover both sides of the goal.

RAY GREEN

Tackling technique

Below The tackle from behind that came under severe scrutiny during the 'referees' revolution' at the start of the 1971-72 Football League season. The challenge is illegal if the tackler only makes contact with the ball after kicking aside the legs of the man in possession. Here, Francis Lee of Manchester City is strongly challenged by the Spurs centre-half Mike England.
Inset Bryan Robson of West Ham feels the full weight of a perfect block tackle from Chelsea defender Paddy Mulligan. Mulligan has won the ball in almost text-book style, making a strong, front-on challenge and forcing the ball away from Robson with the inside of his foot.

The 'referees' revolution' that greeted the start of the 1971-72 Football League season was rooted in a new disciplinary code designed to reinforce the game's fading spirit: 329 players were booked in the first two months of a purge that was particularly painful to those whose game was based on inflicting pain on their immediate opponents.

The key to the new code of behaviour was its attempt to abolish the tackle from behind in which the tackler, because of the angle of his approach, only made contact with the ball after crashing a foot through the back of an opponent's leg. If the tackler managed to reach the ball from behind the man in possession by stretching a leg cleanly at it, then British football adjudged it a fair tackle. But more often skilled screeners of the ball, deliberately protecting it by legal use of their body, were bowled over without ceremony by crippling challenges that simply whipped their legs from under them. If the tackler's next contact had been with the ball, then the referees had allowed play to continue.

Had the 'manliness' been taken out of the British national game?

As player after player fell foul of referees—many for dangerous play but some for the most trivial offences in bizarre circumstances—the new code provoked anger among the clubs, and the controversy reached its climax when Crystal Palace chairman Arthur Wait called for the resignation of the entire League Management Committee. The cry went up that the 'manliness' was being taken out of the British national game. The men who now found it difficult to play were those whose reputations had been founded on coarse challenge and unchecked physical intimidation. Joe Mercer, general manager of Manchester City, was quick to make a significant point: 'A lot of players with a reputation for toughness are being found out. Now that they are being forced to try to tackle properly, it's obvious that they can't tackle at all. They have never learnt how to.'

But, as the fires of discontent began to die, it was seen that the Football League, for all their clumsy mishandling of the situation, had done the game a great service. Nevertheless the ball was still in play to be won, and no player in possession could expect to be free from a fair tackle.

Tackling was a particularly controversial issue in world football because the word had no definition in the laws of the game, and indeed did not even appear in them.

Every country interpreted the laws regarding fair play differently. The British version hung on the belief that it was legal to win the ball from the player in possession by front-on or side-on challenges. As long as the tackler made initial contact with the ball using a powerful thrust of the inside of the foot or the instep or even the toe, the tackle was adjudged to be a fair method of disputing possession of the ball.

But abroad this was not always acceptable. Before the 1970 World Cup in Mexico and following controversial statements from Joao Saldanha, then the Brazilian team manager, Sir Alf Ramsey took a firm stand on what was for him a critical issue.

Back in Rio after a European tour, Saldanha made pointed references to the brutality he had seen and warned that Brazil would react violently if they were threatened by unbridled aggression. Ramsey insisted on fair play. But he defended the physical side of football because he regarded it as part of the game's heritage.

'Tackling is an important part of football,' he said. 'Without it we should be denying the public an essential, exciting feature of the game.'

Football as Ramsey knew it was football the way the British public knew it. They had grown up with an admiration for aggressive endeavour, and defenders who drove in to win the ball fairly with muscular, courageous intent earned as many cheers as the more delicate and artistic ball players.

There was no definite technique, although every coaching manual included a picture of two players poised in exactly similar posture over a stationary ball. The forward hunch of the shoulders. The head down. Knee over the ball. A foot drawn back before driving in. This was the popular picture of what a good tackler was like.

Nothing was further from the truth. Good tacklers are those who win the ball consistently no matter what their technique. But there were essential factors common to all good ball winners. They had to have the desire to win in circumstances which might not always be in their favour. They had to be brave and they had to make use of all their strength.

When Arsenal dominated British football in the thirties they employed Wilf Copping to get the ball, in order that more skilful players could use it. Copping, with his vast expanse of scarred forehead and the bluest of blue chins, was to symbolize a he-man attitude to the game.

Where even a broken leg was no excuse for shirking a tackle

Barnsley born, an ex-miner and as tough as they came, Copping learnt his football in a school where it was claimed that not even a broken leg would be accepted as an excuse for pulling out of a challenge. Tackling was everything to him. He had no illusions about his style, and in later years, when trainer to Southend and Bristol City, he was to say:

'Cowards have no place in football. But if you have to put up with them in your own team, then at least try and make life easier for them, if they can play. My job at Arsenal was to get the ball. I was better at it than anybody else. When I got the ball I gave it to someone who could make use of it.'

When England played Italy at Highbury in 1934 Copping was one of seven Arsenal players in the team. It was a match destined to remain in the memory, and Copping's role was significant. Italy were reigning world champions. England, still complaining over 'broken-time' payments to amateurs, were outside FIFA and had not competed.

The Italians, lionized by Fascist propaganda and the comic caperings of Mussolini, arrived to dispute England's insular self-appointment as masters of football. It proved to be an untidy and at times vicious contest. An Italian elbow broke Eddie Hapgood's nose and the cynicism was to provoke Copping, sending him into a series of cold-eyed tackles which were to ultimately demolish the Italian challenge.

Although it was always argued that Copping was hard but fair, he was no saint: there was no meaner defender in the business. But there could be no doubting the excellence of his technique when presented with the prospect of dispossessing an opponent. Copping seemed to have been hewn from the gritty Yorkshire coal he had worked as a boy. Invariably he looked a good tackler and, in moments of reminiscence, he always sounded like one.

The voice was gruff as though black dust still encrusted his vocal cords, and football to him was all about manliness.

'Tackling,' Copping would growl, 'is all to do with thinking that you can. You don't have to be

Coaching: Learn how to go in hard and win the ball fairly

Tackling is still one of the most effective ways of winning the ball from opponents. Emphasis on team-work and quick interpassing has made tackling that much more difficult, however, because in order to fairly dispossess an opponent, who has control of the ball, the tackler must only go in when he has an excellent chance of winning the ball.

Tackling is without doubt a major technical and tactical weapon in the possession of defenders, but in certain situations it may be equally important to attackers. The actual execution of any movement is always a question of technique; the problem of when and how to use the movement is one of tactics. Although tactics play a more important role in tackling than in any other technical element, the technical side of tackling must never be ignored.

Ask a friend to approach you with a ball at his feet at walking pace. Take up a position as near to him as you can. The standing foot, which is slightly bent at the knee, is placed near to the ball and pointing forward. The tackling foot should be turned outwards so that it is at right angles to the approaching ball. If the tackling leg is slightly bent at the knee, this position is easy to maintain. This foot is then swung back as in the kicking action with the inside of the foot, but the back-swing is shorter. At the moment the inside of the foot makes contact with the ball, the body is inclined forward and balance maintained by the arms. The muscles and joints are tightened to ensure a very firm contact and there should be powerful follow through.

If you have done this correctly, you should now have possession of the ball. Go through this sequence slowly at first, concentrating on putting the weight of your body behind the ball, on making a really firm contact and on going in with determination, otherwise you run a risk of injury. Hanging out a tentative foot, more or less leaving it to look after itself, will only lead to an unsuccessful tackle and a visit to the trainer's room. When you do commit yourself to a direct tackle you will find that it is frequently an advantage to lean in with your shoulder, providing an extra and legitimate means of blocking your opponent.

Now place the ball between you and your friend so that you are both only one pace from it. You both tackle for the ball at the same time. After a while you can make this competitive to see who can win the most number of tackles. You might find that by going in firmly and then trying to lift the ball over your friend's foot you can take full possession.

Your friend can now dribble the ball towards you and attempt to go past. Tactics here are important. Your approach to close him down should be at an angle inviting your friend to go only one way (on to your strong foot and towards the touchline away from danger). You should keep within tackling distance without committing yourself, ready to pounce on a possible mistake, your feet moving quickly to maintain balance. Remember here that your friend will beat you easily if you tackle at the wrong time or out of distance. Work at him with an aggressive attitude, perhaps making an initial play at the ball to try to make him lose control. Then, the moment you see your opportunity, go in really hard and win the ball.

Seek the help of another player. Let him have the ball as a midfield man. Your friend can play as a winger some 20 yards from him and you can be the full-back about 10 yards from the winger. The midfield player plays the ball into an area between you and your friend. The object here is for you to judge quickly whether you can get to the ball before your friend in which case you intercept and play the ball back to the feeder, or whether you can get there at the same time as your friend so that you tackle

immediately; or whether your friend has been favoured so that you will have to work at him to get your tackle in. The first things you will have to do if your friend takes full possession is to close him down quickly so that he cannot get a run at you and so that when he does move he goes into the area where you want him to go.

Move on to a small-sided game, three against three, up to six versus six, and impose the condition that once in possession the player must attempt to beat an opponent by dribbling before he can make a pass. In a confined area, this will give plenty of opportunity for tackles. Eton School play a game called the 'Field Game' in which passing is forbidden. The player in possession dribbles the ball until he loses it or gets a shot in at goal. This is a very hard game physically and again invites plenty of tackling practice under competitive conditions.

The first tackle in the game is important from the psychological point of view. On your first encounter with the player you are marking, display absolute determination and offer the strongest possible opposition. Strength, within the limits of the law, can often undermine your opponent, and get him looking for you instead of concentrating on the ball when controlling it, making it easy for you to dispossess him and clear the danger.

If you lose the first tackle, this will give your opponent confidence and he will give you an uncomfortable time. Avoid spectacular tackles early on and keep your passing within a 'safety-first' limit until you have got the feel of your opponent and the conditions. Once you have dispossessed your opponent, do not give him a chance of recovery. Move away quickly, and play the ball early.

By tackling strongly and fairly, and then passing the ball accurately, you are well on your way to becoming a good defender.

Right The techniques of tackling. 1 A tackle should never be attempted out of range; not only is it almost impossible to put any strength into such a challenge, it also becomes easier for the player in possession to sidestep the tackler. 2 Rather, the tackler should move in closer, looking for the moment when he can put the whole weight of his body behind the attempt to win the ball. 3 In a front-on tackle, the tackling foot should not make contact with the top of the ball, because it becomes impossible once more to challenge with any force. The foot will probably slide over the ball and connect with the opponent's shin, in which case the tackler will be penalized for dangerous play. A mistimed tackle of this nature could severely injure the man on the ball. 4 Instead the tackling foot should be aimed at the centre of the ball, using a similar movement to an exaggerated sidefooted pass. The knee should be turned outwards and the ankle held firm. 5 In tackling from behind, it is important to remember that the first contact must be with the ball, not the back of the legs of the player who is screening the ball. Any tackle that brushes aside the legs to reach the ball will certainly give away a free-kick, and with many sides adept at exploiting set-pieces, conceding free-kicks can become very costly. 6 But if, in challenging from the side or from behind, the tackler plays the ball first, he is tackling fairly and more likely to succeed in playing the ball to safety. 7 The problem of fair play also arises in the technique for winning a bouncing ball. If the foot is raised, with the studs threatening an opponent, then the tackler will be pulled up for dangerous play. 8 But if the foot is twisted to pull the ball down and away from the opponent, there is much less chance of a foul being committed and a much greater chance of the ball being controlled.

Every defender must practise these techniques. Without them he cannot hope to win the ball consistently or fairly for his side.

a giant to be a good tackler.'

The point was taken up by Sir Alf Ramsey many years later when he was quizzed about Nobby Stiles. England's successful World Cup team of 1966 was still being built, and Stiles was a new name to world football. Small, slight and desperately short-sighted, Stiles hardly looked like an international, and Ramsey was asked to supply the simple statistic of weight.

'Nobby is about ten stone,' said the England team manager. But before the figure could be digested, Ramsey added, 'Yes, he's about ten stone—that's until he tackles. Then he's about ten ton!'

Some of the world's great forwards were to suffer from Stiles' aggressive attitude, and there was even a move to have him outlawed in 1966 after one of his tackles had demolished the French forward Simon at Wembley.

Stiles was not alone. Norman Hunter, a lean, back-four defender in the powerful Leeds team which grew out of nothing in the sixties, had an awesome reputation among his friends and foes alike. 'The best tackler I have ever seen,' said the Leeds manager Don Revie. 'When you hear Norman's left foot clicking back, it is like someone cocking a rifle,' said one of Hunter's teammates. 'It's time to get out of the way.'

There was no braver tackler than Tommy Smith of Liverpool, who looked a man when he was 15 and played that way all his career. And Bobby Moore in his more aggressive mood was as good at winning the ball as anyone, and never better than in the Mexico World Cup of 1970.

Bobby Moore rammed his skill down the throats of the Mexican crowd

There was little affection for the England team during that competition. But one marvellously geometric battle against Brazil in Guadalajara was to underline Moore's unarguable status as one of the world's great defenders.

Among the more stirring moments in that match was a break by the Brazilian right-winger Jairzinho. The proportion and muscularity of a middle-weight, added to pace and control, made the Brazilian a fearsome proposition when in full flight.

But as he sped at England's defence early in the second half he found Moore in majestic command of a potentially damaging situation. There was not a hint of desperation—just perfect balance, immaculate timing and a powerful driving challenge which brought England's captain clear with the ball, as Jairzinho's athleticism was suddenly reduced to a flurry of uncontrolled limbs.

The crowd went silent for a second. They had suddenly been taught what a good tackle was all about. It might have been hard for them to take. But take it they had to. Moore had rammed his skill down their throats.

Tackling like this was a critical feature of midfield play, where the ball had to be won consistently if there was to be any domination. When Don Howe, Arsenal's coach and assistant manager, moved from Highbury after the League and Cup double of 1971, he left this message for his former players.

'There's no reason why you shouldn't go on and become an even better team. But you must never forget to make your tackles. You can't play without the ball and First Division teams aren't going to give it to you very often.'

The point was not lost on an Arsenal team in which every player harassed and challenged for possession—especially forwards like John Radford, Ray Kennedy and George Armstrong.

The League's intervention in August 1971 was to force players to amend their attitude and many were disarmed. But the good tacklers—the ones who knew what they were doing, the ones who had been well-schooled, the brave and determined ones—they came through to prove that tackling within the laws remained an exciting and essential feature of football.

DIAGRAM

WILSON (A)

WILSON (B)

WILSON (C)

WILSON (D)

GOROCS (A)

GOROCS (B)

GOROCS (C)

GO ROCS (D)

DIAGRAM/RESEARCH, PATHE NEWS

Full-backs in defence

Above Diagram showing the defensive skills of Ray Wilson, 63 times an England full-back. His speed and positional skill forces Hungary's Gorocs away from goal until he loses control.
Below left Wilson shows his aerial power as he outjumps Uwe Seeler in the 1966 World Cup final.

A well-known story involving Chelsea full-back Eddie McCreadie still causes a laugh in the dressing-room at Stamford Bridge. When chosen to play for Scotland against Spurs in a testimonial match for the widow of John White in 1965, McCreadie was given one specific order: 'Those overlaps you do for Chelsea; we want you to try three of them. But no more than three, mind.'

McCreadie, an instinctive attacker who was a spectacular exponent of the overlap which became so popular in the mid-sixties, laughed at and then ignored what was a crazily specific instruction. But although the sentiments of the advisers to the Scotland team that night were expressed in such a laughable manner, there was more than a glimmer of sense behind the thought. In an era of attacking full-back play it had become easy to forget that the primary task of a defender was still to defend.

Full-backs had to be able to tackle, to win the ball for their side, they had to possess instinctive positional sense both to know when to move infield to cover and when to force their immediate opponent out wide to less menacing positions away from goal, and they had to be strong enough in the air to be able to challenge powerful forwards when put under pressure at the far post. Above all they could not be left floundering and breathless upfield when their own goal was under pressure.

England's success in the 1966 World Cup did much to change the concept of the full-back's role as George Cohen and Ray Wilson consistently surged forward in attack to compensate for the lack of orthodox wingers. It led to a spate of conversions; skilled forwards suddenly found themselves wearing shirts numbered two or three.

Whilst McCreadie was struggling to recover form and fitness at the end of the 1971-72 season after an irritating run of serious injuries, Chelsea seriously considered Peter Houseman at left-back. An intelligent and vastly underrated winger with an educated left foot, Houseman had done well in the position during an emergency a few months earlier.

It prompted Chelsea manager Dave Sexton to say: 'Don't be surprised if I give Peter a long run in the position. He can do it. He's intelligent. He is strong enough to win the ball and he knows exactly when to go into forward positions.'

In promoting the possibility, Sexton had to be sure that Houseman had the necessary qualities to be a more than adequate defender. It was not enough that he could get by under pressure. Unless he could defend he could become a liability.

The blueprint to successful conversions had been seen at Leeds, where Terry Cooper, a young left-winger, had become an England regular at left-back. Yet the flaws which were a natural product of his upbringing as a forward were never completely removed.

Cooper was unquestionably the finest attacking defender in the business when he broke a leg playing against Stoke towards the end of the 1971-72 season. He had the dribbling skills he was born with, the confidence to take people on and a devastating swerve.

Leeds make maximum use of the talent. But they had to live with the fact that Cooper often got them in trouble because of shaky positional play. Cooper was at his most vulnerable when the ball was on the opposite flank. He had a tendency to be drawn too far forward where he could no longer keep an opponent wide on his flank within the area of vision.

This fault was to nearly cost England a goal in the vital opening phase of their first match during the Mexico World Cup. Had Dembrowski been brave enough to attempt a header

RAY GREEN

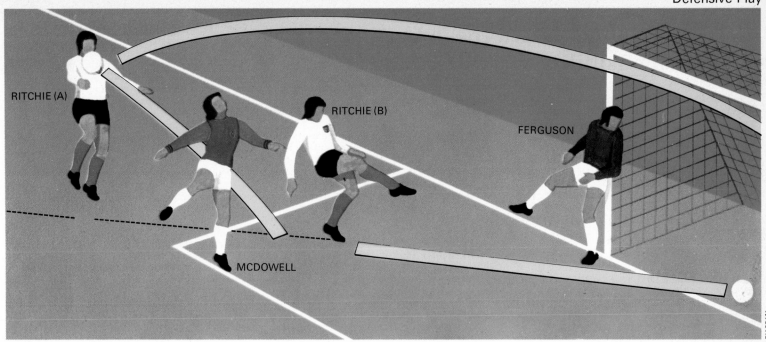

Above *John Ritchie's goal for Stoke against West Ham in the 1971-72 League Cup semi-final illustrates a problem for full-backs. McDowell had been drawn into the middle to cover, leaving Ritchie unmarked to convert a deep cross.*
Below right *Bob McNab moves infield to cover.*

Rumania might have gone ahead.

Another error, two years earlier, had lost England a goal against Scotland at Wembley. Cooper was caught at the far post a yard or two too close to Colin Stein, as the Rangers' striker moved in to meet a cross from Eddie Gray. Committed to a standing jump, Cooper was several inches short of the ball as Stein placed his header wide of Gordon Banks.

The need to eliminate such catastrophes remained very much in the minds of coaches as they pursued more ambitious policies. The era of the complete player was still a long way off.

Arsenal discovered this when bidding to retain their League and Cup double in 1971-72. They began that season with fewer senior players than all but two of the other clubs in the First Division, and with Bob McNab still struggling with a pelvic strain soon to trouble others.

McNab was simply suffering from wear and tear, the strain of continuous top-level combat. Quick and combative, he was vital to Arsenal's defensive structure but there was never a time during that season when he was fully fit.

Once the injury had been correctly diagnosed, Arsenal elected to rest him, confident that they had adequate cover in Irish international Sammy Nelson. Nelson was an accomplished player, especially when going forward. He had good ball control and he used the ball well.

Arsenal used his attacking qualities well but were to discover that they missed McNab's positive tackling and organizational ability. When the pressure was on, McNab was brought back, not fully fit, but fit enough to bring more stability to the defence.

It prompted this comment from a team-mate: 'I feel sorry for Sammy. He's done ever so well. But he just doesn't defend as well as little Bob. You see Bob is a quick thinker. He's sharp. He sees things and he's always yapping.'

Footballers, especially defenders, needed to communicate, to talk and call to each other, warning of danger, advising angles, acting as an extra pair of eyes for each other. This was particularly important for full-backs who were invariably the last man before the goalkeeper.

McNab's alert play helped Arsenal on to their second successive FA Cup Final, but this time they fell to Leeds in a match which fully consoled Paul Reaney for the broken leg that prevented him from playing against Chelsea two years earlier.

Reaney had been chosen to go with England to Mexico and was waiting to play in the Final when he broke a leg playing in a League game at West Ham. By the time he had recovered, Paul Madeley had settled down as the Leeds right-back and had captured the position in the England team. There was no easy way back and Reaney clearly was not as sharp as he had been before his injury. He had never possessed Cooper's smoothness in possession and his attacking sorties were more willing than skilful.

Reaney's goal-line saves come too often to be coincidence

But he had been sharp into the tackle when coming out from a covering position, more positive than Cooper when challenging on crosses from the far flank and less likely to let attackers creep in behind him.

Some of this had gone and Reaney, disillusioned by his omission, asked for a transfer. Leeds manager Don Revie persuaded him to change his mind and the reward was a place in the 1972 Final as a deputy for Cooper whose own injury took on the form of supreme irony.

One of the things Reaney had not lost was the ability to remain calm in critical situations. His goal-line clearances were made too often to be coincidental and there was no better example of this than when he cut off a shot from Alan Ball in the Final with goalkeeper David Harvey stranded on the other post.

Revie said: 'These things don't happen by accident. Paul is good at this. Another player might have drifted off the goal-line in that moment. Paul's judgement was perfect. He rarely lets us down in that sort of situation. We have got to be delighted that he chose to stay with us.'

Another First Division full-back, West Ham's John McDowell, appeared to have been caught out by letting an attacker creep in behind him when John Ritchie scored to put Stoke level in the second leg of the 1971-72 League Cup semi-final. A deep cross found Ritchie unattended at the far post with McDowell left stranded several yards nearer the goalmouth. Yet some critics ignored the problem. Ritchie had escaped from the clutches of centre-half Taylor at the same time that McDowell had to decide to move in to cover the centre of his defence. It resulted in a mix up that eventually cost West Ham a Wembley appearance as Stoke moved forward to meet Chelsea in the final.

When Malcolm Allison moved on to Manchester City as coach, he persuaded manager Joe Mercer to buy Tony Book. Mercer recalled: 'I thought Malcolm was out of his mind. Then he reminded me that I was well into my thirties when Arsenal signed me from Everton just after the War. So I gave in and it turned out to be the best thing we ever did. Tony Book became a magnificent player for City.'

Book rarely involved himself in long, attacking runs. But his use of the ball was immaculate and he was superb in organizing City's defence. Few wingers could draw him into positions where he could be outpaced or outwitted and after two years in the First Division he looked as though he had been playing there all his career.

Full-backs, then, had to remember that they were principally defenders even at a time when they were asked to accept more and more responsibility in attack. The best of them were completely influential and there were few better than Ray Wilson who established himself as England's finest ever left-back, representing his country on more than sixty occasions.

When England were forced to leave without Wilson for the 1968 European Nations Cup in Italy, there was still a possibility that he would recover from injury in time to link up with the squad.

Sir Alf Ramsey was asked: 'What are the chances of Ray getting here?' His reply was significant. 'If Ray can make it I'll go and fetch him on my back. He's that important to us.'

Coaching: Learn the defensive responsibilities of full-back play

Part of the thrill of the football of seventies is seeing full-backs flying down the wings or bearing infield to get into good forward positions. When done at the right time, this can prove very successful, but attack must be put into the proper perspective when dealing with the actual role of the full-back. The full-back is first and foremost a defender. His chief responsibility is to defend his own goal, and his skills must be allied to this main function. The full-back who attacks as a flank striker should be considered a bonus and he should only be allowed to go forward when the situation is favourable.

Basically the full-back is a marker, a ball winner and a supporter in defence and attack. He must be well versed in his knowledge of defensive principles and very experienced in the art of positioning. With complete concentration the good full-back will find himself adjusting his position with every kick of the game.

As a full-back you must master all tackling techniques, work at your heading and control, and concentrate on the game so that you can recognize dangerous situations quickly. Distribution is also important especially in striking long passes early for your forward players.

If pre-match information is limited you will have to pick out the strengths and weaknesses of your immediate opponent and those of the opposition in general as quickly as possible, because your game as a whole will depend largely on the tactics and capabilities of the opposition. You will want to know how fast your immediate opponent is in relation to your own speed. This information will influence how tightly you must mark. If you are quicker than the wing player, then you can afford to mark tighter than if you are slower. If you tightly mark a player who is sharper than you, you are courting disaster; he will be able to get away from you into areas you may not wish him to go.

A clever opponent should be pressured and hustled with aggression as quickly as possible, so you should mark him close when the ball comes over into your vicinity. You should also discover how the winger intends to attack you, find out which is his best foot, whether he is going to attempt to take you on the inside or outside, or whether he intends to use another player for one-two movements. You should also note the winger's main sources of supply and try to anticipate what this supplier is aiming to do. He may be playing to feet so that the winger can have a go at taking you on or he may be dropping them behind your back for a quick winger to chase.

This information will also help you decide exactly how you intend to play your immediate opponent. You will also have to consider the effects of ground conditions on the ball and underfoot. Solving these problems will help you in two of your main functions, marking and the winning of the ball.

Your positioning will also be affected by the performances and problems of your team-mates as well as the tactics of the opposition. Your other full-back may be struggling against an excellent winger. This may mean that the central defenders will have to give closer support and that will mean that you, as the far full-back, will have to come back deeper on the cover. Alternatively the opponents may be playing two central strikers and threatening danger through the middle; this would necessitate the full-backs playing to give more immediate support to the centre of the field, thus leaving their wings somewhat open in an attempt to prevent the greater danger down the middle by making the opponents play the ball out wide. These are only examples. Many decisions have to be made as to what constitutes the most danger. It would, for example, be stupid for the full-back to stand out wide with the winger and allow a midfield player to go through the middle to score. Eliminate the immediate dangers first.

The ball has to be worked for and your training and coaching must develop the techniques of winning the ball. The timing of your tackles, for example, must be influenced and adjusted to changing weather conditions. A sense of vision must be cultivated because some of the best attacking play can come from your distribution. Teams are often vulnerable immediately they lose possession of the ball. If a forward player can anticipate when his full-back is going to intercept a pass and moves before this interception takes place, he can often be clear if the full-back can recognize the movement and plays the ball forward early.

Practice games of attack versus defence should give ample opportunity for you to get to grips with your main responsibilities. During these coaching sessions it is best to work on one thing at a time. For marking, ensure that the ball is played out to wingers as much as possible. For cover, ask the attackers to switch the ball from wing to wing so that you experience the function of moving in to cover the middle after doing a marking job. For immediate support, encourage the attack to break through the middle often with the aid of an extra man. When you gain possession, you must be given a target player or players to find. This will help to cultivate the skill for dropping the ball into space for the target man when he comes to show. It would be good to isolate this skill and practise this with a ball between two exercises.

In the course of the training game, you should be encouraged to move up in immediate support of the ball so that you begin to recognize the positions from which you can move forward. You should also be given experience of playing against varying tactics; for example, you may play against a team without wingers. This means that you are virtually a spare man and you must have experience in this situation so that you can take full advantage of it when it comes along.

The full-back's role is indeed a very interesting and varied one. It gives scope to express one's feelings much more now than ever before, but the key must be to put the priorities in the right place. Never forget that you are primarily in the side to defend your goal.

Top *The West Bromwich Albion full-back has tackled out of range and Leeds' Peter Lorimer has twisted clear to mount a dangerous attack.*

Above *Ron Harris of Chelsea shuttles Sheffield United's Woodward towards the corner-flag. There he can restrict the winger's space.*

HINTON

BOOK (B)

BOOK (A)

DURBAN

DIAGRAM

RAYMONDS

COLORSPORT

The tactics of tackling

Top Diagram of Alan Durban's goal versus Manchester City in December 1971. Derby won 3-1 mainly through Alan Hinton's mastery of Tony Book. **Above left** Durban waits to convert Hinton's cross. **Above** But in the return match at Maine Road the following April, Book amended his tackling tactics, dominated Hinton and City won 2-0.

'Get stuck into him,' the Manchester City crowd roared at their right-back, the veteran Tony Book, as he faced Derby County winger, Alan Hinton, in a crucial First Division match in April 1972. The two teams had battled point for point at the top of the table during the second half of the season, and although City had slipped just out of the range of the title, Derby, the eventual winners, were still on Championship course.

For Book the match had its own significance. The previous December at the Baseball Ground, Derby had won both points in a three-goal first-half display that owed much to Hinton's mastery of Book. After scoring the first goal from the penalty spot, Hinton's speed took him clear of City's right-back and two crosses were headed home by Webster and Durban.

But despite the urgent advice from his home crowd, Book had learned from a painful reminder that tackling is as much a matter of tactics as technique, that *where* and *when* the challenge is made is as important as *how* it is executed. He held off, denying the winger space and only committing himself when he was sure that a colleague was in a position to pick off Hinton should he wriggle clear. The threat was contained and Manchester City gained revenge 2-0.

The ability to understand the tactics of tackling had become a crucial part of a defender's armoury. The principle was clear—if he was exposed and left to face an opponent alone, there was more profit in delaying and backing off than in risking all in a desperate confrontation. For the British defender, applauded and cheered for decades for brisk, spectacular tackles, it was hard to accept.

But the validity of controlled caution could not be disputed, especially after England centre-half Maurice Norman had been humiliated by French centre-forward Raymond Kopa at Hillsborough in the first leg of a European Nations Cup tie in 1962. Norman was under pressure from the moment he left the dressing-room, because the partisan Yorkshire crowd disputed his right to be in the side. Two of the leading contenders for the centre-half position played in Sheffield, Wednesday's Peter Swan and United's Joe Shaw, and the fans were not to allow Norman to forget this. He might have kept his composure, if he had not been faced with an opponent as elusive as Kopa.

Norman plunged into tackle after tackle, and Kopa danced past the flailing legs time after time. England scraped a 1-1 draw through a

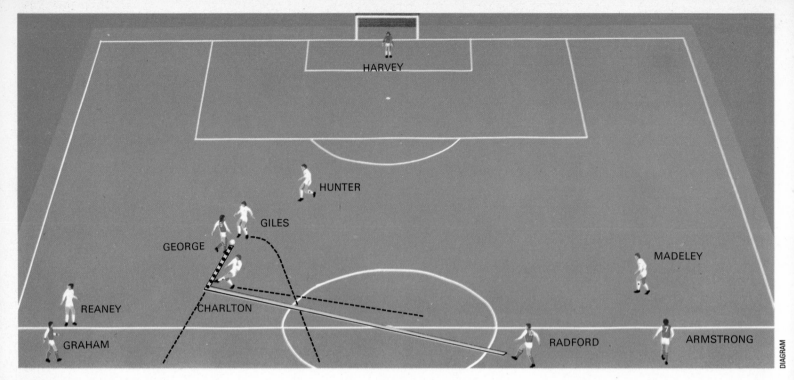

Labels on diagram: HARVEY, HUNTER, GILES, GEORGE, MADELEY, REANEY, CHARLTON, GRAHAM, RADFORD, ARMSTRONG

DIAGRAM

Ron Flowers penalty in a match that proved to be manager Walter Winterbottom's last against foreign opposition. By the time of the second leg, Alf Ramsey was in charge and he was to emphasize the need for defenders to commit themselves to a tackle only when they could do so in relative safety.

Three years later, Ramsey had devised a system that hinged on the use of Nobby Stiles—operating with the back four screening safely behind him—to win the ball. In the 1966 World Cup semi-final, England faced the threat of Eusebio of Portugal, the tournament's leading scorer. Stiles was not posted to follow Eusebio, contrary to speculation. He was there to get in tackles and to provide cover for his fellow defenders when they did the same.

With this insurance the nearest England player always moved in quickly to offer an immediate challenge and the dark-skinned Portuguese was invariably shuttled into cul-de-sacs of defenders where he could eventually be picked off with a comprehensive tackle. Eusebio rarely threatened. The problem had been overcome—a triumph for careful planning and sound application.

Ramsey's philosophy was simple enough. He said: 'If we had sent one man to subdue Eusebio, we ran the threat of that man being put out of the game at a critical moment. That would probably have exposed our back four players to immediate attack, and it was something we set out to avoid. By closing down quickly on Eusebio with the nearest man available, we enabled others to assess the situation.'

Knowing when to tackle as well as knowing how to tackle was to have a significant effect on the career of Jimmy Greaves who, from the moment he made his debut for Chelsea against Spurs in 1957, was clearly destined to become one of the greatest goalscorers in the history of the game. Greaves in his early years as a League player was all quicksilver and excitement, and he could run through a defence with the effectiveness of a laser beam.

But those were the days when defenders, largely unschooled in the arts of careful deployment, threw themselves into Greaves's path, hoping to win the ball with a desperate challenge. Bill Dodgin, later to manage Queen's Park Rangers and Fulham, was then Arsenal's centre-half. A thinking man, he recalled: 'Life was made easy for Jimmy because people committed themselves unnecessarily. Don't get me wrong. Jimmy Greaves, even in the latter stages of his career, was one of the few players I would bother to go and watch, simply because I enjoyed watching him.

'What I'm trying to say is that teams didn't pay enough attention to what he could do unless

Above A split-second incident in the 1972 FA Cup Final emphasized that tackling is as much a matter of tactics as techniques. Radford's pass to George left the Arsenal striker in a one-against-one situation against Hunter. But Hunter did not commit himself; instead he backed off allowing Giles to come back to pressure George.

Above right George was given no time to attack Hunter. Giles' quick recovery had given the other Leeds defenders time to get back. George was forced to turn inside, and he played a square ball out to George Armstrong on the right.
Below Covered by three defenders, Alan Ball safely commits himself to a tackle on Eddie Gray.

RAY GREEN

they set about containing him in the right way. It was pointless just going at him. He had such marvellous close control that he would be there one minute and gone the next. As a defender you had to be patient with him. You had to bide your time, shuttle him away from goal and then pounce.'

The technique became familiar to Greaves as he gradually grew disillusioned with the more demanding features of his profession, and he was to eventually suffer the killing disappointment of missing the World Cup final in 1966.

The final against West Germany was not only memorable because of its historic outcome and the nationalism involved, but for the deliberate design of its strategy. The Germans, fully appreciative of Bobby Charlton's immense influence on the England team, chose to counter him with Franz Beckenbauer whose elegant skills made him almost Charlton's equal. Their strategy was obvious—tight man-to-man marking with the perceptive Willi Schulz deployed as a sweeper at the back.

Beckenbauer took his place in the system, policing Charlton and subduing him as no one else had been able to do during a month of gathering significance for English football.

But when the West Germans had been beaten in the unnerving extension of the contest, criticism was heaped on their manager Helmut Schoen. Schoen, a tall, impressive man who had played with distinction as an international forward, took over the team in 1964 after sitting at the feet of the legendary Sepp Herberger.

He was to avenge himself on England in Mexico four years later and with exactly the same policy which he had used at Wembley in 1966. Time would defend it. And in time he was to say: 'I insist that I was right at Wembley. Bobby Charlton did much to influence the play of the English team. They looked to him for inspiration. He could win a game out of nothing with his marvellous shooting. My plan was to use Beckenbauer to shadow him, because if Beckenbauer won the ball he could do as much damage as Charlton. Considering that he is a creative

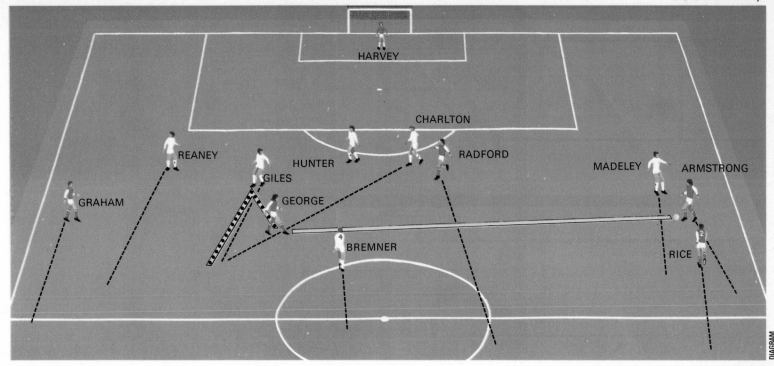

Coaching: Learn when and where to commit yourself to the tackle

The knowledge of when to tackle is of the utmost importance to a player who seeks to dispossess an opponent.

Good positioning in itself will not win the ball. The ball can only be won from an opponent who has possession by a tackle. But a pre-requisite for a tackle is good positioning.

You must obey certain fundamental rules in your positional play—always mark so that you are between your goal and the attacker; always give yourself a chance of interception; and always limit the area in which your opponent can receive the ball. Remember to mark close enough so that you can tackle him as he receives, but not so close that the opponent can lose you by moving away quickly into a dangerous position.

The most important single factor in the tactics of tackling is timing. In principle, the tackle should be made at the first opportunity and ideally just as the opponent is receiving the ball. At this time your opponent's concentration will be focused on controlling the ball, so a quick, unexpected and determined tackle before he has full control will often be successful.

If your opponent has complete control, then the approach must be a cautious one. It is very foolish to rush in and tackle, because a nimble attacker will only leave you stranded and your team-mates with an unnecessary problem. Rather, you must hold off, stalking his every move and trying to pressure him into an error of control when he allows the ball to run too far in front of him whilst dribbling. Once this opportunity presents itself, you should go in without hesitation and make a determined tackle.

This hustling action should be done in an aggressive way. You should try not to allow the attacker to dictate the situation and the area into which he is going, but to keep him on the move ready to pounce on a mistake and to shepherd him away from your goal towards the touchline. The closer you can get him to the touchline, the less area he has to work in. The touchline is your friend. Get him over that and the ball is yours.

This cat-and-mouse game can be practised by two players. Ask a friend to dribble a ball towards you and attempt to beat you. You must concentrate on keeping close to him, not letting him past you, and forcing him to work the ball into the area you wish him to go. Once you have got him going in that direction, look for your tackling opportunity.

Move into an area about 20 yards square with four other players and play three against two. The two players are the defenders who are about to learn the true value of teamwork, because if they do not work together they will be doing an awful lot of chasing. The three players interpass the ball, keeping it within the area and away from the two defenders. The object here is for the defenders to work so that the ball is played into an area that gives them a chance of an interception or tackle. If one of the defenders attacks the player in possession and pressures him into playing the ball, the second defender can anticipate this action and close down on the intended pass and tackle as the receiving player attempts to gain control. This is not an easy game because the player in possession has two players to whom he can pass the ball. The idea is for the defender applying immediate pressure to approach in such a way that he not only makes the player in possession move in one direction, but also cuts out one of the other attackers. The supporting defender positions himself in such a way that he helps in cutting out the same attacker, but is working to get close enough to the attacker who is going to receive the ball so that he can tackle when the pass is actually made.

This can be carried over to the real game when you as a defender must learn to anticipate passes coming at your immediate opponent. Again this is done by good positioning, by being able to see the ball and the player you are marking.

player, he is a good enough marker to do the sort of job I wanted. The worst that could happen was that they would cancel each other out.'

It was a World Cup in Sweden in 1958 which had convinced Dave Bowen of the need to think hard about the way in which great attackers could be contained. Bowen was the captain of a Welsh team which went to Sweden almost by default. They failed to get through from their qualifying group, but were readmitted after a play-off with Israel which decided ·the last of the contestants. Nobody gave Wales a chance but they had John Charles, one of the great all-round players of his time, and the likes of Cliff Jones, Ivor Allchurch and Jack Kelsey.

The Welsh were unlikely contenders. But they were still there in the quarter-finals to face Brazil, but sadly without the marvellously skilful and muscular Charles. Bowen, who was later to achieve the enormous feat of guiding little Northampton Town from the Fourth to the First Division and to manage Wales, recalled:

'Without Big John we knew that we had little chance of meeting the Brazilians on common ground. Jimmy Murphy was our manager and he was well used to dealing with great players as assistant manager to Matt Busby at Manchester United.

'We sat and talked about it. The Brazilians had Didi, Garrincha and this new feller Pele. They could play magical stuff. So we set out to deny them space *behind* us. We let them have the middle of the park. If they couldn't get behind us they couldn't create chances and we went so near to beating them.

'If John had been there he would have got to a cross early in the match and we would have been a goal up. I'm convinced to this day that if we had scored then Brazil wouldn't have gone on to beat Sweden in the final. We had them. They were frustrated simply because we didn't commit ourselves to tackles unless we were back in strength. They finally got a lucky goal from Pele. But if Big John hadn't been butchered by Hungarian tackles in the previous match, Wales would have altered history.'

The lifting of the insidious maximum wage in 1961 led to greater demands being made on professional players. It was no longer enough for forwards to create and score goals. They had to integrate themselves into the team pattern, and in time they were expected to contribute as much to the subjection of opponents as men who had been brought up to do the job.

The point was not overlooked by Arsenal's captain Frank McLintock after an injury to goalkeeper Bob Wilson had enabled Stoke City to recover from impending defeat in an FA Cup semi-final at Villa Park in 1972. Arsenal replaced the injured Wilson with a forward, John Radford, who performed courageously and with some style. But Arsenal were not only short of a keeper, but short of the willing effort with which Radford had pressured the Stoke defenders.

Football by then had become as subtle as that. It was no longer a case of pursuing the obvious as England and in particular, Nobby Stiles, had proved six years earlier.

DIAGRAM

GERRY CRANHAM

Zonal marking

Chelsea's opening game in the 1970-71 League season revealed a change in playing policy which was to temporarily disrupt the career of their Eire international centre-half, John Dempsey. A tall, combative player, Dempsey was signed from Fulham in 1969 and performed convincingly and consistently as one of Chelsea's two central defenders.

But Chelsea were to change their system of marking in defence, and Dempsey found it difficult to adapt. The change was a basic one. Instead of each defender being responsible for policing one particular opponent throughout the game, the man-to-man system, Chelsea adopted the recognized alternative system: in this, each defender marked particular areas of the field picking up

in turn any attacker who entered his zone. And zonal marking was dependent on communication—or instinctive understanding—amongst the defence, for attackers were passed on from one defender to another as they roamed across the pitch.

But Dempsey was essentially a marker, a player who was good at subduing a nominated opponent but who was immediately vulnerable when asked to co-ordinate his positional play with fellow defenders. It was this weakness which led him into trouble when Chelsea manager Dave Sexton chose to amend his team's strategy within a few weeks of winning the FA Cup.

A replay victory over Leeds at Old Trafford, Manchester, had given Chelsea the Cup for the

first time, and Dempsey had no reason then to suspect that there were problems ahead.

Sexton spent part of the following summer watching the World Cup in Mexico. Somewhere along the way and with Europe once again beckoning, he began to re-think his strategy.

Until then Sexton had been sold on a system of man-to-man marking. A forward himself, he recalled the irritation he had felt when being followed and harried throughout a match by one persistent opponent.

At Chelsea, he had an abundance of ball-winning defenders who were more comfortable when given a definite job to do, even when it meant containing outstanding attackers. The job required concentration and a fair degree of aggression. Men like Dempsey, David Webb, Eddie McCreadie and Ron Harris were well equipped for it.

But that summer of 1970 was to have a far-reaching effect on Chelsea's play. European football promised a more subtle design and Sexton set out to cope with it. In pre-season training Sexton introduced his players to the more flexible system with defenders being asked to mark space rather than follow opponents.

It was not new. This system was the basis of England's success in the 1966 World Cup, and, if it could be operated effectively, it had one distinct advantage. It allowed temporarily unemployed defenders greater freedom to attack

Man-to-man marking not only restricted forwards, who were subjected to it, but also confined the markers to a largely defensive role.

All England's leading teams worked to the same system and it was obviously helpful to Sir Alf Ramsey; and his use of defenders in attack became one of the cornerstones of his success.

Although Ramsey made changes among his attackers, his defence remained unaltered throughout the 1966 series, and the key to their effectiveness was their understanding.

George Cohen of Fulham, Jack Charlton of Leeds, Bobby Moore of West Ham, and Everton's Ray Wilson made up the back line of four, and they read each other's play and problems brilliantly.

Between them they divided the width of England's defensive zone into four sections. If an attacker entered Cohen's zone, he had to put him under pressure until he was pushed on into Charlton's zone. This applied across the field with the aggressive Nobby Stiles picking off both passes and players in front of the back four.

Moore's tremendous vision was always a critical factor. He not only sensed where attacks were likely to develop, but he was able to organize the men around him so that England were seldom outnumbered anywhere within range of their goal.

By the time England played themselves through a punishing South American tour in 1969, they had lost both Cohen and Wilson for all

time, but it had done nothing to disturb their understanding and morale.

When they lost to Brazil in Rio it was their only defeat of the tour. Keith Newton and Terry Cooper were then the full-backs, and Cooper in particular benefited from a policy which allowed him considerable freedom as an attacker.

Leeds had signed him as a winger and his dribbling skills were to serve him well. After switching him to full-back, they encouraged him to go forward, and his willingness to do this was a decisive feature of Leeds' success when beating Juventus in the 1971 final of the Fairs Cup.

Italian football was assembled on a principle of man-to-man marking with the insurance of a sweeper tidying up behind them. Comforted by the sweeper's presence, they ordered their men to make swift, urgent tackles and to attack quickly with the ball if they won it. If they lost out in the tackle, there was always a man to cover.

The final was played over two legs and the second encounter at Elland Road underlined the essential features in contrasting systems of play. As Cooper constantly hurried forward in attack, Norman Hunter shuttled across to cover the space he had left and the movement was repeated across the back line—Charlton to cover for Hunter, Paul Reaney to cover for Charlton.

Cooper had a tremendous match, taking players on and totally confusing a team who had never experienced such skill in a defender. But there

would have been little opportunity for Cooper to advance as he did if Leeds had elected for man-to-man marking.

Arsenal built their 'double' success out of a similarly flexible system, and it was Don Howe, taking over as chief coach from Dave Sexton in 1967, who instituted zonal marking. Whereas Sexton had been influenced by his experience as a forward, Howe reacted to his own experience as a defender who had hated being negative.

He said: 'When we used man-to-man marking we were often undermining the team's attacking potential. Take the full-backs, for instance. We were trying to encourage them to get involved in going forward, but the system might lead to them following around an opponent who was not playing well.

'Footballers are creatures of habit. If you ask them to mark a man out of a match and they are good at doing this sort of thing then they will go on doing it. They have to be encouraged to think and this is what we set out to do.'

When Chelsea adopted a similar system it was Dempsey who suffered most. He could not break the habit. Dempsey wanted a man to mark. Marking space and waiting for someone to enter it did not really appeal to him. Dempsey stayed in the side, but only until the middle of September by which time Chelsea's unconvincing form had underlined their confusion.

He was then replaced by Marvin Hinton, a

more astute but less physically aggressive defender. Hinton read the game well and got to the point of attack very quickly. But he was clearly uncomfortable when forwards pushed up on him, and, as a result, he had been unable to hold a permanent place in the team.

Chelsea had occasionally used him as a sweeper, patrolling the spaces behind their markers and he had done the job well. Now he was given a chance to show that he could firmly establish himself at the heart of the defence. He lasted through until the fourth round of the FA Cup when Chelsea surrendered the trophy, losing to Manchester City at Stamford Bridge.

Dempsey came back to a team that had gone a long way to mastering a new technique, and he was to score a crucial goal when Chelsea closed the season in triumph by beating Real Madrid in a replayed final of the Cup Winners Cup.

Thus the more accomplished, the more assured settled for flexibility and only called for the disciplined subjection of one player by another when that player was seen to be outstanding.

Even then the job was done with intelligence. Confronted with the threat of Eusebio's stirring individuality in the 1966 World Cup semi-final against Portugal, the England players elected to shuttle him into cul-de-sacs rather than try to subdue him with one player.

Four years later in Mexico against Brazil, the job of trying to contain Pele was largely taken over by Alan Mullery. But once again, it was intelligent deployment rather than dogged, short-range persistence which proved vital.

Zonal marking called for intelligence and thoughtful application. Some found it easy, others were unable to master it. To John Dempsey's credit he made a competent job of solving the problem when his career was under siege.

Coaching: Develop a system of zonal marking for your club

Zonal defence is a most efficient method of protecting a goal. Defenders divide the area in front of the goal among themselves, each challenging any opponent coming within his own area or zone irrespective of who the attacking player is or which position he is playing.

Before you decide to use any marking system for your team, you must develop an understanding of the method and defensive principles involved. It is generally accepted that four players can cover the width of the field quite adequately and also give defensive support to one another, whilst midfield players can give added support in front of the back four.

To get a broad picture of zonal defence, split the length of the field into three equal parts, then divide the back or defensive third across the pitch into four parts, so that they overlap one another to the extent that apart from smaller zones on the flanks the width of the pitch is covered by two zones. This means that a defender should not be caught with two players in his zone. Any defensive system must be flexible and these zones are only a guide as to the space that must be marked; one would not, for argument's sake, not go into another zone if danger threatened.

One of the important principles of attack is mobility. Players constantly change positions in an effort to break down a defensive system. So in zonal defence you must get used to handing players over to one another as they move from zone to zone. Communication with one another is crucial, the whole system is built on mutual understanding. Build this up from two-a-side games. Play in an area about 30 yards long and 15 yards wide. An imaginary line down the middle will give a rough indication of the zones to cover.

The two players in possession are encouraged to interchange positions from one zone to another. The two defending players must apply the first two principles of defence; first, that of putting pressure on, or delaying the player in possession and second, that of support, or cover, so that there is never a one-against-one situation. Work this practice slowly at first, and go through the movements without a ball. Talk about the best positions to take up in certain situations remembering that you must not violate the first two principles. Then work with a ball at walking pace so that you have plenty of time to think and position yourself before going on to a more realistic pace. Constant practice will give you the necessary experience and confidence to allow players to leave your zone and pick up players entering.

Pressure, cover and balance—the three basics of defence

Increase the size of the pitch and play three against three. Again, imagine a line down the middle for the two zones, but add a third zone in the centre so that the central defender can overlap ensuring cover for both zones. There are now even more possibilities for the attackers to interchange, so once again start gently. Walk through it because this is a good time to introduce the third principle of defence, balance. This applies to the defender furthest away from the ball. Whilst the defender nearest to the player in possession is applying pressure and making it difficult for a pass to be made, the second defender is covering him so that a one-on-one situation does not occur, the third defender is moving round to balance the defence and stop the long, through ball down the middle. He is also in a position where he can apply pressure and delay movement by moving out quickly to the flank player on his side should the play be switched.

Encourage attacking players to interchange so that defenders are forced to talk to one another as they pass players to each other. Now the offside rule must be observed and the furthest defender from the ball is in a good position to dictate when this should be played. Do not rush things at this stage. This is excellent practice, one that will give you tactical understanding, technical experience and conditioning. Work hard at it until you feel confident enough to move into a more realistic practice of attack against defence.

Set this up with four main defenders in zones and a couple of midfield players to defend in front of them. Against them play four forwards with three midfield players to support. Again the attack must be encouraged to interchange positions, but at this stage restrict the midfield players to a supporting role so that they are concerned with switching the play quickly in an effort to get one of the front players free. When defenders intercept the ball they must be encouraged to play it out from the defence as they would in a real match. To help them do this, have a target man around the half-way line in case they want to play long passes out from defence.

Introducing new systems is a long and often tedious process. Teams have often spent a whole season working on something new in training before risking it in the actual game. If you are underprepared, your new tactics might let you down, and may be thrown on the scrap-heap before you have a chance to establish them.

Remember this is one system of play—not necessarily the best method or system for you. But if you understand the principles of defence and if you work hard at building an understanding, there is no reason why zonal marking should not strengthen your defence.

Below Liverpool's left-back Alec Lindsay clears the ball upfield as his colleagues in the back four cover their particular areas in defence.

GERRY CRANHAM

The centre-half

role should his team-mate be beaten.

This was the difference between Charlton and Cherry. For England Charlton had used his exceptional strength in the air to challenge for almost every high ball; Bobby Moore provided the astute cover if ever the Leeds' giant was caught out. For Leeds Norman Hunter, an astute reader of the game, became that second line of defence as Charlton moved to a challenge.

The player who bore more resemblance to Charlton at nearby Huddersfield was centre-half Roy Ellam, another player to interest Revie. His cover was provided by the nimble, mobile Cherry. If Cherry was to have a first-team future at Leeds, it seemed to be Hunter's position that was threatened. And yet he had ended the 1971-72 season with a succession of commanding performances for club and country.

Revie had not been lax in his chase for a centre-half cast more in Charlton's mould. He said: 'We have looked at every centre-half in Britain who might be available to us. The position has been very difficult, almost impossible to fill.' Two years earlier, he had even gambled on John Faulkner, an unknown defender with Isthmian League amateurs Sutton United, who had effectively marked Mick Jones throughout a fourth round FA Cup tie. A serious injury wrecked what chances Faulkner had of making the grade.

Charlton had his own theories as to why no obvious replacement was forthcoming. Always a perceptive thinker, he suggested: 'Once they put another central defender alongside you the job was halved. There was no longer the same sort of responsibility attached to the position of centre-half. It improved the overall pattern of defensive play but it hindered the progress and development of outstanding centre-halves.'

After scrutinizing the talents of every young central defender, Revie finally decided to pay out £30,000 for Cherry's team-mate, the 29-year-old Ellam. But in his own mind he had already considered the possibility of a redeployment, and it was while watching England lose to Northern Ireland at Wembley in May 1972 that he was encouraged to think that it could work. That match stimulated the signing of Cherry.

That night it was an unfamiliar England team. Having beaten Wales in Cardiff the previous Saturday and with a more serious contest to come against Scotland in Glasgow, the England manager gave a chance to hopeful contenders.

But when it was expected that Ramsey would use Colin Todd, Derby's covering defender, to play on the right of Liverpool's left-footed centre-half Larry Lloyd, he surprised everyone by giving the job to Norman Hunter and playing Todd at right-back.

He was to say: 'I have Bobby Moore and Hunter to play alongside the centre-half. I have seen Todd play well at full-back for Derby and I wanted to see whether he had a future in that position.'

What made Don Revie sit up and take notice was the way in which Hunter, heavily left-sided himself, coped with what seemed at the outset to be an entirely alien environment. From that point Revie realized that he could consider Hunter himself as a successor to Charlton.

Symmetry in defence was so important that Revie must have experienced some doubt when Hunter began to play on what for him was the most awkward flank. The doubt was dissolved as Hunter, playing with customary enthusiasm, emerged as one of the few successes in an England defeat which emphasized the frightening shortage of legitimate international material.

A few nights later in a Glasgow hotel, Revie gave a hint of what was to emerge from proof of Hunter's versatility. He said: 'What I saw at Wembley has probably persuaded me to pay a lot of money for a defender within the next month.'

That defender was Trevor Cherry, left-sided but an immediate possibility once Hunter had

---

'He will strengthen our first-team pool. It's as simple as that,' said Leeds manager Don Revie in June 1972, when asked where he intended to use Trevor Cherry, the 24-year-old defender he had just signed from Huddersfield for £100,000.

Nevertheless on the surface it was a surprise move by Revie. He had made no secret of the fact that the main objective of his quest for new players was a replacement centre-half for England veteran Jack Charlton. Cherry had played in Huddersfield's back four, but in a distinctly different role to that of Charlton.

Since there has become a tactical consensus that teams are better prepared to defend by using a line of four defenders, the position of centre-half, or centre-back, has become a dual responsibility. The roles of each of the two central defenders have been defined on two broad bases; first there are lateral distinctions. One player will be more responsible for the right-hand side of the field and the other will tend to play on the left. The second distinction has its roots in the centre-half play of the W-M system in which this player took complete responsibility for the centre of the defence. He marked the centre-forward and moved to meet the ball to make clearances. In a back four, one defender plays along these lines whilst the other marks space to fulfil a covering

COLORSPORT

Left *Jack Charlton shows his power in the air during a Leeds versus Everton match. This willingness to go and meet the ball was an elusive quality as Leeds searched for Charlton's successor.*

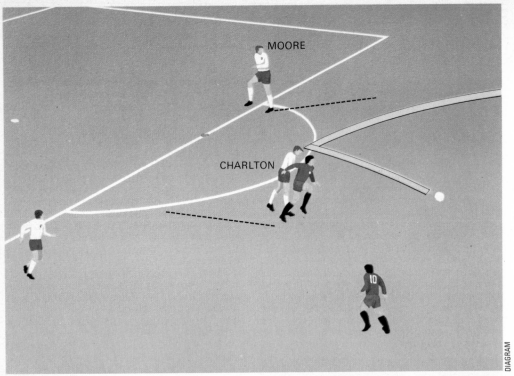

shown that he could operate on the right.

Equally as important had been Hunter's steady improvement in the air throughout the previous two seasons. Leeds needed aerial supremacy in defence. Charlton had given it to them. Hunter might not be able to match him but he would prove more than adequate.

The development of back four play had confronted managers with the problem of blending right and left-sided players at the centre of the defence. Those lucky enough to have a recognized centre-half still had to seek this balance. Derby County, for instance, used Colin Todd on the right side of Roy McFarland, although McFarland was such a well-balanced player that he was happy to have Bobby Moore at his left shoulder in the England team, Moore admitting that he felt more comfortable on that side of the defence. Liverpool stationed the aggressive Tommy Smith on the right side of Larry Lloyd.

Those not so fortunate had to make do without losing this balance. Arsenal had to pull back Frank McLintock, a creative midfield player, to stand alongside the left-sided Peter Simpson in the core of their defence. West Ham used another wing-half, Tommy Taylor, in an attempt to solve a centre-half problem that had been with them since the retirement of Ken Brown. Manchester United experimented with David Sadler, yet another wing-half, and Paul Edwards, a sometime full-back, in an effort to find the right blend.

The danger of having an unbalanced defence had been vividly demonstrated when England lost to West Germany at Wembley the previous month.

Derby's decision to withdraw McFarland from the match had given Ramsey a problem. McFarland had emerged as the most accomplished centre-half in Britain and possibly Europe. He could not easily be replaced.

Ramsey, with the knowledge that the Germans presented little threat in the air, considered, like Revie, a redeployment, and he elected to give Moore the centre-half marking job, bringing Hunter in to take the left side and provide cover through the middle.

But the move failed. Both Moore and Hunter were essentially covering defenders, men whose astute positional play enabled the centre-half to move in and mark tight.

Against the Germans they both responded to instinct. They were invariably caught hanging back when attacks were being built up around the halfway line and as a result the Germans were granted the space in which to launch damaging thrusts from the middle of the field.

Ramsey emphasized the point in the dressing-room at half-time, adding: 'Because we aren't pushing up, there is too much room in the middle of the field. This means that our midfield players aren't able to make contact with theirs.' The problem was to be overcome but there was to be further proof of inadequacy.

England had weathered the storm and drawn level with a goal from Francis Lee when Moore was suddenly threatened with a swift, positive dribble by the German left-winger Siggy Held.

When playing in the Mexico World Cup two years earlier, the England captain had dealt brilliantly with similar individual assaults. But Moore had been playing then where he was most comfortable, between the centre of the defence and the left touchline, not on the other side where he was manifestly unhappy.

His one serious error in Mexico had been made against Brazil when he was drawn into an indecisive tackle on Tostao which left him

Top left *Diagram showing one way in which Charlton and Bobby Moore had differing roles during their time as England's central defenders. Whenever possible Charlton challenged for the ball whilst Moore dropped behind him to provide cover.*

Above left *Against West Germany at Wembley in 1972 Alf Ramsey was forced to play Moore in the more positive role with Norman Hunter covering. But their uncertainty allowed the German forwards to turn and attack the England defence.*

Left *Moore heads clear in that match whilst Hunter takes up his covering position.*

scrambling out of position when Jairzinho scored from a cross pass.

It was Moore's mistake when instinctively turning the ball away to his left and back across the England goal which had led to Hoeness giving the Germans a first-half lead at Wembley.

Now with Held in full flight, he attempted to slide the ball clear and gave away a penalty which put the Germans on the way to a 3-1 lead and a famous victory.

Ramsey's gamble had failed and McFarland's withdrawal—he played two days later in a critical Championship match against Liverpool—was seen to be completely damaging.

Had defences, especially England's, been better organized in the fifties, Derek Ufton might have had a longer run as an international centre-half.

Ufton, chosen from Charlton, then a First Division club, played against the Rest of the World at Wembley in the autumn of 1953. Alf Ramsey's late penalty gave England a 4-4 draw and kept their home record intact until the Hungarians shattered it a few weeks later.

But for Ufton the match often assumed nightmare proportions. In the first half he did what he had been brought up to do and followed the Swedish centre-forward, Gunnar Nordahl. As a result there was a great hole in the middle of England's defence. In the second half, encouraged by Ramsey, he stayed in the middle, and England tightened up.

Ufton is convinced that he played well in the second half. Certainly, sound judges have argued that he was badly let down by players who had assembled false reputations in the England team. But Ufton never played for England again.

Nineteen years later it could have been argued that Mike England of Spurs was the best centre-half in Britain. A tall, well-built Welshman, he had all the equipment needed for the job when he settled down to do it properly. Muscularly resolute, he more than matched most opponents in the air and he tackled his weight.

But England was uncomfortable when asked to stay and mark space instead of following the centre-forward out to the touchline or deep into midfield as Ufton had done at Wembley.

Opponents were not slow to notice this. They lured England out of the middle and sent other players in to attack crosses.

Leeds planned to do this when playing a First Division match at Spurs in March 1972. But England had been talked out of his weakness. He stayed when Leeds tried to pull him out and Don Revie was to say: 'On this performance Mike looked as good as anyone in the position.'

It was possible to detect a wistful note in the remark. But Revie, practical as ever, was already looking elsewhere.

Coaching: The secrets of successful centre-half play

Most goals are scored from within a 15-yard arc of the centre of the goal. Therefore the centre-half, being the most central defender, will find himself heavily involved with every situation that threatens his goal. Also he will often be engaged in repelling attacks before they have acquired strength or in moving intelligently to prevent the quick break.

Because of this function, he must be considered totally as a defender; his defensive qualities should include a dominance in the air, a thorough knowledge of the principles of defensive play, particularly those of tackling, and he should possess a quick brain for reading dangerous situations. Physical attributes of height to win balls in the air, strength of body to win balls in the tackle and speed of movement to cover and win possession by interception highlight his main functions as that of a ball-winner and marker of the opposition's most forward, central striker.

If you are a centre-half, you will be called upon to make quick decisions and the wrong ones may prove fatal. Under these circumstances, you must be prepared to accept responsibility and, at the last resort, learn by trial and error. Possibly your main two problems are judging the ball as it is on its way towards you so that you are not played out of the game, and tackling out of distance which can leave you stranded whilst your opponent moves into a more dangerous situation. Another main problem is knowing when to let your immediate opponent go. You must learn to decide whether you are being lured away to make space for a more dangerous attack. Finally you must master the art of moving up to catch opponents offside.

Good positioning on the opponent will help you with the first of these difficulties. Whilst obeying the principle of marking goalside, mark on a 'dog leg' in relation to the position of the ball. This means coming off your opponent, giving yourself room in which to work on one side of him; this will give you an excellent chance of an interception should the ball be played to him on the side you are marking. If you stand directly behind him you are giving yourself very little chance of any ball other than the one over the top which could have been covered quite adequately from the 'dog leg' position.

If the ball should be played up to your opponent in such a way that it is not possible for you to attack, then do not move in to contest. Get into the habit of only contesting when you have a chance of winning the ball or when you have no choice, such as when you are close to goal. Instead, come off and look for the flick on or pick up the run again if your opponent knocks it back and runs forward. Don't pull off too far so that if he decides to get the ball down, you can move in on him, applying pressure, and preventing him from turning on you and adding to your problems.

As well as keeping goalside of your opponent, you will want to be goalside of the ball and in a position to deal with a threat coming from another player. Very few centre-forwards play up and down the pitch; most are highly mobile players. You must learn to use your vision, not only watching the movement of your own player but that of the whole opposition in general, trying to decide where the main danger is and how you intend to deal with it.

When your opponent moves from the middle in an attempt to work behind the full-back, you must follow, listening for a call from the other full-back telling you to move up and play him offside; if the call doesn't come, decide how far you can afford to follow. It would be foolish to stand out on the touchline with the centre-forward whilst the opposing winger was worming his way through the middle. Even though the centre-forward has moved wide, you can still keep tabs on him and watch the middle by being in a half-cocked position, ready to close down when the danger threatens.

To become dominating in the air, you must have complete confidence in your own judgement of the flight of the ball and where you can make contact. Some players are drawn in by the movement of the opposition. A long ball down the middle can prove dangerous if it is allowed to drop over the top of the centre-half, especially if he has been committed in making an attempt at it. Or a ball dropping to the ground very close to goal when the centre-half has misjudged can be even more dangerous. Knowing this, you must give yourself room in which to work and time to make up your mind. Your final movement to the ball must be well-timed and if you have judged the situation correctly and if you have jumped just that fraction before your opponent, you should be in a commanding position to head away.

At centre-half, you must live by your defensive principles, knowing that in violating them you are taking chances when the golden rule must be, safety first. When you are unsure as to where you are clearing, you must get distance or drive the ball towards the wings. Get to loose balls as quickly as possible, giving yourself more time to use it constructively. Always be positive, either when moving in to win the ball or when backing off. Never allow yourself to be played out of the game by being caught in two minds.

Left Diagram of the 'half-cocked' position the centre-half should adopt if the centre-forward moves wide. From here he can close down on the man with the ball or move wide should his man be fed.
Below Arsenal's central defenders, McLintock and Simpson, pressure Leeds striker Mick Jones.

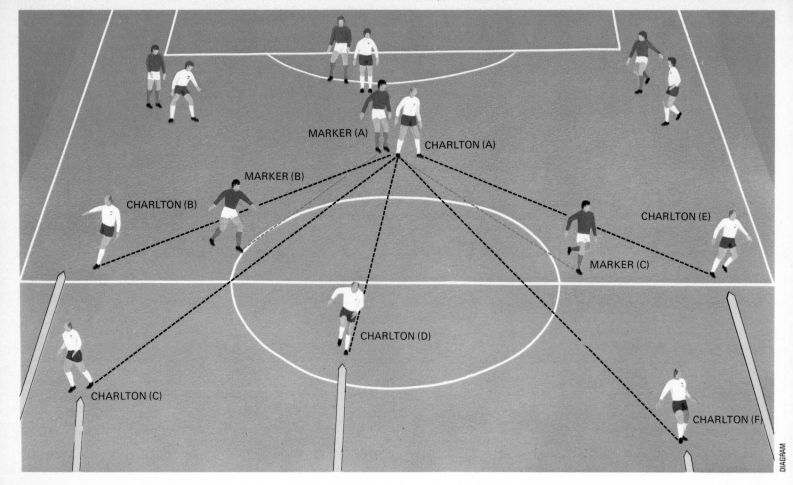

MARKER (A)

CHARLTON (A)

MARKER (B)

CHARLTON (B)

CHARLTON (E)

CHARLTON (D)

MARKER (C)

CHARLTON (C)

CHARLTON (F)

DIAGRAM

Shadow marking

Above *Much of the midfield inspiration of England's 1966 World Cup side came from Bobby Charlton, especially when the opposition allowed him to drop into deep positions to collect the ball.*

Above right *But in the final, West Germany realized how effective Charlton could be, and briefed Franz Beckenbauer to shadow him all over the field. Wherever Charlton went, Beckenbauer followed, and Charlton's contribution to the match was limited. This type of man-for-man marking reduces the game to ten-a-side, but Germany were prepared to sacrifice one player to subdue another.*

Right *Another Charlton thrust is thwarted by Beckenbauer as Tilkowski safely gathers the ball.*

It was a popular misconception in the pre-match ballyhoo which surrounded the 1966 World Cup semi-final that England would counter the sharp menace of Portugal's Eusebio with the doggedly resolute marking of Nobby Stiles; that Stiles would shadow the man from Mozambique from the first to the final whistle, ignoring the temptation to become involved in any play that did not involve Portugal's most feared striker.

Stiles had strong views on that particular role. He said: 'When I am asked to follow players around I am virtually putting myself out of the game. It becomes a matter for great discipline but it's not really football. If you are keeping someone else quiet, you are inevitably quiet yourself. You are reducing the game to a ten-against-ten contest. If you are doing your job well, you and the man who is to be marked don't get a kick at the ball.'

Stiles' contribution to England's 2-1 win was considerable, but Alf Ramsey never restricted the Manchester United player to limiting the threat of Eusebio, playing him as a sweeper in front of the back four defenders. But there were many other managers who strongly adhered to the principle of making the game a ten-a-side contest. And Portugal, hailed universally as the attacking success of a defensive-minded tournament, had brutally been among that number.

When Portugal announced their team to face England in that World Cup semi-final at Wembley, there were two notable omissions. They left out Vicente and Morais, their two most damaging and cynical tacklers, and the decision had a lasting

effect on the overall memory of the competition.

Portugal, with the marvellously athletic Eusebio among their forwards and the thoughtful Coluna in midfield, had gained a reputation for skilfully designed attack.

Eusebio's killing pace and murderous shooting had finally overwhelmed little North Korea in the quarter-finals, and to earn their match against England they had scored 14 goals in four matches. Yet they had relied heavily on men who, when it was necessary, could put a boot in where it hurt.

In a critical group game against Brazil on Merseyside, they had reduced the great Pele to a limping wreck. Unprotected by an English referee, George McCabe, and with little support from an ill-prepared and badly chosen team, Pele was first tackled into anonymity by the mean Vicente and then butchered out of the contest by Morais. It was two wicked fouls by Morais in the space of two yards which brought Brazil's contingent of medical men out to hover worriedly over the greatest of their players as he lay in pain.

But Pele had already been softened up by persistent attention from a man he had long since learned to fear. He had run up against Vicente before, and the memory of what had happened twelve months earlier when Brazil met Portugal in Oporto must have been very much in his mind that evening at Goodison.

In Oporto the previous summer, Vicente had followed Pele to every corner of the field, harassing, niggling and finally producing a tackle which brought Brazil's coaches from the touchline in a galloping protest. A stern, disciplined defender,

Vicente was then to play a key role in the World Cup, but not in the match which was to ultimately set England up for their greatest triumph.

The reasons given for the absence of Vicente and Morais were obscure. It was said that one had a damaged hand, and that the other was suffering from the physical pressures of the group games.

More cynical observers read something more significant in the shape of Portugal's team. The Portuguese were at Wembley, one of the show places of world football. They were facing an England team who had proved to be almost invincible on their ground. Victory would be a great prize. But a defeat tainted with bad temper and unforgivable tackling would prove nothing. It seemed to some that the Portuguese were as much interested in good public relations as they were with winning.

England had no such problems, although Stiles had collected mounting criticism for his combative, unrestrained eagerness to win the ball and there had even been a move to get him expelled from the team.

But Stiles was still there, and one who held the wide belief that he would be given the job of containing Eusebio was Eusebio himself.

Eusebio was well aware of the possibility and no slouch when it came to propaganda. In a pre-match interview, he announced: 'I like Nobby. He is a good player. But I hope he plays properly. I hope it is a good match. A good game of football.'

The inference was obvious. Stiles had a reputation for keeping great players quiet, and Eusebio was no stranger to him. As it turned out England

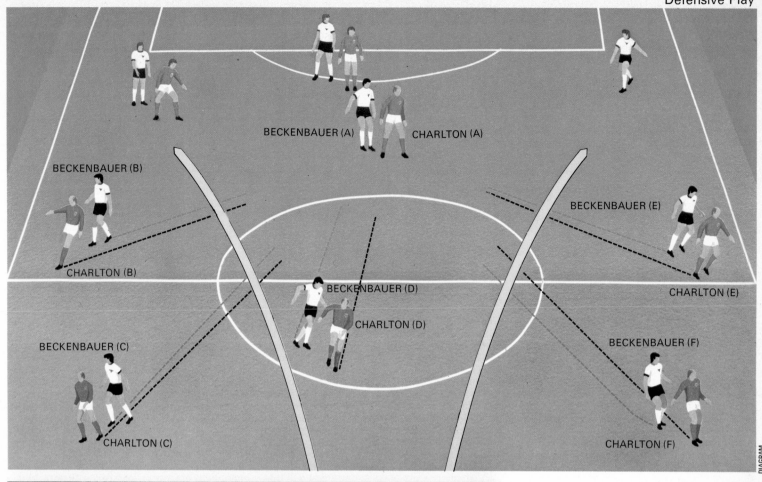

BECKENBAUER (A)　CHARLTON (A)

BECKENBAUER (B)

BECKENBAUER (E)

CHARLTON (B)

BECKENBAUER (D)

CHARLTON (D)

CHARLTON (E)

BECKENBAUER (C)

BECKENBAUER (F)

CHARLTON (C)

CHARLTON (F)

DIAGRAM

SYNDICATION INTERNATIONAL

settled for a collective system of marking whenever Eusebio threatened. He was shuttled into cul-de-sacs of defenders, and when one went in to bite at the ball another lurked, offering cover and insurance against the possibility that the tackle would fail.

Over the years, Pele had to live with the shadow markers, and there were times, as in England, that he was subjected to scandalous treatment. His strength, skill, speed and temperament enabled him to avoid both damaging injury and outbursts of insulting behaviour. But there was one occasion when he was driven beyond the limit of his self-control. Playing for Brazil against Argentina in the 1964 'Little World Cup', he was to explode in the face of abuse.

Two years later following a sensational encounter at Wembley in the World Cup. Sir Alf Ramsey was to refer to the Argentinians as 'animals'. Ramsey was not merely reacting to the immediate strain on his patience. He had been among the spectators that night in Sao Paulo,

when Pele was threatened with serious injury by a disgraceful attempt at putting him out of the match.

When the Argentinians arranged themselves for the kick-off, they had Juan Messiano wearing an eleven shirt. Within seconds of the start, it was seen to be a bandit's mask. Messiano simply sprinted to Pele's side and snarled his intent. For the following twenty-nine minutes, Pele was kicked, tripped, punched and spat upon. In the end he broke. He turned and drove his black forehead into Messiano's face, and the Argentinian was led bleeding to the touchline.

Pele might easily have been sent off. The fact that he was not may well have had its root in the conscience of a Swiss referee who had licensed Messiano's villainy.

Such incidents were not entirely typical of suffocating marking. There were players capable of keeping opponents quiet without resorting to butchery, and George Best was reminded of this when playing for Northern Ireland against Russia

in 1969.

The Irish needed to beat Russia in Belfast to retain a hope of qualifying for Mexico. There were only three teams in their group and they had already beaten Turkey twice when the Russians came to Belfast. It was imperative for the Irish to win at home. And Best with his devastating skills was the man most likely to win the match for them.

But from the start Best was policed by Dzodzuashvili, a determined, composed defender who proved to be an outstanding marker of a great forward. The Russians had studied Best closely. They recognized that his ego prevented him from using other players to free himself from close attention. They knew that the longer the game went on, the more eager Best would become to impose his will on the man detailed to stop him from playing. If that man could retain his concentration, then Best could be subdued.

Dzodzuashvili was well equipped for the job. Compactly built and a neat, swift tackler, he gave Best nothing and the Russians were more than content with a goalless draw. Billy Bingham, then Northern Ireland's team manager, said: 'We wanted George to try and play himself free by using support players. If he had knocked the ball off first time and gone for a return, he would have found the space he needed. But he wouldn't do it. It was something he still had to learn.'

Leeds United were not slow to see this point. When facing Manchester United, they sent Paul Reaney to hunt Best, and Reaney did the job effectively. One of Leeds' complement of full internationals, Reaney was an England full-back. Well-balanced and quick into the tackle, he was to lose some of his edge after breaking a leg just prior to the 1970 FA Cup Final against Chelsea and as a result his place in the team.

But he had a history of success against Best and his manager, Don Revie, made these points: 'If you are going to sit on a player like Best, you must use someone who can match his mobility. Tall players have no chance because Best is so quick on the turn, and he has this ability to come to a full stop when in full flight. Paul was ideal for the job because he was quick and disciplined.'

There were few better markers than the Chelsea captain Ron Harris, although he was to suffer more than most from the Football League's determination to outlaw some of the harder tackles in the 1971-72 season.

Harris was a ruthless player with little respect for the niceties of football. He was successful in subduing players such as Jimmy Greaves and Denis Law at a time when roles were more obvious before teams had devised subtle methods of protecting outstanding individuals from close attention.

In the fifties, West Ham had, in Andy Malcolm, a defender who could claim to have collected some of the more coveted scalps in the business. Johnny Haynes of Fulham rarely got any change from him and admitted that he had no fondness for the man's football.

All the outstanding players were at some time or other subjected to close attention. It was tried without much success against Stanley Matthews. It was used against Bobby Charlton in the 1966 World Cup final and when England met West Germany in Mexico four years later.

The Germans set the elegant Beckenbauer to do the job. Some saw it as an astonishingly ill-judged move. But Helmut Schoen, the German team-manager, argued: 'Beckenbauer was a good marker as well as being an exciting creator. We asked him to play off Charlton. When he won the ball, he was more than capable of doing something with it.'

In Leon particularly, Beckenbauer had been able to illustrate that the shadow role was not wholly restrictive; he found time to move forward and score the first German goal, the shadowing of Charlton momentarily forgotten.

Few forwards had the ability to earn such treatment. But some like Pele in the sixties earned much more. His scars as well as his bank balance were testimony to his outstanding talent.

Coaching: Learn how to mark an opponent out of the game

One of the big differences between top-class football and lower grades is that the higher the standard the harder the work needed to win the ball. Professionals have a high degree of technical and tactical ability which commands the respect of the opposition to such a degree that they will not contest for balls they know they cannot get. Defenders will position themselves in such a way that it is made as difficult as possible for the attackers they are marking to take possession of the ball or make killing passes. They will position themselves so that they can intercept or take possession of a ball successfully or block the path of an opponent to the goal at any moment of the game. It is this skill that you must develop to become an efficient marker.

A defender should take up a position between the goal he is defending and that of the opponent he is marking. Draw an imaginary line from the centre of the goal to the man you are marking. If you stand in this line, you will be in a position to watch the ball and see the opponent out of the corner of your eye at the same time. In this position you can attack the ball if it comes near, or run with your opponent should he suddenly move. This position will also limit the area into which the ball can be played to the marked player.

It is sometimes necessary to deviate from this general principle when marking a player who is a long way from the ball. The far full-back, for instance, may be required to move infield to cover the middle when the ball is on the opposite wing. He will be obeying the principle of keeping goal-side but not necessarily on an imaginary line from the centre of goal. Attackers moving in on near post balls from the wings will have to be marked so that the defender can get to the ball first. This will often mean marking more on a line with the near post.

Ideally you should mark close enough to the attacker so that you can intercept a loose pass by moving forward quickly. This distance between defender and attacker will vary depending on several factors. Speeds of both players will be a big factor. If you feel that you are faster than the man you are marking, you can stand quite close to the attacker. If, on the other hand, the attacker is faster, it would be unwise to mark too closely. Instead, adopt a position from which you can tackle him as he is receiving the ball and have sufficient room to pick up his run should he move.

Another factor is the technical ability of the attacker. If he has excellent ball control, you should mark him tight in an attempt to harass him when he receives the ball. You can often allow a fair amount of space for an inexperienced player and make him try to control the ball, knowing that he will make an error and you can take possession as the ball bounces away. Where the attacker is will also have a bearing on how tight the marking will have to be. Generally speaking, the closer he is to your goal the tighter you must mark. Technically experienced players will only require a very limited space in which to be effective.

A simple practice of defending a post will help you react to an attacker's movement. Place the post in the middle of a circle about two yards in diameter. Stand in front of the post outside the circle with an attacker facing you. The object of the exercise is for the attacker to try to touch the

Below A practice for the shadow. He must prevent an opponent carrying the ball across the front of the penalty area from getting in a shot at goal.
Bottom left Against Brazil in Mexico in 1970, England used Alan Mullery, No 4, to shadow Pele, and the great Brazilian failed to score.
Bottom right Stiles versus Best. The shadow must rarely leave the side of the man he is marking.

post whilst the defender reacts to his movements and attempts to block his path. The attacker must be encouraged to deceive the defender by changing direction and feinting; bodily contact must be avoided.

Using the same techniques, get your friend to dribble a ball across the field just outside the penalty area. In this exercise the object is to keep your body between him and the goal. Get him to change direction quickly, and if he can, get a shot in at goal when you give him too much room or he catches you in a bad position. These exercises are very tiring and should only be done for short spells.

Now move on to a three-a-side game in which man-for-man marking is adopted. This game should be played in an area about 25 yards square with no goals. The players are paired so they know whom they are marking. The player in possession must not be tackled by his nominated opponent, but he can be harassed whilst the other two members mark their immediate opponents and position themselves in such a way that they can intercept the pass when it is made. This is a continuous practice of 'keep ball' with no tackling, and the emphasis is on positioning for interceptions. This is a most strenuous practice, good for conditioning, and again it should only be worked on for short periods.

Move on to another practice for three or four defenders, who are marking man-for-man three or four attackers and defending a goal with a goal-keeper. The attacking players are supported by another player who is unmarked. The idea is for the supporting player to play balls through so that a goal attempt can be made. The defenders mark tight and follow their opponents wherever they go. The attacking players may play the ball between themselves in an attempt to break through, and the supporting player must be on hand should he be required to help them out of trouble, but he cannot go through himself. The object here is for the defenders to gain experience of marking man-for-man, positioning themselves for an interception or tackle.

Five or six-a-side games, conditioned for man-for-man marking, are the final stage in developing your technique. This will also give you experience as to when players should be tightly marked, and when you can afford to let them go. And the more experience you gain in practice, the more effective your marking will be in a match.

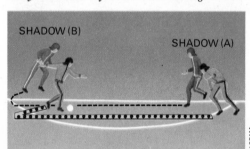

SHADOW (B)

SHADOW (A)

DIAGRAM

SYNDICATION INTERNATIONAL

RAY GREEN

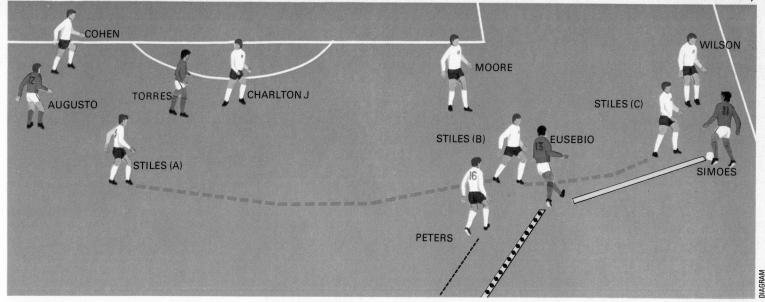

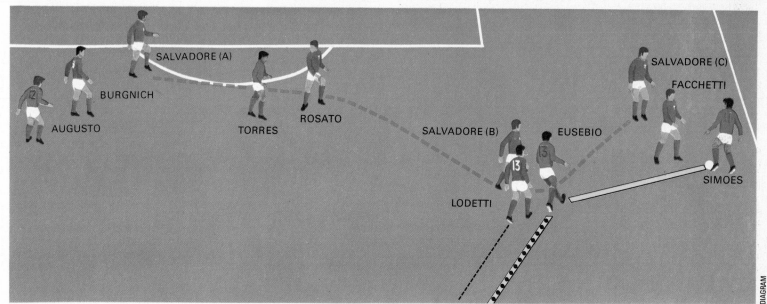

The sweeper

Top In the England team of 1966, Nobby Stiles was played as a sweeper—not in the traditional way behind the back four, but in front of them. He would shuttle across the pitch picking up any opponent who had broken free before that rival could commit a defender in the back four. In the diagram, Stiles forces Eusebio to pass to Simoes, and then moves across to challenge Simoes in turn. He has succeeded in giving Peters time to get back and mark Eusebio, and another crisis in the World Cup semi-final was over.

Above This diagram shows how Italy, and their orthodox sweeper system, would have met the same threat. With their back four marking man-to-man, Italy's sweeper, Salvadore, would have run out from behind the line to hold up Eusebio. Then, when Eusebio's marker had regained his position, Salvadore would have resumed his covering role, ready to meet the new threat from Simoes.

By 1965 Helenio Herrera, then manager of Inter-Milan, stood unrivalled as the high priest of negative, grim-faced, entirely practical football. He had won the European Cup that year, and Inter's success was set on concrete principles of defence.

Inter played with four tight-marking defenders who dogged the paths of nominated opponents throughout the 90 minutes. Behind these four, Herrera deployed an extra defender whose task it was to shuttle from one side of the pitch to the other to cut off any move that had penetrated the man-to-man marking of the four. This was the role of the sweeper.

Herrera was accused of placing a dead hand on the game, but it was an unjust charge. He had not devised the strategy; he merely improved upon it. In fact when he first arrived in Italy he brought with him a philosophy of attacking play, which was an astonishing contrast with what was to follow.

One of Inter's outstanding players at the time was Eddie Firmani, a South African who had

been taken to England by the Charlton Athletic manager, Jimmy Seed. Firmani had an Italian background, and a talent for scoring goals led to his transfer from Charlton to Sampdoria. He was an immediate success, and Italy capped him as an 'oriundo'—a foreigner who qualified because of Italian parentage.

Herrera—when he first came to Italy he wanted to attack

He recalled that when Herrera came to Inter there was every indication that he would pursue an ambitious policy of play which would totally contradict the mood of the Italian game. He said: 'Herrera was seen to be a man who had no interest in trying to take the game to the opposition. This was wrong. He wanted to attack, and when he first came to us we did attack. We carried on like this for a few months and for

a while we played really well. We scored more goals than any other team in the Italian First Division. But then we started to run into some bad results. The transformation was immediate. Herrera took a long look at the situation and set out to play the Italian way better than anyone had played it before. He used Guarneri as a sweeper, and we settled into a pattern of tight man-to-man marking, giving nothing away. Herrera used his players intelligently and he had a knack of employing the right people for particular jobs.'

As a forward Firmani had wrestled with the problem of playing against defences who used the suffocating influence of a sweeper. He said, 'I was usually asked to push up on top of the back man and if the man detailed to mark me

SYNDICATION INTERNATIONAL

BARRATT'S

Above *Italian defenders surround Pele during the 1970 World Cup final. Italy gave Pele a 'shadow' and also had a spare man sweeping at the back.*
Left *When Eusebio, Portugal's menacing forward, threatened England in the 1966 World Cup semi-final, Nobby Stiles (No 4) was usually at hand to prevent danger. But England scorned the man-to-man marking system, and every other England player was expected to do his share in the task of keeping Eusebio out of shooting range.*

for defenders who were committed to making early tackles in midfield. Definite qualities were needed for the sweeper's job. He had to be a good reader of the game. He had to be quick and alert both in his thinking and movement. He had to be willing to push up as a marker if one of his own players had broken forward in attack and it was his responsibility to come out from the back if an opponent advanced quickly from the middle of the field.

Only rarely did British clubs experiment with the Italian philosophy. Burnley dabbled with the possibility of playing a man in his role, and Sheffield United used Joe Shaw as a sweeper for a number of seasons in the fifties. Shaw was a centre-half in name alone. Skilful and perceptive, he covered the spaces behind the other United defenders, cutting off through passes and using his talents to play the ball off quickly when under pressure.

The experiences of West Germany highlighted one reason why many British football thinkers rejected the traditional sweeper. Germany had an outstanding sweeper in Willi Schulz and he was to play with conviction for them. Schulz was brave and would come out to put himself in line with the fiercest shots, apart from displaying an overall excellence. But sometimes Franz Beckenbauer, a highly talented and, in many people's opinion, a world-class midfield player, would take over Schulz's job. Beckenbauer played as a sweeper both for his country and his club, Bayern Munich, but never revealed the same solidity as Schulz.

This could have been disastrous for the Germans when facing Scotland at Hamburg in a World Cup qualifying game in 1969. Scotland needed to win to have any real chance of going forward to the finals in Mexico, and they seemed to be on their way to doing that when Eddie Gray of Leeds United provided the opening for an early goal by Jimmy Johnstone.

Beckenbauer was clearly at fault when he stood watching Gray cut in on goal and was in no man's land when the cross found Johnstone on the far post. Schulz would not have been so indecisive and the Germans knew it. Beckenbauer was back in midfield when the real stuff began in Mexico. Thus, often the use of a sweeper meant a weakening of the team in other departments and it was this which discouraged most British teams from taking up the tactic. But however defensive-minded football became in Britain during the sixties, the only common concession to the sweeper principle was the consistent

came with me it meant that I was engaging two players. It wasn't an easy thing to do because it meant that I was going against a natural instinct to be where the ball was. But this was what the Italian game was all about. It was a thinking game. You planned certain things in training and you were expected to put them into operation during a match. It was cat-and-mouse stuff. One goal was often enough to win and you probed until you got the one goal which mattered.'

Born in the Argentine and brought up in France, Herrera had been no more than an average player, but as a manager, initially in Spain with Barcelona, he established a reputation which was later to command him a salary of around £100,000 a year. An expert in physical and mental preparation, Herrera's concern with winning was never better typified than in that 1965 European Cup final.

Inter's opponents were Benfica, and the

game was played in Milan's own San Siro stadium. But although the Portuguese were without their keeper, Costa Pereira, for most of the second half, Inter made no attempt to improve on a goal scored by their Brazilian winger, Jair. They sat on that goal, maintained their strangling man-to-man marking, and Picchi, a quick, mobile defender, patrolled relentlessly as the sweeper.

The familiar pattern of play in Italy was not, however, imitated in Britain despite a mistaken belief that players such as Bobby Moore and Norman Hunter were being deployed in the role of sweeper.

Moore, Hunter and many others marked space, usually on the left side of their centre-half, and they formed a system of two central defenders who were charged with giving the defence cover through the middle.

The genuine sweeper was the man who patrolled the full width of the field providing insurance use of ball-winning midfield players to pick off attacks in front of rather than behind the back four. This became an essential feature of England's play when winning the 1966 World Cup.

Nobby Stiles was a controversial figure whose fierce tackling was to arouse much ill-feeling among England's opponents. But Sir Alf Ramsey looked more to his ability to read the game and the speed with which he got to potential danger areas.

Stiles' job was to cut off ground passes before Jack Charlton and Bobby Moore could be isolated and attacked at the heart of England's defence. The fact that he was employed in front rather than behind the defensive line meant that he could move forward to join in attacks.

Within what had become a recognized, secure system of defensive play, English football was to produce outstanding back four players. Moore was the best of them, but Hunter, Bobby Moncur of Newcastle, Tommy Smith of Liverpool, Derby's Colin Todd, Spurs' Philip Beal and many

others all did well in the role of the secondary centre-back. Yet in time the system was to have an undermining effect on the production of genuine centre-halves.

There was a definite shortage of players in this position when England began to build for the 1974 World Cup in Munich, and it was significant that the veteran Jack Charlton remained a strong contender for the position despite his advancing years.

Roy McFarland of Derby was established in the England side when they travelled to play Greece in a European Nations Cup match in December 1971, but Ramsey admitted that he would have sent for Charlton had there been any doubts about McFarland's fitness. Ramsey said at the time: 'For one reason or another centre-half-backs are not coming through. Every manager seems to be looking for one and there isn't much cover for the position.'

Charlton saw the problem as an effect of modern strategy. 'When I first came into the

game, a centre-half was expected to accept much more responsibility. You had to be able to cope in the air without the insurance of knowing that someone would be tucking in behind to pick off the ones you missed. You had to be able to deal with attacks down both sides, through the middle, and to pick off those who attacked you with the ball.

'Once they put another central defender alongside you the job was halved. There was no longer the same sort of responsibility attached to it. It improved the overall pattern of defensive play but it hindered the progress and development of outstanding centre-half-backs.'

Charlton's point was valid, but in the seventies there was little sign that British coaches and tacticians would act upon it; the orthodox back four system, based on the marking of areas of the field rather than specified opponents, still prevailed. And the genuine sweeper—so familiar in Europe, remained a rare sight on English grounds.

Coaching: Develop the spare defender system for your team

Teams concede goals because of four main failings: a lack of pressure on the opponent with the ball; a lack of support for the defender in the immediate playing area who is applying the pressure; failing to track down a player running through into a danger area; and giving the ball away in the back third of the field.

When planning tactics, the idea is to cater for these problems, bearing in mind the capabilities of the players in the team. The first and third reasons can be overcome by good man-to-man marking but this does not give you any spare supporting player if the plan is strictly followed; dangerous one-against-one situations can be created against you. To counter this problem some teams adopt a sweeper or mopping-up player who patrols the area behind the main defenders as a reserve defender.

This is a highly specialized job which calls for the ability to read dangerous situations quickly, a cool head when under pressure in order not to give the ball away, techniques to intercept fluently and start up attacking moves by accurate and positive passing and the physical assets of speed, strength and stamina to cope with the great physical demands associated with covering the whole width of the field often at sprint pace.

To introduce this type of tactic into your team it is for once best to start with a full-scale practice match. Both teams should employ man-for-man marking in defence with the exception of one defender who acts as a sweeper, and who patrols as a cover player.

A lot of talking amongst the players must be going on during this practice period because it is essential to get an understanding of the whole picture before breaking the different functions down into parts. A good understanding of what

can happen in a game will help you see what you want to achieve in your small-sided practices.

A three-a-side practice with two players marking man-for-man with the third player supporting when in possession and covering when defending is a good starting point. This game should be played in an area about 40 yards long and 20 yards wide, across the penalty area perhaps. Encourage players to give and go for through balls to give the covering players practice at intercepting and at picking up opponents who have broken clear.

Once possession has been lost it is more than likely that the covering player, plus one of the other players, will have to delay play until the player who went on the through ball has recovered to mark his player once again. This is a very hard exercise physically so play for short, sharp periods.

Another way to improve is a practice for four players and one ball. Two players stand about 40 yards apart, and another two stand almost in between, ten yards in from each of them—the four standing in almost a straight line. One of the players on the end has the ball, and on a signal the player nearest him runs in as if to tackle him. Before he gets too close the player on the ball plays a long pass to the player 40 yards away. As he is receiving the ball, his partner moves in as if to tackle him; he must control the ball and play it long again to the other players who have changed functions. Take your time early in this practice when you are challenging, so that the controlling player has space to make a long, clearing pass. Eventually the practice should become a two-touch movement—one touch to control the ball closely, the second to drive the pass. The changing over of the two pairs simulates the

moving up in support that must be performed in a game. In the practice this must be done quickly because the ball will soon be back.

From these small group activities put the ideas that have come to mind into practice in further full-sided training games. One problem you will have to solve is what is the best action to take when the sweeper has to leave the middle to cover a full-back.

The best method of extra cover here is for the other full-back to leave his man and move infield to cover the area immediately in front of the goal and to keep glancing over his shoulder in case his man makes an unexpected run. By moving into a more central position, he will thicken the cover in the most vital area. This is known as balancing the defence, because he would still be in a good position to close the winger down if play should be suddenly switched. Your winger could help in this respect if he came back just a little deeper. He could make a quick switch in the play more difficult by cutting down the space left to the winger.

Having won the ball and started an attacking movement the sweeper can now move up into line with the main defenders, releasing one of them into midfield to support play on his side of the field. The moment possession is lost, the main defender must come back quickly to his marking job, so releasing the sweeper to do his covering at the back.

By developing this understanding between the defenders in your team, you may well find that the use of some kind of sweeper will tighten things at the back, and will help you to concede fewer goals.

Below *Diagram of a way for sweepers to practise clearing the ball under pressure. Four players stand almost in a line. 1 plays the ball to 4 as he is challenged by 2. 4 plays it back again under pressure from 3. Each player becomes alternately passer and challenger.*

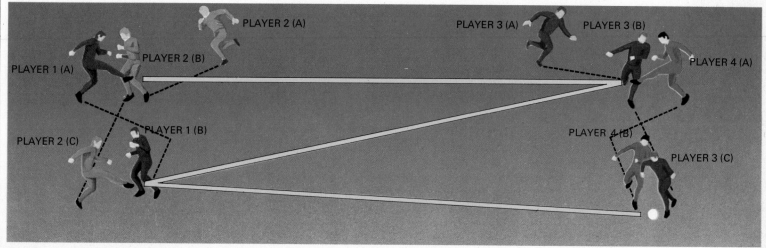

PLAYER 2 (A)   PLAYER 3 (A)   PLAYER 3 (B)

PLAYER 2 (B)

PLAYER 1 (A)   PLAYER 4 (A)

PLAYER 1 (B)

PLAYER 2 (C)   PLAYER 4 (B)

PLAYER 3 (C)

DIAGRAM

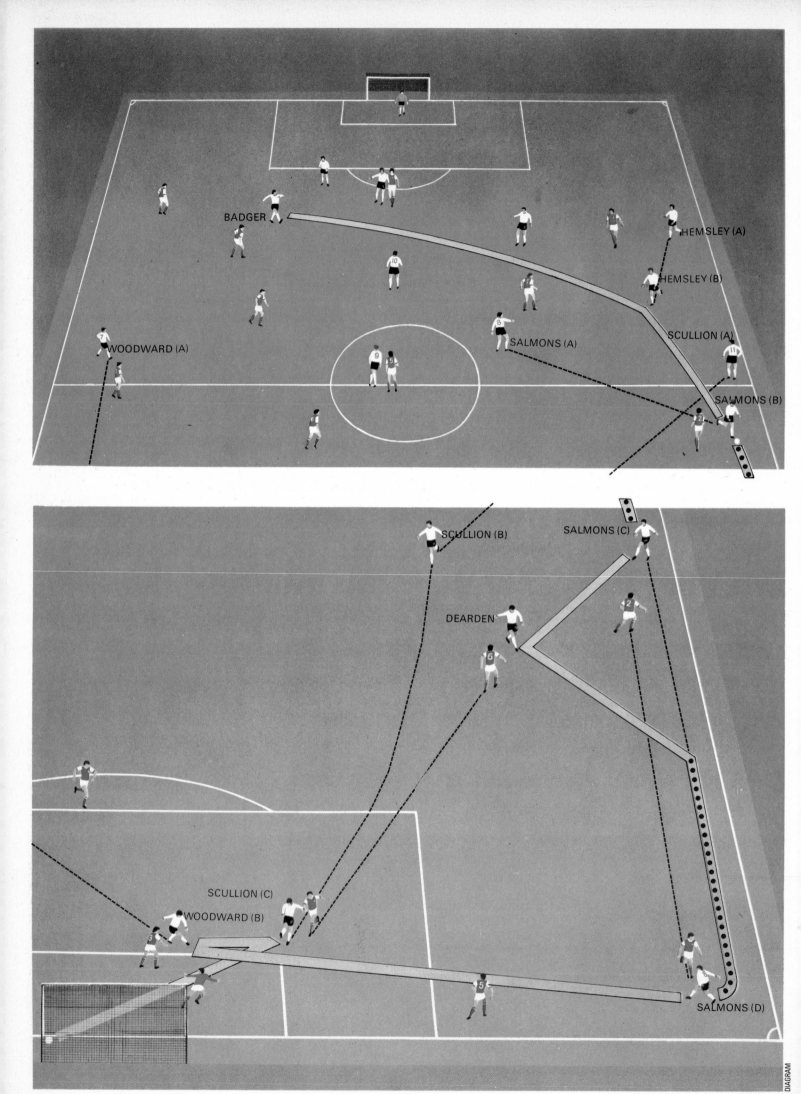

BADGER

HEMSLEY (A)

HEMSLEY (B)

SCULLION (A)

SALMONS (A)

WOODWARD (A)

SALMONS (B)

SCULLION (B)

SALMONS (C)

DEARDEN

SCULLION (C)

WOODWARD (B)

SALMONS (D)

DIAGRAM

The new role of the winger in midfield

It was a dictum held by many other top managers at that time. Leicester paid Chelsea £100,000 in September 1971 to secure the services of Keith Weller, a winger previously with Tottenham Hotspur. As well as possessing the ability to attack defenders on the flanks, he was equipped to do much more. He could cut infield to score goals, and his physical resilience could be put to use in defensive situations or to win the ball in midfield.

A year later Spurs almost doubled that fee to sign Ralph Coates, an England international, from Burnley. Coates had latterly been used by his former club as a midfield player, but he possessed the expensive ability to go past defenders.

Able to defend, graft in midfield—yet still attack on the wings

Tottenham introduced him into their costly line-up as a winger to capitalize on this gift. Able to defend, graft in midfield and still attack down the flanks, Coates characterized the value of the winger of the seventies.

In Woodward and Scullion, who was only playing because of a pre-season injury to Welsh international winger Gilbert Reece, Sheffield United clearly had two wingers conforming to that demanding pattern.

Yet the style of wing-play changed so completely during the sixties that the very position looked at times to be totally obsolete.

For instance, critics of Sir Alf Ramsey's teams, who were unable to resist harsh comment even amid the triumph of 1966, labelled the England team 'Wingless Wonders'.

Martin Peters, in a number eleven shirt, and Alan Ball, wearing a number seven, could not satisfy the yearning for an era when wingers looked and played a conventional touchline role.

In fact, Ramsey included three wingers among the 22 players he chose in 1966 and they all got a game. John Connelly, Terry Paine and Ian Callaghan each played in a group game, but all three had been passed over before the final.

Indeed, by then, wingers who operated almost exclusively along the touchlines had become almost a luxury.

Changes in defensive strategy brought this about. Wingers were immediately denied time

The second week of the 1971-72 Football League season meant a lot to Sheffield United. Newly promoted to the First Division, they set a blistering pace at the top of the table, and on 24 August they scored a thoroughly convincing goal to beat reigning Champions and Cup-holders, Arsenal—at Highbury.

The final pass in the goalscoring movement came from Alan Woodward, a strong, hard-shooting winger coveted by several top clubs, and the ball was tucked resolutely into the corner of Bob Wilson's goal by Stewart Scullion, another winger signed a few months earlier from Watford.

Both Scullion and Woodward were stationed on their touchlines on the half-way line when United's right-back, Len Badger, struck a pass square across field to left-back Ted Hemsley.

They were still behind the ball when Hemsley's forward pass found midfield player Geoff Salmons breaking along the left touchline from the middle of the field. Scullion had drifted inside to make the space.

It was then and only then that these two new-style wingers made decisive breaks themselves. Scullion, from the side of the pitch on which the Sheffield attack was being launched, took a straight line at Arsenal's goal. Woodward, from the opposite flank, had to run further, but he sprinted with the same unswerving determination and at great speed.

Above left As Sheffield United start the move that brought them a win over Arsenal in August 1971 their wingers occupy traditional touchline positions.
Left But as the move progresses they strike infield, and Woodward sets up the chance that Scullion takes.
Below Elated team-mates congratulate Scullion.

Both of them were well inside Arsenal's penalty area when Salmons turned the ball back across goal. Woodward got the first touch and, when he prodded the ball forward, Scullion arrived to provide a conclusive finish. Although the Arsenal left-back, Bob McNab, insisted afterwards that it was a gift goal due to indecision between himself and Wilson, this in no way undermined the significance of the move.

Sir Alf Ramsey, the England team manager, was among a 45,000 crowd who saw United take this lead in the fifth minute before going on to defend that goal with confidence and composure.

He recalls: 'They were a delight to watch. They played intelligent, sensible football and I was very pleased for them.'

Their play was so appealing when set against the negative approach which most teams had come to settle for away from home that there were bound to be errors when critics attempted to examine their style.

The most popular was that John Harris, their manager, was asking his team to attack on a wide front with wingers hugging the touchlines.

But their subsequent play confirmed that United were asking more from them than just the willingness to run and centre. They shared the load in defence, and continually pressured Arsenal's defenders into passing errors by moving in swiftly to offer a challenge.

Before the opening of the season John Harris had been asked why he had signed so many wingers. His reply was significant. 'I have signed footballers,' he said, 'people who can play. We have been asking defenders to display attacking skills. I believe it is better to have good attackers who can also defend.'

RAY GREEN

and space in which to collect the ball when full-backs were sent in to mark them closely. They could no longer turn and take on defenders, and it suddenly needed courage to play in a position which had not previously made any excessive demands on that particular quality.

The change was in many ways remarkable if only because English football had once thrived on its wing-play.

England's most famous footballer for thirty years was Stanley Matthews, a shuffling, immensely gifted dribbler who rarely scored goals himself but who made plenty for his team-mates.

Matthews style was not unique. It was the way in which he used his gifts which set him far apart from the rest. Popularly known as the 'Wizard of the Dribble' he could mesmerize full-backs and then destroy them with a sudden, demoralizing burst of speed.

Like all wingers of his day, Matthews was confined to the touchline where he would be fed the ball by his inside-forwards and wing-halves. He would not be expected to go infield to win the ball for himself. Thus if the inside men and half-backs had off-days Matthews would not often receive the ball.

But what was permissable in the tactical context of the fifties became a scandalous waste of a player in the seventies. Even in the match for which he is most remembered—the 1953 FA Cup Final—Matthews often stood in isolation on his touchline.

Conventional wingers suffocated—by full-backs marking tightly

But in the dying seconds, the score at 3-3, and with extra-time seemingly inevitable, Matthews shuffled in from the right touchline.

His shuffle took on a deadly air, as defenders fell off before him, and Matthews suddenly surged forward. Even at 38 he still had his speed off the mark. He reached the byeline and cut back a low centre away from the packed goalmouth.

Bill Perry, a South African-born forward who was to play for England, had not gone into the

Above left Alan Woodward (striped shirt), a winger coveted by many top clubs, played a major role in Sheffield United's fine start to the 1971-72 season. Above Stanley Matthews, most noted of the orthodox wingers who patrolled the touchlines and were fed the ball rather than having to find it.

ruck. He had waited, delaying his run until the last minute. He was richly rewarded for his patience. The ball came true, he struck a savage shot past Bolton's goalkeeper Stan Hanson, and won Blackpool the Cup.

That type of goal and the skill which made it encouraged wingers to try and develop Matthews approach. It was a pointless exercise.

Tight marking came to suffocate most of them and even Tom Finney, arguably the best all round player to appear in Britain during the period, was used as a deep-lying centre-forward.

Nevertheless there was still value in wingers who had the pace and the will to go at defences. Wolves had two of them, Johnny Hancocks and Jimmy Mullen, and they used them successfully. The style of their team was essentially one of

Coaching: Learn how to work best for your team as a modern wing-player

Getting round the back of defences is one of the most productive forms of attacking strategy, and a team that does this will regularly make itself scoring chances and score goals. Direct wing-play will enable attacks to penetrate behind a line of defenders.

But now wingers come into the game more and work harder than traditional wingers, who used to patrol the touchlines waiting to be given the ball. They have to go and look for the ball, and try to win it from opponents by tackles or interceptions.

A winger must still have the great qualities of the famous 7's and 11's of the past—speed and the ability to get past opponents. But in modern football this is not enough on its own. The winger must be a good all-round performer, who can kick and head the ball well, and who can work back and infield for his side.

Speed is often a natural quality, but you can improve your sprinting ability—in two ways. Because speed is largely a result of how powerful your body is, you can run faster by becoming stronger. Weight training will build up your strength—but do remember that this must only be done under qualified supervision.

If your own football club does not have a set of weights, a local youth club or evening school will probably run weight-training classes. Strength can be built up quickly—especially if you can manage to attend classes two or three times a week.

But you can work on your sprinting on your own. You will be able to move quicker if you can lengthen your stride as soon as you are moving at top speed. Short rapid paces will get you moving smartly, but a longer stride will give you further acceleration.

Mark about 20 yards in the garden or your local park, and check how many strides you take to cover this area—going as hard as you possibly can. Now without lowering the speed at which your legs move, try to reduce the number of strides you take. This means that more ground is being covered by each stride, and—if you can maintain the speed of your leg movement—you must be going faster.

As a winger a lot of your running will be with a ball, so you must practise your dribbling. You can dribble with either the inside or the outside of the foot or with the full instep. More than likely one of these methods will be the natural one for you, but you should work on all three methods so that you become a less predictable player.

Take a ball out with you and walk, jog and

sprint controlling the ball close to you all the time. Constantly change and switch direction. Keep twisting and turning—all the time you are cultivating a feel for the ball, so that it almost becomes a part of you.

Get a friend to come out with you. Make him act as a defender, and try to beat him. Do not be satisfied with one particular trick—because your opponents will soon find you out. As a winger you must consciously try to vary the way that you play. You must practise until you can beat your opponent equally well on the inside or the outside, and can control the ball closely with either foot.

As a winger you will be expected to share the goal-scoring responsibilities of your team. Most of the opportunities that come your way during matches will be at sharp angles to the goal, and you must cultivate your judgement in these situations. Few things can be more infuriating than the sight of a winger who persistently puts the ball into the side-netting. If you aim for the far post with your shots or headers, the keeper may be able to reach the ball, but, if he can only parry it, it will leave a simple chance for a colleague.

At a training session you can practise all these skills in a continuous routine—see diagram. Place the players as follows; as defenders—a goalkeeper, a right-back, a left-back and a centre-half; to attack these defenders two right-wingers, two left-wingers and two centre-forwards, all placed on the half-way line.

Above right Peter Lorimer (white shirt) of Leeds Utd and Johnny Morrissey of Everton, two successful wingers of the seventies, battle for possession. Both are versatile players who can defend bravely and score vital goals, as well as make penetrating, attacking runs along the touchlines.

intimidating directness. Wolves used the long ball, working on the principle that the more often you put the ball in the goalmouth the more likely you were to score.

Hancocks and Mullen not only had to accept responsibility for putting the ball in there but for scoring also. Powerful runners who could centre when at top speed they made many goals for each other with wing-to-wing moves.

Spurs, too, refused to ignore the winger as he was supposed to be. In January 1958 they paid Swansea Town a then record £35,000 for a Welsh international, Cliff Jones, who was to become outstanding during his time.

Jones, the son of an international soccer player and the grandson of a Rugby League international three-quarter, combined the qualities needed in both games.

He was skilful on the ball, he was courageous and he had paralysing pace. But Jones' job, unlike that of Matthews and his counterparts, was not to make goals. It was to terrorize defences by scoring them.

Jones made a notable contribution to Spurs' great years in the early sixties and Dave Mackay, another of their great stars, says of him: 'He was undeniably world class. Every great team has five great players. Cliff Jones was one of ours. He could grab goals out of nothing and when he was at his peak I have never seen anyone as quick over a long distance.'

While Jones was tearing defences apart, Sir Alf Ramsey was detailing an ageing wing-half, Jimmy Leadbetter, to play in a number eleven shirt for Ipswich Town.

Leadbetter was a fine passer, especially with his left foot. Ramsey sent him out to the left wing, made sure that he got a lot of the ball, and the Ipswich team took it from there.

The job of running behind defenders went to two burly forwards, Ray Crawford and Ted Phillips, with the opposite winger Roy Stephenson filling in behind them. A revolution was on its way. As 4-2-4 became 4-3-3 and even 4-4-2 wingers almost disappeared.

When they began to return at the end of the sixties it was with a new sense of responsibility. Outstanding attackers such as George Best and Eddie Gray who could loosely be regarded as wingers were expected to turn their hand to defensive work.

But no one typified modern wing-play better than Arsenal's George Armstrong. A busy, energetic little forward who could centre well with either foot he made many goals for Arsenal when they snatched the 'Double' in 1971. Almost as important from Arsenal's point of view was Armstrong's contribution to holding up the opposition with resolute tackling.

But on the night of 24 August 1971, Armstrong's busy contribution was not enough. The early pretenders to Arsenal's throne, Sheffield United, had two such players in Woodward and Scullion. And Arsenal were beaten by two wingers of the seventies.

The routine begins with the first centre-forward passing the ball to the first right-winger, who dribbles down the touchline, and attacks the left-back. At the same time the centre-forward and the first left-winger race forward into the penalty area—the centre-forward going to the near post, the winger cutting in to the far post. They are marked respectively by the centre-half and the right-back.

The right-winger must now beat his full-back to get a cross in, and the two players racing into the box must try to score or get in a shot from the centre.

The second group of players then repeat the move, but this time it is the left-winger who takes on the right-back to get the cross in, and the second centre-forward and right-winger who try to turn his cross into goal.

The first group then go again, and this time they use the left-winger to take on the full-back and centre the ball. Then the second group go again using their right-winger in this role—and so on.

To make the practice even more realistic, make the three attackers sprint back to the half-way line as soon as they have finished their attack on the goal. This is the sort of chasing forwards, the wingers in particular, will have to do in a game.

As a winger never forget that you have a defensive function. Practise your tackling. Play in the above training routine as a full-back, so that you get the feel of being in a defensive

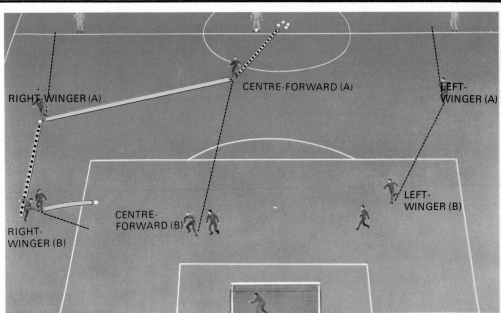

Above Practice for wingers, using two groups of three—two wingers and a striker—to attack a defence. The groups go alternately at goal, trying to score from the winger's cross.

situation. Work on your fitness so that you can cover all the ground that a player who has both attacking and defensive duties must cover.

Practise and practise, and you will have the satisfaction not only of scoring and making goals for your team, but of saving a few as well.

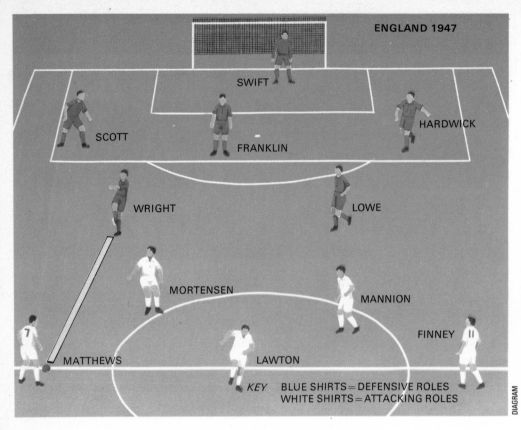
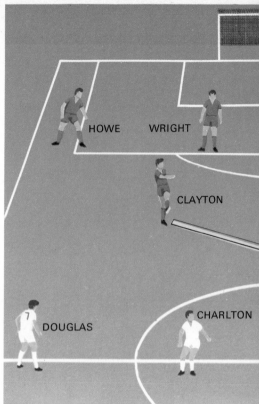

ENGLAND 1947

SWIFT

SCOTT

FRANKLIN

HARDWICK

HOWE   WRIGHT

WRIGHT

LOWE

CLAYTON

MORTENSEN

MANNION

7

CHARLTON

MATTHEWS

FINNEY   11

DOUGLAS

LAWTON

7

KEY   BLUE SHIRTS = DEFENSIVE ROLES
WHITE SHIRTS = ATTACKING ROLES

DIAGRAM

Strategy in midfield

England players returned from a tour of South America in 1969 well aware of two problems that would face them in the coming 12 months: one, that hot and hostile conditions awaited them in Mexico in the following summer, and two, that Everton would swarm all over them in the League during the coming winter.

The England squad had their own experiences of football in Mexico to prepare them for the World Cup ordeal—and they had Alan Ball's word for the tough winter that lay ahead.

Ball's insistence that Everton were cut and dried Champions before the season had even started became one of the running jokes of the tour. Sooner or later every waiting hour in a hotel or airport lounge would be pierced by his shrill voice proclaiming: 'All you've got to play for is second place. Winning? . . . you've no chance. Not with our Panzer Division. That's what I call it, our Panzer Division. . . . Me, Colin and Howard, we're like little tanks. We'll swarm all over you.'

Ball's prophesies are famous for their lack of overdone modesty, and for their absence of qualification. And this time his claim was to be proved only too accurate during the eight-month trudge of the League season, because of the power and influence of Everton's midfield trio.

Everton won the title just as Ball had insisted they would, streaking clear with a nine-point margin over Leeds. And the midfield of Ball, Harvey and Kendall was just as decisive as the ebullient Lancastrian had predicted.

In the 25 years of evolution and then revolution in tactics in football since the Second World War, nowhere was change seen more strikingly than in midfield. Once, the midfield was merely the area through which the ball had to pass between defence and attack, a 'land' where

dwelt men whose sole purpose was to effect the transfer quickly and accurately. By the end of the sixties, midfield had become the area where defeat was avoided, where success was created and, perhaps more important still, where the very shape of a team was decided.

Very simply, perhaps too simply, it could be said that if two of a team's midfield trio were defenders first, then that side would be hard to beat; if two of the three were eager attackers, then the side were hard to hold.

Everton's success was in finding a trio that was both. Ball, Harvey and Kendall, the 'Panzer Division' of Ball's repeated threat, were all small men, all intensely committed, all totally mobile. What else they had in common were quick and agile feet, a love for bold exploratory runs into attack, and an equal ability to get back fast to deliver stinging tackles in defence. All duties were almost equally shared, the old midfield theory of 'one man to get it, another to give it' was completely abandoned. The result was a marvellous, almost perfect combination.

Some statistics support the claim. In that triumphant drive towards the title Everton collected 17 goals—equal to the contribution of an extra fine and gifted forward—from these midfield men. Yet the fact that in the hard-pressed matches away from home they conceded only 15 goals (half the total given away by their nearest challengers, Leeds) says it all about the effect on Everton's defence of a first-line of resistance provided by 'the Panzers'.

A year later, Arsenal were to use five different players to provide their drive towards the title with the same midfield impetus. A scrutiny of their teams well illustrates the manner in which a team can colour its approach to a single game

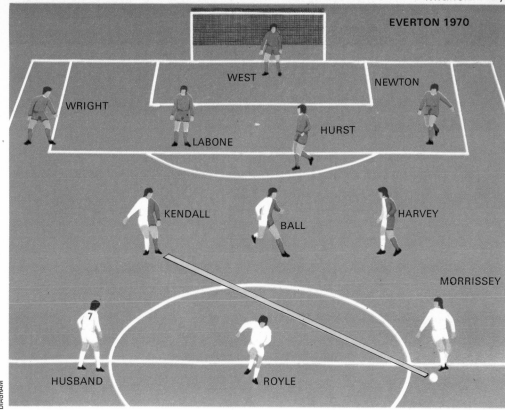

The three diagrams show in a very simplified form the development of how teams have been organized in midfield over a span of 25 years.

Above left In immediate post-War football, attacking and defensive roles were clearly defined, and only rarely were goals scored by players not in the five-man forward line. The England team scored more than 70 goals in post-War matches before a wing-half, Billy Wright, got on to the score-sheet. The wing-half's job was to win the ball, and then to feed passes to the forwards.

Above centre The England team of the late fifties played 4-2-4, but the roles of the two linkmen were still specified clearly—one basically to attack and strike at goal and one to win the ball. For England Ronnie Clayton would do the defensive job, but having won the ball he would look to find Haynes who would set the attack moving.

Above In 1970 Everton won the League Championship with three all-purpose players in midfield. Ball, Kendall and Harvey each had specific duties, but they scored 17 vital League goals between them and consistently supported their strikers.

Left Johnny Haynes (white shirt, left), an attacking midfield player, scored 18 goals for England.

Below left Alan Ball commanded Everton's midfield three, nicknamed 'the Panzer Division'.

or an entire competition by its choice of middle-park players.

Arsenal, ambitious but not yet confident, began an historic season with Kelly and Storey (both defenders first) and Graham (a clear attacker) as their midfield. The points came gradually but surely, and the need changed. Arsenal switched then to a Storey, Sammels, Graham midfield—Sammels, too, was an attacker, and their football flowed a little more easily.

As Arsenal's lead built they could afford the luxury of still more enterprise, and the extrovert, almost irresponsibly confident George replaced Sammels, as the Highbury club spread out to try to win the title in a canter. But the lead dwindled under Leeds' pressure and Kelly, a now-constant substitute, came back to help tighten the team in the last handful of League and Cup matches.

In the final counting it could be seen that Arsenal had gained 23 goals—and thus an historic double—from the sudden strikes of this small army of midfield men. But there are no figures to show how many times Kelly and Storey, or even the one-time forwards like Graham and Sammels, had been back volleying desperate clear-

ances from within the shadow of their own goal.

This final point needs to be emphasized; that no matter where a man had begun his career, once he became a midfield player he was expected to do the lot—the running and the shooting up front where possible, but also the tackling and the heading in defence when needed.

Leeds, Champions in 1969, and runners-up to both Everton and Arsenal, owed their pre-eminence at the time to an equal claim to solidarity in midfield. Giles, a former winger, linked with Bremner to become the inseparable basis of the Yorkshire side. Hockey, a former winger, was the most influential player of promoted Sheffield United's startling return to Division One in season 1971-72; West Ham threw a former full-back, Billy Bonds, into midfield and taught him to attack; Manchester United's new manager, Frank O'Farrell, began rebuilding a famous team in 1971 by switching a former striker, Alan Gowling, and a one-time wing-hugging forward, Willie Morgan, to his midfield.

They came from all quarters, in all sizes, and they brought many different skills and attitudes to their new job, the midfield men of the late sixties and early seventies: and they had to learn first that their old habits and instincts would not be enough. The defender who could only defend was wasted, the forward who could only attack was a liability.

But it was not always so. The years after the Second World War were those of the great England names, Matthews and Finney, Swift and Lawton, Mannion and Carter, and the era of great England victories. In the first 22 games when international football was resumed England scored 75 goals—approaching four goals per game, and scores of 4-0, 5-0 or 6-0 were not uncommon.

Yet, the record clearly shows, scoring was then a job for the forwards. Not until the 75th goal—by Billy Wright against France in Paris in 1949—is a man not wearing a shirt number between 7 and 11 seen as a marksman. Wright, partnered by players like Johnstone, Cockburn, Lowe and Dickinson, was then the typical midfield player of his day.

His job was to win the ball, then to give it either short to his winger, short to the nearest inside-forward, or long and crossfield to the opposite winger. Even in games when England dominated, he shot only rarely—and in the full knowledge that a wing-half who trespassed too readily in forwards' territory was risking abuse as a 'glory hunter'. The lines of demarcation were clear.

It worked the other way, too. The forward, the Carter or Mannion or Mortensen who tracked back to tackle or clear, could be sure of an immense and startled cheer from the terraces and a paragraph all to himself in the newspaper reports—a paragraph that would probably go on to hint that England had played badly to need such unseemly help.

The change was slow in coming. It began in the fifties with the gradual spread of 4-2-4. Now, with one wing-half almost permanently in defence, the remaining wing-half was helped by a forward in midfield. Clayton and Haynes were typical of the partnerships struck for England, and copied in club sides.

Yet still the areas of responsibility were clear: one man to get the ball, another to use it. Clayton played 35 times for England with all the park his preserve, and did not score a single goal; Haynes won 56 caps, and probably made fewer significant tackles. This is not a criticism of either man, nor of those who shared the roles like Revie and Edwards, or Clamp and Shackleton, but rather recognition of a system that regards it as unthinkable that jobs in midfield should overlap.

Nor, at first, did the coming of Sir Alf Ramsey bring change. Eastham had replaced Haynes, Milne, then Stiles, had taken over from Flowers, but one to get it, one to give it, remained the midfield rule.

Not until Ball, a forward who liked to tackle, and later Peters, a wing-half who consistently outflanked his own forwards, made their appearances was a different shape given to football. Once the fans became accustomed to the strange numbering of players, acceptance of the rest was easy: whereas a No 4 up in attack once caused howls of surprise and derision, suddenly there was no 'proper' place for a No 17 or a No 22 —the entire pitch was open to exploitation.

At the start of the 1971-72 season Tottenham's team was given a target of 85 goals in all competitions, to be made up as follows: from Chivers 30, from each of the other two strikers 15, from penalties or headers from big defenders, say another five. That left 20 still to get, and at this point Spurs officials looked hard and meaningfully at their midfield men.

Even ten years earlier the demand would have been greeted with gales of derisory laughter. But, as Everton with their Panzers, and Arsenal with their permutations had proved, a midfield with the players and the plan had become football's area of decision.

Coaching: Learn how to plan your midfield tactics

At all levels of football, what happens in the middle of the field is of crucial importance. This is the 'engine-room' of all teams, where two, three or sometimes four players must work hard, both in attack and defence, to influence the course of a match.

Many sides favour a 4-3-3 or 4-4-2 system, both of which have been criticized for showing a defensive bias, but this need not be valid providing there is an organized balance in midfield. To have this balance in your side you need at least five players who are looking to score goals; thus in a 4-3-3 system two of the three midfield players must be pushing upfield looking to run into forward positions. The third, often a strong player whose task may be to win the ball for your side in the middle, must content himself with a supporting role.

If you have three men in midfield in your side, the most common way to deploy them is in rough areas of responsibility across the field; one will play on the right, one in the centre and one on the left. In most systems it is the two flank players who are looking to move forward and strike at goal, whereas the central man is used as the main supporting player for both attack and defence.

For all aspiring midfield players, fitness is of the utmost importance. Therefore training should never be neglected. Confidence in your own ability to keep running for the whole 90 minutes will generate an appetite for work; you will find yourself wanting the ball the whole time. If you are to play the defensive anchor role, practise your tackling. A simple routine of your friends or team-mates dribbling a ball at you in turn will soon sharpen you up. Go in firmly and want that ball.

As an attacking midfield player you must be looking to move forward into the penalty area to strike at goal. The importance of getting into the box often cannot be stressed enough; to rely on long-range shooting is often to waste a good situation. It obviously has its value, but to get into the box will cause far more danger and result in more goals. Timing when you arrive is important, so start your practices from deep positions in order to cultivate this skill.

Whichever side of the midfield you play, set up a winger on the other side, on the half-way line. Play the ball diagonally long and wide towards the corner flag on the winger's side of the pitch from the half-way line, and make ground to the penalty area whilst the wing player works the ball into a crossing position. The art of this movement is to be moving into the area at the same time as the ball, so making it difficult for an opponent to track you down. Having had a strike at goal you must get back to the half-way line as quickly as possible. To help you do this give the goalkeeper a spare ball in case the ball goes behind. The idea is for the goalkeeper either to make a save or get a ball from the net quickly and then kick it downfield into the centre-circle; you must beat the ball back to the half-way line. Make the practice harder by introducing an opponent to run with you.

Practices of attack versus defence can be built up in this way. Three attackers and three attacking midfield players play against four defenders and two defensive midfield men. This gives you a chance to create space for an attack. Work at different ways to get in at goal. It is important that the front attackers work to create space into which the midfield players can move up.

Overlapping the full-back is often a good way to get round the back into a scoring or crossing position. The right midfield player plays a ball wide to the left front attacker who is immediately supported by the left midfield player. The winger moves the ball infield, taking the full-back with him, leaving space for the supporting midfield player to move down the wing in an overlapping position. The winger plays a reverse pass so that the left midfield player is in a position to cross the ball. The right midfield player can either be in at the far post or run quickly checking in at the near post in front of the centre-forward.

There are obviously many variations to this movement all of which must be co-ordinated with the front players. Through balls can be played direct or via the front players. Practise timing the run by playing the ball square around the half-way line to another midfield player, then sprinting through either to receive the ball back direct or via a front player who has moved wide. Invariably he will need further support for a final push-and-run before being clean through.

Part of the excitement of playing in midfield is that there is so much variety in the play in every match. You may be driving home a goal one minute and clearing off the line at your end the next. Think about the game and develop your fitness and you will be a valuable part of your team's 'engine-room'.

Below *The conversion of front-runner Alan Gowling (second left) and winger Willie Morgan (third left) to strengthen Manchester United's midfield inspired much of the club's revival during the 1971-72 season.*

RAY GREEN

Support play

For a while in the fifties it seemed that Real Madrid would go on winning the European Cup for ever. Their spectacular style had dominated the early years of the competition and, when they went to Glasgow in May 1960 to play their fifth successive final, no other name had been carved in the trophy.

It was a memorable era for them and the game they played. But there was much more to the Spanish team than panache and the arousal of individualism. They had great players, and they used them well. And in Glasgow they introduced a player who was to illustrate one of the most basic of football principles—supporting the man in possession.

Luis Del Sol was then an anonymous figure in a team woven with great names. He did not have the overwhelming stature of di Stefano, the presence of Puskas or the exciting potential of Gento. He was a new name, but di Stefano in particular was aware of his quality.

Di Stefano was the complete player. He had an abundance of skill, endless stamina and tremendous vision. He could create, and he could finish. But in Glasgow, the sorcerer had reached the point where he needed an assistant.

The point was not lost on Walter Winterbottom, then England's team manager and director of coaching. Winterbottom trained his coaches at Lilleshall. And it was on a course there that Winterbottom was to spotlight the value of Del Sol's industry and its place in the modern game.

A film showed the extent of Del Sol's vital contribution

Film of Real's sensational 7-3 victory before a record crowd of 135,000 at Hampden Park revealed three essential points. There was the anxiety which they had to overcome in the opening phase of the contest, the power and accuracy which brought di Stefano four goals and Puskas three. And there was the extent of Del Sol's contribution.

Di Stefano, running with the ball from midfield, his head up and always swivelling to take in the changing picture before him, acted as a candle to a moth for those studying the range of his skills. But Winterbottom looked beyond the immediate area of di Stefano's operation. He spotted the figure who would appear in the film's frame, and then disappear as though fearful of infringing on the master's domain.

But there was a much more practical reason for Del Sol's apparently sporadic involvement. He was making space, offering help, always supporting di Stefano and protecting him from immediate challenge.

Winterbottom recalled: 'It was a significant feature of that match. Di Stefano dominated the play, but Del Sol's contribution was vital. He was simply giving di Stefano the opportunity to find him with the ball if he felt it was necessary. This willingness to run and run again without getting the ball was a rare quality.'

In a game against England when playing for Spain, di Stefano, the adopted Argentinian, was once again to emphasize the need for such players and his particular need to have Del Sol around. England were very much in the match played in Madrid when the Spaniards settled on a substitution. The manager was Hellenio Herrera, a man who was not used to having his orders countermanded. His chosen substitute was stripping down on the line when di Stefano sprinted across to the bench. Sitting there was

Above left As George Best carries the ball forward, team-mate Alan Gowling keeps pace alongside him, maintaining a supporting position.

Centre left Everton built a winning side in the late sixties around midfield men, Ball, Kendall and Harvey. Here Ball, in possession in the 1968 Cup Final, has Kendall, as ever, in support.

Left Paul Madeley on the ball for Leeds while Johnny Giles waits in support in case Madeley needs him. Support is a feature of Leeds' play.

P & L PHOTO SERVICE

COURTESY PATHE NEWS

COLORSPORT

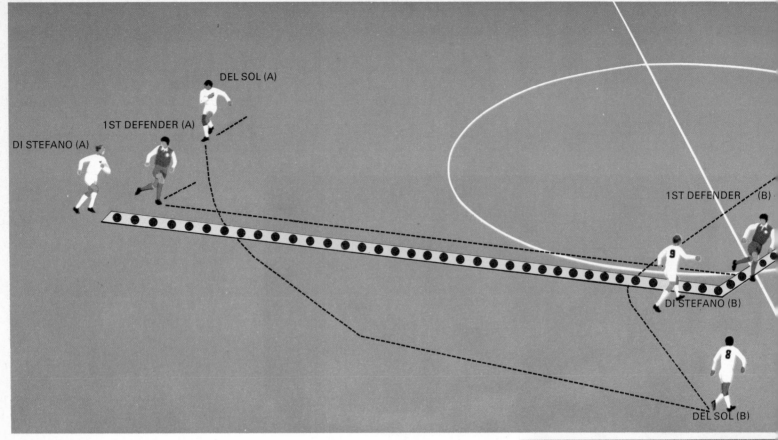

LABELS ON DIAGRAM:
DEL SOL (A)
1ST DEFENDER (A)
DI STEFANO (A)
1ST DEFENDER (B)
DI STEFANO (B)
DEL SOL (B)

Del Sol, and it was Del Sol that di Stefano wanted and Del Sol whom he got.

But support play could take more than one form. It could come in the willingness of a Del Sol or as a more comprehensive part of team tactics. The Belgians, for instance, have a tradition for playing in groups, building attacks from a system of providing a variety of short passing possibilities. It requires players to find space, and accuracy is essential to the pattern.

This was the basis of Spurs' push and run style in the fifties. They varied it with the use of longer passes hit out of defence up to Len Duquemin, a powerful forward who was particularly good at receiving the ball under pressure.

The principle of support began again from there. Team-mates would zone in on Duquemin and, with a range of options made open to him, he could trigger a variety of dangerous raids.

England encountered the Belgian talent for this kind of play at Wembley in October 1964. Sir Alf Ramsey, building for the 1966 World Cup, chose an experimental side which included Terry Venables. It was Venables' first full cap, and it completed a remarkable record of representative honours. He had been capped as a schoolboy, as a youth, as an amateur and he had played in the England Under-23 team. His first senior appearance was hardly a satisfying one.

For it was Venables who found himself involved most frequently as the Belgians assembled their attacks around the principle of supporting each other at close quarters. Venables recalled: 'I found myself running from one to the other without getting a touch at the ball. It was like that training game "piggy in the middle". I was the man in the middle.'

Venables was not short of experience, and the fact that he found himself embarrassed by the situation proved that group support play could be highly effective. Many teams used it as a means of closing down the game after doing enough to win it. It required confidence, and it was not an easy thing to do in England where crowds were used to a more progressive tradition.

More subtle forms of support for the man on the ball gradually became an integral part of play among the best British teams. Spurs, in a later era when they were to win the coveted Cup and League double, did this well. Spurs' target man was Bobby Smith, a barrel-chested, muscular forward who was more than capable of holding

Above Diagram showing the supporting qualities of Luis Del Sol of Real Madrid. In the 1960 European Cup final, di Stefano made a run in which he shuffled and feinted past four Eintracht defenders. All the time Del Sol kept pace, unselfishly darting about, always ready to help.
Right Luis Del Sol in action for Real Madrid.

off a challenge when the ball was driven up to him. Smith's problem was his lack of touch. He could play the ball back to supporting players, but not with any consistent accuracy.

He was relieved of the responsibility when John White, a gifted Scottish international, was signed from Falkirk. White saw situations early. He could sense where the clumsiest of Smith's passes would drop, and he was invariably on hand to receive them. As a result Smith's confidence blossomed, and he was to develop into an England forward.

Leeds United found impetus for their successful run in home and European competition in the consistent use of supporting runs, and John Giles emerged as one of the leading midfield men in Europe.

Giles, stocky, combative and skilful, passed with great accuracy, and saw most of what was going on. His partners in midfield were the fiery and effervescent Billy Bremner and the tall, phlegmatic Paul Madeley. Bremner hunted space ahead of Giles, giving him the chance to open defences with through balls. Madeley was more conservative. He had no convincing pace, but he constantly appeared in the corners of Giles' vision where he could be found with the ball.

Everton built their 1970 Championship winning side around three midfield players who willingly put themselves into supporting positions in all corners of the field. If Alan Ball, a seasoned international, stole much of the limelight, he had two henchmen of similar quality in Howard Kendall and Colin Harvey. Much of Everton's attacking power revolved around the head of Joe Royle. Royle was the target, playing the ball back into the midfield zones, laying the ball off with a skill that often belied his awkward build. Here Ball, Harvey and Kendall would search for the ball insatiably to win possession in vital phases of the game.

Perhaps the most interesting example of support play came earlier when Ferenc Puskas was still scoring spectacular goals for Real

Madrid. In a friendly match against Manchester United at Old Trafford, Puskas was seen to contradict the theory that he was more concerned with his own brilliant individualism than he was with team play.

United's right-back that night was Maurice Setters, and he was confronted with Gento's murderous pace. When jockeying Gento on the touchline, Setters was suddenly aware of Puskas's presence square to his left shoulder. Puskas had moved in to offer Gento the opportunity of playing a one-two along the line.

Gento ignored him, and Puskas departed. He reappeared again in a forward position. Again Gento ignored him. Back came Puskas, again he was ignored. Then, as Gento chose to race Setters to the corner, Puskas adjusted with a thirty-yard run which took him to the edge of the penalty area.

Puskas had made five runs covering something like three hundred yards. He was no longer young. But he was conditioned to the effort. Gustav Sebes, manager of the Hungarian team of the fifties, made this point: 'Puskas was doing that when he was 15, and he will still be trying to do it when he is 35. It's built into him.'

Somewhere along the way it had been built into Del Sol. When 135,000 Scots stood in salute of Real's majesty at Hampden Park in 1960, his was not seen to be the most influential contribution. That opinion might have brought a rare smile from di Stefano.

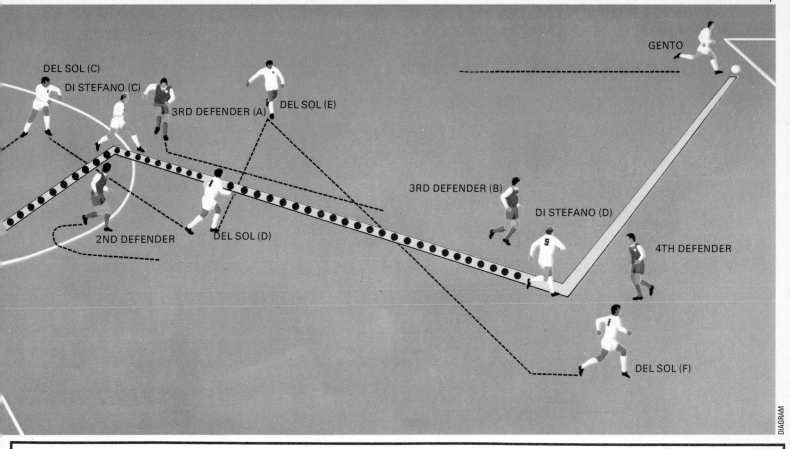

Coaching: Support play—learn how you can help the man on the ball

The first and most important principle in football is that ball possession determines everything. To play, a team must have possession of the ball. To play and be successful, a team must have possession for long periods. The length of these periods and the number of passes that can be strung together will depend on the quality of the passes but, most important, on how well the player on the ball is supported.

The man off the ball determines the shape of play. The player in possession, ideally, should have at least three players at any given moment to whom he can pass.

A simple practice to get players used to the idea of supporting the man on the ball, which can be done at training or in the park amongst a group of four friends, is to have three players interpassing the ball against one defender in an area about 12 yards square. The more the players improve, the smaller the area can become. Possession of the ball will depend on the players off the ball working to make themselves available for passes. This means positioning themselves at an angle so that there is a clear pathway for the ball to travel without a chance of interception. They must also work to position themselves in such a way that they maintain as much space as possible in front of them. While practising in this way, you will find it best to keep to the extremes of the area. Concentrate in passing the ball so that the player who receives the ball can control it very quickly and easily. Once the ball is passed the two players off the ball must re-position themselves in order to support again.

You can make this more difficult by playing 2 against 1 but it becomes an exceptionally difficult practice if you play in a small area. There is only one player off the ball and he has to work very hard. In these practice routines, if you lose the ball to the defender or if you play the ball out of the confined area, you change places with the defender.

As you improve, introduce two more players into the routine. Six players are now involved. Pair up—two pairs play against one pair—4 against 2—and play in an area about 20 yards square. Again the two in the middle are changed when the ball is intercepted or goes out of play. This is a more realistic practice and increases the number of passing possibilities. Keep space in front of you when you are supporting the player with the ball so that you will have time to play the next pass when you get the ball.

This type of small-sided practice cannot be emphasized enough, because the same principles are involved as in the real game, yet the players are involved many more times in a much shorter period. Do not take these practices lightly. This is a key to football. If you get into the habit of playing these games before progressing to a proper game, these skills will serve you well when you play eleven a side.

In an ideal match, the forwards are able to move the ball wherever they require. This can only be achieved if there are supporting players. Every player on the ball requires help.

If a player cannot play forward or receives the ball when facing his own goal, then he must have support from his team-mates coming towards him. The best position is at a slight angle and about 10-15 yards away. This allows for a fair degree of error for the forward in playing the ball back. The supporting player then has the space and time to use the ball in the area directly in front of him.

Practise this in training in an attack-versus-defence routine into one goal. Play six against six. The defence team consists of a goalkeeper, two full-backs, two centre-halves and one defensive midfield player; the attacking team, three front players and three midfield players. One of the attacking midfield players starts the routine by playing the ball up to a front man who acts as a target. The front man must play the ball back to any of his three midfield team-mates who must offer themselves in supporting positions. The defence's midfield player must try and stop this happening. The attacking side goes on to try to score.

As you become more skilled at this, you can introduce another midfield player on the defensive side to make it more competitive.

The key to success is to learn to anticipate play when you are not immediately concerned. Good balls become bad balls when they are unsupported, and good players can look bad players if they are not supported when in possession.

Above *Playing three against one in an enclosed area, about 12 yards square, is good training for support play. By using the full width of the area and keeping on the move, possession should be maintained.*

Improvising in midfield

Right A diagrammatic sequence showing the three phases of midfield tactics employed by Ireland when they beat England 3-2 at Wembley in 1957.
Top Ireland began using both wing-halves, Blanchflower and Peacock, in attack. The full-backs were briefed to spot Haynes' through passes.
Centre But Haynes took charge and when Blanchflower came back to mark him tightly he simply rolled the ball for Edwards to create attacks.
Bottom But by squeezing Haynes out on to the touchline Blanchflower limited his passing angles. And when Peacock dropped back to mark Kevan, and McIlroy and McCrory harrassed Edwards, Ireland restricted the England midfield players.

There was something in the way Northern Ireland filed out at Wembley in November 1957 which immediately encouraged the prospect of an historic victory. They were flying in the face of tradition. The odds were stacked against them. It was thirty years since they had beaten England, they had never won at Wembley and they were facing a team whose impressive form had brought them sixteen successive victories.

But the Irish, gay in their green, looked alive and confident, and there was a smile on the face of their captain, Danny Blanchflower. The smile was to remain for much of the game, and for a long time afterwards, because, by solving a midfield problem and abandoning an original idea in midfield, Blanchflower won a famous battle.

Blanchflower had discussed the game at length with team manager Peter Doherty. The following summer these two were to design a campaign which would make the Irish the surprise team of the 1958 World Cup in Sweden.

Doherty had been one of Britain's great inside-forwards. A player whose skill and style survived the six years of War which almost silenced the game between 1939 and 1945, he had taken over the Irish team and there were old scores to settle. With the irrepressible Blanchflower as his chief aide, Doherty had injected new belief into a side that could only look back on fairly consistent failure.

The Irish were not short of good players. To their skill they added a plan. Blanchflower, Jimmy McIlroy and Bertie Peacock were all formidable midfield players, and it was their eventual redeployment which was to prove critical. Blanchflower recalled later in his own *Book of Football*: 'There was great confidence in our camp. We all had strong feelings that Ireland would win. And as the day approached Peter Doherty and I discussed how we could put this great faith to practical effect. We felt that England had more ability and potential, but that our better team spirit might carry the day. We always believed in attack and decided that we should start the game with that attitude.'

Blanchflower had little time for cautious attitudes. His kind of football was gay and always thoughtful, and he loved probing the mental capacity of the opposition; invariably he was one move ahead of the rest. But at Wembley it was a switch to caution that won the day.

His perception had given Blanchflower an idea which he thought would shape the course of the game. England's general was Johnny Haynes, a master passer and an outstanding professional

Above *Ireland keeper Gregg clears from Tommy Taylor. The Irish defender is centre-half Jackie Blanchflower who had to mark both Taylor and Kevan—at the start of the 1957 international.*
Below *Left-winger Peter McParland leads an Irish attack during the early moments of the match.*

who had the ability to take complete charge. But Blanchflower, mistakenly, had noticed what he regarded as a flaw in Haynes' style.

'One of the most difficult passes to make is the one inside the full-back for the winger to run on to. At that time Johnny's play suggested that he was fascinated with the challenge of that pass and we decided to tempt him. Our full-backs were to encourage it by pretending not to be expecting it, but were ready to anticipate it when it was played.'

The theory was interesting if only because of its timing. At that period full-backs were only halfway towards remodelling their play after years spent pivoting on the centre-half. The pass inside the full-back was to become almost obsolete as defensive play became more organized. But on that day at Wembley it still carried a threat.

It was not the only thing Ireland had to worry about. England had great strength and much experience. They might even have gone forward to win the World Cup the following summer had they not lost the immense talents of Duncan Edwards, Tommy Taylor and Roger Byrne in the Munich air crash three months later.

Blanchflower set out to try and establish control in midfield—an area rapidly being recognized as the most significant area of play. He and Bertie Peacock, a neat, ambitious footballer from Celtic, concentrated on attack, hoping to disturb England's rhythm.

In doing this they left Danny Blanchflower's brother Jackie to cope with the threat of a twin English spearhead made up by Taylor and Derek Kevan. By the late sixties this would have been suicidal. But football was still wandering through the meadows of change, and Blanchflower was always willing to gamble.

'If we could get control in midfield then we could ignore the loitering Kevan. If we could not then we were liable to be ruined by it.'

They nearly were. England took over and Haynes' passes began to rifle through to Taylor and Kevan and the two wingers. When Blanchflower checked back to counter the threat, Haynes

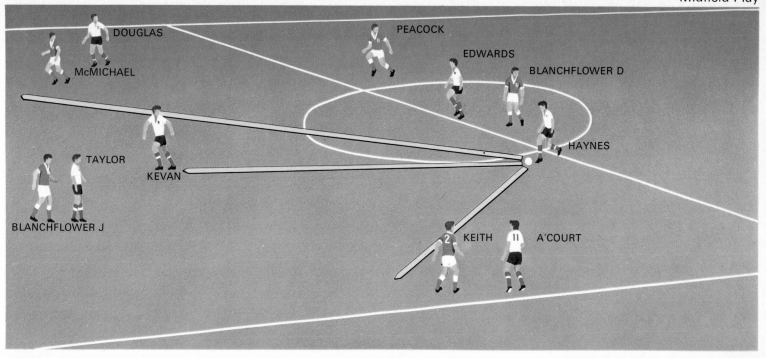

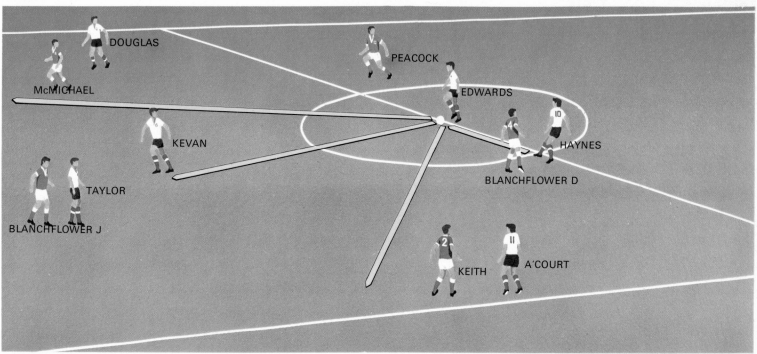

DIAGRAM

87

simply rolled the ball square for the powerful Duncan Edwards to plough forward.

Blanchflower was forced to readjust and to abandon his attacking ideals—an immediate decision based on what was happening at great speed around him. He pulled Peacock in tight to mark Kevan, and started to try to squeeze Haynes on the touchline so confining his passing angles and making them more predictable. It began to work, and confirmed Blanchflower's reputation as a gifted, thinking captain who could bring his intelligence to bear on a game even if it meant admitting a mistake.

But it was a penalty taken by Jimmy McIlroy after he had been brought down by Billy Wright and goalkeeper Eddie Hopkinson which gave Ireland the lead. McIlroy was an extremely talented inside-forward who played brilliantly for his country and his club, Burnley. He walked up, struck the ball against a post and watched it rebound into the net from the diving goalkeeper's back. Blanchflower recalls: 'One of the England players looked at me with fierce claims of luck burning in his eyes. I reassured him, "Brother, when we do it, we do it clever".'

'Ten minutes on top of 30 years seemed an awfully long time'

Early in the second half Alan A'Court equalized for England, but Ireland's system kept them well in the match and Sammy McCrory put them back in front. McCrory's selection had already given the game a certain poignancy. He had never played for Ireland before and he knew that he was unlikely to play again. He took his chance brilliantly before returning to the relative obscurity of Third Division football.

Billy Simpson's diving header from a Billy Bingham cross put the Irish further ahead before Duncan Edwards pulled one back for England. Ireland had to hang on for ten minutes and Blanchflower said: 'It suddenly seemed to me that ten minutes on top of thirty years was an awful long time.' But they held on and the place was alive with Irishmen at the final whistle.

The emotion of the moment may have obscured the fact that the Irish had won a great tactical victory. Their success was due as much to their instant planning as it was to the skills of their players, and the emphasis placed on regaining

ASSOCIATED PRESS

Above England defenders appeal for offside but Simpson's header counted as Ireland's third and winning goal.

midfield was a significant episode.

Haynes was one of the master players of his time and he had able lieutenants. Yet he had now been contained in midfield and it was to become clear that skill alone was not enough. Teams who chose to deploy two players in midfield found themselves outnumbered and West Ham had an interesting experience against Burnley in 1965.

Burnley had assembled their style around the thinking skills of Gordon Harris and Brian O'Neil. They combined well in the middle of the field even if they were occasionally caught too close together, and West Ham were fully expecting to see a familiar pattern. But Burnley had drafted another player into midfield, and it was West Ham who found themselves outnumbered. The answer was to withdraw one of their four attackers and a point had been proved.

It was not the first time West Ham had been forced to amend their strategy to cope with pressing problems in midfield. Preston troubled them in the 1964 FA Cup Final out of clever linking between Nobby Lawton and Alan Spavin.

Preston's system was strictly 4-2-4. West Ham's was similar but with Eddie Bovington, a combative wing-half, operating from a deeper defensive position than either of Preston's linkmen.

It left Ron Boyce to cope with the problem. He was continually by-passed, and at half-time it was decided that Bovington should advance to establish numerical equality. West Ham won the match because they won a critical battle in midfield, and the need to adjust to the demands of the moment in such a crucial area was to become a familiar

pattern.

The more perceptive managers had long recognized the need to have authority in this area. Arsenal had two outstanding half-backs, Jack Crayston and Wilf Copping, when they dominated English football in the thirties, and they were players of contrasting styles.

Crayston was elegant, Copping dour and intimidating. Later trainer to Southend United and Coventry City he recalled: 'My job was to get the ball. Jack's was to use it to good effect. We often found ourselves playing with three players in midfield because Alex James operated from deep positions.'

The ultimate refinement was to have midfield men who could dictate the pattern of team play. The deployment of three players became an accepted principle and Brazil discovered it by accident in Sweden. In the final of that World Cup in 1958 they found themselves under great pressure early on. It was then that Zagalo, their outside-left and ultimately their manager, chose to involve himself in defensive problems. For 20 minutes Brazil played 4-3-3 before most people had thought about it, and by adjusting to the demands of that game they forestalled a shock Sweden victory.

Both Danny Blanchflower and Mario Zagalo, within eight months of each other, had memorably emphasized two of the game's finer points. The midfield was a vital area, and tactical planning essential. But how the players reacted to the dictates of immediate situations was in no way less critical.

Coaching: Be prepared to adapt to solve problems in midfield

Players in midfield are likely to have more problems to solve than any other department. The fact that play is going on all around them, that they are deeply involved whether offensive or defensive play is going on, and that the ball is coming to them from all directions has a large bearing on the number of decisions that have to be made.

The battle is often one of numbers and spare players. To create an extra man in midfield and then carry him through is the aim of many teams. Assuming opposing teams are playing 4-3-3 formation, they both have a spare player at the back. Which player is free varies according to how the three players up front in the opposing team function. If one team plays with two central strikers and one winger then the opposing team have a full-back spare—if on the other hand they play with two wingers and one central striker then a central defender is spare.

Problems can be created in your team when this extra player moves forward into midfield. Immediately you are outnumbered, and if this happens often, the tide of the game will go against you. Your first thought must be to delay the play in order to give time for a front player to recover and help out or to allow the defence to re-adjust itself. Assuming it is the left-back who has moved

up, the idea is to make their spare player the man farthest away from the ball, who is their right-back. The three midfield players push across so that the right midfield player takes the left-back, if the right front player cannot recover. The other two midfield players push over leaving the opposing right midfield player to be picked up by the left front player. This then means that the opposing right full-back is spare, but in such a position that he can cause no immediate problem.

The best way to practise this situation is a team functional exercise into one goal, using one goalkeeper, four back defenders marking three forwards, three midfield players marking three midfield, and two forward players being marked by four defenders.

The teams line up so that the team with only two forward players are defending and so that they are just in the opponents' half of the field. The idea of the exercise is for the goalkeeper to kick a long, high ball down the middle on to the heads of the two central defenders. The two forward players move in to challenge passively so that the ball can be headed wide for the spare full-back to move on to. The problem is then there to solve.

Once you get the idea, play a proper game but use only two forward players to start with so

that a spare man can be established. Every time one of the goalkeepers gets the ball he can find the spare full-back with a throw. The midfield players will learn to cope with this problem and if they are encouraged to talk to one another the problems will gradually ease.

If your team is playing 4-3-3, and meets opponents playing 4-4-2, you will have midfield problems because four players outnumber three in midfield. 4-4-2 usually means that the two strikers play reasonably close together supporting one another and are marked by the two central defenders. Thus you can adjust in one of two ways; either bring back one of your front players to mark in midfield or push forward a full-back. Both methods have advantages and disadvantages. If the full-back moves up then the space behind him will be used by one of their two strikers because long balls will be played over the full-back. Your spare player is then the far full-back who comes round on the cover behind the two central defenders. If the front player is brought back, then an opposing back player can move up as a spare player.

Again you can practise what to do in such situations by creating the problems in training matches. But out on the field it is not only the adjustments that need to be performed skilfully, you must also be able to spot quickly the situations that need such decisions.

It is this ability to read the pattern of a game, as well as your own skills, that will make you a complete midfield player.

Attack in depth

The success of West Germany during the spring and early summer of 1972, when they almost arrogantly won the European Championship, made them undoubted favourites for the 1974 World Cup.

The most popular assumption was that the Germans had resurrected orthodox wing-play in a bid to penetrate defensive tactics which depended to a large extent on getting as many players as possible back behind the ball.

In fact it was much more subtle than that. Certainly the Germans used players who had a natural instinct for attacking along the touch-lines. But they used them to come from the middle of the field wherever they might be most effective.

In a fluid attractive way, Helmut Schoen had solved one of football's basic problems, how to build attacks. Many offensive movements at all levels of the game fail because the forward players position themselves 'flat', in a straight line across the field. This severely limits the area in which an attack can be constructed. A simplified version of the problem is given in Figure 1; if the three attackers remain in a straight line, progress will be limited even if they are supported from behind by players arriving from midfield. If the attackers interpass amongst themselves, they will not be able to progress from a series of square passes; the player who receives the ball can only play it square again or backwards. Any passes into the space beyond the three attackers will be easily swallowed up by the back defenders or the goalkeeper.

Real progress can only be made if movement

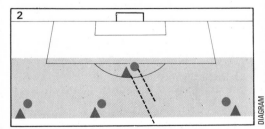

staggers the straight line and creates depth in attack. As Figure 2 shows, this immediately widens the area into which an attacking pass can be played. In the football of the seventies, it became harder for front players to shake off markers when they made forward runs. As Schoen's German team showed, there were greater percentages in urging midfield players to run positively from deeper positions, especially as it was easier for them to remain onside.

There was no better example in their play in 1972 than their vital second goal in the Championship final against Russia in Brussels. Herbert Wimmer broke from the middle of the field as Netzer slipped the ball to Heynckes. Heynckes stabbed it forward into Wimmer's path. His run

carried him clear of the Russian defenders and although the final shot was not struck with power it beat the Russian keeper Rudakov. Possibly he was as surprised as the other defenders at the devastating suddenness of Wimmer's sprint into forward space.

Coaches who used three and even four players across the middle of the field had to be confident that at least two of those players could break quickly to create depth in attack. It was equally important that these players could finish effectively when their forward running brought them chances.

Finding such players became a problem as a mood of caution settled over the game in the sixties. It became difficult to persuade the midfield men that they could safely abandon defensive roles when their team was in possession, and even someone as gifted as Bobby Charlton was often reluctant to do so.

When England were battling to win the World Cup in 1966, it was Charlton's job to break first when long passes were played forward to Geoff Hurst and Roger Hunt. There were times when Charlton did it well, others when he did not do it at all.

It was Alan Mullery's reluctance to do this which led to criticism of his play in Mexico four years later. 'Mullery will never push himself forward into a goalscoring position,' said Malcolm Allison, the Manchester City coach, when appearing on a television panel assembled to dissect England's performance.

But Mullery was to prove them all wrong with

Below Diagram of Herbert Wimmer's goal for West Germany against Russia in the 1972 European Championship final. Sprinting forward from midfield, Wimmer ensured that the German attack had depth and was not built up in a 'flat', straight line. Bottom Wimmer's left foot finishes the move.

NEWTON

MULLERY

MAIER

HURST

LEE

Above Alan Mullery reacted to criticism that he could not break forward and add depth to the England attack with this fine goal against West Germany in Leon during the 1970 World Cup. *Right* He started the move and arrived as the most advanced player to convert Newton's cross.

a marvellous goal in an ultimately fateful quarter-final against the West Germans in Leon. Oppressive heat and a demanding altitude had reduced the effectiveness of the tactic. For instance, Martin Peters found it difficult to maintain contact with the front runners while still functioning as an auxiliary defender.

But in this match both Mullery and Peters were to prove the value of running from a deep position to link up with attacks in the finishing area.

Mullery's goal in the first half was exceptional in that he began the move himself with a long crossfield pass into the path of right-back Keith Newton. From that point he kept running and he eventually arrived in the German penalty area to meet Newton's cross and beat Sepp Maier with a fierce drive into the roof of the net.

Peters' goal early in the second half was entirely in character as he 'ghosted' in on the far side of the German defence to slide in a centre from the opposite flank.

Such moments were rare simply because players became bogged down in the swamp of midfield play, fighting fierce battles for possession and settling for safe, short passes when they won the ball.

Colin Bell of Manchester City proved to be an outstanding exception. Bell waited a long time before he was given the opportunity to come to terms with himself as an England player. He revelled in activity. He had natural stamina and City allowed him to get involved in the flow of play, sensibly freeing him from a restricting role on one side of the field.

Bell scored many fine goals but there was no better example of his effectiveness when coming

from deep positions than in a match against Sheffield United in the spring of 1972. City were playing with enough conviction to suggest that they could emerge as League Champions, although it was Derby County who were to eventually take that honour.

Sheffield United had begun the season as popular recruits to the First Division. They had settled on a policy of attacking play as the most likely means of consolidating their newly-won promotion.

It worked. For a while they led the League and they led it long enough to make themselves secure from anxiety later in the season. By the time they played at Maine Road they had lost their momentum and teams who had attacked them discovered glaring defensive inadequacies. City exposed them again but it took a great goal by Bell to confirm their superiority.

It began when Mike Summerbee, another of City's England internationals, lured three United defenders to one side of the field. Summerbee

coolly waited for someone to break out into the avenue which United had left unguarded. The responsibility for blocking that channel rested with left-winger Scullion, and he was on his way back there when Bell began to sprint forward with the peculiar loping stride which made him such a distinctive player.

Scullion had seen the danger all right. But Bell was too quick for him as he drove himself forward onto Summerbee's square pass before going on to score with a typical flourish.

Another who could do this and finish with great power was John Hollins of Chelsea. Hollins never seemed to be entirely convinced of his potential. He came into the Chelsea team as a 16-year-old during Tommy Docherty's reign, and a high level of fitness and enthusiasm helped to keep him there.

Hollins played for England but he might have done so more often if his passing had been more imaginative. Nevertheless, he proved to be a highly effective midfield player and especially when he could be persuaded to hurry forward as an auxiliary attacker.

Chelsea manager Dave Sexton said: 'I want John to get into forward positions more often. He's got a good shot, he's strong and he's quick. If he puts himself in there, he is likely to pick up chances.' For a while Hollins did this well but there was no consistency of purpose, and it probably prevented him from breaking through as an England regular.

Alan Ball was an England regular and yet he found it difficult to score goals for his country. Ball did not really have the pace to free himself from the middle of the field quickly enough to be dangerous around the penalty area, and yet he was to score an important goal against Scotland at Hampden Park, in May 1972.

He was in fact making something of a comeback. For, three weeks earlier, he had wandered aimlessly around Berlin proclaiming his disenchantment with the game.

England had failed to recover from a 3-1 defeat by West Germany at Wembley and, although they saved face with a draw in the German city, they were out of the European Championship. Ball with his restless pride felt it more than most. This plus the disappointment of losing in the FA Cup Final to Leeds United diluted his enthusiasm for the game.

Sir Alf Ramsey recognized the symptoms. He left Ball out of the opening match of the British Championship against Wales at Cardiff and the little Arsenal forward was still on the substitutes' bench when Northern Ireland played at Wembley three days later.

But the big one was against the Scots. Ramsey and his England regulars were under pressure. Defeat in Glasgow would have amplified the criticism, and in many ways it was a mean match.

England ought to have won it easily. They had enough chances to score four goals, but it was left to Ball to take the one which mattered. For 20 minutes there had been more vicious tackles than intelligent passes. A goal was needed to dampen down the violence and it came when Ball set up a neat move on the edge of the Scottish penalty area.

Having begun it with a pass to Martin Chivers, he kept running to create a penetrating angle. When the ball came back to him he prodded it forward over the line. There was nothing exciting about that goal. But it proved again the value of pushing forward to extend the point of attack.

The Germans did it constantly. Wimmer, a splendidly direct runner, was their most penetrating player in the 1972 European final, his probing sprints from midfield devastating a well-organized marking system. It was an exciting throw-back in concept and the Germans with their eagerness to push players forward were pointing the way ahead.

Coaching: Improve the range of your team's attacking play

Generally there are two major attacking methods, individual attack, of which dribbling, feinting and shooting are the main weapons, and collective attack, which is based on the ability to interpass by kicking, heading and the essential ingredient of positioning to receive the ball.

Football emphasizes the need for collective attack because defensive tactics have developed to such an extent that they have limited the use of individual attack. This does not mean that there is no longer any use for such methods. If a player takes on a defender by using a team-mate as a decoy or a team-mate runs to take the covering defender away, creating a one-against-one situation, an individual is working within the tactics of collective attack.

There are a number of attacking principles which are interrelated and interdependent in successful attacking play, but the first and most important is that possession of the ball determines everything. Possession is dependent upon several factors which are bound by the passing abilities and positional sense of the players. Assuming the player in possession has the ability to pass accurately at the right time into the required space at the correct pace, he is relying on his team-mates taking up positions that enable him to use this ability.

If an attack advances in a straight line, the only way in which the ball can be passed to another player's feet is square. This severely limits the progress of the move. The purpose of positioning off the ball is to disturb the defenders, to exploit the open spaces or to be able to draw away from an opponent. This form of positioning, if done intelligently, will give you depth, and with it strength, in attack.

To give depth at least three players are required. If in a game the outside-right has the ball, the centre-forward should support him by making himself available in a forward position and the right midfield player should support him from a slightly backward of square position. This means that the outside-right has two immediate passing possibilities and the three players will find themselves in some form of triangular formation. With the quick movement of the game the nature of this triangle will change and may be pointing in any direction, but the flatter it becomes the less effective it will be. This will increase the risk of the pass being intercepted.

Three players interpassing the ball quite freely will help to cultivate the positioning technique. The idea here is for the three players to concentrate on maintaining the triangle whilst movement is taking place. Confine this activity to a 15-yard square and introduce one defender. The idea here is for the two players off the ball not to be caught hiding behind the defender. This can become competitive; if the ball is intercepted or goes outside the area, then the last player to have

touched the ball changes functions with the defender.

This practice should be the basis of your positioning technique and you should work hard at it, so much so that it becomes part of your training routine. For experienced players introduce another defender and enlarge the area so that you play three players against two defenders. The defenders take it in turns, changing functions when they have caused the three players to lose possession.

To make space and use it, and to be mobile and fluid, you must keep on the move. Keeping possession will be hard, and it is most likely to be lost by slow, haphazard positioning by the players off the ball. An even-sided game of keep ball in an area suited for the number of players in each team is excellent practice; make a target of so many consecutive passes which will count as a goal.

Although these are excellent practices to cultivate positioning, they do not encourage the principle of penetration which is vital in playing through defences. Play three players against two in an area about 15 yards across and 30 yards long. Set up a small goal at each end and the defending team must play a goalkeeper. When they gain possession, the defending team play the ball back to their goalkeeper whilst the attacking team send one player back to act as goalkeeper and change their functions to that of defenders. The goalkeeper of the team now in possession leaves his goal to make up three players attacking against two defenders and a goalkeeper. The attacking players must remember to maintain the formation of a triangle even though in moving about, the positions they take up have changed.

These movements can be brought into the game using a system of shadow play. A team of eleven players interpass the ball from one end of the field

and mount an attack getting in a finish without any opposition whatsoever. The coach can dribble the ball back so that the team are made to react as in the game by keeping cohesion. When he gets back to the team's defensive area, he loses possession to any player of his choice by passing to him. Immediately the team position themselves and show imagination in their build-up play by switching direction occasionally or going on a dribble past imaginary defenders. Each player must continue to position himself as he would in the game. Now introduce a few opponents who can be quite passive; they should not tackle but just make their presence felt. If they are given possession, by a bad pass or from their own goalkeeper, they are allowed to interpass the ball well into the other half where the team can then dispute possession and away they go again.

There are times during the game that the need for depth is all important. Such an occasion occurs when a player is moving along the bye-line just inside the penalty area. All too often players are over-eager to score; the attack rushes forward and usually flattens out. Such movement leaves the player in possession with only two alternatives, to shoot from a difficult angle or to centre the ball, which gives the defence an equal chance. If the attack moves with some depth, the player coming along the bye-line should have a player in an immediate supporting position to whom he could pull the ball back.

Flatness in attack is a common fault. If you realize the danger of being caught square to the man on the ball, you will add vital depth to your team's attack.

Below The Inter-Milan full-back, Giacinto Facchetti, broke from defence to score against Liverpool in the semi-final of the 1964-65 European Cup. The Inter system of play allows Facchetti freedom to move forward from the back. Because he is particularly adept at timing his runs into forward space, Facchetti adds a new dimension to Inter's attacking play.

The swerved pass from midfield

On the morning of Thursday 10 December 1971, English newspapers reported a competent if undistinguished victory in Greece which ensured that Sir Alf Ramsey's team would go forward to the quarter-finals of the European Championship.

A few hours earlier, while those reports were being printed, Ramsey had witnessed the form of a player who was to help shatter England's belief that they could win the competition.

As he sat watching the match between Borussia Monchengladbach and Inter-Milan in the European Cup on television in the lounge of a hotel outside Athens, he made glowing reference to the football of the West German midfield player Gunter Netzer. That night Netzer almost played the Italians on his own. And it was here that Ramsey saw for the first time his remarkable ability to stimulate attacks with long, swerving passes.

Ramsey muttered his admiration in front of the screen: 'He does everything. He makes things happen. I wouldn't like the job of keeping him quiet.' The comment was prophetic. Within six weeks England knew that they would face West Germany in a quarter-final inevitably charged with fierce nationalism.

Netzer was a new name to the British public. He had not played in the 1966 World Cup final, nor in Leon, Mexico, when the Germans had recovered to beat England during extra time. Yet he was 27, an international veteran with 25 caps who had played against England in a friendly at Wembley in February 1966.

Ramsey knew about him, and he was more than aware that here was a player who had matured out of all recognition in his late twenties. It had taken Netzer a long time to come to terms with the style and discipline called for by West Germany's team manager Helmut Schoen.

Now the chemistry was right. An injury to Overath had guaranteed Netzer an extended run in the national team. Schoen had supplied players who would run for his passes and Netzer's natural confidence and infinite passing skills put it all together in startling fashion.

Defenders are convinced they can clear until the ball curls away

One of his more destructive weapons was that swerving pass, bent into the path of a supporting colleague and with such marvellous accuracy that defenders remained convinced that they could cut the ball out until it curled clear of them at the very last moment.

After England had been put on one side, the Germans went on to contest the final stages of the competition in Belgium—where Netzer decisively confirmed the claim that he had thrust himself amongst the world's great creative players.

Drawn against the Germans in the semi-finals, Belgium chose to play the match in Antwerp, where they hoped that fierce local support would unsettle superior opposition. The Belgians were no fools. They had beaten Italy to qualify and they went at the Germans as though the ball was a secondary consideration.

It was left to Netzer and the superbly composed Franz Beckenbauer to calm it all down, and again they used curling passes to free themselves from the aggressive play which the Belgians mounted in the middle of the field.

Beckenbauer, confident to the point of arrogance, cut and screwed the ball as Netzer shuffled into position for the passes. Netzer, in turn, looked up and curled the ball over and around the burly, Belgian defenders. Gerd Muller's alert header when Netzer floated the ball forward gave the Germans a half-time lead, but there was no respite in a rugged second half.

It took a goal created for Muller by a beautifully weighted, curling through ball to bring the Belgians back to reality. Netzer was the architect. The final lay ahead. Now only Russia stood between the Germans and the championship of Europe.

British players are protected from subtlety by winter conditions

Netzer, his long, lank blond hair streaming out over oddly hunched shoulders, was to demonstrate his skills yet again—and never more vividly than with a 30-yard forward pass which curled delicately around a Russian defender to drop perfectly in front of Muller. For once Muller did not score and a great pass had been sadly devalued.

The Germans went on to win easily, leaving the rest of the world with a problem. The World Cup was two years away. The Germans would be playing at home. How could their football be contained?

Coping with the swerving pass was always a problem, especially for British players who were protected from its subtlety during the hard, damp months of midwinter when passes had to be driven.

Not that it was an alien skill. Colin Bell, Martin Peters, Bobby Charlton, Rodney Marsh, George Graham, Alan Hudson and Johnny Giles were among the accomplished First Division players who were willing to attempt a more devious line with their passes, and Giles in particular used them well. He would bend and curve passes that dropped in to the paths of Leeds front runners, Mick Jones, Allan Clarke and Peter Lorimer, with uncanny accuracy.

Some players used such passes badly, unnecessarily, ignoring the fundamental principle that a good pass presents the man receiving it with no problems of control. The best passes were always those played between two opponents, passes which put those opponents out of the game. Modern defences became so well organized that it was difficult to play such passes over distance with any hope of success. But the best defenders were least comfortable when the ball was angled across them and the pass which swerved presented particular problems.

Helmut Schoen, the German manager, said: 'When our players break forward they are simply putting themselves into space where they can be hit with the ball. They are relying on Netzer to get the ball to them. As long as they are running intelligently, he has the skill to find them. It doesn't matter that we give the ball away now and again. We get so much possession in our games that losing possession around the opposing goal isn't critical.'

While the Germans were emphasizing their quality in the early summer of 1972, there was no doubt that the Dutch had gained control of European club football. After winning the European Cup in 1971, Ajax of Amsterdam defended it successfully in 1972 and with much greater style than they had shown the previous

Top Diagram showing how a Martin Peters swerved pass, curled in from England's left wing, enabled his West Ham colleague Geoff Hurst to glance in the only goal of the 1966 World Cup quarter-final against Argentina at Wembley.
Above Hurst watches his header defeat goalkeeper Roma on its way towards putting England in the World Cup semi-finals for the first time.

year at Wembley.

A superbly confident and appealing team, they were stimulated by the play of two outstanding forwards, Johann Cruyff and Piet Keizer. Cruyff embodied all the qualities of the superstar; young, rich, successful, he could claim greatness and Arsenal were more than willing to support that claim.

Football League Champions in 1971, they were drawn against Ajax in the quarter-finals and immediately despatched a succession of coaches to spy on their Dutch opponents. Frank McLintock recalled: 'It seemed as though everyone in the club had been over to watch this lot. I was expecting the groundsman to come up and warn me about something they did. I knew so much about Cruyff that I felt as though I had been playing against him for years. We were grateful of course. No team has been better prepared for a match like that.

'But I'll tell you this. Even when you know what players are likely to do in certain situations, you can't always budget for them. Alright, free-kicks and corners, long throws, things like that. You can sort them out. But when you run into a Cruyff and you know what he's all about, he can still turn you over.

'Like he's great at this swerving cross when he attacks down his left. He takes players on at great speed and then he cuts the ball with the outside of his right foot. The keeper has got a hell of a problem then because the ball is curling away from him. If he comes out for it he can get stranded and if there is a player hanging out wide on the opposite side, it's curtains.

'We knew Cruyff would do this against us, but we couldn't prevent him from doing it.'

Cruyff was exceptional in that he could get the ball into the air with the outside of his right foot while moving at top speed. Tom Finney, a world-ranking England forward in the years following the Second World War, had a similar talent, but it was one generally more evident in the dryer climate of South America than in Europe.

Peters' perception puts him 'ten years ahead of his time'

European players found greater percentage in swerving the ball with the inside of the foot when playing it over long range, although Bobby Moore often came out of defence to strike passes along his left touchline with the outside of his right foot.

Martin Peters, with Spurs and West Ham, had such a deft touch that his skill when swerving the ball forward often went unnoticed by the public. He showed subtlety in his play even early in his lengthy international career. In the 1966 World Cup quarter-final against Argentina, his perceptive cross swung into the path of Geoff Hurst's run to the near post to create the game's only goal.

Sir Alf Ramsey had said of him: 'Peters is ten years ahead of his time.' That comment was to be used to ridicule Ramsey during the traumatic spring of 1972. But although he was to leave Peters out of the England team, he continued to argue in his defence: 'Peters is always attempting the "killer" pass. There aren't too many players around with that sort of confidence. He can get passes into areas which would be beyond most men.'

Those areas were not beyond Netzer as Europe's best defenders discovered while West Germany assembled the conviction that they could become champions of the world in 1974.

Above right West Germany owed much of their success in the 1972 European Championship to the ability of Gunter Netzer to swerve passes to quick running team-mates. The diagram shows one such move which brought Gerd Muller the vital second goal in the semi-final against Belgium.
Right Muller holds off a Belgian defender who has failed to control the spinning ball.
Inset right Muller turns away in triumph as Netzer's long-range skill again leads to success.

Coaching: Learn to curve your passes around defenders

All players must aim at being masters of the ball. Yet excellent situations may be wasted when, after controlling the ball, the selection or application of the pass has been poor.

The first and most important point is to judge what is on, the next is to make the correct selection as to which type of pass is best suited to the situation, then comes the application of skill. This is basic football, yet very few players have acquired sufficient skill. When such a player emerges, he stands out like a beacon in the night. Johnny Haynes has probably been one of the best passers of the ball in English football. Another has emerged in Germany, Gunter Netzer. He has the ability to use short and long passes with deadly accuracy and timing, but the pass that really puts him in a class above the top players is his ability to bend the ball into areas that straight passes would never reach. They are played with such accuracy that the swerve gives a definite advantage to the player the pass was meant for.

A short study of angles will help understand the value of such passes. Two players run down the left wing about 5 yards apart, the one inside and just slightly ahead acting as a defender. The player with the ball is behind them and about 20 yards infield. His object is to play the ball to the man on the outside so that it reaches him as quickly as possible and so that he can move on with it without checking. If the ball is kicked straight and is aimed, as it should be, to beat the defender on the inside, it will have to travel some considerable distance before the outside player eventually makes contact. This time lapse often gives another defender the opportunity to come across and intercept. This type of pass, to be a good one, must just beat the defender, because if you study the angles, the further the ball is played away from the defender the further it must travel before the player on the outside makes contact. Now think of the advantages the outside man will have if the ball is bent round the inside man when instead of the ball running away from him it is now coming in to him and away from the defender. Now we know that this is on and this is the best pass to suit the situation, application of skill is now the prime factor. Can you do what the situation demands?

To bend the ball to the left with the right foot, you must spin it in an anti-clockwise direction. You can do this by making contact with that part of your foot between the hub of your big toe and the side of the foot. Go out on to a practice ground with a friend, and, if possible, find a goal with space at the back so that you can stand about 30 yards apart with the goal in between. The object of the exercise is to bend the ball round the right hand post using your right foot. This practice will help cultivate the touch you need and you will soon begin to control the amount of spin. Remember to watch the ball carefully as you make an angled approach. Make contact with the right-hand side of the ball, below centre to get it off the floor, and straighten the leg just after contact; there must be a pronounced follow through slightly outside the intended line of flight. Obviously the more spin imparted on the ball the more vicious the bend will be.

Move on to practise finding a moving target. Both of you now stand on the same side of the goal, slightly wider than the posts and about 20 yards away from them. The one on the right has the ball, the player on the left makes a run towards the left hand post. As he nears this post, the player with the ball plays it so that it curls round the right hand post for the running player to move on to. Having done that, the player who has kicked the ball follows up so that again both players are on the same side, but this time they work back to their original position by changing functions.

The receiving player must concentrate on the ball in order to read the amount of spin, so that he can anticipate the reaction of the ball as it bounces. The player making the pass must concentrate on giving the ball in such a way that the receiver has an advantage. In order to do this it may be necessary to be able to bend the ball both ways, to be able to bend it early or slightly delay this action. This touch will come with practice and experience.

The longer pass which bends later in flight is an extremely useful ball to play from the wing position into the near post or up to a front runner who is running diagonally across aiming to get at the back of an opposing full-back. This longish kick is best performed with the inside of the instep. Again an angled approach is best because a full swing is necessary if you want to get a powerful follow through. The ball is struck with a firm ankle and slightly out of centre according to how late you require the bend.

Now work a functional practice with two small groups of players; one group stands just to the right of the centre and about 15 yards inside one half of the field. The other group stands with a ball each, about halfway inside the other half. The object here is the front players to make a diagonal run towards the left-hand corner flag and for the players with the balls to find that movement with a ball that bends rather late in flight; it should be aimed to drop in and run alongside the front player, making it easy for him to work the ball by either going on with it or checking and bringing it back so that he can attack the goal. Increase the number of players so that the front player is being marked. This is a real test of accuracy once the defender is allowed to be active.

An excellent practice which takes a little organizing is for eight players and requires an area of approximately half a pitch split into two zones. It is a game of four a side, but two attackers marked by two defenders must remain in each half of the pitch. The condition of the game is that it must start with a diagonal run and a ball bent into that run. From then on, it is a pure two against two in that zone. Whilst these four players are engaged with the play the four waiting at the other end must re-organize themselves so that the moment the defending two have gained possession at the playing end they are in a position to make their diagonal runs. This can be done in one of two ways, either one player stands on the halfway line and is ready to go in and support his team-mate who is making the diagonal run or both players can go on diagonal runs across one another. The defender in possession must then try to find the best of these runs.

This is very demanding physically so a third pair can be introduced on each side so that each pair can have a rest period and learn by watching from the outside. You are only a short step from increasing the number so that finally a complete game can be built up from the original exercise of one player going on a diagonal run receiving a swerved ball.

Once you have mastered the knack of swerving your passes, do not become obsessed with this technique; in most situations the straight, direct pass is the most effective move. But when the situation is right, the shrewdly swerved ball can open up any defence.

Below left A training routine for two players to improve the technique of swerving the ball. In turn they each curl the ball round the post into the path of the other's run. One of the advantages of the swerved pass is that, correctly used, it can make it easier for the receiver to control.

Below Bobby Charlton and inset Johnny Giles have dictated many games from midfield for Manchester United and Leeds United because of their ability to open up tight defences with curved passes. Even though the direct route to a colleague is covered they are able to find him by bending the pass.

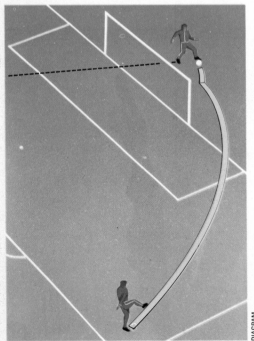

Left Diagram showing a free-kick routine which surprised Burnley in the early sixties. Burnley were one of the first sides to spot the value of planning for every situation, and they created a host of free-kick moves. But one they rejected, Spurs used against them—and scored.
Below left Jimmy Adamson (right) masterminded much of Burnley's originality at free-kicks.

Burnley speciality and a pattern for others to follow—especially ideas for kicks that worked the ball round the wall.

Jimmy Adamson, later to manage the club, was then Burnley's captain and he never forgot the lesson. He said: 'Alan would always encourage us to think. He wanted us to speak up if we had an idea and free-kicks were like champagne to us.' Burnley had small forwards at the time and it was pointless trying to play balls to them in the air. Going around the wall became a challenge and Burnley had more ways of doing it than most of their rivals. Adamson said: 'You name it and we had a plan for it. But the free-kick I remember most is one which Alan wouldn't wear until it rebounded against us in a match against Spurs.

'Jimmy McIlroy and I had worked this one out where the ball was knocked in to a runner from the other side. We set a player up to the left of the wall and he knew that the ball would be clipped in to him. His job was to play it off first time behind the defenders. The first man to move ran over the ball and off to the right. The next man took the kick. His job was to hit the target man and the target man's job was to help it on first time. The runner would collect the lay-off behind the wall. Alan had a look at it and decided that it was too complicated and that was that.

'We forgot about it until we ran into Spurs one day and they scored a goal with the very same move. Alan was big enough to admit that he had been wrong but although we tried it ourselves there was always something missing. It was no longer original and the Burnley team at that time was all about originality.'

Adamson and McIlroy— the inspiration behind Burnley's originality

With players such as Adamson and McIlroy around no one knew what Burnley might attempt next. Adamson said: 'People were giving more thought to the game and the first of the thinkers were bound to make an impression. The interesting thing was to go on a coaching course, to be there when players were asked to contribute. It proved that there was a wealth of ideas and our job was to encourage them.'

Free-kicks were fascinating because they created situations at which attackers knew where defenders would be, and they presented a rare opportunity of using pre-planned moves. Some wore out very quickly as they were recognized by shrewd observers but others lasted long enough to be decisive because there were players willing to work hard at them.

Getting around the wall was always a problem but some teams managed it and in this respect Burnley were outstanding. Chelsea developed the technique towards the latter stages of the sixties, and they benefited from the influence of Burnley.

Chelsea began the 1966-67 season by scoring a remarkable free-kick goal against West Ham at Upton Park. Three West Ham players, Bobby Moore, Martin Peters and Geoff Hurst had appeared in England's World Cup winning team the previous month and they were tuned in to subtlety and cunning. But they were left stranded when John Hollins struck a memorable goal set up for him by Bobby Tambling and Eddie McCreadie.

Tambling and McCreadie stood over the ball apparently arguing. Tambling had run forward as though to shoot, but McCreadie had appeared to distract him. As the discussions continued, Tambling suddenly slipped the ball through McCreadie's legs to the lurking Hollins. Hollins

Free-kicks around the wall

When Alan Brown looked back on his days as manager of Burnley he recalled a hesitant knock on an office door and a fresh-faced kid with a free-kick to sell. 'He just stood there,' said Brown, 'and I said, "Speak up" and he mumbled something about a way of getting round the defensive wall. He explained it and then began to back away. But I took him out where the first

team were training. I set it up and it worked. We used that free-kick in First Division football. It proved to me that everyone was worth listening to if they had something to say.'

Burnley were acknowledged to be among the forerunners in a new brigade of football thinkers and, particularly at set-pieces, they were full of ideas. Free-kicks within range of goal became a

STANDEN

HOLLINS (B)

McCREADIE

TAMBLING

HOLLINS (A)

DIAGRAM

could shoot with great purpose and he shot well enough to take a vital goal.

Five years later, in the autumn of 1971, Chelsea went close to scoring with another shrewd free-kick against Spurs at Stamford Bridge. Where Hollins had been the finisher he was now the decoy. Running to the left of Spurs' wall he left Alan Hudson to play the ball wide on the opposite side, and Peter Osgood, running sharply behind the wall, was just wide with a header.

Leeds had sent their assistant manager, Maurice Lindley, to watch that match and the move was not lost on him. When Chelsea attempted the move a fortnight later Paul Madeley was told to run with Osgood, and he cut off the ploy at birth.

Arsenal had an acute problem with thinking teams who were seeking space at free-kicks when

Jack Kelsey was their goalkeeper. A Welsh international, Kelsey had an eccentric approach to the problem of setting players up to block one side of his goal. Kelsey insisted that he should be able to see the ball from the moment that it was struck and that the wall should be positioned to guard the far post, whilst he covered the near post.

It was a contradiction of the theory that the roles should be reversed and he was instantly vulnerable when the ball was played in to an attacker who had sprinted on after running wide of defenders.

England in the 1966 World Cup attempted the very free-kick which rebounded on Burnley but it never worked properly. A lot depended on the initiative of the players involved and Danny Blanchflower had much to say on that subject:

Above Diagram of a Hollins goal for Chelsea against West Ham in 1966; decoy work at a free-kick set up a shot that flew wide of the wall.

'Good free-kicks are all about accuracy and confidence. If you haven't got the confidence to try them then you are wasting your time. When I was captain of Spurs we had something to suit every situation. We tried to go around the wall whenever we could and we had players who could pick up chances out of nothing. You can create the perfect opening but if there is no one to finish it then you are wasting your time.'

That charge could never be directed at Spurs in their double era and Blanchflower was the architect of some remarkable goals. He said: 'You need only to look at the faces of players who have been involved in a successful free-kick to realize

Coaching: Create routines for going round the wall

In football, teams have to work for their goals. Since the majority of goals are scored from within a 15-yard radius of the goal, the task must be to make chances for players in that area. These opportunities rarely come easily.

The chance to be able to place the ball down 20 yards or so from the goal when you are awarded a free-kick—knowing that opponents must be 10 yards away and cannot move until you have taken the kick—must be an ideal situation from which to plan the scoring of goals. You may only have a couple of free-kicks in each game, so perfection is vital and this can only be achieved through constant planning and practice during training sessions.

The principles involved are: surprise, either by keeping the opposing team guessing right up to the last moment or by taking the kick quickly before they have time to adjust themselves; simplicity, by keeping ideas as straightforward as possible, because the more players involved and the more passes made the greater the chance of breakdown;

complete understanding, with every player knowing exactly what is going on even though he may not be directly involved; timing of the movement, by constantly practising to get players into the right spaces at the right time. Accuracy is also obviously important because the ball must be delivered into the right place at the right pace at exactly the right moment. It may sound complicated, but if all the players understand exactly what each has to do and they have complete confidence in one another, the chances of success are high.

When free-kicks are awarded in or around the penalty area, the defending team will usually form a wall of players. A free-kick directly in line with the centre of the goalmouth would necessitate four or more players in the wall, but the number decreases with the increasing acuteness of the angle. A movement designed to get the ball round or wide of the wall is a basic way to destroy this defence.

To start with you need two players able to think

clearly and quickly under pressure to take the kicks. They must be able to read the variety of situations, which will be dictated to them by the positioning of the ball and the defenders. They must be accurate passers of the ball. If you have a player with a very powerful shot, he can be used if the ball is played wide of the wall. Many ways can be used to disguise your intention. The two players on the ball can chat, whilst one of them moves his body so that his back is towards the space to be used and his legs are open. The other player toe-ends the ball through the legs into the path of the third player. Alternatively one of the two players can place the ball, but as he walks over it he back-heels to set up the shot.

Another method is to place a colleague just in front of the wall. The two players taking the free-kick run at the ball, one behind the other. The defenders might think that the first one is going to run over the ball and the second one to play it. Instead, the first player plays the ball to the feet of the player standing in front of the wall and runs wide for a possible return. As he does this, the second player quickly moves wide the other side so that the player in front of the wall has two alternatives for a lay-off. Whichever one recovers the ball is now in a position for a

COLORSPORT

Above *Northern Ireland's Jimmy Nicholson cele-brates his goal against Russia in 1971—a 25-yard drive around the wall after a quick free-kick.*

the joy they get out of it. When you have worked at a thing in practice and it comes off in a game there is nothing quite like it. It's a thrill all on its own. You have put one over on the opposition when they have got time to prepare themselves. It troubles me when I see teams wasting free-kicks. They should always be attempting something.'

It was a tribute to defences in the late sixties and early seventies that fewer goals were being scored in situations which began with the ball dead and the initiative with one team. But Northern Ireland cracked the tough, unsmiling defence of Russia with a goal from just such a situation in a European Nations Cup tie in

October 1971 in Belfast. In Jimmy Nicholson, a Matt Busby product who had helped Huddersfield Town back into the First Division, the Irish had a player around whose power shooting free-kick ploys could be built. When a Russian defender was penalized on the Ireland left some thirty yards from the visitors' goal, the familiar wall was set up. David Clements tapped the kick wide to the wall's right into Nicholson's path. The midfield man drilled a low drive into the bottom left-hand corner of the net.

But as such goals became rarer Leeds manager Don Revie said: 'If we lose a goal at a free-kick, if the opposition get around our wall, then I want to know why. We should not be surprised because our observers are trained to spot every possibility.'

Nevertheless such moves sometimes worked and

the general scarcity of goals meant that no idea was discarded until it was proved to be totally unproductive, although the televising of matches made many ideas out-dated quickly.

Alan Brown always had his door open when at Burnley and anyone was entitled to have his say, and football had become a game for thinkers. Malcolm Allison, appointed Manchester City's team manager in November 1971, said about the general philosophy of free-kicks:

'Deception, disguise, false running, false calling, general hustle and bustle will hide the most obvious plans. Attackers have the advantage. They are bound to be moving first. Defenders must be moving more slowly. Think about it.'

A lot of teams did, chances were made, and sometimes goals of undoubted satisfaction to the participants were scored as a result.

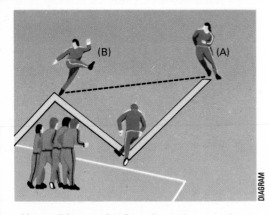

DIAGRAM

Above *Diagram showing a free-kick move using an attacker in front of the wall. All free-kick plans should be continually practised in training.*

first-time shot.

A third method again involves the two players on the ball. One walks towards it and on a pre-arranged signal, like on the fourth step, the second player pushes the ball past him and wide of the wall for him to sprint on to and shoot at

goal with power and precision.

Your winger may be quick off the mark, so get him to stand almost level with the wall and fairly wide. Invariably he will be marked by the opposing winger, but the attention of the defenders can be diverted if one of the two players on the ball suddenly runs past the other side of the wall calling for the ball. The ball is then played for your winger to run on to and have a crack at goal.

If their winger does come back to mark your winger then your full-back is often spare. Now if your winger runs quickly across the wall taking the player marking him away, your full-back can move quickly into the space left as the ball is played. He should now be in a position either to carry on for a shot or get a cross in behind the wall.

With all of these ideas only two or three players are directly involved. The remaining players, knowing what is going on, should make sure that the space to be used is left vacant and that they always move in quickly to follow up the movement or shot in case there is a ricochet or a post is hit.

The best way to introduce the ideas into your team is first to discuss which methods are to be used and which players are going to be involved.

Work on one idea first. Walk over it without a ball so that players can concentrate on co-ordinating the movement. When this is right, work with a ball, again moving very slowly to get the timing. Gradually, increase the pace until you are work-ing at match tempo. Discuss alternatives in case a defender is marking the space you wish to use. Introduce this in exactly the same manner. Find a simple way to communicate to the other players so they know which idea is to be used, like number-ing the routines. From this one situation, you may work on several alternatives catering for all eventualities, so no matter how the opposing team arrange their players you have a plan to beat them.

Having worked at these during training sessions and gradually built up your plans, play an occasional re-start game when the coach awards free-kicks when and wherever he wants. The defenders may know what is going on so they must act passively. Remember at this stage you are working at all the principles except surprise, which will only come when you have developed a complete understanding and when you are play-ing against strangers.

Then, when it matters, in a proper game, your industry will pay the right dividends.

Free-kicks through the wall

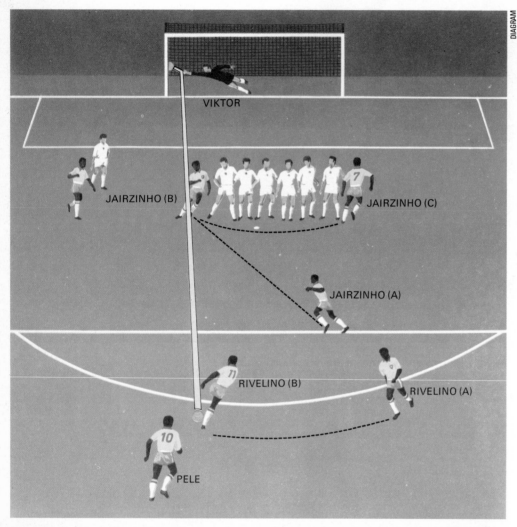

Having opened their campaign in the 1970 Mexico World Cup with a cautious yet quietly convincing victory over Rumania, the England players and their manager, Sir Alf Ramsey, found themselves suddenly confronted with a problem that demanded immediate discussion and ultimately a decision.

As they gathered for breakfast around the swimming pool of the Guadalajara Hilton Hotel on the morning of 4 June, there was one topic of discussion—Brazil's opening match in the tournament against Czechoslovakia the previous day.

Brazil had won in spectacular style, scoring four exciting goals, although their porous defence had allowed the East Europeans to take an early lead. But one aspect of the Brazilians' play dominated the early morning chatter of the England players—their murderous use of free-kicks awarded within range of goal.

It took Brazil only 24 minutes to reveal their gift of exploiting set-piece situations. They still trailed 1-0 because of their leaky defence. But in that 24th minute they fashioned a goal of cunning and impertinence.

Pele, his appetite for international football revived, was brought down as he tried to manoeuvre across the penalty area, and the Brazilians gathered in animated discussion and elaborate gesture.

The Czechs nervously pulled each other into a protective screen. In the thin air of Mexico the ball would travel at great speed and swerve would be more pronounced. The Brazilians had the talent to take advantage of it.

Pele shaped up to take the kick himself, as a six-man line of Czechs braced themselves for the impact, with goalkeeper Viktor fidgeting on his line.

The wall was correctly set, guarding the area from the centre of the goal to the post nearest to where the kick was to be taken.

How a series of insolent inventions startled keepers in important internationals

The last man on that side overlapped the post by the full width of his body, and it seemed that the Brazilians would have to try and take advantage of the fact that only four opponents were left outside the wall to deal with a pass played across goal.

But the Brazilians had something more subtle —and certainly more deadly—in mind. While Pele was engaged in distraction by chatting eagerly to Gerson, Jairzinho crept in to attach himself to the wall at the point where Viktor was responsible for the safety of the goal.

The preliminaries were over. Rivelino, one of the new stars, suddenly sprinted at the ball almost at right angles and struck a savage, swerving shot straight at Jairzinho.

Jairzinho leaped aside, and the ball swept on to find the net just inside Viktor's right hand post.

It could legitimately be argued that Viktor's positioning had been poor, but Jairzinho's presence at the end of the wall had undoubtedly been a distraction. It was a move of killing quality.

In fact, Brazil had not cornered the market on this ploy. Peru had scored a similar goal against

Above left Diagram of Rivelino's goal from a free-kick in the World Cup match against Czechoslovakia in 1970. Jairzinho was the key player. While the Czech wall were wondering whether Pele would take the kick, Jairzinho joined the end of the wall. Rivelino made a deceptively oblique run in to take the kick, and as he shot Jairzinho leapt aside. The ball crashed into the net.
Left Goalkeeper Viktor's view as the shot passes through the wall. Rivelino is fifth from the right.

Bulgaria 24 hours earlier, and it was significant that the Peruvians were managed by the former Brazilian forward, Didi, master of the swerving free-kick in the Brazil World Cup winning sides of 1958 and 1962.

The England players had seen both those goals, and the two who showed most concern were goal-keeper Gordon Banks and captain Bobby Moore.

Moore said at the time: 'We rarely use more than four players in the wall because we feel that it would leave us vulnerable if the ball is switched across goal. If we had five players in the wall, our other defenders would be outnumbered if the free-kick is passed to another attacker. Normally, we can confidently keep to four because of Gordon Banks' sound positioning and agility.

'On the other hand these people present special problems because of their skill at bending and dipping the ball. We mustn't leave Banksie with

Above Rivelino prepares to take another free-kick in the 1970 World Cup final against Italy. Jairzinho has attached himself to the wall, and is now covering part of the goal. He has only to step aside and Rivelino's shot has an unobstructed route to the left-hand side of the net. However, on this occasion the move was thwarted by the wall.

Right Joining a wall is not always an easy matter. Alan Birchenall meets strong resistance from a determined line of Arsenal defenders.

Above Diagram of Brazil's goal against England at Wembley in 1963 from a long-range free-kick. England's three-man wall was not enough to stop Pepe's left-footed shot 'bending' in on goal.

Below Banks stands transfixed as Pepe's swerving free-kick from 35 yards completely deceives him. It was Brazil's only goal of the game, and England managed a 1-1 draw with the 1962 World Champions.

too much to do or it could be fatal.'

The basic principle of disrupting players gathered to prevent a direct shot at goal was not new. But in the Mexico World Cup, where physical contact was discouraged and consistently penalized, the plan took on more potency.

In Europe, for instance, a player standing within touching distance of marshalled defenders was unlikely to emerge with less than a bruised back and scarred calf muscles. In Mexico, it was different. Penalty-kicks were likely to be given for less.

It was Moore who made the major contribution —Moore, out of his skill and experience, who produced the most effective counter when England faced Brazil the following Sunday.

It was clear from their opening game that the Brazilians would work unceasingly to create situations which would encourage unwary referees to award them free-kicks in shooting positions.

Eusebio, the famed Portuguese forward, had employed a similar tactic when playing for Benfica against Manchester United in the 1968 European Cup final. Pele, who used to collapse in disgust at the heart of a dribble, had long since mastered the art of winning free-kicks.

No one, however, could doubt the legitimacy of a free-kick awarded against Terry Cooper when he drilled Jairzinho down just outside England's area.

Jairzinho rose from the scurrying attentions of Brazil's trainers to take his place at the end of the wall, as he had done against the Czechs, with the charade going on around him.

Once again Rivelino ran at right angles to strike a shot of wicked design. But, as Jairzinho leaped aside, he merely uncovered the unruffled figure of Moore standing behind him.

As the shot bored through, the England captain killed it as though he was dealing with a ball of cotton wool, moved forward and found Martin Peters with the calmest of passes.

Banks said later: 'After talking about it, Bobby decided that he should accept responsibility for tucking in behind the end of the wall. It meant that I would be even more unsighted, but it was worth taking the chance because of Bobby's confidence and skill. They didn't try it again, did they?'

Because of their special talents, the Brazilians have emerged as the outstanding exponents of free-kick situations, and there is more than one outstanding example of their success.

They achieved little that was memorable in their general play in 1966. Their squad was badly selected and totally discouraged by the physical play they knew would be allowed in Europe.

Nevertheless, they scored two outstanding free-kicks against Bulgaria, one from the incomparable Pele, the other from the immensely gifted Garrincha in his last World Cup.

When faced by only four players in the Bulgarian wall, Pele jumped clear of the floor to get the spin he needed to beat goalkeeper Naidenov with a vicious low curve.

Garrincha's effort was even more spectacular, confirming the extent of instinctive skill which made him one of the greatest forwards seen in the game. From 25 yards the Bulgarians were entitled to feel safe. They were not. Garrincha not only struck the ball with great hostility but managed to impart a prodigious swerve that changed the direction of the shot by several feet. When it entered the net Naidenov could be named among the spectators.

When England met Brazil at Wembley in 1963, Ramsey, in his first year as team manager, warned the young Banks of the danger which could come from skilfully flighted free-kicks.

Banks was warned and alert—but still beaten by Pepe's curving shot

But Banks was convincingly beaten when Pepe struck a curving shot behind the keeper's right shoulder.

With goals harder to come by in the sixties, every team turned to the possibility of scoring from free-kick moves and the simplest of them proved the most effective.

If the defenders chosen to stand in the wall have been well selected, if they are consistently willing to stand firm in the face of the fiercest shot, there is little chance that the wall will be broken.

So the attackers turn to deception. From the Brazilians' point of view in Mexico it was important that Jairzinho detached himself at the right time, and that Rivelino struck the ball with utmost power and reasonable accuracy.

Yet, in the Football League, few players have chosen or been allowed to choose such extravagant methods at free-kicks. Every team has its ploys, but no one has followed the example of Terry Venables while playing for Chelsea in the sixties. In a European competition match, Venables was faced by the inevitable wall of defenders. They were less than the stipulated ten yards from the ball. With histrionic irritation, Venables began to pace out the proper distance. After seven paces he met the wall and pushed his way through it. The wall parted. 'Now, John,' he yelled to John Hollins. Hollins pushed the ball through the split wall, and Venables slammed it into the net.

The referee, who had blown for the kick to be taken, awarded the goal—while the Chelsea players collapsed in laughter at Venables' cheek.

It is this sort of inventiveness at free-kicks that characterized Brazil's play in post-War international football. Every opponent they met devised ways of countering them, but consistently Brazil came up with new ideas. British teams invent, but rarely succeed. The skills are not lacking, but perhaps their insolent application is. Or it may be that, in home football, defenders are simply too knowing to be fooled.

Coaching: Develop the cheek to try and pierce the wall

At all levels of football free-kicks on the edge of an opponent's penalty area provide chances to score—if the attack is well organized. The opposition will line up a wall of defenders, and to get a shot at goal the wall must be evaded. The wall can be beaten by going over the top—by chipping the ball, and by going around it—passing to a colleague wide of the wall who can have an unobscured shot at goal. The attacker-in-the-wall method is a classic way of getting the ball *through* the wall.

The move has three basic elements—getting the attacker into the wall, timing his movement out of the wall, and directing the shot through the gap that has been made.

Before considering the use of this tactic in your team, you must have a player who has this ability to direct his shot accurately. Again, the best practice is making a mark, some two or three feet square, on a wall or a fence and hitting the ball at this mark from a distance of 20 yards. Kick the ball with the instep, and keep your ankle firm.

Before you start, drop the ball from your hands and kick it before it hits the ground; this will give you the feel of how you should kick the ball. By keeping your ankle firm you will bring the right muscles into play. Now place the ball on the ground, as though it was a free-kick. Keep your eye on the ball at the moment of impact so that you make contact with the part of the ball intended. Keep the knee over the ball to keep the shot low and, after you have made contact, follow through. Practise this until you can hit this target at will—remembering you are after both speed and accuracy.

When you have become proficient at hitting a hard, straight drive at the target, you can move on to develop a swerve into your shot. This will add to the goalkeeper's problems. To make your shot swerve, you are aiming to impart spin on to the ball without any loss of power. Kick around first with a plastic ball; this will swerve more than a proper football, but it will give you the feel of swerving a ball. Then place the proper ball on the ground so that any three adjoining panels vertically face you. If you are aiming to hit a straight shot at goal, you will be trying to make contact with the middle of the three panels. Assuming you are right-footed, the ball will swerve to the *right* if you hit the *left-hand* panel, striking the ball firmly with the outside of your instep. It will swerve to the *left* if you strike the *right-hand* panel with a full instep.

Practise swerving the ball at your target. It will be difficult and require hours of patient work, but an ability to swerve a ball will pay many dividends in all aspects of play as well as in the taking of free-kicks.

In this particular free-kick, the problem is to get a team-mate, or perhaps two, into the wall. Defenders will not like the idea of attackers standing in or with their own wall, but it is not against the laws of the game—unless, of course, they push their way in. The easiest and most successful way is to have your attacker so close to the defenders that, on a signal, he can attach himself to the *end of the wall*—just before the kick is taken. This will give the defenders no time to re-orientate themselves, and will distract the goalkeeper, whose view of the ball will be obscured by the attacker. Timing is vital. If the attacker moves too soon the defence will have time to readjust; if he moves too late, the whole move breaks down. The same sort of timing is necessary when the attacker detaches himself from the end of the wall. If he goes too soon the gap he has created will be covered; if he goes too late he is likely to block the shot himself.

Practise the timing by going through the free-kick routine with stationary defenders. When you have mastered this, make them active, and continue to practise until every player knows what is expected of him. Only by total understanding will the move succeed.

When, and only when, you have proficiently performed the move in this exercise, move on to a 'game-situation' practice. Start playing training matches exclusively for practising free-kicks. Whenever the ball, during the course of play, is just outside the penalty area tell the referee to blow for a free-kick. Then try your routine of putting an attacker in the wall. This time it is not a static practice shot. In the context of your training game, you have only this chance to get it right, and score a goal. It will be good practice too, for defenders as well as attackers. You will be surprised at how players, who have mastered their play in the static practice, forget things when the situation they have been practising occurs in a game. By working out these problems in a training game, these players will perform more reliably when the free-kick situation occurs in an official match.

You will probably have other free-kick plans worked out, as well as the ploy of putting an attacker in the wall. Give each idea a number, so that, whenever you get a free-kick in your training game, the player taking the free-kick can let his team-mates know which tactic he wants to use, by calling out this number.

Repeat your practices so that, when a chance comes in a game, you are prepared.

Below A guide to swerving the ball. It will swerve in the direction of the arrows if you make right-footed contact with the marked, orange panels.

Below Fritz Walter of Germany swerves his shot around an unconventional Turkish wall during the 1954 World Cup. Germany won the match 4-1.

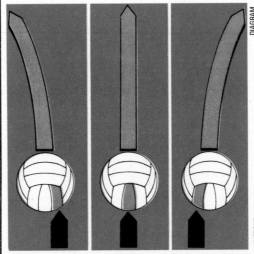

PELE GARRINCHA

NAIDENOV

ALCINDO

JAIRZINHO

DIAGRAM

Free-kicks over the wall

ASSOCIATED PRESS

Brazil's spectacular success with two free-kicks against Bulgaria in their opening game of the 1966 World Cup reinforced the popular belief that the reigning world champions could successfully defend their crown in England.

Shrewd observers felt otherwise. Among them was Malcolm Allison, coach to Manchester City and enough of a gambler to bet against the Brazilians when they appeared in their next group game against Hungary.

Allison, who had watched the Brazilians in training, said confidently: 'They don't look right. They don't look fit. Some of them seem to be playing from memory.'

His doubts were to be vividly borne out as the champions failed to qualify and went home in tearful disgrace. Yet in that opening game they had managed to conceal the cracks in their morale and strategy from an adoring public.

Brazil came to England with a deserved reputation for killing free-kicks. But it was their second goal against Bulgaria that added a new dimension to their repertoire. Pele had already sent a slicing shot wide of the line of defenders past keeper Naidenov, when right-winger Garrincha rose from a butchering tackle to confound defensive theories. He swerved the free-kick in at the near post over the top of the wall.

Garrincha, with his legs bowed in parallel, looked to be a grotesque parody of an athlete. But there was an astonishing overdrive built into the deformity of his physique and he could perform prodigious feats of ball control.

By the time he appeared in England he was well past his best. Almost illiterate and unable to cope with the adulation heaped upon him at home, Garrincha was about to fade into the colourful folklore of Brazilian football.

But he left Merseyside with something to remember in the 64th minute of an undistinguished match. From nearly 30 yards he struck the ball with great venom and cunning, the wall in front of him set some three yards along from the angle of the penalty area.

The ball carried over the Bulgarians, swerved wickedly in flight and found that part of the goal which had looked to be least vulnerable. It was an astonishing goal which confirmed the theory that it was no longer possible to erect a completely efficient barrier against the more skilful and imaginative takers of free-kicks. Garrincha had gone over the wall, a feat which was beyond the majority.

Coaches had long since decided that it was suicidal to offer professional players a free sight of goal anywhere below 30 yards range.

Professionals clubbed the ball so powerfully that if they were on target even the best goalkeepers were struggling.

The answer was a human barrier which closed off the area between the centre of the goal and the upright nearest to the line of shot. The goalkeeper's main responsibility was the other half, that part which could be opened up by a square pass or threatened by a delicate chip.

In most cases the technique was effective enough. But there were players with the wit and the confidence to try and exploit the unexpected. One of them was George Cummins. A wiry southern Irishman, he entered First Division football with Everton but was to play with rare distinction for Luton Town in the late fifties.

Cummins' main assets were his dribbling skills and a marvellous left foot. He was expert at floating passes forward through the air and with a better temperament might have made a much greater impact on his times.

It was in a game against Manchester United at Luton that he was to demonstrate his mastery of the ball. United's defence gathered themselves quickly when Luton were given a free-kick just outside the penalty area.

They went through the pattern which had become familiar. The wall was set to overlap

102

HARTFORD　　CANTELLO

STEPNEY

ASTLE (B)

ASTLE (A)

DIAGRAM

NO PORS

GEOFF WRIGHT

Opposite top *Garrincha added a new dimension to Brazil's considerable repertoire of free-kicks when he sent a vicious curving shot over the wall against Bulgaria at Goodison Park during the 1966 World Cup finals.*
Opposite centre *The Bulgarian wall turns in disbelief. The wall was set to cover the near post and Garrincha's swerve had defied it.*
Above *In 1972, the West Bromwich Albion midfield pair, Len Cantello and Asa Hartford, devised a way of lifting the ball over the wall in two stages. Against Manchester United, Cantello lifted a free-kick into the air with his toe and Hartford struck a dipping volley over the line of defenders. Alex Stepney, covering the other side of the goal, could not reach the shot and it struck the underside of the bar and bounced out.*
Left *But centre-forward Jeff Astle had followed up alertly and he headed in the rebound. The goal was a fine example of the surprise value of going over the wall—if the ploy is performed with skill and imagination.*

goalkeeper Harry Gregg's near post and other defenders moved about quickly to counter the possibility that Cummins would attempt to chip the ball into an unguarded space around the far post for someone to try a header.

Cummins had something much more devious and astonishing in mind. As Gregg crouched, wary not to position himself behind the wall where he could not cut off an angle, Cummins strode forward and chipped the ball over the wall and into the goal. Gregg could not believe it had happened. Not only had the shot cleared a line of tall defenders and still dipped under the bar, it had actually bounced before the line as it carried on to the back of the net.

A quick analysis of the feat showed that the angle of trajectory had been quite unbelievable. The ball had cleared the wall and dropped at a sharp angle in the space of some 20 yards. Cummins, who never repeated the feat in a competitive match, was to say:

'I always knew that it was possible. But until that day I had never succeeded in getting enough backspin. You are trying to get the ball to stand up straight. Golfers do it with a club with a face which is almost at right angles to the shaft and a sharp edge. In training I had been able to get the ball down far enough to creep

under the crossbar.'

Cummins had a rival. Tommy Harmer, a superbly talented but criminally underrated inside-forward, had never been able to establish himself as the player he could have been.

A brilliant ball artist, he was never guilty of being obsessed with his touch. But a frail physique discouraged Spurs from using him as a regular first-team player and he eventually drifted on to play for Watford in the Third Division.

Chelsea, looking for someone to inspire their young players, brought him back to big-time football and he was to score the goal which guaranteed Chelsea's return to the First Division when they won at Sunderland in the last but one game of the 1962-63 season.

Harmer's ball skills were a constant source of astonishment for young Chelsea players who were proud of their own talents. Terry Venables was to say: 'You felt you could do special things with the ball until Tommy got under way. He was in a class of his own. But he didn't want to show off. He was a thinking player. Skill for skill's sake didn't appeal to him at all.'

What did appeal to Harmer was the challenge presented by an urgent discussion during a training session at Stamford Bridge.

Chelsea were uncertain about a goal they had

conceded at a free-kick. They felt that maybe goalkeeper Peter Bonetti had been stationed too near the middle of the goal and that he could afford to move a fraction nearer his far post.

The near post was an area for the magicians in the game and the Chelsea players felt that it was impossible for any player to score here. Harmer, already changed into his street clothes, listened with great interest. 'What do you think, Tom?' asked one of the Chelsea players. 'I don't know,' replied Harmer as he shuffled forward, nervously chewing the fingers of his right hand.

It was a characteristic habit. An outward expression of the man's examining mind. The ball rested where the coach had left it. Harmer approached it at an angle, drove a black leather shoe down sharply and watched helplessly as the ball dipped viciously over the wall and carried into the goal.

Harmer turned away, almost embarrassed by his success, barely noticing the admiring looks of his young colleagues. He was that sort of man. One or two sceptics in the bunch of spectators questioned the feat as a fluke. Harmer, still embarrassed and chewing his fingers, replaced the ball and scored again.

Few players could have equalled that skill, but in the early seventies in the Midlands two notable attempts were made to get the ball over the wall in two stages. At Coventry, midfield player Willie Carr flicked the ball up donkey-style for team-mate Ernie Hunt to volley over the wall and into the Everton net in October 1970. It was a move later to be outlawed by the International Board who ruled that Carr had not kicked the ball in the accepted sense of the word.

But early in 1972 Len Cantello and Asa Hartford of West Bromwich Albion scored against Manchester United at the Hawthorns using a legal variation of the Coventry move. Cantello lifted the ball by stabbing his toe beneath it. Hartford hit the volley. The ball flew over the wall and dipped enough to strike the United crossbar. Jeff Astle, alert for such an opening, followed up to nod in the rebound.

In volleying, backspin can be imparted to the ball to make it dip and swerve even over short distances. Once the ball has been lifted into the air, the problem of propelling it over the defensive line and down under the bar lessens considerably.

Yet players rarely showed the inclination to gamble on what seemed to be long odds. A much more common tactic was to try and lift the ball over for another player drifting in behind the wall. It was no longer necessary to think about pace or accuracy. It was no longer a chip but a lift with the end of the toe—a more exaggerated version of Cantello's stabbing movement.

Danny Blanchflower and then Martin Peters used it for Spurs, and Chelsea would send Peter Osgood in sharply from the far side of goal to connect with a ball lifted over the wall by the alert and skilful Alan Hudson.

It was still a very special talent, one that bordered on the realms of amazing. Those who could perform it were not forgotten in a hurry, especially by defenders deceived by the ploy.

Coaching: Vary your team's free-kicks by going over the wall

It is possible to dip and swerve a ball directly from the ground and over the defensive wall accurately enough to beat a goalkeeper, although it requires a high degree of skill.

This kick is performed by striking the ball firmly with the inside of the toe with the foot pointing forward. This action, when the ball is struck on one side rather than dead centre imparts a tremendous spin which will make the ball swerve. If the ball is struck with the inside of the right toe, the ball will spin anti-clockwise and swerve to the left. It is possible, with a pronounced follow through, after a very angled approach, to impart some top spin as well which will cause the ball to dip in flight. This means that you are able to play a ball firmly into the top corner of the goal, over the top of the wall and away from the goalkeeper.

Before you go rushing off to practise, you must realize that it will take a long time before you are proficient enough to attempt this in a game. If you are unsuccessful in a match and the percentages are against you, you may have wasted a situation which could have been utilized more reliably with another method.

This is a good method to practise on your own. Hang a tracksuit top from the crossbar up in a corner and see if you can get the required movement in the air and hit the target. Try it against the wind and you will see it move a lot more. Keep this one up your sleeve until you are reasonably sure of success.

Coventry City found another method of getting over the wall. They got a player to donkey-kick it upwards by grasping the ball between the ankles and back-flicking it into the air. Another player prepared himself to volley the ball, as it was coming down, over the wall into the top corner of the goal. Several other teams had tried this by flicking the ball in the air using the toes of one foot. This without any doubt has distinct possibilities because a full volley using the full instep can be hit powerfully and be violently dipped in the air. The donkey-kick is now illegal but practise lifting the ball with your toe. Also work on the full volley by throwing the ball in the air, allowing it to bounce then striking it firmly with the instep before it bounces again. Move on to work with a partner and try to co-ordinate both movements. Of course it is difficult, but again, very little is possible without dedicated practice.

Apart from the direct shot, it can also be profitable to lift the ball over the wall to a team-mate. Some teams afford cover to this area behind the wall but often they do it at the expense of covering another area. It is well worth organizing methods of getting into this vital space.

This can be done in several ways, but it all depends on the player who is chipping or lifting the ball over the top. Place a player on the end of the opponents' wall; as the ball is flicked over all he has to do is turn and he is on to it ready to volley it home.

Instead of standing on the end he may be walking slowly to be first on the ball behind the wall. This can then be done as a decoy movement. One player stands on the end of the wall whilst another player stands wide of the ball. On a signal, the one standing wide of the ball runs quickly across the front of the wall away from the player standing on the end of the wall. This can distract attention away from this player who, when the ball is chipped over, is free to turn and get on to the ball. Remember you will be offside if you are level with the back defender. Just take a quick look along the back to make sure you are onside.

This can lead into another method, with the use of two players acting as a decoy for one another. These two players stand some 7 yards to the side of the ball, one on each side so that they are about 14 yards apart; they will probably be quite loosely marked. On a signal they run and cross over in front of the wall making for the areas to the side and behind the wall. The player on the ball selects which player is most likely to have the best chance and plays it over the wall to him.

The ball played over the wall and towards the far post can be very difficult to clear and can give an excellent chance of a goal. The players off the ball must stagger their positions outside the far post but no one should be so far out that he cannot make the six-yard box to meet the ball. Instead of chipping the ball at the far post which could be an easy ball for the goalkeeper to collect, play it very firmly. The idea here is for the players off the ball to get in front of the opponents marking them. Theoretically, if they miss it, so will the player marking. If three players can stagger their approaches they will get in first, and the odds are that one will make contact. All that is required now is a deflected header past the keeper. They may have to be brave and dive for the ball. Providing the running is well-timed and the ball is accurate, a very definite threat is laid at your opponents' goal.

Your team may prefer to work your free-kicks wide of the wall or even find a way through it, but if you have a few routines for going over the wall you are widening the scope of your attack.

Even though the percentages are against you succeeding if you strike directly at goal, this chip into the top corner over the wall may well catch unwary opponents by surprise.

Above *Practise chipping the ball over an imaginary wall, using a suspended track-suit.*

Above *Alan Ball, playing for Everton, lifts a free-kick over the Sheffield United wall and aims to find a colleague. Space is often left behind the wall by less-than-alert defences.*

Defensive tactics at free-kicks

1953 was Coronation year and there was romance in the air. Hilary stood in triumph at the summit of Everest. Gordon Richards rode his first Derby winner. And it seemed that the whole world was applauding when Stanley Matthews, with a classic pass to Bill Perry, completed a Blackpool triumph in the dying seconds of an astonishing FA Cup Final against Bolton Wanderers.

Matthews gleaned most of the credit for Blackpool's fight back from a 3-1 deficit with his mesmeric contribution to the game's momentous climax. But it had been centre-forward Stan Mortensen, scorer of the first three goals, who had taken more consistent advantage of lax defensive play from a rapidly tiring Bolton side. His third goal was a direct result of the Bolton defence being unable to organize itself to protect keeper Hanson's goal from a direct free-kick on the edge of the penalty area.

As Mortensen prepared to take the kick, five Bolton defenders immediately closed up, shoulder to shoulder, barring the threat of a direct shot at goal. Mortensen could command none of the swerve or dip which was to be a feature of such free-kicks in the years to come. But he had power and he elected to use it. He simply strode forward and drove a right-foot shot straight into the roof of Bolton's goal.

Mortensen claimed later that he had seen a gap and had aimed for it. But the wall had been badly set leaving Hanson's near post unshielded and right-back Ball turned away allowing the fierce shot to pass behind his back.

What this goal proved was the need to pay careful attention in such situations, and the need increased as more and more players began to experiment with highly sophisticated kicking

Almost a certain goal if players are allowed a free shot from 20 yards

techniques. There was a fundamental principle involved. Professional players who had developed power could almost guarantee to score from up to 25-yard range if they were allowed a clear sight of goal.

In order to deny them that advantage, defenders arranged themselves as a first line of cover, protecting as much as they could of the near side of their goal. If the angle was narrow, two players could provide an effective barrier. But as the angle increased so it was necessary to extend the width of the wall.

A free-kick directly in front of goal, especially when a renowned striker is involved, calls for four or even five players to present themselves as a barricade. The end man overlaps the nearest post along the possible angle of strike and the goal-keeper positions himself to cover from the middle to the far side.

Those who make up the wall have to be carefully chosen. There are basic requirements. Courage is essential. But although defenders are likely to display more of that, it is not practical to use them all up because of the threat which could come from attempts to create openings with well-planned moves.

Trained men are needed to repel that possibility and if more than five men are stationed before the shot the remainder will find themselves outnumbered. So brave forwards are the more likely recruits when danger threatens.

It has now become the goalkeeper's responsibility to position the wall correctly, although he needs the help of an outfield player to establish a complete area of cover. This led to problems for players in the Football League when firmer refereeing was introduced at the start of the

Above left Blackpool's Stan Mortensen flashes a free-kick into the Bolton net to level the scores at 3-3 in the 1953 FA Cup Final at Wembley.

Left As the diagram shows, Bolton paid the penalty for poor defensive tactics at the free-kick. The wall was not set correctly to cover the near post and right-back Ball increased the gap by turning inside the flight of the shot.

COLORSPORT

COLORSPORT

Above *Gerd Muller, the West Germany striker, twists away from the England wall in the 1972 international in Berlin. In such situations a defender must move to mark the run off the ball.*
Below *Alan Hudson scored for Chelsea against Stoke City in 1972 because the wall, having covered against the possibility of a direct shot, failed to recognize and move to cover the secondary threat.*

Inset right *Gordon Banks fulfils the keeper's role of lining up the England wall to protect his goal against a Welsh free-kick at Cardiff in 1972.*
Above right *The referee pulls back the England wall in the same match. By standing less than ten yards from a free-kick, defenders guard against the kick being taken quickly but, of course, risk being booked for ungentlemanly conduct.*

1971-72 season.

Wingers, especially, had grown used to racing back at free-kicks to line up the defensive screen. Attackers themselves, they could eliminate the possible angle of shot by carefully lining up along the full arc of flight. Under the new system this was seen to be ungentlemanly conduct, and it became necessary to think hard about the technique. The answer was simple enough. Instead of standing over the ball, the player now stood behind the grouping attackers.

The goalkeeper's governing influence in such situations gave Arsenal particular problems when Jack Kelsey, an outstanding Welsh international, took over from George Swindin in the mid-fifties. Kelsey not only flew successfully to save hundreds of shots but also in the face of accepted theory. For whereas every other keeper in the business settled happily for near post cover, Kelsey reversed the principle. He wanted to see the ball from the moment it was struck and was happier with the wall covering his far post.

When chosen to play for London against Barcelona in the early, more definitive years of the Fairs Cup, Kelsey offered his theory to the then Spurs' captain Danny Blanchflower. Blanchflower would have none of it. He asked Kelsey to set his wall and then proceeded to flight a succession of accurate chips into the top far corner of the goal. And yet Kelsey remained true to his beliefs despite persistent dispute.

It was inevitable that gamemanship should enter into the techniques which were formulated to provide certain cover at every free-kick situation. Football's folklore provides an example of what managers and coaches were determined to prevent as the game took on more professional techniques.

In the FA Cup Final of 1930, Arsenal, emerging as the most powerful force in the land, scored their first goal as a result of the quick thinking which characterized the play of their inside-left Alex James.

James was to prove himself a master player, a superbly creative forward whose wide vision and devastating use of the ball over long range contributed more to Arsenal's success than any other single factor. He came to Arsenal from Preston with a reputation for scoring goals. The character of his game was to change dramatically in the following years. But in a Cup Final which was to herald Arsenal's ten-year domination of English football, he scored a goal which was all about instinct and cunning.

As Huddersfield stood back at a free-kick,

FARMER

HUDSON (B)

HOLLINS

HUDSON (A)

DIAGRAM

James slipped the ball quickly to the youthful Cliff Bastin, took a return pass in his stride and scored.

In order to prevent such happenings, teams detailed one player to settle over the ball whenever a free-kick was given so that it could not be taken until the defensive system had been ordered. In time it would lead to confusion and disorder when players doggedly refused to retreat the mandatory ten yards from the ball. FIFA, the game's international governing body, instructed their referees to take firm action with players who refused to conform to the law, but as late as 1972 it was still causing problems.

When Spurs met AC Milan in the semi-finals of the new-styled EUFA Cup in April of that year there was an extension of the traditional conflict between two distinct attitudes.

Spurs playing the first of two legs at home relied on sustained pressure designed to pin down the Italians close to goal. Milan, conditioned to resisting such pressure, soaked it up and broke out to take the lead with a shot from Benetti, whose tackling had previously looked the outstanding feature of his play. Benetti was not alone. Milan's cynicism was seen in every corner of the pitch and it finally led to the expulsion of one of their midfield men, Sogliano.

For that match, Spurs recalled Alan Mullery. When it seemed that Mullery was finished with top-flight football he was brought back to resume as captain, and he was to score a critical goal in the second leg which helped his club through to an all-England final against Wolves.

Mullery's vigorous protest when held up by Sogliano's refusal to retreat from a second-half free-kick at White Hart Lane led to the Spanish referee taking immediate and damaging action. Throughout the match Milan had used delaying tactics to ensure that their best equipped players were back in strength to cope with centres flighted at the heads of Spurs' attackers. But the referee had by then had enough and Sogliano was sent from the action.

A few weeks earlier, Arsenal coach Steve Burtenshaw had noted the devilish use which Piet Keizer, the Ajax winger, made of free-kicks close to goal. Keizer used cut and dip to bypass the wall. Arsenal's answer was to detach a player from the end nearest to the middle of the goal as soon as the ball was played. His job was to come forward swiftly and threaten.

It was not pretty but it was effective. Arsenal went out of the European Cup but not because of any flaw in their defensive technique when confronted with the threat of close free-kicks.

Coaching: Learn how to tighten your defence against free-kicks

Teams lacking organization when conceding free-kicks, particularly close to the edge of their penalty area, are very vulnerable. Pre-match planning and coaching has developed to such a degree that, unless defences understand what is going on and how they are going to cope, they must expect to concede goals.

For defenders it is a matter of deciding which players present the immediate danger. From a free-kick 40-45 yards from goal, the forward players are more dangerous than the ball, because a shot is not feasible from such a range, so they must be marked tightly. This means that the defenders must concentrate on keeping the forwards as far from the goal as possible by pushing forward to the edge of the penalty area. If the ball is played into the goal area, the goalkeeper should reach it. If it is played shorter, then it has got to be a very good header to beat the goalkeeper.

If a forward does meet the free-kick, the defenders not involved in contesting for the first ball must concentrate on looking for the second ball which now becomes the danger.

When these longer kicks are taken from the touchline area, defenders must make a point of being just that much in front of the man they are marking to enable them to move in first for the near post ball or jump and harrass for the ball that is chipped high.

The closer the kick is to your goal the more immediate is the danger from a direct shot, especially if it is a direct free-kick. A wall or human barrier must be presented to the ball in such a way that it limits the area of the goal into which the ball can be shot the first time. The number of players in the wall varies according to the distance and the angle, but the principles remain constant. It is important that the goalkeeper can see the ball when it is actually kicked so he is better positioned near the far post. From this position he can move forward quickly to the near post; he would not be able to move backwards so rapidly.

The wall will guard against the direct shot to the near post and the goalkeeper the shot to the far post. This means that three of the four immediate dangers have been catered for. They are the direct shots into both corners and the chip to the far post. The fourth problem is the chip into the near post, over the wall, and the keeper must be prepared to move forward and across his goal quickly to deal with it.

If the anchor man of the wall, the first player to line up on a direct line with the near post, is not covering it fully, then a fifth problem exists—the ball bent round the wall inside the near post. To help eliminate this problem the anchor man should be lined up so that the near post is over his inside shoulder. Once the goalkeeper has lined him up, this key player should remain static so that the other members of the wall just fall in alongside him.

Speed of organization is important at this stage. It will make things easier and quicker if it is agreed in advance that certain players will always form the wall. During your coaching sessions this can be sorted out so that every player knows exactly the part he has to play in the event of a free-kick being conceded close to your goal.

Having attempted to eliminate the direct threats, secondary areas must be protected, especially by close man-for-man marking of attacking players who constitute a threat to your goals.

Players selected to form the wall must be courageous. The wall players should stand tight against one another leaving no gaps and it is advisable to guard vulnerable parts of the body with the hands. The chin should be tucked in and neck muscles tensed in preparation for heading away the shot. If the ball is played short to one side, the wall must close down *en bloc* as quickly as possible on the player playing the second ball.

As soon as the referee has signalled an infringement, the forwards must come back and it should be the duty of one of them to run behind the ball in order to check the anchor man is in position and that the ball has not been moved to change the angle. The main striker can cope with the area to the inside of the wall should the ball be passed sideways. The defending winger on the other flank should come back to mark his opposite wingman. The other main defenders, instead of being in the wall, should be doing the jobs they do best which is marking and contesting for the ball.

Different teams adopt different tactics as to who does which job. Your preparation should be done in your pre-season work when the weather allows you to stand and discuss the problems. Once a pattern has been decided upon, your practice games can be conditioned so that re-start situations can be worked on. The wall players can be taken with the goalkeeper as a unit and players encouraged to score direct.

Below The wall correctly set, covering the near post, with the anchor player lined up so that the post is over his inside shoulder.

The throw-in

Above Liverpool's Peter Cormack controls a Steve Heighway throw-in against Leeds in 1972. Heighway waits for the return pass. At throw-ins possession can be carelessly wasted if the thrower is inaccurate or not mentally in tune with what the receiver is hoping to achieve; this will complicate what should be a simple situation.

'There are First Division players around today who can't even do this properly,' said Spurs manager Bill Nicholson, miming a throw-in for two reporters in his club's car park.

It was April 1972. Spurs had not had a bad season. They were in the final of the EUFA Cup against Wolves. But Nicholson's irritation with deficient technique was legendary.

He could not excuse the inadequacy which some players showed when performing what was in theory the simplest of football skills. 'You would think that any mug could pick the ball up and throw it so that there was no problem in getting it under control. But no, they throw it here, and here and here.' As he spoke Nicholson picked out points on his body which were rarely employed by players when receiving a pass. The shoulders, the hips, the throat.

The tirade continued as Nicholson warmed to his favourite subject. Skill. The simple application of technique for the good of the team. 'I could bring any player on my staff out here now, draw a chalk mark on the wall and they would hit it every time if I asked them to throw the ball. But watch some of them in a match. They stop thinking. They don't look. I can excuse players who make errors under pressure. But who is under pressure when they are taking a throw-in?'

Nicholson's was not an uncommon experience. Managers throughout the business shared it. The technique of taking a throw-in was so uncomplicated that they could hardly be expected to devote much time to it in training. Only the specialists, men such as Martin Chivers and Ian Hutchinson who could reach the penalty spot with long-range throws, were allowed time to practise.

Why waste time on something which any schoolboy should have been able to do? Yet throw-ins broke down simply because there were those, at every level of the game, who made them hard work. On the other hand team play from throw-ins commanded much attention. Because throw-ins are frequent in every match it is bad play if possession is lost when returning the ball from

Left *Three methods of retaining possession from throw-ins. The ball* **top** *thrown into the receiver's feet and then returned to the thrower is the most common; but it depends on the thrower making it easy for his team-mate to control the ball and play it back. A cross-over play* **centre** *is a useful way to make space, particularly when the opposition is marking tight. Two players interchange and the thrower selects the one who has created more room. Feint play by the receiver* **bottom** *is another ruse that can lose a marker. In this diagram the receiver moves in very close to the thrower pulling his marker with him. Suddenly he checks and sprints clear as the thrower aims the ball into his path.*

the touchline.

The more thinking players had not only devised methods of keeping the ball but of manipulating situations which could be the springboards for decisive attacks.

Spurs, with a long established reputation for taking killing advantage of moments when the ball was dead and in their favour, had figured prominently in this. The high priests had been Danny Blanchflower and Tommy Harmer. Blanchflower, the artful, intellectual Irishman. Harmer, the shy but instinctively quick-witted Cockney. Contrasting personalities, but sharing the common factors of skill and football intelligence.

Spurs and Burnley give a new meaning to the throw-in

Harmer's devilish talent for conjuring up astonishing levels of flight and trajectory delighted the elegant Blanchflower. Between them they fashioned a whole series of deceiving tricks which brought a new meaning to throw-ins.

As they were found out so they produced other moves. They were restless creators at a time when there were not too many of their kind around. Blanchflower's favourite was the 'argument'. Harmer described it perfectly:

'In those days teams always pulled inside-forwards back to mark their opposite numbers at a throw. This meant that the half-back marked the winger, leaving the full-back free as cover. It was very difficult to work out of this sort of marking.

'The winger had the job of marking your spare full-back and the man who was taking the throw. It was a terrible job really, impossible. How can one man mark two players at once?

'Most teams taking a throw settled for having their full-back lying deep so that he could come into space and collect the ball long before the opposing winger could get at him.

'But this meant that you were only starting again. You had possession alright. But there had been no penetration. The other lot were still all goal-side of the ball.

'Our idea was to get someone free into a forward position. Most teams used a cross-over thing. The winger running infield and the inside forward going down the touchline. You were looking for a yard start. Sometimes it worked if the markers were caught off balance. But not always.

'So Danny started this thing about arguing over who was going to take the throw. He used to do it with Terry Medwin. Medwin would pick the ball up and shape up to throw it. Then along

would come Danny to demand the ball.

'They would make out like they were having a real barney. You know, trying to tug the ball away from each other. Then when the other team had been kidded into relaxing, either Danny or Meddy would sprint down the line, whichever of them was left slung the ball in. It's amazing how many times it worked. How many times we got someone free and behind the defence.'

There were much simpler ploys. Some teams would send players in close around the thrower, drawing the markers in and leaving space behind them, for someone coming at speed from the opposite flank. By standing well back from the thrower, space could be created for him to receive a return pass, ensuring possession and a point from which something might be created.

The return pass could only be made accurately if the ball was thrown in correctly to feet or head. It was the inability to do this which incensed Nicholson. Movement was always essential if the throw-in was to have any true value. Players who stood still and waited simply made life easy for their opponents.

Blanchflower's eagerness to exploit throw-ins was matched by a fellow Irishman, Jimmy McIlroy of Burnley. They were the arch-thinkers in an Irish team which flowered splendidly, with good football and traditional blarney, to make an enormous impression, against all the odds, during the 1958 World Cup in Sweden.

Spurs and Burnley, encouraged by their respective managers Nicholson and Alan Brown, were the two First Division teams most likely to come up with something new in the late fifties and early sixties. Intelligent use of free-kicks, corners and throw-ins was the champagne of their game. Such moments appealed to Blanchflower and McIlroy more than most.

McIlroy's favourite, like Blanchflower's, hinged on the ability to act out a part during the heat of a game. He would make a deliberate run towards the thrower, demanding that the ball be given to him quickly. The thrower, well prepared, would hesitate and McIlroy would admonish him for apparently failing to take advantage of the moment.

McIlroy's next move was to relax completely, bending down to adjust the tape holding up one of his stockings. Then with the game at a full stop, he would suddenly sprint clear collecting the ball in his stride.

The trick had a funny sequel when it was tried at Norwich by Scottish forward Jimmy Moran. Moran had copied it from McIlroy and he took it to his new club.

'We talked about it in training and the lad taking the throw knew exactly what he was supposed to do. So, early in the game I came sprinting in and gave him the rucking for not taking the throw quickly. Then I bent down to fiddle with my tie up. Just as planned. I was just about to launch myself off on a run when the ball hit me in the face. It was a wet day and I went down as though someone had whacked me one. I didn't bother with it again.'

Quick throw-ins were worth trying in advanced positions where it was not always essential to retain possession. These were the areas where chances could be taken, where there might be more profit in a gamble than in playing safe.

In defensive areas, safety was of prime importance. Opponents closed down so quickly that a throw-in close to the corner flag became a problem. It was difficult to work the ball clear and the team taking the throw had to recognize that they were temporarily outnumbered.

Unless teams had tremendous confidence in the control technique and dribbling skills of players in the zone they invariably settled for throwing the ball along the touchline.

It usually meant that they gained another throw further from goal and it was a popular tactic especially when hanging on late in a match.

Tight marking at throw-ins was particularly profitable at lower levels of football where deficiencies in ball control offered greater opportunities of gaining possession.

The effect of tight marking was diluted higher up the scale and yet, as Nicholson so vigorously pointed out, it was still possible to hustle players into errors simply because throw-ins were often badly performed.

His point was well supported by the Leeds manager Don Revie who said: 'However much a team achieves in this business you are always having to work at the little things. It is when the little things go wrong that the team starts to fall apart.

'We have always paid a lot of attention to throw-ins because after all they are the most common means of returning the ball into play. If you haven't got them right, if you are careless with them, you are asking for trouble. We haven't been lucky enough to have someone who could throw a long way. Someone like a Chivers.

'So we concentrated on making sure that we at least started with the advantage of having possession. There is no excuse for not being able to throw the ball where you want it to go.'

Some teams conceded possession at throw-ins, more concerned with not being caught out by the sort of thoughtful moves which Blanchflower inspired at Spurs. On the other hand Leeds emphasized the value of closing down tight when winning at Spurs early in the 1969-70 season.

A goal ahead they put the issue beyond doubt when pressure following a throw-in led to a careless square pass by the Spurs centre-half Mike England. An interception by Johnny Giles led to the goal which ensured a Leeds victory.

Needless to say, Bill Nicholson was not at all pleased.

Coaching: Learn to retain possession at throw-ins

So often a team in possession at a throw-in literally throws away the advantage they have. Since every throw-in provides a chance to start an attacking movement, retaining possession is very important.

There are several ways in which this can be done. First, the ball can be thrown to an unmarked player in a space. There is better chance of success with this method if the throw-in is taken quickly. The nearest player, irrespective of his position, should be prepared to take the throw, giving the ball to an unmarked team-mate providing, of course, that he is prepared to receive it.

A supporting full-back or a player who has moved quickly from another area and arrives unmarked and in space are often in the best position to receive such a throw. Space is of the utmost importance inasmuch that it means time available to use the ball. It can be created by speed off the mark and surprise, movement that enables you to lose a marking opponent.

To create extra surprise, you should feint to move in one direction, get your opponent moving that way, then suddenly move off in another direction for the ball to be thrown to you in the space you have created.

An interchange of positions and decoy movements is another way to make space. Two players quickly switch positions and the thrower selects the player who has created most space. Alternatively one player runs, calling for the ball, and creates space for a colleague where he started his run from.

Although this may sound simple, timing is crucial and you must practise to become successful. The position of the throw will influence your choice of throw-in. For instance, if the throw is taken opposite your own penalty area you may make use of your goalkeeper. In midfield you may use an unmarked player or play the ball back to the thrower. Close to the opponents' goal-line you could work to free a colleague for a possible striking opportunity.

Considerable time should be spent on the accuracy of the throw. This is so often neglected and yet is a major cause of failure. The ball should be thrown direct to head or feet and not allowed to bounce up to the stomach area where it will take more time to control. This is the most important technical consideration. The most important tactical consideration is that the players concerned are tuned in on the same wavelength. They must be thinking the same tactics.

Start your practice with a ball between two and aim to become accurate with your throw. Make sure, too, that you throw in accordance with the laws of the game. If in any doubt consult your coach or a booklet on the laws.

The player off the ball should stand about 15 yards away from you and you should throw the ball so that he can volley or half-volley it back using the inside of the foot. A useful practice which will give you movement is for the receiver to move off quickly for a return ball. When he receives the ball a second time, he picks it up and commences the practice again with the functions changed.

When you have gained some degree of accuracy the player off the ball should move away and to the side of the thrower, then quickly come back into the same position to receive the ball. Now you must concentrate on the timing of the accurate throw. The other player must receive the ball just as he moves into the space he has created.

Many other movements can be performed in order to create space. Try moving in close to the thrower, then suddenly move away for the ball to be thrown into your movement over your head. This can be very successful when there is no cover on the player who is marking you. Once you have acquired a certain amount of skill try it with a player marking you. He remains passive at first until you have a better understanding with your colleague.

The object of the exercise is to get the ball back to the thrower or to get away from the marker with the ball. Now increase the possibilities by bringing in another two players who have been practising the same movements. One player acts as a winger standing some 15 to 20 yards down the touchline being marked by a full-back, the other as a midfield player standing 15 to 20 yards square infield marked by an opposing midfield player. On a signal the two players suddenly switch positions in an attempt to throw off the tight marking. The thrower should throw the ball to the movement that has made more space and the player should continue to make an attack on a goal.

In a match your throw-ins will be influenced by the way your opponents mark and the position of the throw. Remember to throw the ball in quickly when the situation presents itself because defenders sometimes move slowly into positions. Also remember that you cannot be offside direct from a throw-in and that the opponents have a numerical advantage of one player. This player often acts as a double cover making it more difficult for the team taking the throw. This is the traditional method of marking, wing-half marking winger, inside-forward marking inside-forward and the opposite winger operating between thrower and the full-back.

This means that the ball can be thrown direct to the full-back if the winger is marking the thrower. But if he marks the full-back, it can be thrown to the inside-forward and back to the thrower and if the winger leaves the full-back to stop the ball going back to the thrower just after it has been thrown, then the inside-forward changes his mind quickly and passes back to the full-back.

Improvement will be almost immediate but success will not come overnight. Work and be patient and above all have confidence in the knowledge that practice will bear fruit. Where previously you had been giving the ball away you are now taking advantage of the fact that you have the game in your hands.

Left *Chelsea's Eddie McCreadie throws the ball down the touchline to Chris Garland. Not tightly marked, Garland is well-positioned to receive the ball, having avoided the temptation to be drawn in too close to the thrower.*

RAY GREEN

The long throw

A football tradition that massed attacks should be led *in person* by a team's biggest and most dangerous striker was calmly set aside by three of the most successful sides in season 1970-71. At moments when rivals looked intensely vulnerable, gifted marksmen John Radford, Martin Chivers and Ian Hutchinson were absent from the goalmouth—by order.

Arsenal, Spurs and Chelsea had gambled on missing goal-chances that these big men might have taken, because coaches had discovered in each of them an ability to throw a football a prodigious distance.

Other men could take free-kicks and corners, and Radford, Chivers and Hutchinson could be relied upon to compete successfully in the muscular battles to connect with such centres. But unlike most other players, they had the destructive knack of hurling a ball two-handed from the touchline to the penalty spot or even beyond.

So, forced to choose between having them waiting in the goalmouth on the off-chance that a throw-in might lead to a centre, or waving them to the touchlines knowing that the throws would carry to the heart of the rivals' defence, the coaches of these top London clubs each decided to make these goal scorers into goal-makers.

A classic example of the effectiveness of the move came when Spurs beat Nottingham Forest in the fifth round of the 1970-71 FA Cup. Chivers had already put his side ahead when Spurs forced a throw-in on their right flank some 30 yards from the Forest corner flag. Chivers, as usual, was deputed to take the throw. As he picked up the ball, Alan Gilzean, Spurs' tall Scottish international, was loitering innocently at the far side of a crowded goal area. He was tightly marked. Chivers threw the ball towards the goalmouth, but to the near side of the goal area. Suddenly, with perfect and practised timing, Gilzean sprinted 12 yards and was the first to reach the ball with his left temple, skilfully directing it behind him with sufficient power to send it gliding towards the far side of the goal. The ball beat keeper Barron's dive at the far post. Spurs were 2-0 up, and on their way to the sixth round.

That Gilzean scored from so delicate an angle was a testimony to his deft touch—as a Spurs player said after the game: 'Gilly's got a head like a threepenny bit.' But even had his header been less precise, the move was still very dangerous once Gilzean had got his head to the ball. The deflection could have made a goal for an in-rushing colleague—in the Forest match Alan Mullery was lurking for such a chance—but whether the target forward scores himself or makes the opening for another player, the long

FOX PHOTOS

PETER ROBINSON

Left *Alan Gilzean (fourth from the right, white shirt) moves away in triumph as his glancing header from a long throw by Martin Chivers (far left) beats Nottingham Forest keeper, Jim Barron.*
Below *Diagram of the Spurs long throw method.*
Above *Bobby Woodruff measures the length of his long throw when he played for Crystal Palace.*

DIAGRAM (RESEARCH LONDON WEEKEND TELEVISION)

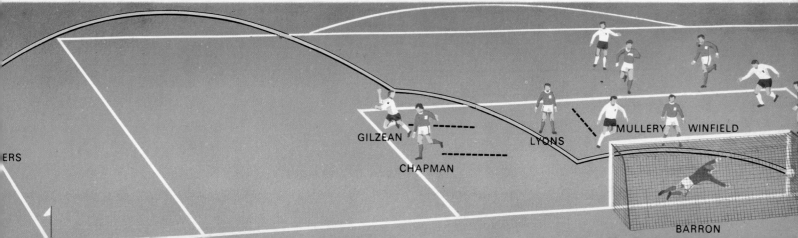

GILZEAN CHAPMAN LYONS MULLERY WINFIELD BARRON

throw is plainly a weapon which is effective only if its two prongs are sharpened by practice.

It is not sufficient simply to have a player in the side who can throw a ball 40 yards. That is only one of the skills required. What must accompany the throw is the clever deployment of colleagues waiting in the goal-mouth. Without this, the long throw is as lame as a weak corner kick.

Spurs used the exciting aerial talents of Gilzean and, sometimes, Martin Peters. Gilzean could direct and deflect the ball at amazing angles. Most of Spurs' long throws were aimed at him. The opposition knew this but, by timing his runs and using other players as decoys, Gilzean was still able to make his penetrating flicks to unbalance defences. Once the deflection had been made, other players would hurl themselves into the goal area to snap up the chance.

Having discovered Hutchinson's gifts in a pre-1969-70 season experiment with their entire staff, Chelsea, too, looked for organization in the penalty area to obtain the most damaging effect from their new weapon. If they lacked a target man with the artistry of Gilzean, then they compensated with a squad of big, determined players, particularly Osgood, Webb and Dempsey, who could be thrown forward in waves to meet Hutchinson's throws.

Hutchinson, a bargain signing from the then non-League Cambridge United, drew full advantage from his long arms and loose-jointed shoulders. He astonished his manager, Dave Sexton, in training—'I have seen Ian hit the top of the far post with a ball thrown from the touchline during a practice session.'

One of his gigantic heaves won Chelsea their first FA Cup. Under severe pressure from Peter Osgood, Jack Charlton mistimed his clearance from the throw, sending the ball over David Harvey to where the fearless Webb risked all as he forced it over the line.

Hutchinson's gigantic throw-in won Chelsea their first FA Cup

Arsenal won the 'double' in 1970-71 with a whole range of skills, but in their repertoire was the long throw. Radford's version of the move had more in common with Chivers' than Hutchinson's. The Arsenal centre-forward would aim his throw at the head of the elegant George Graham, whose touch in the air was only equalled by his touch on the ground. The pair almost put Arsenal ahead in the Cup Final when only a combination of Ray Clemence's hands and the cross-bar stopped Graham's

header crossing the line. Nor was the technique confined to the bigger clubs. Luton, for example, used the powerful throwing of another fine marksman, Malcolm Macdonald, in their challenge for Second Division honours.

As with any profitable tactical ploy, its success was quickly followed by defensive counter-moves.

In a bid to check the danger, managers and coaches began to deploy defenders in front of the attacker detailed to try and glance the ball across goal; this proved an effective answer. When Arsenal met Spurs in the match which decided the 1970-71 League Championship, John Radford, the Gunners' long throw man, made no impression. His target was George Graham, but Spurs delegated Alan Mullery to stand in front of Graham. The result was that Graham was beaten to the ball at five out of six throws.

Leeds preferred to attack Hutchinson at the source, rather than the target man in the penalty area. When the two teams met in the League in the 1969-70 season, Don Revie, concerned over Hutchinson's astonishing throwing distance, detailed Allan Clarke, a forward, to station himself in front of Hutchinson when he was winding up to release the ball.

Revie assumed that Clarke's presence would put Hutchinson off, decreasing his distance or

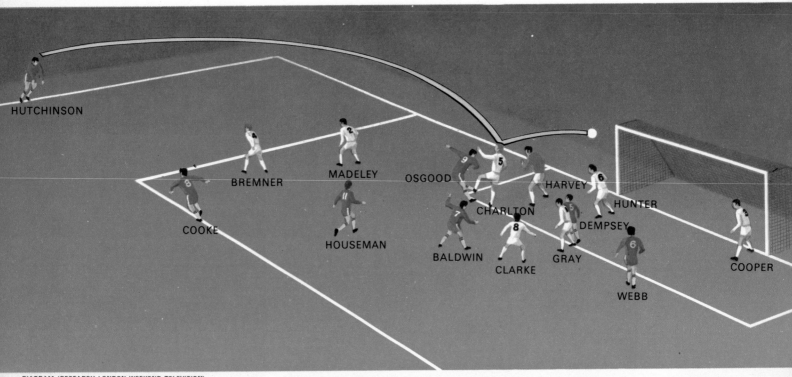

DIAGRAM (RESEARCH LONDON WEEKEND TELEVISION)

pressuring him into a foul throw. For the throw to be valid, both feet must be on the ground at the moment of release and on or behind the touchline. The ball must be propelled with both hands and it must not be released in front of the head. Hutchinson had to get all this right, and still clear Clarke.

Yet Clarke's presence posed no problems for Hutchinson, and one immense throw led to a Chelsea goal. This time there were two touches, one from Dempsey and one from Webb, before the third, a blistering volley from Osgood, finished the move decisively.

Leeds won that game 5-2. For them it was a splendid away win, but Osgood's goal revealed a weakness that Hutchinson so successfully exploited in the 1970 Cup Final.

Revie was more successful later with a tactic that created a mental barrier for the Chelsea man. Whenever Hutchinson prepared to take a throw, the nearest Leeds player would gesture to the linesman to watch carefully the throwing technique. Because he became obsessed with making sure that his throw was a fair one, Hutchinson lost both length and accuracy.

Many teams have subjected the target players to the same pressures that had proved effective at corners and free-kicks. As the target player made his run to the ball, a defender simply blocked him. In the turmoil of a packed penalty area, referees found it hard to distinguish between the accidental collision and deliberate obstruction.

Such measures only became necessary in the late sixties and early seventies when sides were exacting the full potential from the move. The long throw itself was far from a novel idea. Sam Weaver, an excellent wing-half with Newcastle United and England in the thirties, was the first noted exponent, and later Dave Mackay exploited the move in the Spurs 'double' team. Other players such as Bobby Woodruff, Mike Bailey and John Hollins more than half recognized the possibilities of projecting a 40 yard throw into the heart of a defence.

The attacking move that always catches keepers in two minds

Surprisingly, teams in the 1970 World Cup finals made little use of the ploy—most throw-ins being simply used as a way of keeping possession. Some teams, England among them, did not have a recognized thrower in their squad. Yet had Chivers captured his 1970-71 form earlier, Alf Ramsey might very likely have used the big centre-forward's massive strength to throw dangerous balls that, in the thin air of Mexico, would have reached beyond the far post.

Like all tactics, the long throw loses some of its value if it is over-employed : there is value in retaining some measure of surprise. The very fact that opponents expected a long throw encouraged perceptive players to make use of alternatives. Indeed, the expert often became a different sort of danger as defenders left him unmarked by the touchline, expecting him to be moving to take the throw.

Yet properly used it justifies the decision of Bill Nicholson, Dave Sexton and Don Howe to pull out their big men. As a move it gives goalkeepers continual difficulties. Bob Wilson, the Arsenal keeper summed it up like this: 'Unlike a corner kick, the long throw comes in at a peculiar trajectory. Hutchinson, for instance, gets the ball in flat, which makes it extremely difficult for the keeper to make contact. When the ball is aimed at the near post and at the head of another attacker the goalkeeper is caught in two minds. He doesn't know whether to go and fight for it and risk the possibility of being passed by a deflection header or to stay and deal with the possibility of a shot from a wider angle.'

In an era of defensive sophistication, a move that catches goalkeepers in 'two minds' deserves further cultivation.

Above Ian Hutchinson summons all his power as he hurls another long throw into the goalmouth.
Above left Diagram of the Hutchinson throw that led to the FA Cup going to Stamford Bridge for the first time in Chelsea's history. From the throw, Jack Charlton can only back head the ball over his goalkeeper towards the far post.
Below left At the far post David Webb forces the ball over the line for the winning goal.
Below The courageous Webb finishes the move.

Coaching: Add length and accuracy to your throw-in

The success of the long throw depends both on the length and accuracy of the throw and the understanding and organization between the thrower and his team-mates in the goalmouth.
How to improve your throw: First make sure that you are certain of what constitutes a fair throw-in. Remember to keep your feet on the ground, take both hands behind the head before you throw and do not step on to the field of play until you have released the ball.

Then concentrate on accuracy. During your training sessions practise with a partner until you are satisfied that you can throw the ball to his head or feet accurately so that your team-mate can play it easily first time. When you are satisfied that you can accurately hit this standing target, get your friend to move about, perhaps pretending to go one way and then darting off in another direction, while again you practise getting the ball to him in such a way that he has immediate control. Talk with him about what you are doing and what possibilities lie just between the two of you. This will help develop the understanding so necessary for match play.

Above Dave Mackay was the first player in the 'sixties to exploit the use of the long throw.

Now you are ready to move on to develop the length of your throw. One way to do this is to work on your throwing technique. Remember you throw with your back as well as your arms so try to develop a whiplash movement with your body as you deliver the ball. As you release it, get as much power as you can behind the ball by using your fingers as well as your hands and arms. Finally follow through powerfully with your arms.

Practise with a medicine ball instead of a football. Obviously the extra weight will make it harder to get distance, but it will develop all the right muscles. This is a simple form of weight-training. More sophisticated exercises with weights will undoubtedly increase the body strength needed for the long throw, but they must only be done under proper supervision.

You cannot become a long throw expert overnight, but by constant practice and application you will always be able to increase the distances you can throw.
How to practise your long throw tactics: Assuming you can now throw a good length, start to plan your tactics. These must be based on the ability you have in your side. Do not allow tactics to dictate to your team.

You will need a target player who can make space for himself by moving away from the area into which you are dropping your throw, and who can then run back into the space at the time the ball is delivered. This skill will have been developed in your practice when you were throwing at a team-mate who was constantly darting about.

To start your practice, first go through the move without the ball and without opposition. Every player must know his job, first the target man, then other players moving up to be in position for a deflection. Then go through it with the ball, but still without opposition. Every time you repeat the move you should try to finish with a scoring shot. Now introduce defenders. At first they must remain passive so that the attacking players get the feel of 'company' without too much pressure. Again each move should end with a goal being scored. Keep practising until you achieve this.

When every attacking player fully understands his role, make the defenders active. Progress at this stage may be slow, and constant practice is a necessity. You must also have a strong belief in what you are doing. When you are rewarded for your efforts by scoring a goal in an official match, you will realize that all the work has been worthwhile.

Remember, goals from long throws need many skills, and the basic quality, courage.

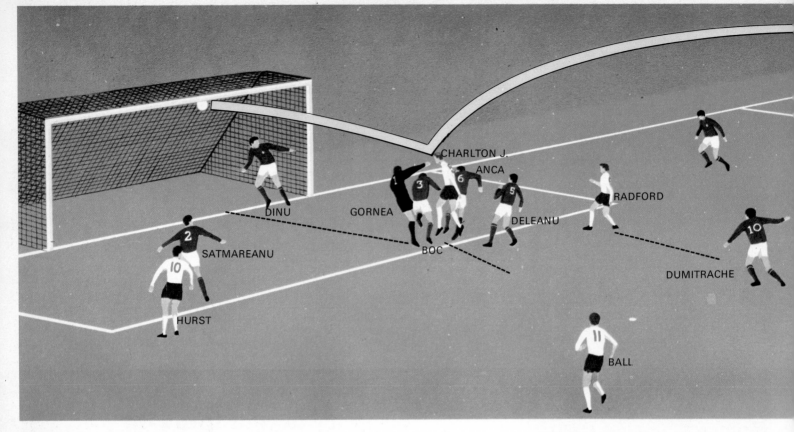

Labels on illustration: DINU, SATMAREANU, HURST, GORNEA, CHARLTON J., ANCA, DELEANU, BOC, RADFORD, DUMITRACHE, BALL

The corner-kick

For six seasons Sir Alf Ramsey built his England defence around Jack Charlton. Tall and inelegant, but always aggressively effective, Charlton rebuffed challenges from the best of the world's strikers. During the same period his uncompromising defensive skills stabilized his club side, Leeds United, as they grew from being close to the Third Division into one of the most consistently successful sides in Europe.

But both Ramsey and Don Revie, the Leeds manager, found that their centre-half possessed a second value, as a powerful attacker, to exploit a football situation that was becoming an increasingly important route to goal—the corner-kick.

As tightly meshed defences threatened to envelop and stifle free attacking football in the middle sixties, the sides that rose to the top, such as Leeds and Liverpool, were those who worked hardest to convert corners and free-kicks into goals.

Jack Charlton's intimidating presence at every Leeds and England corner-kick became a familiar and even provocative sight. More often than not he would stand shoulder to shoulder with the goalkeeper directly beneath the crossbar. His head would stand out as a target for the man taking the corner even amongst a forest of large defenders.

Goalkeepers, particularly those from abroad unused to physical contact, were unsure of how to handle him. His part in an England attack that often found goals awkward to come by was invaluable. One example came in 1969 when he moved upfield for a corner in the international against Rumania at Wembley.

The corner was to be taken by brother Bobby, whose ability to pick out Jack's head was almost extra-sensory. Jack took up position towards the near post, this time on the edge of the goal area. Bobby took the corner from England's right wing. And it was totally accurate. Although he was surrounded by sturdy defenders, and although keeper Gornea came out to claim the ball, Jack Charlton climbed upwards to turn the ball into the goal.

It was the only goal England scored that night despite constant pressure. By using a player who could drop corners into the goalmouth wherever he liked, and by deploying their forces carefully in that region, a defensive stronghold was breached.

Charlton's advance up the field, often designed to unsettle and unsight the keeper, led to Leeds being accused of flagrant gamesmanship when they finally broke through to beat Arsenal in the 1968 Football League Cup final.

Leeds had never won a major honour during 50 years of trying. They managed it at last at Wembley when Charlton's aggressive interference at a corner led to a superb volleyed goal from left-back Terry Cooper. Arsenal claimed that Jim Furnell, their goalkeeper, was impeded. But Charlton defended the accusation that he was elbowing and impeding the goalkeeper, pointing out instead that he was the victim of illegal attempts to prevent him making contact with the ball.

'Opponents pick me up as I approach their penalty area, and I get pushed and shoved while waiting for the ball to come over. I must have qualified for fifty penalty kicks, and never got one of them. If it was thought that I was upsetting goalkeepers, there was no rule which said I could not stand on the goal-line.'

The development of tall defenders at corner-kicks was not in itself a new tactic. Arsenal looked to be on their way out of the FA Cup in a semi-final against Chelsea in 1950 when Les Compton, a powerfully built centre-half, moved forward as his more famous brother Denis prepared to take a left-wing corner.

Joe Mercer, then Arsenal's captain, tried to wave the elder Compton back, but he ignored the instruction, went on into Chelsea's area and arrived in time to head an historic equalizer. Arsenal won the replay, and went on to beat Liverpool in the Final.

Mercer recalls: 'If big Les had obeyed my instruction, we would almost certainly have gone out of the Cup. It was one of the moments of inspiration which made the game what it is. I was more concerned with hanging on in the hope that we could draw level. But Les clearly felt it was time to try something. All credit to him.'

Compton's goal was seen as an oddity. But 15 years later, Leeds and others were purposefully using all their tall men to try to scale defences when they seemed to be at their least vulnerable.

Gordon Banks, England's goalkeeper who was popularly regarded as the world's best, makes a significant comment about the period.

'There were very few occasions when it was possible to come out and take the ball cleanly. You were surrounded by players of both teams, and I was more often than not satisfied to get a fist to the ball. Having done that, you had to get back into position quickly, because, unless the ball had been got away cleanly, it would come straight back.'

Big, belligerent men pushed up—to spread panic in the area

Chelsea made continual use of this sort of belligerent pressure. They had tall, muscular forwards in Peter Osgood and Ian Hutchinson, and they supported them by sending in the the the tallest of their defenders, David Webb and John Dempsey.

The tactic was successful if players were able to spread panic in the penalty area. If the big men could make vague contact, or if the ball was knocked down loose by a hurried clearance, there were always quick players around to take advantage.

Above *Diagram showing Jack Charlton at Rumania's near post nodding home brother Bobby's corner to put England ahead in the 1969 international.*
Top right *A close-up view of Charlton outjumping Rumanian keeper Gornea to head home.*
Right *Brian Kidd heads in a George Best corner in the 71-72 League game versus Crystal Palace.*
Below right *Diagram of Kidd's goal. Best drove his corner to the far post. Keeper Jackson did not go for it, and was beaten by Kidd's power.*

Bobby Charlton swung in countless, wickedly swerving crosses from the corner flags, and inswingers of this type presented goalkeepers with great problems.

And George Best, his Manchester United colleague, learned from this. As the might of United rose again at the start of the 1971-72 season under the managership of Frank O'Farrell, Best took a significant left-wing corner in a match at Selhurst Park against Crystal Palace. It was an inswinger, struck deep to the far post. Brian Kidd rose amongst the rugged South London defenders to head the ball home, and set United on their way to an important 3-1 win.

There was often value in dropping corners short by prearrangement with a forward who would move to beat the ball before glancing it back at an angle across goal.

Corners would also be driven high to the far side of the penalty area from where they could be headed back across goal, so forcing defenders to turn, denying them the advantage of facing the ball.

There was value to be found in playing them short, within the protective ten yards allowed by the laws. By clever manoeuvring the kicker and a supporting player could create an angle for a shot or a more decisive centre, and there was sometimes a chance for an advancing defender to arrive in time for an unhindered shot.

Other coaches settled for getting the ball straight into the goalmouth, especially when they were aware that there were players who would fight for it.

By varying the angle of flight and using players as decoys, chances could often be made for men who were at their best in the air when they could rise to meet the ball undisturbed by challenge.

Ron Greenwood, manager of West Ham, indicated the need for defenders to be constantly aware of their responsibility for going to meet the ball in these situations.

He said: 'The defender should not concern himself with what his immediate opponent is doing if he feels that he can make contact with the ball. This is what he should be concerned with. If he gets to the ball first, he has done his job. If he waits for a forward to make his move, he is in danger of arriving too late to make an effective challenge.'

Stoke City could have benefited from Greenwood's instruction when conceding a vital goal in an FA Cup semi-final replay against Arsenal at Villa Park in the spring of 1971.

The crucial first blow came when George Armstrong, an accurate and confident striker of the ball, drove a right-wing corner out to the edge of the Stoke penalty area.

Two Arsenal players made their moves early, and the Stoke defenders were deceived by their runs at the near post. But the ball was driven deliberately behind them to a point where George Graham was arriving after delaying his run.

Graham, who was more stylish than aggressive, managed to put these two qualities together, rising magnificently to head the ball into the top left corner of Stoke's goal with such power that even Banks' superb reflexes were useless.

Ron Davies rifled in the corner—a header from all of 15 yards

The outswinging corner led to spectacular goals like that. Inswingers usually led to scrambles and deflections, because attackers were following the ball in. When the ball was hit away from goal into the path of an advancing player its velocity was increased if it was struck cleanly.

There was no clearer example of this than a goal by Ron Davies of Southampton for Wales against Scotland at Wrexham in the 1969 Home International championship.

Davies was among the most threatening headers in the business, and he proved his power with one that was rifled into the Scottish goal from all of 15 yards.

For many years defenders had seemed to have most things in their favour at corners. They had no need to be accurate when challenging for the ball whereas forwards were restricted to a target of eight yards by eight feet.

The balance was altered by belligerent attitudes from attackers. It was no longer enough to guard against known experts in the air. Anything could happen in a crowded penalty area from a corner-kick and often did.

Coaching: Increase your side's scoring power from corner-kicks

The use of corner-kicks must play an important part in every team's attacking plans. Corners have become such a crucial way of making scoring chances and sensible coaches explore the many alternative methods for taking the kicks.

If you are going to take the corners for your team, crossing the ball is the skill you must practise. Generally speaking, a corner taken right-footed from the right-wing and a left-footed corner from the left-wing and will curl away from the goal—an outswinger. A left-footed corner from the right-wing and a right-footed corner from the left-wing should curl towards the goal—an inswinger. If you are to take corners for your side practise taking them with both feet and from both sides of the field. Your team's basic tactic might be to take outswingers, but if you are playing against a suspect goalkeeper the inswinging corner can put him under tremendous pressure. Against a dominating keeper, the outswinger might be more successful.

To take accurate corners you will have to work on your basic kicking technique to get the necessary power. Hit the ball firmly keeping the ankle firm, and keep your eye on the ball at the moment of contact.

Most of the time you will be trying to loft the ball. This can be achieved by placing the non-kicking foot slightly behind the ball rather than alongside it, and by leaning the body backwards as the kicking foot nears the ball. Contact should be made with the instep. Spend time in the park with a friend or at training sessions practising corners—concentrating on getting power and loft into your kick.

Although short corners run the added risk that you might lose the ball even before you get your cross into the goalmouth, they have the advantage of enticing defenders away from the goal area—thus giving attackers more space to work in. With this in mind it is a sound idea to start planning your corner tactics with a short corner move.

Work in small groups before attempting it in a practice game. Two players stand at the corner, one with the ball, the other a yard away, standing on the goal-line facing infield. That way he can see everything that is going on. These two players first make sure that the defender (if there is only one) is standing ten yards away. The player taking the corner plays it to his team-mate and moves infield, so that he cannot be offside—as the ball can only be played back to him. The player with the ball now attacks the defender, and according to the action of the defender either passes the ball infield to the other player who can take it forward into the penalty area to shoot or cross, or he takes the defender on himself and moves up on the bye-line before crossing or pulling the ball back.

Once you have mastered this move, think of how your opponents would try to stop it. They will send another player to help the one defending, making two against two. The most likely player to do this is the opponent's winger. If this happens then the corner can be played to your full-back on that side of the field who should be left free (see diagrams). He can either shoot or cross the ball. If this move works successfully the defending team may now be forced to send another defender from the goal area out to the corner so that their winger can mark the full-back, making three against three. When this happens, you have drawn at least two defenders out of the middle so now it is best to play a long corner into the goal area.

It is important to work on the way you position players in the penalty area. The bigger men are of most use on the far post whereas the smaller and often quicker players can be used for near post running. It is a good idea to have a tall player on the goal-line looking for the cross which is close to the goal.

With this to aim for, corners can be played in different ways. One is the ball power-swerved inside the near post. This obviously has to be very accurate and will require much practice, but with a tall player on the line who could make contact with it the practice is well worth the effort.

The second type of long kick can be played to players taking up formation just inside the opposite corner of the penalty area looking for an outswinging ball just beyond the reach of the keeper which might tempt him to leave his line. This concentration of players can move simultaneously on to the ball, in the hope that by sheer weight of numbers one player might be able to head forcibly towards goal.

These tactics must be built slowly. Take them step by step—move by move until all the players know what they are doing. When you are happy with your progress, play games in which every time the defending side put the ball out of play in their own half, a corner is awarded.

Treat corners seriously. They are a main route to goals.

Below The perfect inswinging corner. Alan Woodward's flag-kick goes straight into the Leicester City goal.
Bottom Diagrams of how two attackers can beat a defender and three can beat two at short corners.

NEVILLE CHADWICK

DIAGRAM

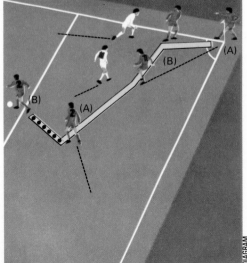

DIAGRAM

Defensive tactics at corners

Chelsea's victory at Sunderland in their penultimate Division Two game of the 1962-63 season virtually ensured that there would be First Division football played at Stamford Bridge the following August.

It was a game that stuck in the memory of Chelsea fans for two reasons; first, Tommy Docherty had gambled on a curious line-up, mixing youthful skill and veteran expertise; second, the winning goal came from little Tommy Harmer, the oldest of Docherty's reshuffled pack, scored with what one journalist described as 'an unprintable part of his anatomy'.

The fans would have been well advised to recall a third factor that was equally crucial to the success of the visit to Roker Park, the way in which the blue-shirted defenders neutralized the menace of Sunderland's Charlie Hurley at corner-kicks.

Hurley, a tall, magnificently built, yet nimble centre-half, had been christened 'King Charlie'. His impressive skill and deft touch made him much more than just a destructive defender.

But it was his power in the air which prompted Chelsea to adopt a totally cynical approach when he advanced to offer himself at corners in their penalty area.

Whenever Hurley moved forward he found himself hustled and impeded. When he crossed the halfway line he stepped into a minefield of body-checks which prevented him from taking up a position where he could present a genuine threat.

He must have been fouled 20 times when the ball was 30 or 40 yards away. If Hurley did reach the penalty area he found himself baulked and jostled to such an extent that he was rarely able to get off the floor. But an indulgent referee offered no protection. Chelsea were simply taking advantage of an attitude which was to become all too common in the game.

It had not always been so. For decades defenders defended and forwards attacked, and rarely at corner-kicks were these demarcations broken. The two full-backs guarded the line, one at each post, the centre-half marked the centre-forward and the wing-halves picked up the remaining opposing attackers, who rarely numbered more than two. The goalkeeper, unhampered by milling bodies, could move out comfortably and freely to punch or catch.

Any alteration to this pattern was so rare that it stood out. Leslie Compton, the big Arsenal centre-half who doubled as a county cricketer with his illustrious brother Denis, was one who fancied his chances at corner-kicks. It was a skill that was to earn him a Cup Winners medal in 1950, because, rare as it was for defenders to go forward at corners, it was even rarer for a forward to go back and mark them.

In the semi-final Arsenal met Chelsea and trailed by two goals. But Chelsea forfeited their lead simply because their defence at corners betrayed them. A Freddie Cox corner was allowed to swirl straight into the goal to pull one back and then Compton strolled forward to head in the equalizer from another Cox flag-kick. Just how unorthodox Compton had been can be judged from Joe Mercer's reaction as he saw his centre-half begin to move upfield. Mercer, the skipper, yelled at Compton to stay where he was—even though his side were trailing in the last few minutes of a Cup semi-final. Fortunately for Arsenal, Compton disobeyed. The Gunners won the replay and then beat Liverpool in the Final.

With goals harder to come by, more and more teams began to pay much closer attention to the possibilities which could come from determined assaults at set-pieces.

The chance to put the ball into the goal-mouth, to put defenders under great pressure and to keep that pressure on was not overlooked.

Defending against such tactics, when there was not only the danger of being outfought by powerful headwork but of being beaten to knock-downs by eager, determined attackers, forced managers to take deliberate and often ruthless steps.

Tall forwards with known prowess and determination in the air were brought back to help out at corners just as they were at free-kicks. The traditional policy of guarding the posts with full-backs was modified to ensure that the tallest and the strongest players were available to compete for the initial cross. Some teams even chose

Left The aftermath of Terry Cooper's match-winning goal for Leeds United against Arsenal in the 1968 League Cup final. Keeper Furnell looks up in protest against the challenge from Charlton that had prevented him reaching Gray's corner.
Below Diagram of the move. With Furnell beaten, Graham was well positioned to head off the line, but his clearance fell straight to Cooper.

COOPER
CHARLTON
GRAHAM
FURNELL

Above *Diagram illustrating a goal scored by Joe Royle for Everton against West Ham in 1970 when he was allowed to move in front of centre-half Stephenson to head in a corner. Ron Greenwood, the West Ham manager, later commented that defenders had become so obsessed with marking that they forgot the basics of going to meet the ball.* **Left** *This time Stephenson beats Royle to clear.*

only to protect the post nearest to the line of flight.

Corner-kicks were no longer unthinking skirmishes with the ball driven hopefully into the penalty area. Where the goalkeeper had once been confident of getting out to deal with most of them he now found himself baulked to such a degree that Arsenal's Bob Wilson was to say in 1970, 'I can't remember the last time I was able to get right out and catch the ball cleanly at a point where I was nearer the edge of the penalty area than my own goal-line. The best I can hope to do now is to get a touch and trust that I can get the ball far enough away from goal to be sure of getting back to deal with it if it gets knocked in again.'

Jim Furnell, Wilson's predecessor in the Arsenal goal, knew what it was to suffer from pressure tactics in critical circumstances. Playing against Leeds in the 1968 League Cup final, he found himself hemmed in on his goal-line by the then inevitable presence of England's centre-half Jack Charlton.

Charlton had become familiar in the role. He claimed that the Laws did not forbid him to stand in front of the keeper, blocking his line of vision, and that it was up to the keeper to take evasive action. Charlton felt that he was justified and recalled the fact that he had suffered continuously from foul tactics when coming up to take an orthodox station at corners.

He said: 'During the 1966 World Cup I was

fouled every time I went upfield in this way. I don't think I ever got a free-kick in my favour. It seems that referees will always give defenders the benefit of the doubt. They ignore the fact that the people who are detailed to jump with you are never jumping for the ball. They are simply body-checking you in the air. So why shouldn't I attempt something else?'

Charlton's change in tactics was undoubtedly provocative, and it led to controversy when Terry Cooper won the League Cup for Leeds with a powerful shot driven back into goal following a scrambled clearance at a corner-kick.

Pressed by Charlton, Furnell was unable to make contact with an inswinging corner from his left, and George Graham's half-header off the line carried to Cooper lurking some 20 yards infield and wide of the far post. Cooper steadied himself and drove a winning goal through the players packing the penalty area.

Arsenal did not play well that day but Furnell insisted that the Leeds goal was invalid because Charlton had deliberately prevented him from reaching the original centre.

Goalkeepers never really overcame this tactic although more efficient refereeing was to reduce some of its effectiveness. Free-kicks against players who made no attempt to play the ball when jumping with keepers became more frequent and this did relieve the overall pressure.

The technique of bringing back tall forwards to counter this threat went some way to aiding pressured keepers. But it did not always work out. When Liverpool paid a visit to Highbury in the late sixties, Tony Hateley, their controversial centre-forward whose one claim to fame was an exceptional ability in the air, was under orders to drop back for corners. He rose to meet one kick with perfect timing but with a warped sense of direction probably induced by a slight nudge, his forceful header crashed past Tommy Lawrence into his own goal.

The risk of a mistake such as Hateley's just had to be taken against teams who could muster a whole troup of big men. In the 1972 Home International Championship, Wales were armed in this way, calling on six-footers of the calibre

of Ron Davies, John Toshack, Wyn Davies, Mike England, John Roberts, Terry Hennessey and Terry Yorath. That Wales failed to score once in the whole competition was more an indictment of their complete inability to play worthwhile crosses than any weakness in the tactic itself.

Derby County, when establishing themselves in the First Division, were not really equipped to defend against a powerful aerial attack. Playing at Chelsea in the early part of the 1970-71 season they were seen to use Willie Carlin, at five feet four inches the smallest League player, as a guard at an upright.

This was immediately taken up by a BBC Television commentator as a curious and barely understandable deployment. What he overlooked was that Carlin's job was to protect the foot of the post. Anything over head height was the goalkeeper's responsibility. And in putting their smallest player on the post Derby had freed a full-back to contest the high ball around the penalty spot.

But whichever defender stands on the line, he must move forward quickly once the ball has been safely cleared beyond the point where a scoring shot is still a possibility; by doing this unwary attackers will be left in offside positions. Knowing exactly when to move out was a product of timing and experience and often the subject of one man's orders. Had Leeds' defence moved out too quickly against Arsenal in the 1972 FA Cup Final they might not have emerged as winners in the competition's centenary year.

Alan Ball's instant return shot, following a corner, was angled well out of goalkeeper David Harvey's reach, and low to his right. But Arsenal cheers were stifled when Paul Reaney, still sensibly stationed on that post, coolly cleared the ball from the line.

England were to suffer significantly from equally sound positioning when attempting to retrieve an almost lost cause in the quarter-finals of the 1972 European Championship against West Germany in Berlin.

Trailing 3-1 from the first match at Wembley and with a team picked for strength in the middle of the field, England needed an early goal.

They nearly got one when Alan Ball's inswinging corner-kick was helped across goal by Rodney Marsh to Martin Chivers. Chivers bent low into the chance but his header was deflected from the line by Hottges and England were denied a breakthrough.

Tactics apart, defenders had to conform to well-tried techniques when coping with corners. They needed to station themselves where they could see both their immediate opponent and the flight of the ball in order to cope with the dual responsibilities of defending at corner-kicks.

They would get more height with a jump taken from a short run than they would from a stationary position and they had to be first when going to meet the ball.

This last point was made with startling clarity when Joe Royle, Everton's tall, young centre-forward, scored from Alan Ball's corner-kick against West Ham at Upton Park in October 1970.

Instead of moving to meet the cross, Alan Stephenson, West Ham's centre-half, allowed Royle to make the first move and he was still a yard short when a powerful header was driven past goalkeeper Peter Grotier, deputizing for the injured Bobby Ferguson.

In the post-match discussion, Ron Greenwood saw the goal as highlighting a problem in making defenders efficient at corner-kicks: 'They become so obsessed with watching their man, that they forget the basic principle of getting the ball away.' That, after all, is what defence at corner-kicks is all about.

Coaching: Improve your defensive play at corner-kicks

The traditional defensive line-up at corner-kicks illustrates at least four defensive principles: cover, double cover, man-for-man marking and concentration in defence. Attacking players in scoring positions must be tightly marked, the goalkeeper should have adequate cover should he leave his charge and, because of the dangers from direct attempts on goal, he should have double cover in the form of a defender on each post.

At a corner, the goalkeeper, because he can handle the ball, is the key defender. He should position himself so that he can see what is going on; he must take notice of the kick being taken and the movement of opponents, especially those close to his goal. This is best done from the far post and just infield, which allows one defender to stand at the near post and another on the goal-line at the far post. The keeper should be prepared to come for all balls played into the goal area except those driven in to the near post; the defender on that post is often best situated to deal with these.

He should also take command and issue instructions on every ball played into the penalty area. The fact that he is on the far post gives him a commanding position to deal with balls dropping in close to goal. He has only to move back a few yards to deal with the ball struck well to the far post, yet he can move quickly forward for balls falling shorter. He should attempt to catch the ball if possible, or, if heavily pressured, he should punch into areas where the ball cannot be volleyed back by an opponent. The best areas are towards the touchlines, well away from the front of his goal. The keeper should call to let his defenders know he is leaving his line so that they can move out of his way and give him extra cover should he mishandle.

This positioning may alter slightly if there is a direct danger from a ball swerved in on the near post. Some teams send up a big defender to stand on the goal-line in this region. The goalkeeper may feel more comfortable if he moves into a more central position to cope with this danger; this means that the defender on the far post may have to move out to meet balls played deep to the far post. The goalkeeper should have ample opportunities to practise these tactics so that an understanding can be made between him and his fellow defenders.

Defenders should mark man for man with a special emphasis on dangerous players. Opponents known to be good headers of a ball must be marked by the best men in the air in the defending team. This will have to be decided before the corner is taken so that each danger man can be marked really tightly in order to prevent him taking a free jump at the ball. The marking should be on a dog-leg basis. This means that each defender should be goalside and slightly in front of the attacker he is marking. This position will help the defender to get in first on the short ball and also allow him to move back and challenge in the air for balls played slightly over him. This technique should be practised often within normal training and coaching sessions because of its importance in defending against cross balls.

Opposing defenders coming up for corners must also be watched closely. Forwards must be prepared to follow their men and either continue to mark until the danger has passed or hand them over to his own defenders.

Goals are scored from corner-kicks mainly because a defender has failed to track an attacker coming in late, or has failed to jump with him, or has been late to cover the second ball, the one that either is knocked on or down by one attacker for another to finish off. Practice is essential, not only for the individual but also collectively in order to cope with these problems. Vary the types of corner-kicks; this will also assist in your tactics when attacking.

Right Diagram illustrating the correct marking position at corner-kicks. A defender should stand goalside and slightly forward of his man. From this position he can watch his opponent and the ball and be in first to head away the cross.

Below A scene from the Leeds versus Juventus Fairs Cup final shows perfectly the pushing and obstruction that takes place at corner-kicks.

JOHNSTON

MERRICK

WRIGHT (A)

WRIGHT (B)

10

PUSKAS (B)   PUSKAS (A)

DIAGRAM/RESEARCH—PATHE NEWS

Once a week, when Billy Wright was their manager, the Arsenal players had a film show. The films were, of course, of football matches, and chosen to illustrate a particular tactical point. But whatever was shown on the screen at Highbury, the Arsenal players clamoured to see one goal above all others.

The requests for the goal, scored by Ferenc Puskas for Hungary in their 6-3 rout of England in November 1953, were an 'in' joke for Arsenal, because the film showed the great inside-forward utterly deceiving Wright before he cracked the ball past Gil Merrick. But the goal *deserved* to be seen over and over again—as a memorable piece of opportunism.

Wright, who later left football to take an executive position in television, recalled: 'The boys loved to see that one. They were being mischievous of course. Whenever we studied films, the England-Hungary one was top of the list with them. Seeing the 'Boss' embarrassed by Puskas was all part of the scene. But even though I cringed every time I saw myself scampering yards in the wrong direction it didn't alter my admiration for Puskas' skill.'

It happened on a day which proved to be the moment of truth for British football. Deficiencies born out of insularity and conceit were vividly exposed as a great Hungarian team tore England apart, destroying the belief that they were invincible at Wembley.

Ferenc Puskas, Hungary's captain, scored twice. But it was the first of his goals which remains the most famous because the very manner of its execution captured the full flourish of Hungarian skill and confidence.

The fact that it involved the almost contemptuous dismissal of Billy Wright was in every way significant.

Wright was more than just England's captain. Blond, sturdy, fit, uncompromising but unswervingly fair, he typified the best type of British professional player. The sight of him groping

Billy Wright's groping underlined England's total humiliation

in total confusion underlined the extent of England's humiliation.

A popular theory at that time was that continental players could not shoot.

Hidegkuti, another of Hungary's great forwards, destroyed it within a minute against England when he finished a fine move with a savage goal. England fought back and equalized through Jackie Sewell, but within half an hour they were trailing 4-1. It was the third goal which remains the most memorable.

England were back in strength when Czibor took a pass from Kocsis and flew at left-back Eckersley. Czibor went for the byeline before cutting a low diagonal pass into the penalty area, and into Puskas' path.

Puskas seemed to have run too early, and received the ball outside the near post, leaving himself with no apparent angle for a shot.

COURTESY PATHE NEWS

Above left Diagram of Ferenc Puskas destroying England and Billy Wright at Wembley in 1953.
Left Wright charges in, but Puskas pulls the ball back away from him using the sole of his left foot.
Right The move sets up Puskas to shoot past Merrick.

the box

Blatantly left-footed, he was running right, and England reacted to the angle.

Billy Wright was famous for the swiftness with which he pounced in the tackle. He pounced, calculating that Puskas could only continue moving in the direction in which he was running. But England's captain merely found himself flailing at thin air.

Puskas checked, dragged the ball back with the studs of his left boot and watched Wright go galloping by. Then with no more than a flicker of adjustment to his balance he rifled an instant shot beyond Merrick's left shoulder. It was over so quickly that Wright still had his back to Puskas when the ball hit the net.

Puskas, dragging the ball back, watched Wright gallop past

The sheer audacity of it stunned England's defenders. Puskas had been surrounded by them and had been threatened with extinction. Yet he had looked totally detached.

He went into that match comparatively unheralded outside his own country. His fame as a great goalscorer was to blossom even though Hungary's greatness died with the Budapest uprising a few years later.

Real Madrid claimed him in exile and there were to be countless examples of his tremendous finishing powers in the years that followed. But it was his first goal at Wembley which assured him of immortality in England.

Unlike other great goalscorers, Puskas had no great pace. But he had an extremely sensitive touch, immense power of shot, absolute confidence and tremendous determination.

All great goalscorers have been able to call on most of these qualities but the one common to them all is the latter.

Gustav Sebes, coach of that great Hungarian team has said: 'When we were building our teams we discarded players whose ability was equal to that of Puskas and the rest. We let them go because they were suspect in temperament. They had to prove their determination and aggression on top of their skill.'

Jimmy Greaves, Denis Law, and George Best all emerged as great opportunists in British football, displaying single-mindedness and determination in the tightest of situations.

If Greaves' courage was sometimes masked by a tendency to wander the field with disinterest, it was nevertheless undeniable.

Eddie Hopkinson, a fine goalkeeper with Bolton and England, recalls: 'Jimmy's eyes went cold when he was in front of goal. He was only concerned with one thing—putting the ball into the back of the net, and he invariably did. He had this tremendous ability to put absolutely everything out of his mind.'

Greaves not only scored great goals, he also got a lot of them. He displayed all the essential qualities of the great finisher—tremendous balance, quick reflexes, perfect timing, sense of anticipation, and he was marvellously alert

Above right Denis Law twists acrobatically to volley a cross at goal. Law's ability to adjust himself like a gymnast in the goal-area made him a constant scorer of opportunist goals—at a time when tough defences were dominating the First Division.

DIAGRAM, RESEARCH—LONDON WEEKEND TELEVISION

Labels on diagram: BONDS, WOODS, GREAVES (A), HAMMOND, MORRIS, BOYCE, COLLARD, GREAVES (B), SIVELL, ROBSON, 6, JEFFERSON, BELL, MILLS, 3, 9, HURST

to opportunity. He struck his shots with a minimum of back lift and there was a marvellous economy about it all.

Greaves had no time for the frills of football. He was never seen juggling with the ball during the pre-match kick-in. He just shot for goal. It was the essence of his game.

He spent his last season with West Ham. By then he had lost much of his zest for football. But one goal scored against Ipswich was entirely in character with his illustrious career.

There were at least a dozen players in Ipswich's goalmouth when a volleyed shot from Ron Boyce bounced down and back from the underside of the cross bar.

Greaves did not seem to move with any great speed. The crucial factor was that he moved first. Three strides took him to the ball and he put it away before anyone could get to him.

It is impossible to give a footballer this quality of anticipation, the alertness which is distinctive among the great goalscorers.

Greaves himself said: 'I never knew why, but I found myself reacting to possibility. Some sort of sixth sense enabled me to be on hand to punish errors.'

Denis Law's goals were a testimony to his speed of reflex and his extrovert willingness to put himself at the ball when others would be put off by an awareness of physical danger.

Playing for Manchester United against Sunderland in the second replay of a fifth round FA Cup tie in 1964 he came from nowhere to snatch an equalizer when it seemed that Sunderland might reach the quarter-finals of the competition.

It was a miserable night at Huddersfield. Law was back on the ground where he had first entered English football as a spindly teenager from Aberdeen. What was left of the turf glistened with rain, and each tackle was made

Above Diagram showing the art of football's supreme opportunist, Jimmy Greaves, against Ipswich in 1971. He was the first to move to a rebound and score. Above right Greaves (partly hidden) scores.

in a cloud of spray.

Sunderland went in front on the hour with a goal from an alert little forward, Nick Sharkey. Had they held their lead for five minutes, Manchester United might have found life difficult.

Law was in no mood for such aggravation. In United's next attack David Herd, a muscular striker, sped swiftly to the right corner flag and centred on the run.

When the ball was struck, Law was still poised on the edge of the penalty area. When it skipped out of goalkeeper Jim Montgomery's hands on the near post, Law was on top of the chance and stabbed home an equalizer. Within ten minutes United were leading 4-1, and ran

Coaching: Improve your sharpness inside the penalty-area

Scoring goals is at the same time one of the hardest and one of the most stimulating tasks in football. The tremendous exhilaration is reflected by players who leap about and punch the air when they have scored. To score often needs quick reactions when opportunities present themselves. Players like Jimmy Greaves may be born and not made, but every player can increase his sharpness in front of goal.

In the six-yard box things happen especially quickly. The attacking player will want to get to the ball first, but as well as concentrating on its movement, he has to be aware of the position of defenders, especially the goalkeeper, and, above all, the position of the goal in relation to himself.

This awareness stems from the simple ability to see out of the corner of your eye. Check this by looking at an object directly in front of you; now note what else you can see without taking your eyes from the object. It is almost possible to notice things at right angles to you.

Start cultivating this ability with the ball coming directly at you rather than at an angle. If you are on your own, find yourself a wall that you can mark targets on. Make various marks about a foot square and number each of them. Stand about fifteen yards away from the wall and hit the ball firmly against it. As it bounces

back to you, play it first-time at one of the targets. As you move in on the ball cultivate the habit of 'seeing' the target without taking your eye off the ball.

Take a friend out to practise with you and you can adapt this routine. Play the ball to your partner, he plays it back to you—like a wall-pass or a one-two—and you shoot at the target. Remember that you must nominate which target you are trying to hit before you start. As the ball rebounds from your shot, your friend should control it, play a wall-pass with you and then he shoots at his nominated target. Then you collect the rebound and so on.

If you have another friend with you, put him in goal so that you now have a goalkeeper to beat. A practice competition is always a good way to sharpen your skills. Chalk a target about six yards wide and four feet high on the wall. The ball must be played first-time as it rebounds from the wall and it must hit the target.

It is a practise for two players. Start the competition by striking the ball from about ten yards and hitting the target. As it rebounds your opponent must hit it back first-time at the target. You gain a point every time he misses the target, and, of course, he gets one every time you miss. The object, then, is not only to hit the target, but to hit it in such a way that it rebounds

awkwardly for your opponent. To play this properly you will have to concentrate on the ball, but also be aware of the goal and the position of your opponent.

At a training session with your club you can practise coming in to meet the ball at an angle. With your goalkeeper in goal, split the rest of your squad into four equal groups. Each group should contain at least three players.

Place a group in each corner of the penalty area with the two groups almost on the goal-line having a ball per player. Start with the group on the goal-line to the goalkeeper's left. The first player in that group plays a low cross to the near post, and the first player in the group 180 degrees away across at the far corner of the penalty area sprints in to connect with the ball at the near post, trying to turn it past the keeper. Then the first player in the group on the goal-line to the keeper's right crosses a ball to his near post and the first player in the fourth group races in to try at goal. Carry this practice through until everyone has had half a dozen cracks at goal.

At the near post you should aim to make contact about six yards out and just inside the post. On your way in try to assess the position of the keeper out of the corner of your eye, and try to place the ball wide of him. Remember to keep the ball low and go for accuracy. The best kick is in fact with the inside of the foot to make it almost a pass into the goal.

Although this is a relatively simple practice, it will build up your confidence and help you to

WESTMINSTER PRESS

out comfortable 5-1 winners.

Montgomery had every reason to curse Law's electric reactions. In the first replay at Sunderland he made a hash of a goal-kick, and the ball barely carried to the edge of the penalty area. Although he was policed by Charlie Hurley, a powerful Eire centre-half, then in his prime,

Movements timed to the last stride—such was the alertness of Law

Law reached the ball first to punish Montgomery's error with a scoring shot.

Had he hit the ball a shade inside the penalty box, the goal would not have counted—as goal-kicks that do not go out of the area have to be re-taken. But Law's alertness incorporated an ability to time his movements perfectly.

The difference between meeting the ball just outside and just inside the area was only a matter of half a stride or a fraction of a second. But Law timed it to perfection—as in so many of his goals.

As the edge to Law's blade, while not blunted, failed to cut so regularly, his team-mate at Old Trafford, George Best, began to show similarly smart reactions to goalscoring chances.

Supreme confidence and skill enabled him to score a typical goal in a European Cup semi-final against Real Madrid in 1968.

Closely marked he began a run across field from the right-hand corner of the penalty area when John Aston prepared to centre from the opposite wing. Best checked, almost as though dismissing the possibility that he could get involved in the move.

It was the perfect deception, causing his marker to relax. Then from a standing start,

Best accelerated away to meet the low pass which Aston cut into him. He was still at right angles to goal when he drove a killing shot on the turn. An astonishing feature of the goal was that the ball had bobbled up as Best swung into it. He simply made an adjustment abandoning his original intention to hit the ball off the floor. It was a superb volley which brought the Old Trafford crowd to their feet, and deservedly won the game.

Above all else, it was this ability to adjust which characterized Puskas, Greaves, Law and all the great goalscorers. However, wherever and whenever the ball came to them, with the merest whiff of a goal in the air, they could adjust both physically—twisting their bodies into the best possible position—and mentally—by assuming a cool, killer frame of mind—to the needs of the situation. Great goalscorers will always be great players.

keep calm when the real chance occurs in a game. You can vary the practice by making the players on the goal-line play their crosses to the far post. Here you will discover that the best target to place your headers or volleys is just inside the post furthest from you.

The final variation is to have two players moving in for the cross—one at each post. If the ball is played to the far post the player at the near post turns and looks for the knocked down header that needs finishing off.

So far no defenders have interfered with your efforts to get the ball into the goal. Introduce defenders into your practice and your skills will be sharpened even further. Stand about ten yards from the goal with a defender marking you. Get a third player to play the ball into different positions in the penalty area so that you have to beat your opponent to get a quick shot in at goal.

You can increase the pressure on this activity by getting several players to play balls into the area near goal, so that as soon as you have got one shot in there is another ball played in for you to fight for. You can vary this by playing two against two in this situation.

Another variation is to get your winger to cross balls to an unmarked forward at the far post. As he heads the ball down you try to beat the defender marking you to turn it into goal. Here you will learn quickly that to get into position too early is a mistake. If you are a little late moving, a diving header or a lunge will often compensate. But to be in too early will only result

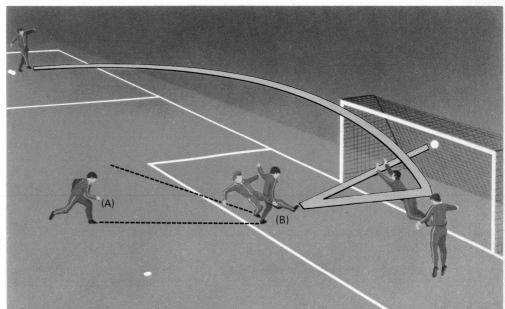

Above Opportunism can be practised. Try to beat a defender to a series of headers from crosses—and score.

DIAGRAM

in loss of mobility when you have to stand still waiting for the ball.

The greatest asset of all is to *want* to get the ball into the net. You will require courage, coolness, accuracy, speed of both thought and

movement. But if you continually work on your skills—and really want to score goals, whether they go in off your shin, thigh, chest or even the back of your neck, you will regularly enjoy the greatest feeling in football.

LAWLER JEANDUPEUX CHIVERS STIERLI BLAETTLER MADELEY KUNZLI MCFARLAND MOORE BANKS COOPER

The near post header

England's reputation for being able to resist the world's most skilful attackers was severely dented when they conceded two goals against Switzerland in October 1971.

Superior fitness finally saw them through a critical Nations Cup tie in Basle, but not before they had been embarrassed by the fluent quality of Swiss teamwork and one memorable scoring header—a superb effort at England's near post.

The fitness was beginning to take effect as England approached half-time leading 2-1. It was then that the Swiss were revived by a goal from their most threatening attacker, Fritz Kunzli.

Kunzli had good cause to regard his effort as an outstanding point in his career. To score he had to outwit Gordon Banks and Bobby Moore, England's two most experienced defenders, and to display a considerable degree of courage. Sir Alf Ramsey knew that he was not short of that.

He had seen Kunzli flash across the front of Turkish defenders to get his head to a centre dropped short when watching the Swiss three weeks earlier. The point was not ignored. Ramsey said at the time: 'This man is dangerous. He thinks quickly, and he will go to meet the ball played in at the near post. It is something we shall have to guard against.'

England's team manager conveyed the warning to his players, but saw them disregard it at a vital stage in the match. Most of Switzerland's dangerous attacks had developed along the left, and they threatened again when midfield player Kuhn carried the ball forward. He found left-back Stierli pushing up ahead of him on the touchline. Stierli wasted no time in making his centre, drilling it first time, head high, into the England penalty area.

From a standing start Kunzli cut across in front of Moore towards the near post as

Banks scurried back to meet the danger. It was Kunzli who got there first, and, although Banks got a touch to the header, he could not prevent it crossing the line.

It was a fine goal, but not a novel one. England had made much use of the move themselves and had learned to be wary of it.

No one more so than Bobby Moore. He had seen the technique developed at his own club, West Ham, and he knew those factors which were vital to scoring and preventing goals in such situations.

He knew, for instance, that the cross had to go in early just as Stierli had played it, and that it was to be aimed at space and not at a player. As a defender he had learned that it was necessary to move in and mark that space; to be first to the ball regardless of what the attackers were doing.

He had seen many make the mistake of not doing this when his clubmates Geoff Hurst and Martin Peters had created and taken chances with cunning and skill.

West Ham were thinkers. It was part of their tradition to try and be a move ahead of the rest, and they already were when the use of space in front of the near post was suddenly spotlighted in the 1966 World Cup.

In beating a rusting Brazilian team in Liverpool the Hungarians had capitalized on sending players in to meet short centres. One devastating volley from Farkas had watching coaches making hurried notes, but England had no need for schooling. They had Hurst and Peters, and that was to prove significant.

Left opposite Diagram showing how Switzerland unlocked the England defence with a near post header in Basle in October 1971. Left-back Stierli crossed the ball quickly and centre-forward Kunzli nipped in front of Bobby Moore to power his header past Gordon Banks.
Left Kunzli's header on its way into the net.
Left below A close understanding, built up at West Ham, between Geoff Hurst and Martin Peters served England well. Here Hurst's near post header from Peters' cross beats Argentina in 1966.

To reach the semi-finals of the competition they had to overcome an intimidating Argentine side at Wembley. The sending off of Rattin, the Argentinian captain, and the gross cynicism of their play obscured the fact that England scored one of the finest goals in the series.

Their delinquent attitude apart, there was much to be said for the Argentinians. After Rattin's controversial departure they settled down to play with a firm resolve, and England were hard pushed to dominate ten men who managed to convey the impression that a substitute had been slipped in unnoticed.

When it seemed as though England would never score, they did. Ray Wilson sent Peters along the left, and Ramsey's most adaptable player floated his centre in front of the defenders.

The pieces fell rapidly into place. Peters was not looking for Hurst. He was aiming at space confident that Hurst would attempt to find it. He did. Peters said afterwards. 'I did not know where Geoff was, but I was sure that he would be looking for the ball in that area.' He swung the ball in, high towards the near post.

As Roma pressed to the near side of his goal, he suddenly found Hurst flashing across and upwards. The Argentinian goalkeeper pawed at the ball. But it was little more than a desperate gesture. Hurst had already got the vital touch with his head, and the ball nestled in the far side of the goal. The move was to be repeated many times by these two players in the years which followed, and until Peters departed to Tottenham it was a telling feature of West Ham's play. In Peters' last full season at Upton Park the roles were reversed, with Hurst playing in the crosses and Peters combining stealth and courage to meet them at the near post. They combined memorably in a League game against Manchester City, but Peters gives Hurst the accolade for the best near post header he has ever seen.

The best near post header Martin Peters had ever seen

It happened in Brussels. England met Belgium in February 1970 as part of their Mexican World Cup preparations. It was a match of some importance because the Belgians were seen as powerful contenders among the European teams who had qualified for Mexico.

By winning, England confirmed their own potential, and it was another Hurst-Peters move which gave them ascendancy. Peters drifted wide along the Belgian left unseen until the danger was evident. By this time he had perfected spin as well as accuracy. The ball was curled deliberately in, and Hurst on the run thrust his head in to complete the offering.

Hurst was involved so consistently in such moves that he seemed to do it by instinct. But the technique was far more deliberate.

For several seasons Hurst had Francis Lee of Manchester City as his striking partner in England's attack, but Lee encountered problems in adjusting to the needs of his more experienced team-mate. He said: 'I was used to looking up when I got into positions that I could cross from. But if I didn't see anyone in the middle I wouldn't hit it across. If I crossed it, and there was no one there to meet it, I would look a bad player.'

But Hurst's counter was simple: 'You play the ball into that area. Leave the problem of how

TRAPPENIERS

HEYLENS

OSGOOD

JECK

HURST

VAN MOER

DOCKX

THESSEN

DEWALQUE

HUGHES

PETERS

to meet it to me. Don't worry if you can't see me, I'll be there or thereabouts.'

They got it right when playing against Uruguay in Montevideo in 1969. Lee played the ball from the right wing towards space at the near post, and Hurst arrived to score—with a volley, but the same technique was involved.

Hurst said: 'It is not easy for a player to appreciate that he can safely put the ball in short when his colleagues look as though they are waiting for it to be hit to the far side of the goal.

'If he drops it short and no one comes he is liable to criticism from the crowd. This is why it is vital to understand each other, to trust each other.

'Martin had no doubts about it because he knew that I would make an effort to get there. The vital thing for me was that I moved late. If I went too early then the man marking me would have a chance to adjust. The timing had to be just right. Half a yard was enough to get a touch.'

Chelsea were among the teams who made use of the ploy, and it was to prove immensely valuable to them when winning the FA Cup in 1970.

A goal down with time running out, they were awarded a free-kick wide on Leeds' right. Leeds, strangely in view of their discipline, made the error of not sending two men out to stand ten yards from the ball as Ron Harris prepared to take the kick. There was only Peter Lorimer, and he was half-way.

Harris turned the ball to John Hollins, and when he swept it into the goalmouth Ian Hutchinson thundered across Jack Charlton to beat Gary Sprake on the near post.

It is doubtful whether there was much design involved in the goal. The urgency and emotion involved in the moment suggests that the centre was entirely speculative and that it was Hutchinson's willingness which made the goal. An aggressive, courageous player, he was willing to put himself in on the half chance, and his equalizing goal came from little more than that.

The use of centres to the near post was a significant development of a technique used by the Brazilians when winning the 1958 World Cup in Sweden.

That it should go largely unnoticed in England at the time was an indication of the stagnation of management at that time. But it was not lost on the Welsh players who surprised everyone by reaching the quarter-finals before losing by one goal to the eventual winners.

Coaching: Develop the habit of running to the near post in the hunt for goals

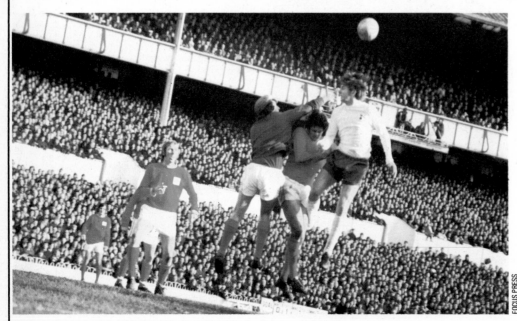

Being able to attack at the near post will give a team the quality of variety in their attacking play. If the ball can be got to a forward at the near post, and he reacts positively, then there is a good chance of a goal.

For the move to work the forward must work hard on his heading skills. But the work will pay dividends. Most likely the header to fit the situation will be a glancing effort, although if the forward reaches the ball inside the near post a powerful effort aimed just inside that post might well do the trick.

A ball suspended on a length of string or thong is the best device for brushing up your heading skills. You can practise on your own as often as you like. Get as much body power into your headers as you can, and make contact with your forehead. Always try to develop the habit

Left *Martin Peters looks to get in a near post header for Spurs against Nottingham Forest.*
Right opposite *A suspended ball is an important piece of equipment for practising heading techniques. Here one player tries to reach the ball before another—as in a near post situation.*

Left opposite *Diagram of Geoff Hurst scoring with a near post header for England versus Belgium in Brussels in 1970—once more bravely throwing himself in to meet a cross from Peters.*
Above *Derby County's John O'Hare gets in a header at Chelsea's near post despite the close attentions of defender Marvin Hinton.*
Right *Hurst's goalscoring header against Belgium. Martin Peters has said that this particular effort was the best near post header he had ever seen. It was England's second goal in a match they won 3-1.*

Dave Bowen, the Arsenal captain, led the Welsh team and recalls: 'Didi, their great midfield player, would come through and knock in balls which seemed to be going nowhere. They would be hit into space between our goalkeeper, Jack Kelsey, and the bye-line corner of the penalty area. Then just as Jack would go across preparing to collect the ball for a goal kick, someone would arrive in front of him. Then it was confusion.'

This unprotected area became known as 'dead space' among coaches and managers. The ability of players like Peters to find it with their passes and the willingness and cunning of men like Hurst to go into it made it come alive. Defenders learned to guard against such threats but they could never be certain—as Bobby Moore found out against Switzerland in Basle.

of 'throwing your eyes at the ball' and you will not be caught out by any late movement of a ball in flight. Begin on the suspended ball by letting it hang still. Practise making firm contact, and then work up to deflections—the sort you will need at the near post—by flicking and turning the head at the point of impact.

Now make the suspended ball swing and, as it comes at you, turn your head and flick the ball—so that it carries on behind you. Attack the ball: do not let it just bounce off your temple. Get a friend to practise with you. Let him head the ball; as it swings back you deflect the ball off either to one side or the other. After your deflection the ball will swing back, and your pal steps in again. He makes another firm header, and then you move in again to deflect the ball as it swings back once more—and so on. To keep going you will need to develop good timing.

To reach near post crosses in a match you will have to steal a few inches on the defender who is marking you, so get your pal to act as a defender. Let him stand slightly to the side and in front of you, but he must not move until you do. Set the ball swinging, then try to get a header at it before him. This will develop your sense of timing. Progressively raise the ball higher off the ground so that you have not only got to concentrate on getting to the ball first and sending it in the required direction, but also jumping above the ball to head it downwards.

The time spent on the suspended ball will stand you in good stead when you move on to a training session. A good team practice for large numbers is an even-sided game played with the hands, like basketball, but goals can only be scored by headers. This leads to realistic goalmouth situations and sets up a succession of good heading opportunities.

But when the heading skills have been developed, the near post move should be practised as a team routine. Begin simply. Set up a full-back, a winger, a centre-forward and the goalkeeper. The goalkeeper throws the ball to the right full-back on the half-way line near the touch line. He plays the ball down the line to the winger, who turns and runs towards the corner-flag while the full-back comes up in support. When the winger gets about five yards from the bye-line, he turns and lays it back for the full-back to cross first time to the near post where the centre-forward has moved to get a header in at the goal. Defenders can be brought into this activity, but remember that when you are working on a specific skill it is easy for opponents to cut it out, so make sure the defenders act in a passive manner while the attackers are getting a feel of the situation. Gradually build up the practice until it involves most of the team. Play attack against defence into one goal, with say seven attackers playing the four or five defenders. The attackers should keep the ball wide, using the extra men, and aim the crosses into the near post area.

But above all what you need to win the ball at the near post is courage. To gain those few vital inches in front of the defence you may have to fling yourself in headlong to reach the ball. . . . It will be played in to the near post area, that is the job of your team-mates. Your task is to put yourself in first and to go in with wholehearted determination. Be brave, and you will score some great goals.

BALL

MARSH

BELL (A)

First-time football

One England move in the international against Yugoslavia at Wembley in October 1972 gladdened the heart of Sir Alf Ramsey. The England team manager was gradually rebuilding for an assault on the 1974 World Cup. But he faced a familiar problem as senior players withdrew through injuries and club calls.

England had to be content with a 1-1 draw and might easily have lost in the last 15 minutes. Yet one decisive series of passes, early in the second half, might have spared Ramsey's anxiety.

Rodney Marsh's challenge set England free and a first-time pass from Colin Bell found Alan Ball. Ball instantly knocked another pass forward to Mike Channon and the Southampton forward, playing in his first senior international, laid it immediately square to Bell striding up on his left in support. It was sweet stuff. Bell strode on but an immaculate build-up, all first-time passes, was spoiled by a shot struck just wide of the far post.

Moments like this encouraged coaches to believe that progressive first-time passing was not beyond the talents of truly outstanding players. And that when such movements were combined, few defences could withstand the strain.

Of all the players used by Leeds United in the formative years of Don Revie's distinguished management, none proved more influential in this way than Bobby Collins. Only as tall as a jockey

and weighing barely ten stone, Collins was nevertheless one of the fiercest competitors in the business. His tackling was venomous. His playing attitudes mean. But he had an abundance of skill, marvellous vision and two of the best feet in the game.

Collins laced up the smallest boots in the club. It was immaculate timing and phenomenal strength ratio which enabled him to strike passes accurately over long distances. His short range passing was superb. Quick, simple, economical. He was, in fact, a master of first-time passing, what professionals term 'one-touch play'.

Les Cocker, the Leeds trainer-coach and one of Sir Alf Ramsey's assistants during the World Cups of 1966 and 1970, said this of Collins: 'We hear a lot about players who are regarded as a "professionals' professional". This feller fits the bill perfectly. He knows the game backwards. He sees things during the pressure of a match which some players wouldn't see from the stands. Above all, he is probably the best first-time passer around.

'To really appreciate that you have to watch him in five-a-side games. When we restrict those games to one-touch at the ball, he simply runs them. His head seems to be on a swivel. He takes in all the angles and knocks the ball around perfectly.'

Collins was 31 when Leeds signed him from Everton in March 1962. Many sound judges felt that he was over the hill. But over the next four years he was to help Leeds emerge as one of the most feared clubs in Europe.

Leeds were to find a more than adequate successor in Johnny Giles, who came from Manchester United in 1963. What Giles learned from Collins was the need to apply himself more ruthlessly to the task of winning matches. He learned well. And like Collins he mastered the art of linking quickly and simply with his teammates.

First-time passing was regarded as the ultimate in team play. It frustrated the opposition and when put together properly it created some of the most memorable of inter-passing movements. The ability to make accurate contact with the ball first time was not in itself enough. The pass had to be accurate, thoughtful and backed up by a sharp awareness of what might be happening elsewhere.

'Keep it simple. Keep it quick,' was Arthur Rowe's instruction to his players at Spurs when founding the style which was to revive a great club in the fifties. Rowe's philosophy was based on the understanding of an uncomplicated fact. The ball could travel at greater speed than a running man. If his players moved the ball accurately and supported each other intelligently then penetrating movements could be set up in any area of the field.

That tradition was to live on at Spurs long

Above Diagram illustrating how England tore through the Yugoslavia defence with a series of first-time passes at Wembley in October 1972. The ball flowed from Marsh to Bell and then to Ball. Ball immediately found Channon, who laid the ball to the supporting Bell. Every pass was made instantly, but the move was denied a perfect finish when Bell pulled his shot past the far post.
Right Chelsea's Chris Garland sends in a first-time volley against Sheffield United. So often the pace of top-class football allows players only one touch at the ball.

MARIC

CHANNON

BELL (C)

BELL (B)

DIAGRAM

after Rowe had left them. It could be seen distinctively in later years when they dominated with a team which won the double in 1961. By then Spurs had acquired more variety. But they still liked to play the ball rapidly out of defence and no one served an apprenticeship at White Hart Lane without learning to appreciate the value of instant passing.

Dave Mackay, whose warrior approach and infinite skills made him one of the great players in Spurs' history, had few peers when knocking the ball off first time. Bill Nicholson was to say of him: 'This man has a tremendous range of kicking skills. He could play the ball long, short. He could volley, half volley. Strike it in full flight. Swerve it. Dip it. He could do the lot'. This talent was to serve Mackay well when he left Spurs to help Brian Clough bring Derby County back from the wilderness.

Clough had signed Roy McFarland, a promising young centre-half from Tranmere. With Mackay alongside him, McFarland was to develop into the best centre-half in Britain; to play for England and to confirm the extent of Clough's judgement.

McFarland was more than aware of the debt he owed to Mackay. 'He really was unbelievable. The Boss played him on my left side and a lot of teams tried to expose Dave. You could see their reason-

ing. If they could get at Dave, put him under pressure, they might get him turning. But Dave was too shrewd for them. Before anyone could get on top of him he would get the ball off. The great thing was that he never put people in trouble. He used to say that he had tremendous confidence in us because he knew we were skilful enough to take first-time passes. But really he never did put us in the cart. I don't think I've ever seen anybody who could use a first-time pass better than he did.'

Denis Law's reputation as one of the sharpest finishers in world football may have concealed the fact that he made almost as many goals as he took. Law's reflexes took him to the ball before most defenders. His quick thinking and his sure touch often led to goals for players bustling in support. A flick. A tap. A devastating prod into unguarded space. These were the weapons which Law used so skilfully around the penalty areas of Europe.

Confidence was vital to such skill. And it was confidence which coaches worked to establish when ordering one-touch sessions during training. The good players assessed situations before they received the ball. They positioned themselves so they could make immediate contact with a colleague, and moved off so that they could link up again.

When England met West Germany in the second leg of the European Championship semi-final during the spring of 1972 both teams held practice sessions in Berlin's historic Olympic Stadium.

Both managers, England's Sir Alf Ramsey and Germany's Helmut Schoen, concentrated on passing. But it was significant that, while the English players were eager for two touches at the ball, the Germans were happy to settle for one.

Schoen clustered all the outfield players in his squad within a tight area barely more than twenty yards square. Five of them were stationed within the square. The rest around its edges. The ball was moved first time. The players within the square tried to intercept. The tackling was fierce.

RAY GREEN

The degree of skill, significantly high.

From there the Germans moved out to work over a much larger area but always playing the ball first time. They used three balls among fifteen players. On the move. Short first-time passes. Long ones.

West Ham manager Ron Greenwood had used a similar practice for many years and, although his team struggled to emulate their success of the mid-sixties, their play always appealed.

However, it was clear that no team could hope to function entirely on the principle of instant communication. There had to be variety and those who did not have it proved to be vulnerable.

Everton were far from vulnerable when using Alan Ball, Howard Kendall and Colin Harvey as their midfield trio. But they did not ignore the value of longer passes up to their tall centre-forward Joe Royle.

Quick-thinking defenders could get themselves out of trouble by playing the ball off first time and running to collect a return. Quick-thinking forwards could avoid close marking in the same way.

Brazil's squad of substitutes always remained on the field while their team rested through half-time intervals during the 1970 World Cup. They played one-touch constantly and with amazing skill. Volleying the ball off to each other, while on the move around a circle.

It seemed to be part of them. Such fluency was never as common in Britain. But there were players who could control a game with a minimum of possession. And when England for the only time in the game really ripped through Yugoslavia on a mild October night, the value of such players was unquestionable. It was only by the development of such skill that England had a real chance of beating teams who defended in depth.

Coaching: Develop the control for one-touch play

Many players are reluctant to play the ball off first time. Sometimes this may be because there is no supporting player, but more often they have not the necessary confidence in their ability to play it quickly and accurately. Good ball control, then, is the ability to play a ball first time in the required direction.

Try a simple practice with a ball between two of you; stand about 15 yards from your partner and play the ball to feet first time every time. This sounds very easy but to begin with twenty passes without the ball going astray will be quite good, especially if you manage to keep the ball moving crisply along the ground and send it accurately to each other.

You will find in this practice that invariably you play the ball badly when you are forced to stretch for it. This means that either the ball has been played inaccurately to you or you have failed to get your body in the correct position through taking this simple exercise too easily.

You will also find that even though you are watching the ball—which is essential if you are to strike it cleanly—you can still see your partner out of the corner of your eye. This awareness enables you to play the ball to your partner when he moves off after playing the ball to you. This introduction of movement is the natural progression from doing this exercise in static positions.

The ball does not always come to you along the ground; it has to be laid off first time on the full or sometimes on the half-volley. Ask your partner to chip the ball to you from about 25 yards so that it is just dropping short of you. The idea here is for you to move forward and play the ball back with the inside of your foot, either as it hits the ground, the half-volley, or before it does, the full volley.

Either way, the ball must be returned so that your partner can chip the ball accurately back to you again. This then becomes a first time pass-

ing practice requiring a high degree of 'touch' and 'feel'. Present your foot squarely to the ball; it must drop so that after a couple of bounces it is rolling along to the foot your partner wishes to chip it with. Again, this is a straightforward exercise but it does require skill and concentration.

This type of practice is excellent for cultivating technique as a warming-up exercise, and it will also pay dividends in a match in helping to change the pace of the game. It is impossible as well as undesirable to play the ball first time all the time, but first-time play is essential to break through tight defences by quickly changing the pace.

Work on this in groups of four, playing three against one in a twelve-yard square. Condition the exercise so that the ball has to be played first time for six consecutive passes before a player is allowed to put his foot on it to slow the play down. This means the players off the ball must concentrate on supporting the ball quickly, knowing it is going to be played first time. They must also make sure they are not in too close and that they themselves have space in which to work.

The player receiving the ball must be aware of the movement, not only of his two supporters but also of the defender, so that he is able to select the best pass available to him. Having decided where he is going to play the ball, he must position and prepare his body to play the ball in that direction. Then in making the pass, he must consider the needs of the receiver because he in his turn has got to play the ball first time as well. This exercise should form the basis of your first-time passing; you should never tire of this or find it disinteresting because so much good can come out of it.

Groups of five players with one ball can work another routine in the centre circle. Six positions should be marked on the edge of the circle, with a skittle, one for each player and a spare. The object of the exercise is for the player with the ball to pass to any other player and immediately run to the spare position.

The player receiving the ball must play it first time to somebody else and again sprint to the spare position which now is where the first player was standing. This continuous practice of first-time passing and running makes players aware of finding space. You can step up the pace by introducing a defender.

This will make players aware of movement, more appreciative to the tactical considerations given to the pass and encourage an early selection of the pass to be made.

Once players are aware of space and support, a six-a-side game, in which everyone must play the ball first time is excellent practice. A full-sided game of one-touch is the next step, and, if necessary, this condition can be limited to certain areas of the field, depending on where the team requires it the most.

Variation of play is essential to a good team; without it a team becomes stereotyped and easy for the opposition to anticipate. One-touch football gives you this and is a natural ingredient to quickening the pace of a game.

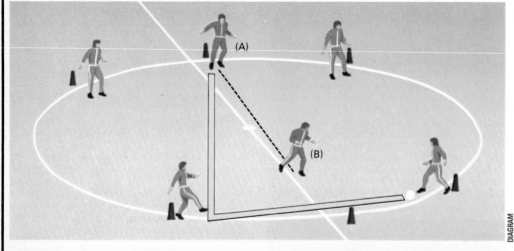

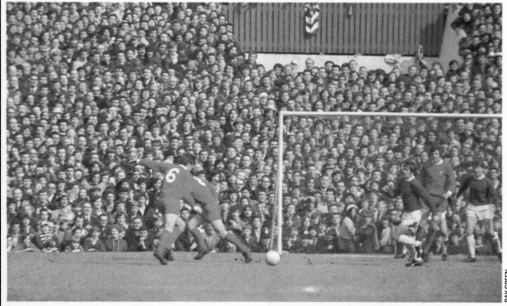

Above left A continuous one-touch practice. Five players stand by six skittles on the edge of the centre-circle. The ball is interpassed first time and after each pass the man who has played the ball sprints to the spare skittle.

Left Emlyn Hughes shoots first time versus Everton.

Attack from the back

Two goals—struck on the same day in 1971—in two First Division matches emphasized what was becoming a valuable asset to the attacking repertoire of any team. A goal by centre-back Graham Cross for Leicester at Upton Park against West Ham and one by Joe Kirkup, Southampton's right-back, against Wolves at Molineux showed the value of defenders spurting forward into offensive positions.

Cross's goal was of immense importance both to his team and himself. Leicester, dangerously situated at the wrong end of the First Division table, had held a succession of exuberant West Ham attacks for most of the game. Then Cross slipped just as he was about to foil another eager raid. The ball fell invitingly at the feet of Geoff Hurst, and eighty minutes of toil appeared to be wasted as the England striker took full advantage.

But as Leicester threw everything into a desperate attempt to reclaim a point, Cross made amends in full. As Keith Weller prepared to take a long throw from the right flank, Cross began his move upfield. His initial run was to make himself available in case Weller decided to throw the ball short. But when another Leicester player moved in close with the same idea, Cross swerved away and sprinted on into the West Ham penalty area.

The throw created the intended confusion. The ball fell to Leicester's Rodney Fern. He lifted the ball towards the goal over his shoulder and Cross reached it just before John McDowell. He smacked it past Bobby Ferguson, and Leicester had saved their point.

In the after-match discussions, the West Ham players remonstrated among themselves about the way in which the equalizer was scored. Someone should have been marking Cross. But the goal highlighted the advantage defenders have in such situations. In theory a defender moving up the field should be accompanied by a marking attacker coming back to help. But the nearer the defender gets towards his opponents goal the more likely the attacker is to leave him to one of his own team's defenders.

Kirkup's goal did not have as much influence on the result of the game—Wolves won 4-2—but it made its point even more clearly. He had been drawn over to the left-back position in his marking of the Wolves left-winger when he won the ball. As he played the ball forward, he saw the opportunity to push forward in support of his attack.

Nobody sensed any danger—Joe Kirkup punished the error

Southampton built this particular foray down their right flank. But Kirkup kept moving forward from the left. The move looked promising enough for him to venture into the penalty area. And as the cross came over Kirkup was standing all alone on the edge of the six-yard box. If he was surprised, he recovered well and headed the ball home.

No forward had run with him, and as he came into the area the defenders had left him to each other. No one sensed the danger, and Kirkup punished the error.

Liverpool were finally struck out of the European Cup in 1965 by a goal of the same type which stands comparison with any of the great ones scored in the competition. They had been drawn against the redoubtable Inter-Milan.

But at Anfield with the crammed Kop booming at their backs the Italians were in trouble. Liverpool went at them with marvellous eagerness and persistence to establish a 3-1 lead which seemed to be defendable in another famous stadium, San Siro, Milan.

Mistakes undermined Liverpool's form in the second leg. But one great goal settled the issue. It was scored by Facchetti, a tall, athletic left-back who combined a Corinthian elegance with professionalism.

As Liverpool were clinging on with the aggregate scores now level, Facchetti suddenly broke clear into an attacking position. He scored many fine goals with similar bursts, but none better than this one.

Tommy Lawrence, Liverpool's much underrated goalkeeper, came out to narrow the angle as the Italian arrived with the ball in an inside-right position on the edge of the penalty area. Lawrence

DIAGRAM (RESEARCH LONDON WEEKEND TELEVISION)

Left Diagram showing how Leicester City defender Graham Cross moved forward from his position in the back four to score a vital, equalizing goal against West Ham in October 1971. The Leicester players massed underneath a long throw from Keith Weller. The ball flew over two West Ham defenders and came to Rodney Fern. A quick hook over his shoulder found Cross momentarily unmarked, and he rammed the ball past Ferguson.

was wasting his time. Facchetti struck the ball in full flight, and no forward could have done better.

The stunning excellence of Facchetti's finishing emphasized the importance of defenders who were willing to work at becoming attackers.

Some did it in great style, taking full advantage of talents which would have seemed more obvious in other positions. Some were simply called up to use their height and heading ability in dead-ball situations where they had a distinct advantage. Some simply relied upon strong-willed determination to put themselves among the goalscorers.

When Leeds beat Arsenal in the final of the 1967 League Cup they won their first major trophy with a volleyed goal from a defender, left-back Terry Cooper. And by the time Arsenal had recovered from that setback to win the League and

Below *Joe Kirkup (centre, striped shirt) in a familiar position defending on Southampton's goal-line against a Manchester City attack.*
Below right *But, as the diagram shows, Kirkup can attack as well. In a 1971 League game at Molineux he escaped the Wolves marking to grab a goal for himself. He started the move and stole forward unmarked to head in the resultant cross from Southampton skipper Terry Paine.*

the Cup in 1971, they had been grateful for many fine goals from their captain, defender Frank McLintock. McLintock had spent the major part of his career as an attacking midfield player. He was past 30 when Arsenal moved him into their back four, where he played with great assurance and perception.

McLintock's instinct for striking at goal was never allowed to rust

But an instinct for striking the ball with certainty was never allowed to rust. He said: 'It's not something you lose overnight. Opportunity to score goals naturally decreased when I had to accept more defensive responsibility. But I was encouraged to go forward whenever we had established control in certain situations.'

Indeed McLintock began the 1971-72 season with a goal against Chelsea at Highbury, and followed it up two games later by scoring against Manchester United. This particular effort confirmed his value in a crowded penalty area. John Radford's long throw was backheaded on by George Graham, and McLintock, following up,

was able to use his determination to get in a scoring shot.

No one did better in this respect than David Webb, a burly, immensely spirited player who joined Chelsea from Southampton. Chelsea, with a long throw expert in Ian Hutchinson and accurate dead-ball kickers in Peter Houseman and Charlie Cooke, continually summoned up tall defenders to crowd and panic the opposition in the penalty area.

Webb's belligerent challenge brought him many important goals but none more so than the winner in extra time against Leeds United in the FA Cup Final of 1970.

His chief assistant was John Dempsey, an English-born centre-half who qualified through parentage as an Eire international. Dempsey got his reward for persistence in the replay of the 1971 Cup Winners Cup against Real Madrid in Athens. The first match was stalemate. The second began to run Chelsea's way when Dempsey came up to challenge for a left-wing corner-kick. He got the first, crucial touch at the ball, and adjusted his position so quickly amid a scramble that he was able to volley a brilliant, unstoppable goal.

The vital thing is that defenders should regard themselves as attackers when they are

launched into forward positions.

Leeds encouraged their men to go all the way, and coach Syd Owen said: 'They have got to get involved. If you press on, you will always win something. It might only be a throw-in. But you are putting pressure on the opposition. Defenders who opt out, and play the ball square to someone else might as well not bother. When you go, you have got to go all the way.'

Jack Charlton scored many fine goals for Leeds out of his willingness to get involved in the opposing goalmouth, and he was matched in this respect by another England player, Liverpool full-back Chris Lawler.

Not one for goalmouth scrambles—Moore lurked for hurried clearances

Lawler introduced this element of stealth into his scoring activities. He timed his arrival well, catching opposing defenders completely unaware. He was strong, and he could finish well on the floor and in the air. Undiluted determination did the rest.

Power contributed largely to the scoring

prowess of other defenders. England's captain Bobby Moore was not lacking in this respect. He struck the ball firmly when backing up behind attackers, and he hit some memorable goals.

Moore was an accomplished volleyer. The skill needed confidence to be truly effective, and England's captain, with his apparently implacable temperament, was never short of it. Unlike Webb and McLintock, he rarely involved himself in the rough and tumble of goalmouth scrambles. Moore was more likely to be found lurking just outside the penalty area waiting to pounce on hurried clearances. The ability to hit the ball firmly and accurately while it was still in the air served him well.

But the very mechanics of kicking when related to defensive technique prevented many defenders from taking full advantage of goalscoring situations. Most defenders in English football were asked to bypass the middle of the field with a lofted ball up to target men. They became conditioned to giving the ball air, and it betrayed them in front of opponents' goals.

Even in an era when full-backs began to play an increasingly important role as attackers, they shot consistently over the top of the target, and indeed the crowds expected them to. 'A typical

Above Graham Cross saves a point for Leicester City at Upton Park. **1** Bonds is marking Cross as Fern prepares to hook the ball towards the West Ham goal. **2** But Cross escapes to reach it before McDowell and put it past Ferguson. **3** Cross raises his arms in triumph as Birchenall rushes in to add his congratulations. Taylor (extreme right) cannot believe it. **4** and **5** The Leicester players reflect the overflowing joy that a late equalizer away from home can bring to a team near the bottom of the table.

full-back's shot,' became a clichéd remark of TV and radio commentators.

But for coaches the message was clear. More and more clubs devoted training time to encourage defenders to move forward positively, and the coaches could prove that defenders could get into positions sometimes denied to forwards, and so they had to be able to finish. Both Graham Cross and Joe Kirkup showed that they had benefited from their coaches' encouragement, and they gained the most satisfying of football's rewards for their efforts.

And when, on 9 October 1971, Leicester City and Southampton scored, the men who put the ball in the net were almost as significant as the goals themselves.

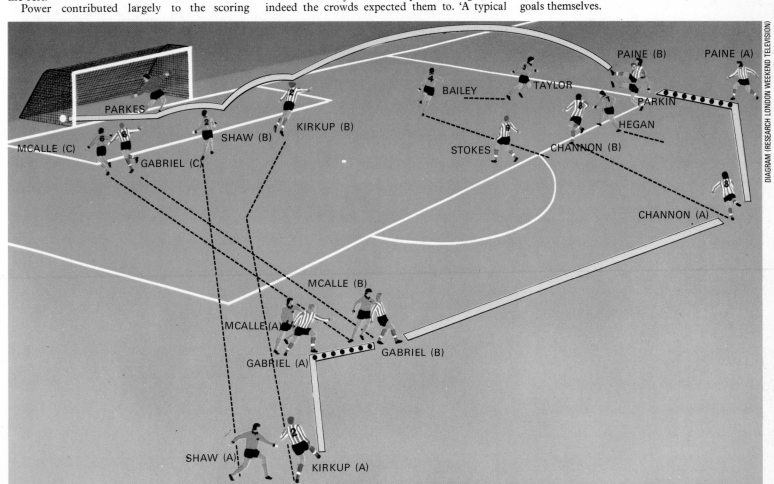

Coaching: Look to come forward from the back and seek out goalscoring situations

The object of football is to score goals, and to score more goals than the opposition. There is no greater joy than seeing a shot hit the back of the net, and every player, no matter which position he plays, gets a terrific feeling when he knocks the ball in. But nobody gets a greater feeling when scoring than a defender.

Players moving through from the back can often cause the most problems. They sometimes escape the net of tight marking defenders and get unnoticed into good positions.

The best opportunities are going to come when you, as a defender, intercept a pass intended for your immediate opponent, and carry on through the interception. This now puts you in a clear position and free. By running at a defender and playing a one-two with a team-mate you stand a strong chance of being put clear by the return pass.

If you want this type of tactic in your team the other players must be prepared to cover this defender. You cannot expect him to be going through looking for goals one moment and be chasing back to defend his own goal the next. You expect him to get back as quickly as he can, but you must afford him plenty of cover until he does.

Begin your preparation for this move by practising your ball control against a wall on your own. Play a good chip up on the wall, move forward quickly to control the rebound and continue moving forward. Different types of control may be necessary to get into the habit of controlling the ball as it comes, without checking your stride.

In training you can put the time you have spent practising on your own to good purpose. Put the keeper in goal, place a player just outside the penalty area to lay the ball off, position yourself on the half-way line and send a partner with the ball to the goal-line opposite you. Your partner chips the ball towards you as you move forward to meet it, as though you were making an interception. Control it quickly. Then carry on, play the ball to the player outside the box then sprint through for a return ball to shoot past the keeper. Your partner jogs down to the half-way line, while you are going through the move. After your shot you retrieve the ball, chip it from the goal-line down to him and he goes through the move. Then he chips to you, and so on.

You can make the practice more realistic once you grow in confidence by getting the player on the half-way line to control the chip and then run at the player outside the box who now acts as a defender. Whilst he is doing this the player who made the chip ball from the goal-line moves up so that he can be used for the one-two.

This function is in complete contrast with the defender's normal duties and obviously the situation is not always quite so clear-cut. However, the principles are the same, and you must learn to take full advantage of the situation, to attack the opposing defenders whenever possible when you are free. Good situations are often wasted because the defender is afraid to go too far forward in case he loses the ball. But if he knows that he will be covered, then he must be encouraged to go all the way.

The tactic of bringing defenders forward can now be brought into team practices. This can be done by setting up a practice game to be played into one goal. Put your keeper in this goal. The game is played by eight players attacking the goal

which is defended by six others. The attacking side line their eight up as follows—two wingers, a centre-forward, two supporting midfield players, and, most important. *three defenders* lined across the pitch behind their team-mates. The defending team must deploy their forces in this way—five players must mark the two wingers, the centre-forward and the two midfield players; this leaves one of their team over to look after the three key defenders.

The movement, then, is straightforward. The goalkeeper punts the ball downfield where it is collected by one of those three defenders. The defender in possession then tries to break through to shoot at goal by playing one-twos with any of his team-mates. If the players actually defending win the ball they have to play it up to their one front man who keeps possession until he is robbed by one of the three who again moves forward to attack.

This is a difficult but realistic practice, and will help defenders to read situations when they

might move forward quickly. Mobility by the front players is vital to create this space for the back players to move into.

Of course opportunities will come from closer in when the full-backs, who have been pushing up, intercept bad goalkeeping or a defender's clearance some 30 yards out. This will often call for first time passing and very quick movement to catch opponents off-balance and disorganized. Opportunities will also come from set pieces (throw-ins, corners, and free kicks) when back-players move quickly forward unmarked.

To perform these tactics efficiently requires very good physical condition and a high standard of technique and tactical understanding, but it certainly is a weapon worth cultivating. For when a game is tight, it can be swung suddenly in your favour by such bold tactics.

Encourage your defenders to go forward when possible. Make sure that they know that colleagues will cover them when they push up. It will all add variety to your team's attacking play.

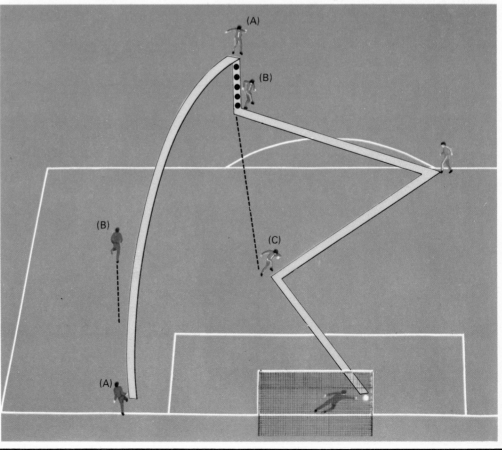

Above right *Everton's auxiliary centre-half, John Hurst, has moved upfield to head home past the Nottingham Forest defence at the City Ground.*
Right *Diagram of a practice to help defenders attack. One player chips a ball from the bye-line to a team-mate downfield. He controls it, plays a one-two with a third man and shoots. He now plays a chip to the first man who has run downfield, and the move goes on continuously.*

Blind-side running

The goal Peters scored for England against West Germany in Leon during the 1970 World Cup was an outstanding example of this skill. England, a goal up, were pressing Germany hard when Hurst picked up a pass just in the German half and to the right of the field.

Ball offered himself for a short pass, but Hurst dwelt on the ball long enough to give the galloping Keith Newton time to make ground along the wing. Then Hurst's pass put the full-back clear. Every German eye swung to the left where Newton was clear, then followed the centre which swung in over the top of Lee who had sprinted, shouting, to the near post.

But it was Peters, who had been on the half-way line on the left when the move began, who came sneaking through at the far post to stick a boot beyond a tackle and steer England into a two-goal lead.

Peters said later: 'I get my share of this sort of goal. I suppose this is what my play is all about. I had to make up a lot of ground to get there, and I had to do it in a way that was not going to tip off the Germans.

'With me it is instinct. I just try to work out where the ball will land and try to reach the spot at the same time. The thing is to come in from behind, to bend the run if necessary so as to keep out of the range of vision of the defenders who are watching the ball.

'This is one case where it doesn't pay to advertise. So I don't shout for the ball, or make a big fuss about moving. I try to look as though I am just loping about without any real purpose —though I know exactly where I am hoping to be at the end of the run.'

What helps Peters greatly is his style of running and his build. Smaller men have to put a lot more apparent effort into sprinting hard;

Below Diagram showing how Martin Peters sneaked in on the blind side of the West Germany defence to put England two ahead in Leon in 1970.

The shocking and tragic death of Spurs and Scotland forward John White in 1964—he was killed by lightning on a golf course—provoked a thousand tributes from his fellow footballers. None was more sincere than that of a rival defender who said: 'Now I can stop looking for a secret trapdoor on the Tottenham pitch.'

In a phrase the rival had captured the essential quality of White's brilliant play, the ability to arrive unseen into positions of deadly merit. No post-War footballer has equalled White's ability to capitalize on what the coaches call 'blind-side running'.

In the great Spurs team of the time White was known as 'the Ghost'. A typical Tottenham move would begin with White taking a pass on the fringe of his defence and rolling it deftly to a team-mate on the wing. And it would end with White taking or making a pass in the opposition area, leading to a goal.

And later, when the goal was being dissected or described, few rivals and few spectators could recall exactly when and by what means he had covered the ground between the two goal areas; or where he had been and what he had been doing as the move gained impetus. Thus came the semi-serious theory that he had slid down a trapdoor to emerge at the other end of the tunnel.

There were worse ways to describe his style.

Tony Kay, a Sheffield Wednesday and England wing-half of the period, had a rather more down-to-earth explanation for White's uncanny progress: 'It's the eyes,' he once said. 'When you mark Johnny White, he's staring at you all the time, almost as though he is trying to hypnotize you. You are marking him, say, and you are backing away when they have got the ball. You are not worried, because he's there where you can seen him. But sooner or later you have to glance across to see where the ball is—and when you look back he's gone.

'He waits for that split-second when your eyes wander, and then he slips away in behind you. All the time he's edging away to the corner of your vision, watching you, waiting for your eyes to flicker. Suddenly he's not there any more—and you've got a hard chase to get him again. That's when he does the damage.'

White's death left a gap that was eventually filled by another man equally adept at finding space on the blind side of defenders, Martin Peters. Peters came to Tottenham with a reputation made at West Ham and with England for subtle midfield play—and again it was an ability to slide unannounced into critical areas to score goals that was an essential of his play.

DIAGRAM

135

when Alan Ball, for example, or Francis Lee makes a run the world knows it—short, pumping legs and driving arms attract the eye. They could not be more conspicuous if they wore cow-bells around their necks.

But Peters has long legs, and a flowing, economical way of running that covers the ground with such seemingly little effort—and looks no

Below Peters scores past a static West Germany defence. He had made a carefully timed run from the half-way line to meet Keith Newton's cross.
Centre Diagram showing how Manchester City's Colin Bell appeared on Marvin Hinton's blind side and put Chelsea out of the 1971 FA Cup. Hinton let Young's cross run to apparent safety, but Bell timed his run into the space perfectly.
Bottom Bell blasts his shot past Peter Bonetti.

different whether he is merely loping into position or sprinting in for a shot at goal.

Another Peters' goal, against Nottingham Forest in October 1971, illustrated his happy knack of moving long distances unobserved. Full-back Cyril Knowles had the ball at the half-way line on the left. Peters was a few yards away and being closely marked. Knowles elected to send in a long centre aimed at the far side of Forest's goal—and every defender turned under the ball to watch the danger switch, apparently, to the far side.

'As soon as the man marking me turned towards goal, I set off,' Peters recalled. 'I kept my speed down to let him stay in front of me for a few paces, then I shot past him on the left as he half-turned to look at me over his right shoulder.' The yard Peters gained by this subtle manoeuvre

was decisive a second or two later, for when Gilzean headed the centre back across goal Peters was there, still just ahead of his straining pursuer, to steer the ball into goal.

Another player dominant in the late sixties who owed his success to an ability to insinuate himself amid rival defences like a knife between the ribs was Manchester City's England man, Colin Bell. He had the same long, lean build as Peters, and possessed a similar ability to cover ground without flamboyant effort.

An archetypal Bell goal in January 1971 des-troyed Chelsea's hope of retaining the FA Cup they had won the previous spring. Chelsea were a goal down, but fighting splendidly to recover, in a fourth-round match at Stamford Bridge when Bell took a pass in the middle of the field.

He swept the ball out to Neil Young on the

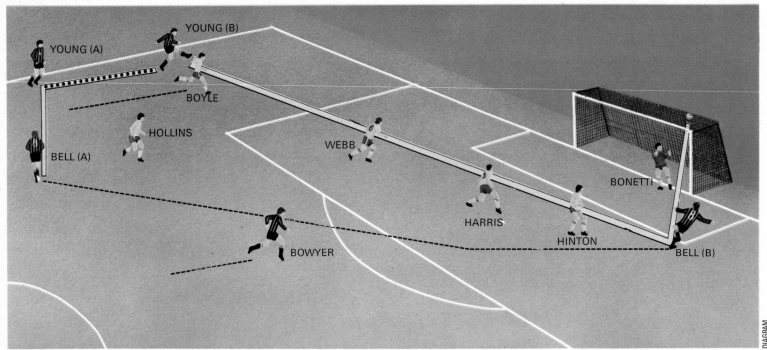

left wing, moved a pace or two forward as though he would run in support, then turned almost wearily away from the scene of the action. Young made a little ground on the left, hesitated, then swung over a low centre which flew across the face of the Chelsea defenders running hard towards their own goal.

The farthest Chelsea defender was Marvin Hinton, a player noted for his cool nerve. As the ball swept towards his feet he could have done any one of a number of things: he could have collected it, steered it back to his goal-keeper, or simply booted it behind for a corner.

Instead, he allowed the ball to run, and then stood aghast as Colin Bell came in behind him to score sweetly. For days afterwards, as they looked back on the inevitable defeat, Chelsea fans moaned: 'Why didn't Hinton *look!*'

Hinton had a complete answer. 'I *had* looked. A second or so before the ball reached me I had glanced over my shoulder to make sure no one was coming in from their right. The pitch was clear behind me, so I knew I could let the ball run, and then turn and collect it away from danger. At least, I thought I could.'

What Hinton had not allowed for, like countless defenders before and since, was Bell's insight. From the moment he had released his pass to Young he had been drifting across field, not apparently running hard, not with any obvious urgency or purpose, but still covering ground at speed.

And, as soon as he saw space developing on Hinton's right, he quickened his pace to get round the flank of the retreating defence. The timing of the run was perfection—so was the

reading of the situation that enabled him to project the flight of the centre, and predict the consequence of Hinton's comforting glance.

Some great attacking players can never go unwatched about their business. The strength of men like Hurst, Chivers or Dougan, the busy commitment of forwards like Best, Lee, and Law will always make them a magnet for the eyes and attentions of rivals. Men like these have to get their goals despite close marking.

But players such as Peters and Bell, and to some extent Graham, Clarke and Robson, will continue to collect their share of goals, because they watch the watchers, because of their cunning employment of the unexpected. They are happy to let the others take the eye as they continue to prove that it is possible to disappear from view—without using a trapdoor!

Coaching: Learn to time your run and steal goals from the opposition

The essence of positional play in football is running. Movement creates movement. A player should always be willing to run into positions which threaten most danger to the opponents' goal, even when the odds are against him receiving the ball. He will cause unrest in the defence which will make things easier for his team-mates. When attacking, running off the ball means getting into a position which enables the player on the ball to make the most positive pass possible in the situation. And often the best runs off the ball are those made on the 'blind' side of defenders.

In order to make any runs you must be fit; the better your physical condition the quicker you will tire your immediate opponent. So if you want to be a good off-the-ball mover, be conscientious about your training. A good exercise to encourage movement and cultivate the ability to lose opponents is 'shadow movement'. You can practise this with a friend; one player is followed by his partner, the defender. While moving forward at a jogging pace, the player in front suddenly stops, then moves unexpectedly or changes direction quickly in an attempt to get away from the defender. The defender should follow as closely as he can. This will also be excellent reflex training for the defender in

close marking one particular opponent.

Defenders are happy to play against teams with limited movement. Movement that takes place in front of them will often cause problems providing the movement is quick and intelligent. However, they are put under most pressure when movement takes place behind them. Ideally a defender wants to be able to see the ball and watch his immediate opponent at the same time. The art of intelligent positioning is to make the defender as uncomfortable as possible by working on his back or blind side. Defenders detest being made to turn and run back towards their own goal. They are also under pressure when they allow their immediate opponent to turn and run at them with the ball. This is called attacking the defender.

With all this in mind, work on an exercise which involves four players, one ball and an area about 30 yards long and 10 yards wide. The four players pair up. One pair will be working in direct opposition to each other, whilst the other pair split up and wait one on each end of the area acting as supporting players. The idea is for one of the pair working in the middle to work the ball with the player resting at one end in order to play to the player 'resting' at the other end. His partner must mark him tight and

try to win the ball so that he can then have possession and work the exercise himself. The two pairs change over after a while depending on how hard they have worked. One minute will be ample for a pair working really hard.

Several attempts will have to be made before you really get the idea, but persevere, it will be worthwhile. You will soon learn to position yourself diagonally from the supporting player to whom you are passing. Encourage the defender to come in close by passing the ball to feet a couple of times before playing and sprinting on the blind side to collect the return through ball, then play it to the other player. You then move quickly into a diagonal position ready to go again. If your opponent comes in really tight, then, without any preliminary passing, you look immediately for a direct ball on the back side of the marking player. If he does not come in tight, turn and take him on.

This exercise can be taken on to the field. One player has the ball on the half-way line, and two others, one defender marking one attacker, stand about 20 yards away facing the ball. Play the ball to the attacker who plays it back. Now your partner sprints on the back side of the defender to collect the through ball and to go on at goal.

Once you have the idea of this exercise, bring in another two players. You now have two defenders marking two attackers who are supported by the player on the half-way line. The idea here is that you play the ball up to one of the attackers so that he is encouraged to come off his marker to meet the ball. Immediately you do this one of two things will happen. If the defender does not come close, the player receiving the ball will be able to turn and run at the defender whilst the other attacker sprints on the back side of him. What you have here in fact is two players attacking one defender. If the defender follows and comes tight, then the ball is played back to the supporting player who can play it through for the other attacker, who has run on the blind side of his own defender, to collect and shoot. No matter what happens the idea is to get on the blind side of defenders. The timing of the running here is absolutely essential because of the danger of being offside.

Once you have got an understanding of the principles and co-ordinated the timing of the run with the delivery of the ball, then there is no limit to the runs that can be made. Perhaps your outside-right has the ball. There is nothing to stop the outside-left coming across on the blind side of the defenders to meet a ball coming into the penalty area. Obviously he will have his immediate defender to deal with first, but if he is quick and has timed his run in well on the ball, then he may be in a shooting position or he can turn the ball back for somebody else to have a crack at the goal.

Timing is the essence; keep one eye on the ball and one eye on your marker and the moment you know you can lose him get away. Then you will be in a position to steal a shot at goal if the ball is played to you, and the other defenders will be wondering where you came from.

Below Another Martin Peters 'stolen' goal as he arrives at the back of the Nottingham Forest defence. His ability to steal into the goalmouth made him a worthy successor to Spurs' legendary John White.
Bottom A one-a-side practice for blind-side running. Possession is kept by using two static players at the ends of the pitch. A blind-side run will free a player to regain the ball from the ends.

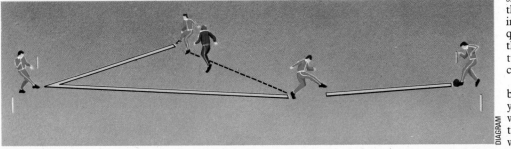

Above Diagram of Bobby Charlton's thrilling run and shot against Mexico that brought England's vital first goal in the 1966 World Cup finals.

The long shot

By the time Bobby Charlton took his place in England's team for the opening game of the 1966 World Cup he had become more a scorer of great goals than a great goalscorer.

Although he was to eventually overtake Jimmy Greaves as England's leading marksman, Charlton's seasonal tally for Manchester United had gradually begun to fall off as defences became more organized.

But whenever smothering defenders gave him an extra second's time and room to launch the high back-swing of the leg that gave him his power, he could crack long-range shots of quite devastating force.

Long-range shooting had been discouraging in English football. Defenders moved swiftly and bravely to block the fiercest efforts and the standard of goalkeeping was higher than anywhere else in the world. But in the summer of 1966 it was the long shot—from Charlton's explosive right boot—that proved decisive as England edged their way towards their greatest triumph.

To make the most of the destructive suddenness of Charlton's shooting, space had to be made for it. Sir Alf Ramsey worked to provide that space by employing players who were in turn willing to work at taking defenders away from Charlton's path, as he arrived from his role in the middle of the field.

But, for all Ramsey's effort, England found themselves suffocated by Uruguay's deliberately negative attitude in the opening game. And they were doing little better in their second match against a Mexican side who showed none of the cocky assurance they were to display in their own country four years later. They were given little hope of qualifying out of England's group and they quickly confirmed that they were of the same opinion.

The ball was pushed to Diaz from the kick-off, and he immediately thumped it deep into England's half. It was not the start of a Mexican attack. It was the signal for a retreat. While the England players paused in astonishment the

Mexicans simply turned and fell back before re-assembling around their own penalty area.

It was a depressing sight, not only for the public but for the England players who were coming to accept that goals would be hard to score in the competition. Someone needed to do something special, and it was fitting that Charlton should suddenly summon up his immense talents to score one of his greatest goals.

The Mexicans were entitled to feel reasonably secure when Charlton took the ball near the half-way line. He dismissed an immediate challenge with a contemptuous swerve, and set off at speed towards the Mexican goal. There was still no real threat. But the Mexicans had not budgeted for Charlton's power.

Defenders stood off him, no doubt hoping that Charlton would either elect to pass or abdicate from the responsibility of trying to finish what he had begun; he did neither. He veered fractionally to his right and then drove the ball almost angrily against the stanchion supporting the net on the far side of the goal. It was one of the great moments of his great career, and it set England firmly on their way to World Cup glory.

When helping England to defend the trophy in Mexico four years later, Charlton was unable to repeat the majesty of that moment, although thin air increased the velocity of well struck shots and goalkeepers were continually troubled by the prospect.

Again England found goals hard to come by, but this time it was the Brazilians who were to nourish the belief that there was a percentage in shooting from long range.

'Thrilled—by the willingness of Brazil to shoot on sight'

Don Revie of Leeds was one of the British managers who travelled to Mexico. He said at the time: 'I think we were all thrilled by the willingness of the Brazilians to shoot at every opportunity. The atmosphere favoured this. But there is no reason why we shouldn't have a go more often at home.'

It was not long before Leeds showed that the lesson had not been lost on their manager. Peter Lorimer, their burly Scots right-winger was already listed as probably the hardest kicker of a dead ball in the country. He was a menace with free-kicks, and Leeds encouraged him to shoot whenever he had a sight of goal.

But the point was not lost on John Giles, an astute, inventive and combative midfield player not renowned for the power of his shooting. But Giles was not employed as a goalscorer. Short and stocky he was the team's general. He pulled the strings, and made most of the penetrating passes. However, he was a fine striker of the ball, and he had tremendous vision.

This vision led to opportunity when he scored for Leeds against Crystal Palace in March 1971. Giles was in an inside-right position and some thirty yards from goal when he suddenly struck the ball left-footed at the Palace goal.

It was a curious shot. It began as though it would be high and wide but then it curled wickedly late in flight. John Jackson, the Palace goalkeeper, was totally deceived as the ball found the top, far corner of his net. Certainly Giles had some good fortune. But the goal was a reward for his initiative and an example of what could be achieved by players who were willing to try the unorthodox rather than settle for the obvious.

Leeds took their cue from the Brazilians but they were merely resurrecting a feature of football that has always provided crowds with great thrills. When Benfica of Portugal beat Real Madrid of Spain 5-3 in the 1962 European Cup final many of the goals were scored from outside the penalty area. Ferenc Puskas, the great Hungarian forward, scored a ferocious hat-trick for Real, yet finished on the losing side.

The referee for that match was Leo Horn, a Dutchman whose career had taken him all over the world. After that final, played in Amsterdam's

Top Bobby Charlton's right-footed 30-yard drive flashes into the Mexican net. **Centre** Diagram showing how Johnny Giles of Leeds Utd used a long shot to score against Crystal Palace. **Above** John Jackson is well beaten as Giles' fine effort swerves into the Palace goal.

Olympic stadium, Horn said: 'I cannot recall such tremendous shooting. The wonder was that only eight goals were scored. Everyone seemed to be on target that night, and the ball was being struck with tremendous power.'

And yet it was a long time before English teams recognized the threat or the power they had at their disposal. They shot but without any real conviction until managers began to encourage the technique of shooting on sight.

It was the willingness to do this which made Arsenal's Charlie George one of the most exciting prospects in the British game in the 1970-71 season. George was brought through carefully until Arsenal felt that he was ready to take his place in the hurly-burly of League football. But he really arrived as Arsenal were pushing forward towards the League Championship.

A neat, swift kicking action enabled him to pick up shots out of nowhere, and he was to score many fine goals.

Much of his success was to do with encouragement. Forwards will shoot as long as they feel that their efforts are appreciated. Arsenal gave George the licence to keep on trying. It did not matter that he was not always on target. It was more important that the opposition should be continually threatened.

David Herd, a burly forward who led Manchester United's attack in the early sixties, paved the way for many goals because his instant power forced goalkeepers to make fumbling saves. If they did not take the ball cleanly they found Denis Law on top of them to take advantage of his electric reactions with close in goals.

Similarly when Chelsea emerged as a power

with a fine young team they had no better shot than Bobby Tambling. Tambling was essentially left-footed. His strong point was that he was invariably on target even when shooting from wide angles and in full flight. Pele with his mastery of spin and swerve scored over 1,000 goals most of which were struck with tremendous power, and power of shot brought Eusebio of Portugal to the forefront of the world's forwards.

As the seventies dawned, more and more clubs began to encourage their top shots to keep on having a go. Players began to advance from midfield with shots rather than passes in mind. It could only increase the public's anticipation of thrill, and as Bobby Charlton's legendary power began to wane, the prospect of a host of crowd-thrilling successors looked bright.

Coaching: Add power and confidence to your long-range shooting

A goal scored from long range is one of the most exciting sights in football. A cracking drive that bulges the back of the net will bring exhilaration to both the players and the spectators.

Power and accuracy in the long shot are of combined importance. One is of little value without the other. World class players have the ability to select and hit a fairly small target from outside the penalty area with power, but generally speaking a player who can hit a ball with power and either score or force the goalkeeper to save nine times out of ten is a rarity—yet the technique can be acquired.

You will be surprised at the amount of power that can be built up with constant practice, providing that your muscles are strong enough, especially the thigh muscles. A few trips to the gym for weight-training under expert guidance will be well worth while.

Start your practice in pairs, stand about thirty-five to forty yards apart and drive the ball as hard as you can at one another. The ball can be stationary because here you are concentrating on power and the basic kicking action which is most important at this stage. In theory a kick is divided into its various separate yet combined move-

ments—(a) the position before you kick the ball (b) the back swing of the kicking foot (c) contact (d) the follow-through. In practice separation of this kind is, of course, very difficult because a kick is a continuous series of movements. Check that your non-kicking foot is about nine inches from and parallel with the ball. Check that you make very firm contact with the full instep or the outside of the instep. Make sure that your knee is over the ball on contact and the follow-through is smooth. To help accuracy, watch the ball closely so that the instep makes contact with the middle of the ball and that the foot travels on a line with the target.

You can introduce a team-mate into the practice to act as goalkeeper between the two of you. Imagine a goal around him. The good thing here is that if you beat the keeper the ball will go to your partner on the other side for his turn to shoot.

Of course every player likes to shoot at real goals, so the next practice to improve power and accuracy starts on the half-way line. Play the ball forward about twenty-five yards then move on to the ball and drive it at the goal. You are shooting from thirty yards so power is vital. It will be hard to score, so concentrate on being on

target. If you miss the target think of why whilst you are running to retrieve the ball. The chances are that you kicked across the line.

To vary your practices is good and introducing competition will often improve your concentration. Stronger players could try a game of two touch—where you are only allowed to play the ball twice or you forfeit possession—against your pal on a full size pitch. The idea is that you try to score with every shot. When your pal tries to score in your goal you must stop the ball with one touch, your next touch must be a shot at his goal. You will find yourself shooting from your own half and that will really take some power. In a team training session several pairs can play on the same pitch as long as they keep to their own ball. This is an excellent practice for fitness as well.

Most scoring opportunities from a distance come from balls being played back away from goals. The ball might be played by a team-mate or it might be a clearance from an opposing defender. Either way you will be coming on to the ball and a first-time shot will often take the goalkeeper by surprise or find him unsighted. Good initial practice is to have a group of your team-mates on the side of the goal area playing balls back for the rest of the lads to have shots in turn from just outside the penalty area. The shots should be hit first time.

The service can vary. Some should go in the air so that a full volley or half volley can be attempted. This type of shot causes the ball to dip, making it difficult for the keeper to deal with.

This situation can be made more realistic by having wing-players crossing balls to a defender who heads the ball away. Two or three midfield players can be some thirty yards out. The object here is for one of the midfield players to get to the ball quickly and have a first-time shot. Gradually build this practice so that you have two or three defenders and a couple of attacking players going for the cross. The attacking players can try to score from the crosses but if the defending players get the ball away the midfield players can quickly on to the ball and shoot from twenty yards.

By this time you will have solved a problem as to which foot is best to use on balls coming across your line of movement. Most players find that they can generate more power when they allow the ball to run across them and then strike it with the far foot. But if there is a chance that the opponent might intercept get used to striking the ball with either foot.

The last problem is a psychological one. In a proper match—under pressure—some of your long shots will go wildly off-target. But do not worry; this happens at the highest level, so whenever the opportunity presents itself, keep cracking away at goal.

If your shot goes nearer the corner-flag than the goal, remember at least you have had a go. The next one might go in.

Left Practise the long shot. The group on the right plays balls for the marksmen to hit at goal.

Creating two against one

England's shock 3-1 defeat by West Germany in the European Championship quarter-final at Wembley in the spring of 1972 aroused fierce criticism of Sir Alf Ramsey and the policies which he had firmly applied since building up to the World Cup final six years earlier.

It was argued that had England played at Wembley in the first leg with the same fierce dedication they later revealed in drawing 0-0 in Berlin, then the overall result might have been entirely different. The assumption was a fair one when taking into account the space which the Germans were allowed in the first match and the astonishing indolence displayed by some members of the England team.

But none of this could obscure the inadequate technique which was made even more obvious by the precise excellence of Germany's counter-attacking. English football was suddenly seen to be laboured and heavy-footed. In contrast the Germans displayed a sharpness of thought and application which suggested that they had legitimate claims to being the best of the world's teams. The ability to get two attackers in against one defender was really what good team play was all about and the Germans seemed to do it instinctively.

This was never more evident than when they broke into space from midfield, using pace and control to create situations in which an opposing defender was immediately outnumbered.

Much of the German play was based on first-time passing. They always had men offering themselves as targets and it was towards this end that they worked in training—movement, accuracy and passes delivered at just the right time and at the correct speed. It was all very impressive but never more so than when build-up play led to incisive attacks around the edge of England's penalty area.

Good players refuse to be drawn—they have to be committed

Improved defensive techniques and the recognition of the need for restraint had served to demolish what had become a cliche among coaches. It was simply pointless instructing players to draw a man. Good players refused to be drawn. They had to be committed.

The German midfield star Gunther Netzer needed no bidding in this respect. Using his tremendous acceleration, he flew at opponents and it was clearly a natural part of his game. When he had freed himself from immediate challenge with the confidence which came to all great players, Netzer immediately hunted out a defender who was already occupied.

Netzer's willingness to attack defenders, to force them to make a decision, was soon evident at Wembley. Picking the ball up deep, he made a strong run through the centre of the field and attacked Norman Hunter. Hunter was committed and, for a few seconds, Muller was left unmarked. Only desperate defence by Hughes and Banks prevented a score as Netzer laid the ball to his centre-forward. He had created a two-against-one situation and throughout the match he attempted similar threatening moves.

Hunter had not been allowed to fall off, to retreat, while keeping both Netzer and Muller in vision. He found two men attacking him at speed and the man he had been detailed to mark was in a position to break free.

Few players in English football revealed the same facility although there were occasionally glittering examples of it. Before Arsenal won through to the FA Cup Final from a controversial replay against Stoke City at Everton in April 1972, they were threatened for 20 minutes by

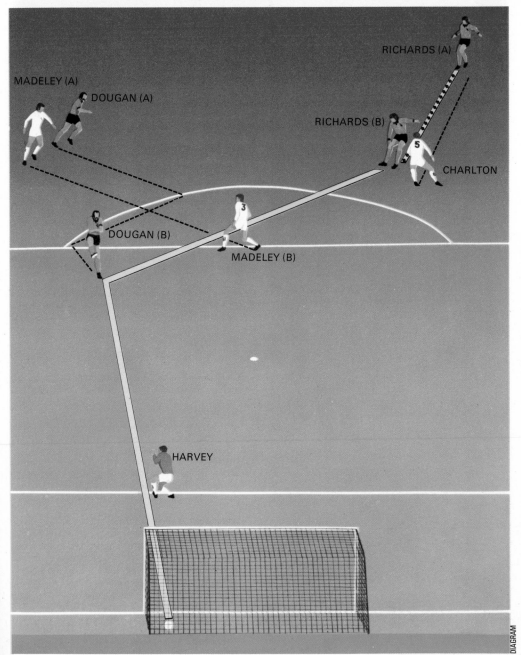

Above left Derek Dougan of Wolves puts the ball past Leeds' Harvey at Molineux in May 1972.
Left The goal resulted from John Richards running at the Leeds defence. Madeley, the covering defender, was isolated leaving Dougan in space. Richards timed his final pass perfectly.

Left *John Ritchie of Stoke heads just wide of the Arsenal goal in the 1972 FA Cup semi-final replay. The cross came from right-back Marsh, set free by Eastham who had created a two-against-one situation on Arsenal left-back McNab.*
Centre left *Chelsea's Garland scores against Spurs in another 1972 semi-final—the League Cup.*
Bottom left *An aggressive run by Charlie Cooke gave Garland the chance to cut in and shoot. He attacked left-back Knowles who was already marking Garland. With Knowles' attention diverted, Garland took the ball from Cooke and found himself in enough space to strike for goal.*

some classic play from George Eastham.

Eastham had returned from South Africa the previous autumn to reclaim the prominence he had once had as a much younger man. A softening of attitude in the First Division brought about by firmer refereeing enabled Eastham to use his neat close-quarter skills and superb passing to good effect.

It was his goal which won the League Cup final against Chelsea the previous March and at Everton he was bidding for a return to Wembley.

Things looked good for Eastham and Stoke when a foul by Arsenal's goalkeeper Geoff Barnett gave Jimmy Greenhoff the chance to hit a confident penalty-kick. They looked even better when Eastham, changing wings, began to operate along Arsenal's left flank where he had the opportunity to take advantage of space.

Arsenal's midfield man on that side was George Graham, a fluent attacker but not the best of defenders. As Graham pushed forward in eager pursuit of an equalizer, Eastham with apparent innocence drifted into the space that had been left unattended.

But when Eastham got the ball, and he got a lot of it, Arsenal were in trouble. He had the cunning to conceal the direction of his final pass, the skill to delay the action until full-back Marsh had joined the assault, and the perfection of line and pace which put the ball perfectly into Marsh's path.

Eastham's ability to create two against one almost destroys Arsenal

The man under fire was left full-back Bob McNab who was to say later: 'I wasn't sure what to do for the best. If I had closed down on Eastham too early, he might have destroyed me because he was still very quick when he brought the ball at you.

'I elected to stay in space, but even then George caused us problems. He was flying at me and he knew just when to release the ball so that you were stranded somewhere between trying to cut off the pass and turning to pick off the supporting player.'

Had John Ritchie's header, from one Marsh cross, gone inside and not outside an upright, and if Peter Dobing had been quick enough to sense the direction of one brilliant reverse pass from Eastham, then Arsenal would have been way beyond recovery.

But they survived for Charlie George to benefit from a controversial penalty decision and for John Radford to snatch the winner from George's pass, with Stoke appealing vainly for what seemed to be an obvious offside. Nevertheless Eastham, if only for a brief spell, had emphasized that he had few equals in situations which were invariably wasted in England.

Chelsea also reached Wembley in 1972, to contest the League Cup final, and they fashioned a significant goal in the second leg of their semi-final by creating a two-against-one situation. In a competitive local derby against Spurs, the aggregate score was level when Charlie Cooke attacked Tottenham's left-back Cyril Knowles.

Knowles was already occupied, marking striker Chris Garland, but his attention was transferred to Cooke when Garland took the ball from his team-mate and cut inside. He ran across the penalty area and beat Pat Jennings with a well-

GARLAND (A)   COOKE
KNOWLES
PRATT
GARLAND (B)
BEAL
HOUSEMAN
EVANS
ENGLAND
JENNINGS

Coaching: Learn the art of isolating defenders

The basis of good football is to create a spare or extra player wherever the ball is. This means that the player on the ball has an alternative. He can either take on his immediate opponent or pass to the spare man. Basically, it is a question of creating a situation in which two players are directly against only one opponent.

Because there is an even number of players on each side it becomes a game of cat-and-mouse. One of two things has got to happen. Either the player in possession must go by his immediate opponent and then run quickly at another opponent so that this opponent has two players to deal with—or one of the players off the ball has got to lose his marking opponent (just a fraction of a second will do) and move in to support the player on the ball.

Give yourself a feel of what you are trying to do by playing two against one in a 10-yard square. This is a very demanding game physically because there must be a lot of movement. The player off the ball has got to work really hard to make sure he is available to accept a pass; he must ensure that he does not get caught for too long hidden behind the defender. This positional sense of moving in to support just at the right time is absolutely essential.

There is a lot of work to be done in this exercise; it is not one to be taken lightly, done for a few minutes and forgotten, because it should be the basis of all passing movements. If you find the exercise too difficult to start with, add another player and make it three against one. The same principles will apply. Once you get the idea you will make it more effective if the player with the ball can get a run at the defender before passing. This is called committing the defender.

Extend the area now to 20 yards long by 10 yards wide. The object of this exercise is for the two players to attack the one defender until one of them is free with the ball so that he can dribble it over the end line. This means you are attacking in a set direction as in a game. You will find that if you can run at the defender and at the same time lure him away from your team-mate he will have more space in which to work when you pass him the ball.

There are many ways in which two players can beat one—the wall pass, blind side running and overlapping play are all very good methods—but the principle remains constant. The defender must be attacked by the two players and made to commit himself. Again there is a tremendous amount of work to be done, and by talking about it and trying different ways it can be made very interesting. An experienced eye can quickly recognize whether players have done the necessary work and whether they have an understanding of the situation.

Having formed some basis of two against one, the object is to create this situation in a game of two against two. It would be preferable at this stage to go back to working in an area about twelve yards square. Working on the same principles of supporting the player on the ball or making pairs with him, the object is to keep possession of the ball. Even though the man off the ball is under pressure from his marking player he can make himself free and available to accept a pass by moving away, creating space for himself, then checking back into that space at the right time. The man on the ball may pass it and sprint by

Below The overlapping Pat Rice supports George Armstrong to create two against one on Paul Madeley during the 1972 FA Cup Final.
Bottom Playing two against one in training helps players recognize such situations in matches.

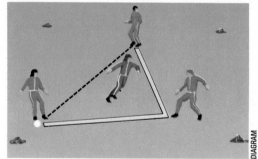

his opponent for a return pass. Alternatively he may use the player off the ball as a decoy and deceive his opponent by feinting to give the pass, then sprinting past him into space with the ball under control.

Move again into the larger 20 by 10 yard area, and continue the two against two practice. This time, however, you have a line to attack and one to defend when you lose possession. The principle that movement creates movement has never been so important as it is now. The two players have got to work for a position from where they can attack one defender. Working to get himself free, the player off the ball must be prepared to do a lot of unselfish running. The ball must be interpassed until an opportunity is seen to make a break using one of the methods you found successful when playing two against one.

Functional practices should now be introduced so that players are functioning in the areas they would normally work. The full-back starts by playing the ball up the line to his wingman. The winger works the ball infield, leaving space for the full-back to move in for an overlapping play. This is better performed in the front third of the field so that the full-back can get round the back for a cross.

Another functional practice involves the centre-forward being marked by the centre-half. A long ball is played up to the centre-forward and an attacking midfield player marked by a defensive midfield player moves in to support. The two attacking players work for an opening which will leave one of them free for a shot at goal.

You will often find it necessary to go back to your original practices when the timing is not quite right. You may find the checking back technique hard to grasp. If you do, you can break down the practice so that you are being marked by an opponent and supported by a player with a ball. The object here is to run quickly away from your supporter taking the player marking with you. You then apply the brakes hard and check back towards your supporting player who must play the ball to you at precisely the time you check in. If he delays it, then your marker will come tight, making it difficult for you.

How many times have you come in after a game, having had a roasting and saying, 'they seemed to have more players on the field than us.' The truth is that they were prepared to work much harder than you and that they had developed a knowledge of the principles of the game.

If you can keep working to make pairs on the field you cannot go far wrong; if you can recognize when you have two players to their one and attack him you really are in business.

---

struck left-footed drive. Martin Peters equalized for Spurs with a penalty, but Chelsea went to Wembley when Alan Hudson's last-minute free-kick deceived the Spurs defence.

Numerical advantage gained out of firm tackling or a careless pass was all too often overlooked by players who seemed unable to apply the lessons driven at them in training. More often players seemed obsessed with finding space away from the ball rather than moving close in support in positions where they could isolate defenders.

In the 1972 Cup Final, for instance, Arsenal had one great opportunity of creating a chance when they had three forwards up on three Leeds defenders. But it remained three to three. No attempt was made to isolate one man with sharp, direct running and positive thinking. Charlie George was finally held up and pushed back by Norman Hunter's shrewd stationing and the chance was lost before it could be exploited.

But 48 hours later, Leeds were not granted the same good fortune. After the FA Cup win they went looking for the League Championship at Wolverhampton, where they only needed a draw to overtake Derby County who had already set a 58 points target.

For 20 minutes Leeds played brilliantly. Composed, relaxed, they pushed the ball around and if they had scored then it might well have settled the issue and clinched the double.

But when they were denied a penalty by a linesman who ignored Bernard Shaw's handball they lost their heads long enough for Wolves to take the lead.

It was Wolves' second goal, after half-time, which put paid to Leeds' hopes. Paul Reaney's careless pass led to a break by John Richards, and it was direct running at the heart of the Leeds defence which helped to create a classic goal.

Derek Dougan played his part by first aiming to bisect the line of Richards' run around about the edge of the penalty area. Paul Madeley, the Leeds left-back, was pulled in on cover, but was left flat-footed when Dougan checked before drifting out wide. Richards released the ball at just the right time and Dougan, now unmarked, shot a confident goal past David Harvey.

Within a minute Billy Bremner had pulled one back for Leeds. But it was not their night. A brilliantly contrived and splendidly taken goal had made the task too difficult. Wolves won. Liverpool drew at Arsenal and it was Derby's Championship for the first time in their history.

Arsenal, double winners the previous season, were left with nothing. They had run out of steam in the Championship, because of their exertions in the European Cup and they were beaten in the FA Cup Final by Leeds.

It was Ajax, later to beat Inter-Milan in the final becoming Europe's premier club for the second successive season, who ended Arsenal's dream of adding the European Cup to their long honours list.

And it was Ajax and their brilliant forward Johann Cruyff who had helped to emphasize the value of using speed, intelligence and sharp accuracy to outwit and confine defenders.

In the first leg of a quarter-final played in Amsterdam, there were times when Arsenal were depending entirely on their high morale.

Cruyff, getting great joy from his superb skills, flew at them and George Graham recalled: 'He was going by me as though I was a shadow on the grass. He comes at you at great speed and does this sort of shuffle without breaking stride. It's not a swerve. It's more of a sidestep. When he goes by he attacks players with the ball and commits them to a challenge they don't want to make.

'I like to think that I'm not bad at using two-against-one but this bloke's a bit special.'

England were to discover that the Germans were a bit special too. Germany's goals required more than a flicker of good luck. But it in no way diminished the quality of their close-quarter skill which for vital seconds enabled attackers to outnumber defenders.

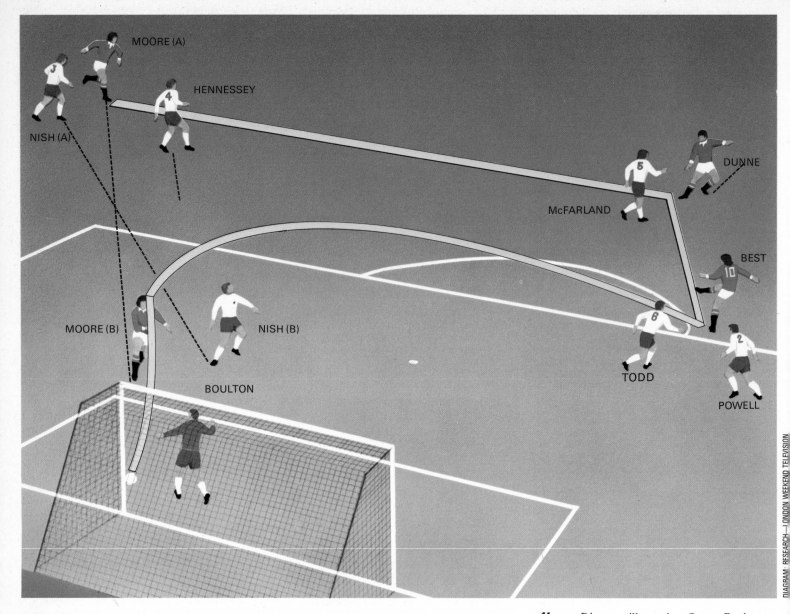

Labels on diagram: MOORE (A), HENNESSEY, NISH (A), NISH (B), MOORE (B), BOULTON, McFARLAND, DUNNE, BEST, TODD, POWELL

DIAGRAM: RESEARCH—LONDON WEEKEND TELEVISION

Penetration in attack

Above *Diagram illustrating George Best's penetrating pass that made Ian Moore's goal in Manchester United's 3-0 win over Derby in 1972.*

Above right *Moore flings himself through the air to head United into the lead, salutes the crowd and then turns to congratulate the man who made the goal. It set United, who had begun the season badly, on their way to their first win—ironically against the Champions.*

Below right *United had lost their way partly because of a lack of penetration in their build-up. Passes had been played in front of defenders rather than between them. Bobby Charlton's long crossfield passes often lacked this vital quality.*

Manchester United's record after six weeks of the 1972-73 season was in every way depressing. Bottom of the First-Division, they had only one victory from eleven League games. Even more worrying for a club whose post-War reputation had been founded on brilliant attacking play was the failure of their forwards.

Their attack had rarely functioned. Lacking was the usual incisive thrust that had become a hallmark of Old Trafford's great teams. No one could play the penetrating pass, the ball that by-passed defenders and took them out of the game. And without such penetration, United and their fans suffered.

Yet in attack United had George Best, apparently revitalized following the personal trauma which had persuaded him to retire temporarily from the game the previous summer. They had Ian Moore, signed a few months earlier from Nottingham Forest. Bobby Charlton and Denis Law, although into the autumn of their careers, were still significant performers. There was Brian Kidd, a member of England's World Cup squad in Mexico and the exciting young Irishman, Sammy McIlroy.

But they were seen to be a blunted force. Frank O'Farrell's recognition of his team's deficiencies was crystallized by his announcement that £1,000,000 would have to be spent to put things in order. Some £200,000 of that was soon to be spent on Ted Macdougall, whose goalscoring feats for Bournemouth in the Third Division had brought him to the forefront of wanted players.

But before Macdougall arrived at Old Trafford there was already a new face among the forwards and United had broken through to win their first League game of the season. Wyn Davies, an uncomplicated Welsh international centre-forward who was more likely to upset defences with his persistent aerial challenge than any definitive sharpness near goal, was signed from Manchester City in a rare deal between the clubs.

Davies made his debut in Bobby Charlton's testimonial game against Celtic, when a 60,000 crowd waited in vain for a sign that United could recapture their scoring touch.

Best did not play in that match. But when he returned to face Derby County the following Saturday, he was to inspire moves which gave United's followers a flicker of encouragement.

The negative passing that had dulled United's edge was inevitably common to all struggling teams. Poor form bred lack of confidence. Players were unwilling to chance a pass which might present the ball to the opposition. They settled for safe angles and their play suffered.

Instead of looking for opportunities to penetrate either by running the ball along the flanks or by slotting it between defenders, they settled for passes across the field, hoping that one of their talented individuals could make something out of nothing.

Ron Greenwood, West Ham's manager and one of the most influential of modern coaches, had always argued a simple but critical point: 'The best pass is the one played between two opponents. The pass which puts people out of the game. You cannot hope to achieve anything unless this is recognized.'

United had lost this art. This type of pass was rarely attempted, and when it was there were too few players willing to try and co-ordinate their

which bisected Terry Hennessey and Nish. Morgan, creeping blind side, was through, gathering pace once he had received the ball. Running on with defenders trailing frantically in his wake, Morgan kept his head, drew Boulton out and placed the ball carefully into an empty goal.

Moments such as this had become rare because modern defences refused to allow themselves to be caught square and without cover. There was little percentage in the long through pass as Jim Baxter discovered when he first arrived in England after a marvellous if undisciplined career with Rangers of Glasgow.

Baxter with his classical style and sophisticated passing typified the traditions of Scottish football. Elegant, thoughtful and impressively accurate, he could slide passes into areas which were beyond the vision of most players.

But in England he discovered that the game was hard work. His favourite, killing pass, inside the full-back for the winger to collect in full stride, was invariably cut out by intelligent covering. With a less extravagant life style, Baxter might have made the adjustments necessary to a successful career in England. But he never really gave the impression that he was willing to change.

Long, through passes had been a feature of Chelsea's play when the enthusiastic Tommy Docherty mustered a squad of young players in the mid-sixties. Barry Bridges, Bobby Tambling and George Graham ran eagerly into forward space and Terry Venables encouraged them to keep on running with a constant supply of lengthy, well-weighted passes.

West Ham, when they had the mercurial Johnny Byrne dovetailing up front with Geoff Hurst, were perhaps the most positive of England's teams. Byrne's immaculate control and Hurst's powerful onward running, perfectly timed, marvellously synchronized with the forward pass, was a problem which few defences solved.

But there were outstanding forwards who never mastered the most destructive pass in the business. Bobby Charlton was a classic example.

running into the space. Malcolm Musgrove, United's coach, said: 'Our play is flat because we are not looking to get in behind defenders. We don't support the man on the ball as well as we should.'

And yet against Derby, in that first victory of a troubled season, United and in particular George Best produced two outstanding examples of penetrating play.

The first involved Best and Ian Moore. Moore, a swift, powerful runner, was essentially an individualist. He had no great instinct for team play. With the ball at his feet, he could outrun most full-backs and at his best his finishing was devastating. And it was his willingness to seek a return pass behind Derby's left flank and Best's vision which enabled Moore to take a valuable goal.

Derby, the reigning Champions, had troubles of their own. They too had begun badly. But it was unfair to fault their defence for a goal which was the product of flair and initiative.

Best, heavily marked when the ball found him on the edge of Derby's penalty area, flicked it up and over the line of white-shirted defenders. Moore, moving in from his right, found himself with a chance to fight for it in the air. He got there first, heading a goal over the top of goalkeeper Boulton who had come hurrying from his line. Moore had beaten full-back David Nish to the ball. It was a classic case of a player running at the right time to connect with a pass played into forward space.

But the true moment of excellence was still to come. Once again Best was the instigator of a memorable move as he collected a ball just inside Derby's half with United now two in front.

Willie Morgan was forward of him and drifting in from the right touchline. Best slid into a pass

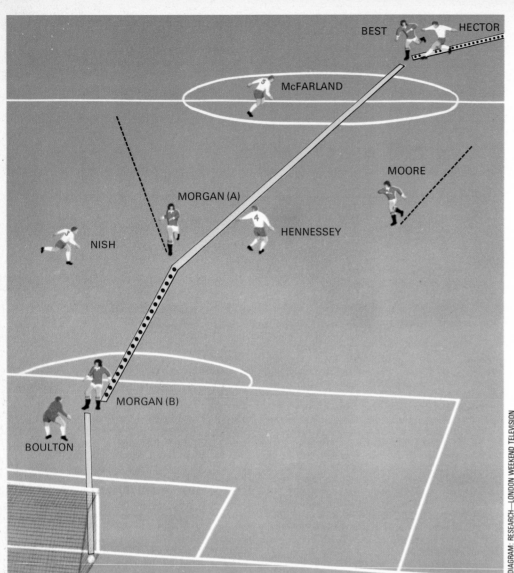

BEST · HECTER · McFARLAND · MOORE · MORGAN (A) · NISH · HENNESSEY · MORGAN (B) · BOULTON

DIAGRAM: RESEARCH—LONDON WEEKEND TELEVISION

Charlton appeared 106 times for England and yet even when his international career was over he was still prone to hit careless forward balls which achieved nothing.

He conceded the point, revealing an odd quirk in his make-up. 'When I was a kid at school the teacher would bring up my long passing in team talks. "Don't forget that Bobby can hit the ball a long way. Look out for his long passes." I suppose I was proud of my ability to do that and I've never really got it out of my system.

'Jimmy Murphy, who was assistant manager at Old Trafford, used to spend hours trying to make me see the wisdom of bringing the game down, of using shorter passes when the other type wasn't on.

'"Look at it this way Bob," he would say. "You might destroy them with one long ball. On the other hand it is more than likely that it will be cut out and half our team are out of the game. Use this pass by all means but only when there is a fair chance of it paying off."

'I could see what he was getting at. But I went on doing the long stuff. In time I learned not to overdo it. But there were still many occasions when I knew I was wrong.'

Ferenc Puskas, captain of a great Hungarian team in the fifties, always said: 'Look for the far man first. If the pass is on then play it. If not settle for something simpler.' It was a simple instruction.

Short passing figured prominently in a popular concept of good football. It was a mistaken belief, if such passes had no end product beyond a fruitless scramble around the penalty area.

Penetration was always vital whether it was achieved by incisive running or by shrewdly directed and well-timed passes. The length of the pass was not significant. Long or short it could only be destructive if it put opponents out of the game.

Left *United's third goal against Derby was a perfect example of a pass that plays opponents out of the game. Best's through pass destroyed the Derby defence and Morgan ran on to score.*
Below *Best, number 10, raises his hands in triumph as Morgan's shot ends up in the Derby net.*

RAY GREEN

Coaching : Learn the pass that puts opponents out of the game

'Play the easy ball' is always sound advice to a young player but unless he is careful, in these days of overloaded midfield, he can fall into the error of constantly playing the ball square and in front of opponents. This only has the effect of transferring the play from one side of the pitch to the other without seriously troubling the opposition.

The success of offensive football depends largely on exercising certain principles. To stretch defenders across the pitch, width in attacking play is essential, to overcome tight man-for-man marking, mobility in attack is necessary, to create passing possibilities and maintain possession, depth is an indispensable element in the success of an attack. But the penetrating pass, more than any other factor, can play opponents out of the game and devastate a defence.

The player in possession should ideally have at least three players at any given moment to which he can pass. His choice of pass will be dependent upon several factors, but invariably his best pass is the one which puts most opponents out of the game, as long as there is a strong chance of retaining possession.

Start your practice for penetration with two of your team-mates. Stand about 30 yards from one of them with a ball, whilst the third player acts as a defender and stands in the middle facing the player without the ball. The idea here is for you to chip the ball over the middle man to the other player who must control it quickly and return it to you. The defender, once the ball has passed over his head, should attempt to close down the receiver and prevent him from returning it. The player receiving should work quickly for a passing angle by taking the ball to one side as he makes his first control before the defender can get in too tight. After a while, change round so that you all get a feel of working for the passing angle to play a penetrating pass.

Once you have got the idea, use the same exercise to attack a goal. The idea here is for the player playing the penetrating pass to sprint to support the ball he has played. He should collect the knock off ball and continue to shoot at goal. Once this has happened he should retrieve the ball in order to restart the exercise so that each player's function changes.

It is so important to support the penetrating pass. For example, in another practice a defender plays a longish ball up to a front striker who is about 30 yards from goal. Because the striker is marked tightly by a defender this ball must be accurate. The pass will be played over a midfield player who is also marked. The midfield player must now move in to support his striker immediately the ball has gone past him. From here on, it becomes two versus two and must be played according to the demands of the situation in order to make a strike at goal.

This basic exercise means that you are hitting your most forward players and setting up a quick strike. It can be a physically demanding practice so it will help your fitness. Work in groups of pairs continually changing functions.

Another supporting player and marker can be introduced to create more passing possibilities and a three-versus-three situation. This will broaden the outlook and create the sort of situations you will encounter in a match.

A small-sided, conditioned game will also help you realize the benefits and highlight the requirements of penetrating passes. The condition is that you must find your front target player from the back. This means that the moment possession has been gained by the back players the target player must be making himself available and the midfield players must be preparing to support. Even though the opposing players know what you intend doing, they can do little about it, providing the timing of the movement into space is good and the ball played accurately into that space.

Timing of the movement is essential and will only come through practice. This will almost certainly help your team to strike quickly by playing balls through the back of defenders after it has been played back to the midfield supporting players by the target player. This search for penetration is an excellent launching pad for an attack, and an indispensable part of successful offensive play.

Below As Liverpool's Steve Heighway carries the ball towards the Crystal Palace defenders, he looks for passing possibilities. The most telling pass might be the one to Kevin Keegan, number 7, who is looking to find space ahead of Heighway in the heart of the defence.

***Bottom** A practice to cultivate the penetrating pass. A defender plays a long ball up to a forward, who is immediately supported by a midfield player. As soon as the midfield player has the ball, the two attackers try to get in a strike at goal. Both attackers are marked so this now becomes a two-against-two situation, all started by a penetrating forward pass that has by-passed opponents.*

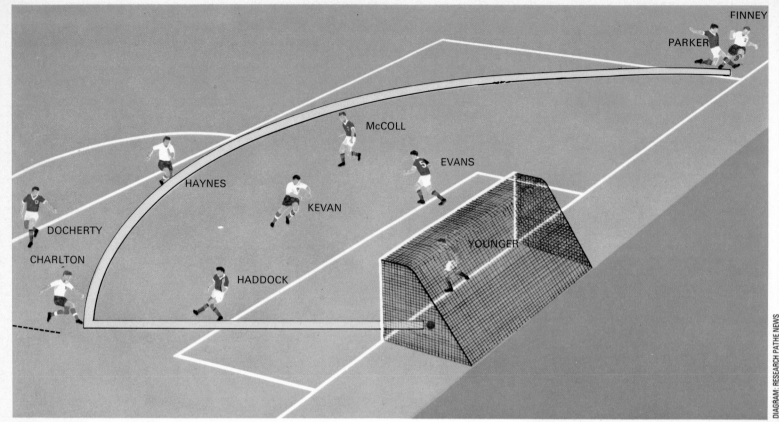

Labels on diagram: FINNEY, PARKER, McCOLL, EVANS, HAYNES, KEVAN, DOCHERTY, CHARLTON, HADDOCK, YOUNGER

DIAGRAM: RESEARCH PATHE NEWS

Volleying at goal

'Why didn't you pick Bobby Charlton?' asked Walter Winterbottom's son when he greeted his father after the 1958 World Cup in Sweden. A boy was merely echoing the thoughts of a nation. The kindly, studious Winterbottom had been charged with assembling a team capable of winning football's greatest prize and he had chosen not to call on his most exciting prospect.

Throughout that series the teenage Charlton, a survivor of the Munich air crash a few months earlier, had sat in brooding isolation while England struggled through their group before losing to Russia in a play-off. Discontent, even disgust, gathered out of his rejection and much of it was due to Charlton's dramatic entry into international football the previous April.

Chosen to play against Scotland at Hampden Park, Glasgow, he had scored a goal of such devastating suddenness that it was clear that a new English star was in the heavens; and he scored it with a killing volley.

Fully blond then and with a fresh-faced innocence which obscured the tragedy he had suffered, Charlton rifled in a shot which did more to spread gloom among the massed ranks of the Scottish followers than anything else England did on the day. England won 4-0 but it was Charlton's effort which indicated that there was a new name to spread concern in the Scottish camp.

Charlton's selection had been controversial but popular. He had recovered from Munich to play his part in a revival which was to carry Manchester United forward to the FA Cup Final at Wembley on a wave of sympathy. He had already displayed a talent for hostile shooting, and it was the confidence to strike the ball when it was still in the air which brought him such a memorable goal on his international debut.

The architect was Tom Finney, a player of infinite talent who was arguably England's greatest forward during the fifteen years following the Second World War. Finney's flair and liquid swerve opened up an untidy Scottish defence and a perfect centre to the far side of the penalty box found Charlton in full flight about ten yards from goal.

Tommy Docherty, then a pugnacious wing-half with Preston and later to become Scotland's team manager, takes up the story: 'Bobby spurted away from me and, as the ball came in hip high, he hit a perfect volley. Tommy Younger was our goalkeeper that day. He was still diving when the ball hit the net. I would say that it was the best volley I have ever seen.'

A majestic goal that registered Charlton in the minds of the public

A goal of such majestic proportion had to register Bobby Charlton in the minds of the public. He was seen as the saviour of an England team then struggling to score goals and a certainty to gain a place in Sweden. But then he played against Yugoslavia in a pre-World Cup tour. It was from Yugoslavia that Manchester United had set off for home on a fateful journey the previous February. England were destroyed by five clear goals, and it was sensed among the squad that Charlton was in danger of having his career threatened at a critical stage of his development.

Charlton eventually established himself in the England team and not only overtook Wright's record of 105 caps but scored 49 goals to become

Top Diagram of Bobby Charlton's first goal for England—a blistering right-foot volley from an accurate cross by left-winger Tom Finney.
Above Charlton's volley rockets past Scotland's keeper, Tommy Younger. The game was played at Hampden Park in 1958, and England won 4-0.

England's all-time record marksman. His shooting was always spectacular and his ability to volley served him well over the years.

Players who could strike the ball whilst it was in the air without needing to have it under control in their stride had an even greater part to play in the game as defences began to tighten up in the fifties. But post-War football had hardly got under way when a Wembley audience was a witness to the value of instant power.

'We'll be back,' said manager Jimmy Seed after Charlton Athletic had lost to Derby County in the 1946 Cup Final. The promise was kept. Charlton

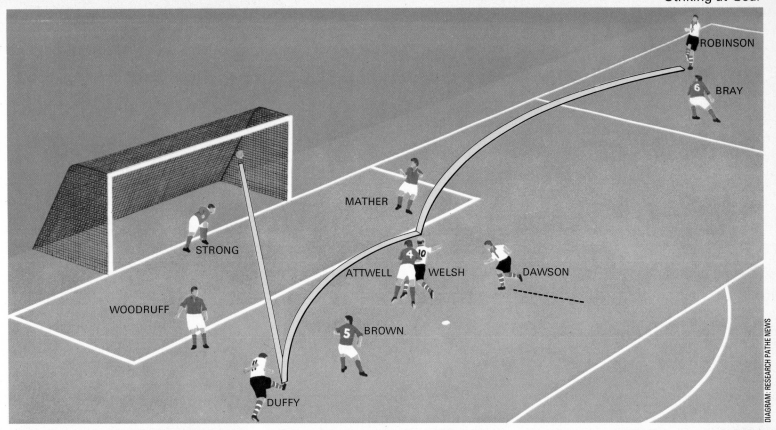

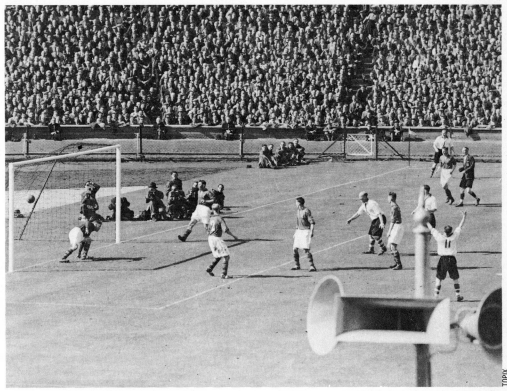

fought their way through to Wembley the following season, and this time they left in triumph. It was a dull Final. Burnley, a dour, defensive side, gave nothing away, and Charlton lacked the cunning and enterprise needed to open up the match. It dragged into extra time, but then created a moment of drama which embellished the competition's history.

Burnley, with their strategy built around the unsmiling play of their centre-half, Alan Brown, seemed in no trouble when Bill Robinson, a balding veteran forward, centred from the right touchline. Don Welsh, a former England forward in the evening of his career, challenged in the air but could only get the faintest touch and the ball flicked through.

Chris Duffy, an unlikely looking little Scottish winger with a talent for taking vital goals, met the chance in full stride and Burnley's goalkeeper, Strong, stood helpless before a wicked volley.

For a second and more, Wembley was silent. Players on both sides seemed frozen by the suddenness of it all. Duffy was the first to react. Realizing the enormity of his feat, he turned and sprinted, going nowhere in particular as the excitement took complete control of his mind and limbs. Pursued by a posse of team-mates, he was finally arrested in full flight when he leapt into the arms of a burly full-back, Jack Shreeve. Football draws its life-blood from such moments of sudden drama.

But it was a long while before deliberate attempts were made to exploit a rare talent for scoring goals out of nowhere. Volleying was an art which required a sure touch and total confidence. Few players were better at it than Colin Bell whose skill and prodigious stamina served Manchester City well when Joe Mercer and Malcolm Allison combined to build an influential team.

Bell lacked Charlton's fluency, but there was

Top The FA Cup won with a volley. Diagram showing Chris Duffy's last-minute effort which won Charlton the Cup in 1947. Robinson crossed, Welsh back-headed and Duffy volleyed home.
Above Strong in the Burnley goal is left helpless as Duffy's killing shot bulges the net.

no doubting his quality. Breaking from midfield he would arrive in full flight on the far side of goal, and he was always willing to chance his arm.

In 1970, Chelsea felt the whiplash of his skill with a volley hit from an angle which suggested to his opponents that they had no need to fear an assault. Bell's action was classic, leaning heavily on to his left foot to take the ball hip high with a full swing of his right.

Martin Peters, first with West Ham and then with Spurs, showed an equal talent for striking the ball in the air and, with a fraction of luck, might have prevented Arsenal from winning the Football

League Championship in their final game of the 1970-71 competition.

Arsenal were still wrestling for supremacy in a match from which they needed a goalless draw to finish ahead of Leeds when Peters swooped on to a pass from Martin Chivers.

The ball sat up on the bounce and Peters struck it with heavy top spin at Arsenal's goal without breaking his stride. Arsenal's goalkeeper, Bob Wilson, pawed helplessly at the ball, destroyed by the power and dip. But Peters was just off line. His shot struck the top of the stanchion supporting the net and Arsenal survived.

Sir Alf Ramsey, England's team manager, watched the match and said: 'That is the kind of thing which makes Peters an exceptional player. Few would have attempted that shot and everything about it was calculated. It required great skill and confidence. It was a masterly effort and deserved better.'

Peter Lorimer of Leeds needed no encouragement to go for volleys, and this willingness, plus his immense power, brought him a spectacular goal when playing against Manchester City at Elland Road in the autumn of 1971.

Injuries had undermined Leeds' challenge and they needed the sort of boost which came when Lorimer, sneaking through on to a long forward pass, went to the left of City's defenders before hugely dipping a volley beyond the giant goalkeeper, Joe Corrigan.

When the England team trained before a European Nations Cup tie against Greece in December 1971, all their forwards were seen to be volleying at goal. The skill was appealing to players with outstanding skill and it would have been surprising if Manchester United's George Best had not used it.

For all his brilliant ball control, Best was essentially a great finisher and he proved this with a devastating goal in a European Cup tie against Real Madrid in 1968. Much of Best's skill as a finisher stemmed from his ability and willingness to meet the ball whilst it was still hanging in the air:

Peter Bonetti, one of England's top goalkeepers in the sixties and seventies, said: 'Everyone seems to be hitting volleys at you these days. Forwards love to beat you with them in training and they acquire the confidence to do this in matches. It makes a goalkeeper's life harder because you never know what to expect.'

Nevertheless, good volleying remained a specialist art. Those who did it well were usually special players—as special as Bobby Charlton was when he first presented himself at the beginning of a momentous international career.

Coaching: Practise striking the ball while it is in the air

Goalkeepers are often taken by surprise by a first-time shot. When an attacking player stops the ball, it not only gives a defending player a chance to close him down but it also gives the keeper a chance to re-orientate and prepare himself for the shot. Goalscoring opportunities have been lost because of a player's reluctance to shoot first time. And a large proportion of first-time shooting will involve hitting the ball when it is off the ground—volleying.

Begin your practice with a ball on a string. Hold the string so that the ball is about 12 inches from the ground. Make contact with the ball by using the full instep, keeping the ankle firm and the toes pointed down. When you have struck the ball, allow your arm to move away from the body so that the pace of the ball is absorbed; it will then swing for you to kick again. Practise kicking with different parts of the foot and at different angles.

Then, lengthen the string and suspend the ball from high overhead. Your body is now free and the use of your arms will naturally help you to balance and co-ordinate your movements. Set the ball hanging about 12 to 14 inches from the ground and stand about 18 to 20 inches behind the ball. Make contact as before—not too hard, but

Right Volley tennis played over benches in a gymnasium sharpens the volleying technique.
Below Dave Mackay exhibits the classic volleying position as he clears the ball from George Best.

hard enough to get the feel; touch is of the utmost importance. As the ball swings back to you, kick it again; this will help cultivate the timing of the kick. It is also a good idea here to try to kick the ball with a short back-swing of the leg because often you will not have time for a long swing. Gradually increase the power of your shot. Keep your toes well down and be conscious of where you are trying to put the ball.

Most of the volley chances at goal will come from balls being centred from the wings. This

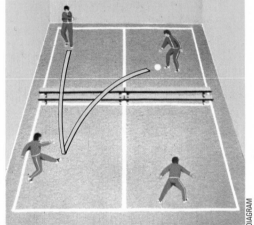

means that the ball will approach you on a different course from the one you are going to send it on. This is more difficult and you must concentrate on keeping your eye on the ball and holding your head steady. If your head is moving about, you will not get a clear picture of the ball; this is most important if you are going to make contact clearly. Pivot on the standing leg as you strike the ball, and make your kicking leg swing on an arc that brings it in a horizontal line on to the ball or even downwards on to it. If you are not very careful, the ball will almost certainly fly high and over the bar.

To practise this, allow the ball on the string to swing just a shade higher, about knee high. As you direct the ball downwards, swing your foot almost parallel with the ground and follow through downwards towards the ground. Some players favour contact with the outside of the instep. Try it; you may find it suits you too.

On your own, throw the ball about ten feet in the air, allow it to bounce once, then volley the ball at a target before it bounces a second time. Next, stand side-on to the target and, before the ball bounces a second time, make a firm contact as you pivot on the non-kicking foot.

Work with a friend next. Ask him to throw the ball in front of you. After taking a few paces to get to the ball, strike it firmly with the instep, keeping the knee well up to direct the ball down. Make sure your head is steady and that you watch the ball closely.

Progress can now be made to a more difficult service. Your friend can stand about 20 yards in front of you. He either chips or throws the ball for you to volley it before it bounces and send it to the target. Have confidence here, because if the contact is not clean you may hurt your foot.

An enjoyable game to help improve your volleying is volley tennis. The rules are the same as for lawn tennis and can be played on a tennis court or a similar area with a net. The ball must be volleyed over so that it bounces in the opponents' court. Your opponent can either volley it back first time or control it with his body so that it does not bounce a second time before he volleys it back. Three-a-side is very good practice and fun.

But practice in game situations under pressure is essential. Three players can work together. One crosses the ball deep to the far post for another one to head for the third member to volley past the goalkeeper. A fourth member could act as opposition to the volleyer. He marks the player coming in from the edge of the penalty area, remaining passive at first, but becoming more and more active as the skill progresses.

There are many practices of this nature, but whatever you do remember to get into the line of flight and to meet the ball quickly. Aim to hit the ball cleanly, and try to crack the ball down on to the target. Volleying is a skill that requires constant practising, but the effort will be worthwhile. For when a half-clearance drops towards you, the ball will be in the back of the net in the time it takes others to control it before they shoot.

Running off the ball

Above Diagram of how Geoff Hurst's decoy running made a goal for Clyde Best against Stoke in 1971. Hurst's first run distracted the defenders around Best; his second deceived Banks.
Left Hurst lunges and Best's header slips in.

selfless movement. It was not lost on England team manager Sir Alf Ramsey who included the West Ham forward in two controversial matches against the Swiss in the European Nations Cup.

Ramsey used an incident in a match between West Ham and Stoke at Upton Park to defend a player who had performed valiantly for him over the years. Ramsey saw the match on television. Hurst did not score but his decisive movement beneath a free-kick played in by Bobby Moore led to a goal by Best.

As Moore shaped up to loft the ball from the West Ham right into the Stoke penalty area, Hurst, stationed opposite the far post, turned to sprint as though expecting the ball to come in short to the near post.

Instead Moore drove it wide to the far post where Best was lurking with an eager forehead, and Stoke, thrown into confusion by Hurst's run, were instantly in trouble. Even then they might have survived had Hurst not been willing to run yet again, this time in towards goal. England goalkeeper Gordon Banks was a good bet to save Best's header until he was put off by Hurst. As he raced in, Banks clearly thought the striker would turn the ball in, and he flung himself to his right. Hurst dummied and the ball rolled in past Banks' left hand.

John Lyall, West Ham's coach, recalled: 'That was really Geoff's goal. In fact he might even have got a touch at it. But when we asked him he was happy to let Clyde have it. That's Geoff. He's dedicated to the team cause and he will run to make openings for others.'

Players willing to run without prospect of getting the ball were few and far between. The effort had no real appeal, and yet it was vital to productive team play.

Spurs proved this during their years of dominance in the early sixties when the late John White consistently lured opponents into false positions. No one benefitted more from this than Danny Blanchflower. A superb user of the pass who could use every conceivable kind of pass,

Since winning the European Cup Winners Cup with an extravagant display of refined football, West Ham United had established a reputation as a thinking side. With a brooding refusal to involve himself in the cynical aspects of the game, manager Ron Greenwood created a pattern of play that bordered on the intellectual. And as Greenwood thought, his players followed. Amongst a host of individual skills, a willingness to run for each other stood out. And in the skill of decoy running West Ham possessed an outstanding performer.

Geoff Hurst, England's hat-trick hero in the

1966 World Cup final, had been for many seasons one of the more intelligent attackers in the business. But as West Ham consolidated in 1971 with fine victories in both the League and the League Cup, Hurst was seen to have entered an interesting phase in his career.

Always a willing, unselfish player, he began to devote himself to the team cause, and Clyde Best, a brawny Bermudan, began to score goals consistently. Hurst's dedication was so complete that many critics considered him to be playing badly.

What they overlooked was his cunning and

COATES (B)

COATES (A)

KNOWLES

LOMBARDO (A)

CERESER

FOSSATI (B)

LOMBARDO (B)

FOSSATI (A)

ZECCHINI

CHIVERS

AGROPPI

GILZEAN

CASTELLINI

Above *Diagram of a near miss by Alan Gilzean for Spurs versus Torino in 1971. Gilzean had space made for him by Cyril Knowles' decoy run which drew defenders towards the Spurs' full-back.*
Left *Gilzean causes more trouble for Torino.*

Blanchflower in the autumn of his career had to have space in which to play.

White, by sprinting from a position square with the touchline towards the corner flag, opened up that space by taking his marker with him. He was simply altering the shape of the triangle. Blanchflower would move forward to accept the space White had left and the ball would be played in to him from the winger. This move became an integral part of Spurs' play and all the best teams used it as a build-up process.

Later generations of Spurs players were quick to spot the usefulness of decoy running. In 1971 in an Anglo-Italian League Cup Winners Cup tie against Torino at White Hart Lane, Spurs mounted attacks in waves, fully utilizing the overlapping skills of left-back Cyril Knowles in their build-up. And when Ralph Coates, eagerly probing for openings, put his foot on the ball in the inside-left position, Knowles was ready to be included in the attack once more. There were two defenders between Coates and the penalty area, and, as Knowles hurtled past his team-mate once more along the touchline, it looked as though the midfield man would use him to get behind the Italians' defence. The Torino defenders had more than half an eye open to the danger, and moved right to cover the threat.

Coates took full advantage, using Knowles as

a decoy. A quick centre found Alan Gilzean half a yard free from the distracted defence. The Scot put his header just wide, but the message was clear.

Les Cocker, Leeds' trainer and one of the two taken to the Mexico World Cup by Ramsey, recalled a spectacular example which involved Bobby Collins.

Collins was a fierce competitor. One of the smallest players in the League, he had skilled feet and much cunning. It was the cunning which led to a critical goal for his club.

Cocker said: 'The ball had gone out to Albert Johanneson on the left wing, when Bobby suddenly set off towards the corner flag. He took one man with him and then deliberately ran across the face of another. By the time he reached the corner he had both of them within touching distance.

'As the space opened up Albert cut inside and scored. Bobby was all smiles. The cheeky so-and-so then turned and shook hands with the two men he had lured away. He was like that.'

Decoy running served England well during the 1966 World Cup, and no one worked harder to create openings than Roger Hunt. Hunt got most of his goals by picking up chances in crowded penalty areas. But it was his powerful, positive running at the van of the attack which proved of most value to England. Bobby Charlton was well aware of that.

Hunt's running opened the way for Charlton's hostile shooting

Charlton's hostile shooting was a critical factor throughout the 1966 series at Wembley, but he would not have had the opportunity to score great goals had Hunt and Hurst not run for him. Charlton was ordered to press forward from midfield whenever the ball had been pitched forward to the strikers. He was supposed to get up with them before Alan Ball and Martin Peters who were the other midfield men.

He did not always do it to Ramsey's satisfaction, but he did it often to add memorable goals to glittering records of his career.

One of these was scored against Mexico when England were being firmly resisted by opponents who were only interested in survival. Taking up the story, Charlton said: 'I got the ball on the half-way line and my first thought was to get it forward quickly. When I looked up, Roger Hunt was streaming off on a cross-run, and half the Mexicans seemed to have gone with him. I just kept on running. When I got within range I was able to drive the ball into the far side of the goal. It was a great moment for me, but Roger deserved a lot of the credit.'

This sort of running had to be decisive if it was to be truly effective, and it was never more deadly than when used close to goal. Arsenal proved the point when winning a European Cup tie against Grasshoppers in Zurich in 1971.

The match was barely five minutes old when George Graham intercepted a Swiss clearance and then set George Armstrong free.

Armstrong's reaction was instant and purposeful. He struck out at the goal-line and centred superbly on the run. The ball came in low, and it was then that John Radford and Ray Kennedy, Arsenal's burly strikers, confirmed the extent of their understanding and comradeship.

Radford pitched in powerfully to meet the ball, and succeeded in taking two defenders with him. Instead of making contact, he allowed the ball to run through behind him and Kennedy, arriving late, drove in a scoring left-foot shot.

Dead-ball situations close to goal encouraged the use of decoy movement to disturb defensive arrangement although most coaches recognized the fallibility of complicated moves.

But there was nothing complicated about Hurst's activity against Stoke and he was well rewarded for his industry. And, despite his critics, it was no surprise to find him still cropping up in the England squad in 1971.

Coaching: Learn to run off the ball, and make chances for your team

How many times have you heard that it is the man off the ball that plays the football? It is a very true saying—put a world class player in a poor team and he will struggle. Every player requires help and if his team-mates are not running into the right space at the right time then passes cannot be made and possession will be lost. Players who are willing to make unselfish runs purposely to create space for other players are of immense value. These are the real 90 minute players.

If you aim to be in this group of players then physical condition is of utmost importance. Work hard at your training sessions and do not miss them. At any level of football, thorough preparation cannot be over-emphasized.

You can begin to practise the art of running off the ball in a simple exercise with a friend. Play the ball to him from about 15 yards, then sprint forward and diagonally across the front of him. He feints to play the ball through to you, then suddenly moves off in a sprint with the ball away from where you have run. You are acting as a decoy for him drawing away imaginary opponents. He then plays the ball to you, and he goes off on a decoy run whilst you move off with the ball. From this, move on to introduce a defender. Play two players against one, with you marking one player who has a supporting player about 15 yards away. The ball is played up to the player you are marking. He plays it off to the supporting player and runs about four yards wide. The supporting player then runs at you. As he is doing this the player off the ball sprints around the back of you calling for a pass. Now your attention is attracted by this run and you cannot concentrate entirely on the man running at you. The man in possession now has a better chance to take you on and get in a shot at goal. But the decoy run is of no value unless it is positive; the decoy man must make the defender think he wants the ball. The run must also be timed so that if the man with the ball wants to use the runner he can. With practice you will be able to perform this so that if you wanted to play the ball through, the decoy runner would be on side. Practise the two against one routine, con-

tinually changing functions, then move on to two against two.

Play in an area about 35 yards long and 15 yards wide. The team in possession must interpass the ball until one of them has the ball in a position to take on one of the opponents. The tactic here is for the second player to run at the same opponent getting on his blind side, because one of two things is going to happen. Either he will be free to take the through ball or he will have created space for the man on the ball to take on the one defender. What happens will depend on whether the second opponent allows the decoy runner to go free or goes with him.

In order to get in a position where you can get a run at an opponent, one of the inter-passing players must move back into plenty of space. If the two opponents are working correctly they should be covering one another to prevent this one-against-one situation. The object of this practice is to destroy the covering position.

Free-kicks give you an excellent opportunity to use decoy work to good effect. It gives you a good chance to work out movements from static positions.

One example is a free-kick routine from a position just outside the penalty area. The opposition might put three players in the wall and their winger might well come back to mark your winger. This means your full-back on that side of the field is spare. The winger, on a signal, runs across the front of the wall calling for the ball, attracting the attention of the opposing winger. The ball is then played into the space created by the winger's movement for the full-back to move on to. He can now get at the back of the wall or cross to the near or far post. This movement can be equally successful within the run of play when a midfield player is moving through into the opponents' half with the ball and the full-back breaks free from his winger. Your winger quickly runs infield creating the space for the full-back.

Practice this movement and you will see that other ideas will come to mind. Once you think about movement off the ball you are certainly on the right track.

Below Two diagrams of two-a-side practice for decoy running. The man off the ball holds the key. If his marker goes with him, the man on the ball has space to beat his man. If not, the pass is on.

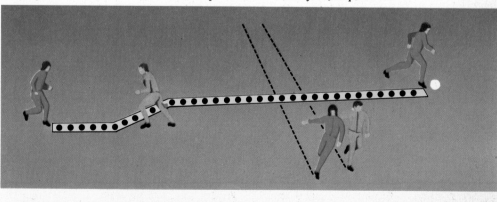

DIAGRAM

The chip

In the sweltering heat of Lisbon on a May Sunday in 1964, Portugal and England appeared to have settled for a draw. It had been an open, entertaining match in which both attacks had found space in which to manoeuvre.

The giant Jose Torres had given the home side an early lead which goals by Bobby Charlton and Johnny Byrne had overtaken at half-time. Torres struck an equalizer and the elusive Eusebio restored Portugal's advantage, but Byrne had popped up to restore the balance. It seemed like stalemate. Three-all would not be a bad result for either side.

And that is the way it would have remained if 'Budgie' Byrne had not found the energy to score a memorable goal only two minutes from time. Indeed such a magnificent climax seemed impossible even up to the point when Peter Thompson's cross from the right wing found Byrne outside Portugal's penalty area. There were still three defenders barring his route in on goalkeeper Pereira.

Undaunted, Byrne slipped past one. The other two bore down upon him. Byrne checked, the defenders checked and for a second the picture froze, the action condensed into a few square yards just inside the area. Then, as of one mind, the defenders moved towards him, shutting down what space remained, and clearly confident that Pereira would not be troubled. At that second 'Budgie' stabbed his right foot under the ball and played it forward. It flew over one opponent and found its way into the top corner of the net past Pereira's left hand. Like a golfer with a nine-iron in his hand, he had executed the perfect chip. That it brought him his hat-trick, that it won the match was almost incidental. The goal would have been totally memorable if England had been five up or behind.

The chip, the ability to propel the ball over opponents, can be used in any facet of play. Few men though, possess the impudent skill of Byrne to use it as a direct shot at goal. The ball travels too slowly and the margin of error is too great. More often the chip plays a secondary role in goalscoring; passes floated into the goalmouth open the way to goal if they are struck accurately.

When West Germany emerged as European Champions in 1972, they revealed a wide range of skill. Much of it was supplied by the midfield talents of Gunter Netzer of Borussia Monchengladbach. Netzer's passing over middle and long range was exemplary. He could drive swerving passes to mobile team-mates and his sense of vision was emphasized by his use of the chip.

To win the European Championship, West Germany had to overcome Belgium in front of their home crowd. It was not going to be easy and in an atmosphere of claxons and sirens they dared not fall behind. Netzer's comprehension of the positioning of striker Gerd Muller saw to that. As the visitors settled to their work in the first half, they built up a gentle, casual attack. The ball was played almost indifferently across the front of the Belgian defence, from Netzer, on the right, infield to Beckenbauer then left to Brietner. Back it flowed, Brietner gently to Beckenbauer and then back to Netzer.

As Wimmer moved wider to distract the defenders around Netzer, Muller made his move across the penalty area towards the near post. Netzer spotted it. His well-struck chip dropped over a succession of helpless white-shirted defenders on to Muller's head. He only needed to make contact to deflect the ball past the indecisive Piot. Muller scored again with Netzer's assistance in the second half and West Germany were in the final.

Trevor Brooking of West Ham had showed something of Netzer's audacity in scoring an original goal against Spurs at Upton Park in April 1972. Brooking, an intelligent footballer with a convincing academic background which was almost unique among professional players, had advanced as far as England Under-23 international recognition, but he seemed to lack conviction about his own ability.

Spurs chose to rest some established stars. One of those given respite was Mike England, the powerful Welshman whose form at centre-half during the previous six weeks had more than adequately countered the theory that he had drifted beyond his best days in the game.

His deputy was Peter Collins, a determined and aggressive young defender. He had none of England's style but he displayed a willingness which made him a forbidding proposition for attackers who tried to match him for strength.

Brooking found him out. Not with muscularity, not with perseverance. Simply with a sudden burst of the instinctive talent that always lay dormant beneath the diffidence which seemed to confound the theory that academic ability could have any profound influence on the state of the professional game.

Brooking had drifted wide on the right side of Spurs' defence when Bobby Moore cleverly broke up an attack with an interception that was a testimony to his awareness. The pass which followed confirmed that Moore had few equals when presented with the possibility of a penetrating counter-attack from a deep defensive position. It was delivered with the outside of Moore's right foot, and it uncovered Brooking in an instantly threatening area. He took maximum advantage of the opportunity.

Brooking creates a moment of sheer joy for Ron Greenwood

Collins shuttled across to contest the angle. A more experienced defender might have held Brooking up, denying him the opportunity to create an opening where contact with the ball could prove to be destructive.

But Collins, all enthusiasm and commitment, allowed himself to be lured into a cardinal error. He allowed Brooking to manoeuvre into the penalty area and to where a devastating chip was an immediate possibility.

The paradoxical nature of Brooking's make-up was now demonstrated in vivid fashion. He had the skill to attempt the spectacular and the intelligence to recognize that it was possible.

Turning across Collins, he sighted on the top far corner of Pat Jennings' goal and chipped the ball there with unerring accuracy.

It was a moment of sheer joy for West Ham manager Ron Greenwood who had continually expounded the principle of intellect when related to the professional player. Brooking was fallible, unsure of his presence in a sphere which paid no account to brains unless they were accompanied by the reality of success.

He was not alone with his uncertainty. But he had a renowned predecessor in Danny Blanch-

Above *Diagram illustrating the immaculate chip with which Johnny Byrne clinched England's 4-3 win over Portugal in Lisbon in May 1964.*
Above right *A perceptive chip from Gunter Netzer enabled Gerd Muller to put West Germany in front in the 1972 European Nations Championship semi-final against Belgium in Antwerp.*
Right *Muller turns away as his header provides the perfect finish to Netzer's skilful pass.*

flower whose thoroughly professional attitude from an enquiring background had confounded the argument that great players were completely reliable by instinct.

Blanchflower, with Spurs and Northern Ireland, embodied the true arts of the game. Few players could match his ability to drift the ball through the air, chipping into the path of running attackers as Netzer was to do for West Germany in their exciting spring and summer of 1972.

Rodney Marsh, with Fulham, Queen's Park Rangers and Manchester City, also possessed audacity beyond question; indeed he often earned criticism for attempting too much. There was something of the Byrne in his make-up as a player, the instinctive ability to take the pace of the ball and drop it to feet, a skill sadly lacking in the British game. Almost as if as a tribute to 'Budgie', Marsh conjured a goal in his fashion at Upton Park, the scene of much of Byrne's magic. The occasion was Geoff Hurst's testimonial match and Marsh brought the house down with a chip up and over the goalkeeper when he was only a few yards out in front of goal.

The Arsenal manager, Bertie Mee, recognized the same sort of potential in Charlie George. He predicted sensational achievement for the precocious striker when he said: 'This chap is going to look up one day and score a goal from the halfway line.'

Elaborating on the possibility that George could execute such an outstanding feat, he said: 'He has the vision, the power and the range to bring off what has been regarded as the impossible. He will score from the halfway line because he

PIOT

MULLER

BECKENBAUER

NETZER

DIAGRAM/RESEARCH—LONDON WEEKEND TELEVISION

SVEN SIMON

believes he can and because he has the equipment to do it.'

The target was not unique. Pele, perhaps the greatest of all players, had attempted it during the 1970 World Cup with a chip shot aimed from the centre circle.

George had none of Pele's extensive experience to call on. He fell short of the great Brazilian's enormous validity in the world game. His aggressive, even abusive conduct threatened to undermine the possibility that he could establish himself as an international figure.

But he could play. There was a distinctive economy in the short backlift which allowed George to produce explosive shots when left with a minimum of time and space. The scoring chip even from the halfway line was not beyond him.

Didi, the elegant, dusky general of Brazil's football between 1958 and 1962 employed similar techniques with devastating effect, proving that it was almost impossible to subdue players who had the vision and confidence to try and penetrate the immediate barrier.

Franz Beckenbauer, when advancing from his role as a covering defender behind West Germany's markers, revealed a similar instinct for the unexpected, using the chip pass to find advancing team-mates.

Eddie Gray and John Giles used the chip with continuing success for Leeds United. George

Best and Denis Law were not lacking in confidence when they sensed they could determine a result with efforts bordering on the miraculous and the completely audacious.

Nevertheless it was always necessary for the great player to choose the right moment. Rodney Marsh went for a chip when playing against Scotland at Hampden Park in the decisive encounter of the 1972 British Championship.

A simple pass square to Colin Bell or Martin Chivers would have settled the issue beyond doubt. Marsh's chip was safely fielded by the Scottish goalkeeper and it registered immediate doubt. International football was intolerant of audacity unless it proved to be decisive.

Coaching: Develop the chip technique to lift the ball over defences

However good a player becomes it is not always possible to pass the ball along the ground to the feet of a team-mate. Good defenders position themselves to make passing more difficult by limiting the number of passing possibilities the player in possession has and preventing the ball going into a danger area. When such a situation presents itself the player with the ball has two choices: either he plays the ball away from the danger, which pleases the defender, or he has got to get the ball up into the air and over the top so that it drops into the space behind the defender.

The closer the defender is to him the more steeply the ball has to climb in order to gain height quickly enough not to be intercepted. This means that this type of chipped pass is mainly used over short distances as distinct from the lofted pass which can be used over longer distances. The chip has an advantage over the long, lofted pass because in getting the ball in the air steeply it is possible to impart backspin. This checks its speed on landing so that it does not go running on out of control into touch or

to a defender. It also means that the ball can be dropped into tighter situations.

There are two ways in which the ball can be made to rise quickly. One is with the full instep. The toe is stabbed beneath the ball so that the angle between the toes and instep makes contact, sending the ball upwards steeply and imparting backspin. The ankle is only slightly extended and is held firm. The contact must be aimed at the lowest possible point on the ball and the approach is in line with the intended line of flight. Limit your follow through, kicking the ball so that the leg is straight just after impact. Although this type of kick is difficult to master it is well worth practising because when you are proficient you will have the ability to really drop the ball accurately.

The second method involves the use of the inside of the instep with the ankle extended and the approach made from an angle so that your foot swings fully through the lower part of the ball. The touch required is often very delicate so the action must be positive, with the head held very

steady to help make the contact clean. A scooping action with the foot must be avoided at all costs.

Practise on your own to start with against a fairly high wall. Work on both methods because the important thing is to get the ball up sharply. This is easier when the ball is moving towards you, so begin your practice by pushing the ball against the wall with the inside of your foot so that it rebounds to you rolling along the ground. When using the inside of your instep make sure you approach the ball at an angle so that the kicking foot can be extended outwards allowing the inside of your instep to swing through the lower part of the ball. As with all kicking techniques keep your ankle firm, focus your eyes on the ball at impact and follow through on a line with the target. The non-kicking foot must be up almost level with the ball but not too close otherwise you will impart an unwanted spin.

You will be able to see the ball spin for yourself and this is a sure indication of how well you have struck it. The spin should be a true backspin and the trajectory of the pass must be straight.

A good practice now would be to chip the ball up on to the wall aiming at a target; then as it rebounds to you, trap pass the ball along the ground using the inside of your foot so that it rebounds again but this time along the floor in a position for you to chip it up again first time. This then becomes a one-touch, continuous practice.

When you feel confident enough, enlist the aid of two of your team-mates who would also like to improve their chipping technique. Stand in a straight line so that the two end players are about 30 yards apart, one with a ball, and the middle player stands about 20 yards from the player with the ball. If you are the player with the ball, pass it along the ground to the player in the middle and then prepare yourself for the return. As the middle player passes back to you, he moves in and acts as a defender. Now you have to chip the ball first time over his head to the far player. Then you move into the middle changing functions with the original middle man to make a continuous practice possible.

Obviously it is not always possible in a match to have the ball played to you before chipping, so vary this practice. Instead of playing the ball to the middle man the receiving player has to control the ball quickly and chip before the middle man closes down tight. Remember to move in quickly to close down the player you have chipped the ball to.

Try some functional practices. Run through at a goalkeeper and as he leaves his line to narrow the angle, chip the ball over him into goal. This you will find difficult because the ball will be running away from you, so concentrate hard on getting your technique right.

A wing player can combine with a midfield player. The wingman plays the ball infield and slightly backwards to his supporting midfield player who chips it first time down the wing for the winger to chase. Having done that, the midfield player moves into a position near goal to finish off a chip from the winger who dribbles the ball along the bye-line before chipping it across. The winger must look up before crossing.

This type of practice will give you a good understanding and will help you do whatever the situation demands where it matters—in a match.

PLAYER A

PLAYER B

PLAYER C

DIAGRAM

SPORTOGRAPHY

Top Practise chipping in threes. A plays the ball to B, receives it back and chips first time to C. He then starts off the routine once more.

Above Rodney Marsh draws back his foot before cheekily chipping the ball over the keeper for a spectacular goal in Geoff Hurst's testimonial game.

The through pass

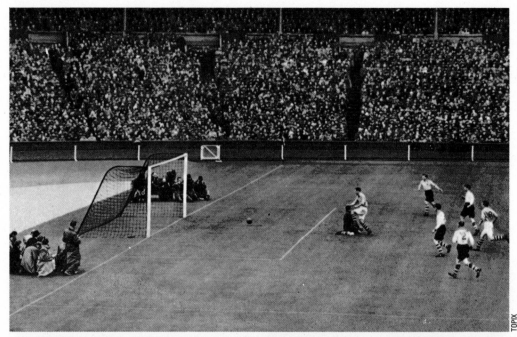

When Arsenal and Liverpool emerged from the FA Cup semi-finals in the spring of 1971 to contest another Wembley Final, both clubs were able to celebrate an anniversary. 21 years earlier they had met in similar circumstances to fight for the same trophy. Arsenal won the 1950 game by two clear goals, but then they took advantage of a style of play and a type of pass that tactical evolution had severely restricted during the 21-year interim.

A central figure in the Arsenal team was a little Scottish inside-forward, Jimmy Logie, and his mastery of the through pass undermined the Liverpool defence. Liverpool adopted the defensive tactic of the time with the full-backs covering the centre-half, and Logie was able to exploit the space to send his forwards racing clear of the defenders and still onside.

The team Arsenal paraded against Liverpool at Wembley in 1950 contained great names. Joe Mercer was their captain; Laurie Scott and Wally Barnes were international full-backs. Alex Forbes was all red-haired aggression in midfield, and there were forwards who could win matches.

One of them was Reg Lewis, dark, easy-going, a supreme stylist who would have played for England if the war had not taken the best of his years. Lewis scored both Arsenal's goals in that Final and the first of them emphasized Logie's instant reaction and creative skill.

After 18 minutes, Arsenal worked the classic strike of that time. Peter Goring, a willing, under-rated forward, went to the left of Liverpool's defence, taking away centre-half Laurie Hughes, and there was a gap for Logie and Lewis to exploit. Logie's through pass was immaculate, Lewis ran at the right time so avoiding the danger of being caught offside and, as Cyril Sidlow came from his goal-line, Lewis calmly drove the ball past him.

Logie had been an important figure in Arsenal's history before leaving Highbury beneath a cloud of bitterness and dispute. In fact, within four years of playing for Arsenal in the 1952 FA Cup Final against Newcastle and for Scotland against Northern Ireland he had disappeared into Southern League football.

The sight of him selling papers in London's West End was to stir the conscience, and Logie's respectability was restored when he was appointed to the security staff of a television company. But it could not completely obscure the tragedy of his decline. It was not uncommon to see great footballers lost in sad circumstances. Largely unschooled, they were unprepared for the stunning anti-climax which came with retirement, and many of them, especially the Celts, were to suffer from the self-destructive element in their make-up.

Johnny Haynes—a career built on the ability to make the through pass

The through ball which Logie used with such devastating effect was later to lose much of its value. When defences began to push up quickly to the half-way line, offside became a more threatening factor and keepers were trained to move quickly to the edge of the penalty area.

Johnny Haynes, the first £100-a-week footballer after the maximum wage was removed in 1961, built a career on the ability to slice open defences with a through pass.

Haynes went to Fulham as a teenager and he was to stay with them for his Football League life which included an impressive period as England's controlling midfield player. Haynes had no claims to being a great dribbler. But like Logie, he could turn when defenders were tight with him and his most penetrating passes were nourished by his vision. It was said that he became obsessed with the ball aimed inside the full-back for a winger galloping into space, but Haynes was merely taking advantage of a situation which was very much in his favour.

Hungary's destruction of England at Wembley in 1953 was largely based on the knowledge that England's system of play encouraged the use of

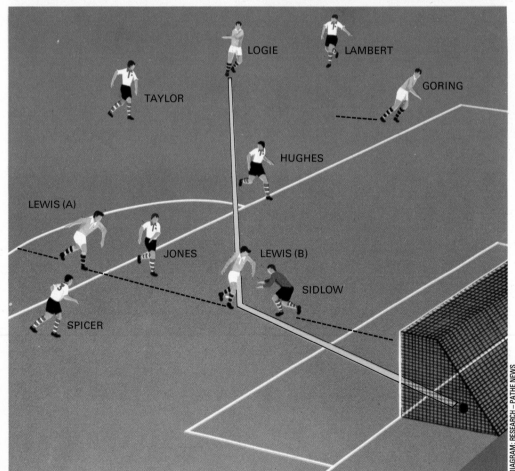

Top Reg Lewis converts Jimmy Logie's through pass to put Arsenal 1-0 ahead in the 1950 FA Cup Final against Liverpool. Although Logie's pass was cleverly timed and perfectly weighted, the prevailing system of covering full-backs made defences particularly vulnerable to the through ball.

Above Diagram illustrating the build-up to Lewis' goal. Logie's pass was played into the space beyond Lewis and left-half Jones, and Lewis reacted first. As goalkeeper Sidlow came out, the Arsenal inside-left guided the ball past him with the outside of his right foot.

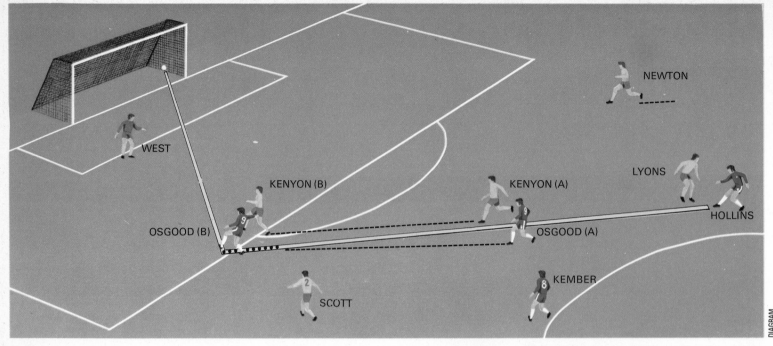

Labels on diagram: WEST · NEWTON · KENYON (B) · KENYON (A) · LYONS · OSGOOD (B) · OSGOOD (A) · HOLLINS · SCOTT · KEMBER

DIAGRAM

AIGLON

Above *Diagram showing Peter Osgood scoring for Chelsea against Everton in 1972 from a perfect through pass played by John Hollins. With defences tightened by sophisticated covering, the through ball has become much harder to execute. Not only must the pass be played with timing and accuracy, but the player making the forward run must also move positively and intelligently.*

Left *As Everton's Gordon West comes off his line, Osgood left-foots the ball past him. Kenyon who had been by-passed by the precision of Hollins' through pass gives up the chase.*

through balls. Walter Winterbottom, then England's team manager, recalled: 'They could rush players into forward positions because there was no danger of them being caught offside. Hidegkuti went deep and it was Puskas and Kocsis who went into the forward space. In the end we learned how to deal with the problem, but we weren't geared to it at the time'.

Eleven years later in 1964, England were to suffer another defeat, this time against Scotland in Glasgow. It was the beginning of Sir Alf Ramsey's reign as team manager, and he had taken the controversial decision to leave out Jimmy Greaves, then the most prolific goalscorer in British football.

Alan Gilzean's header gave Scotland victory, but not before they had survived twenty minutes of early pressure and two devastating through balls from George Eastham. Eastham, frail and seemingly ill-equipped for the rigours of top-class football, had been at the centre of the controversy which led to the removal of the maximum wage. After refusing to re-sign for Newcastle in 1960, he had stayed out of the game for six months before signing for Arsenal.

He had become the first regular successor to Haynes whose international career ended in 1962 when he suffered a bad knee injury in a car crash. Haynes had been the focal point of England's football under Walter Winterbottom. Eastham was being asked to fit into Ramsey's search for an all-purpose team.

At the time there was no definite pattern. Greaves, who had scored four times in his previous international match against Northern Ireland, gave way to Roger Hunt whose powerful forward running had been an impressive feature of Liverpool's play.

But Hunt squandered two marvellous chances made for him by Eastham's ability to thread a perfect pass into space behind defenders. Greaves was recalled for a match against Uruguay a month later, yet it was to be Hunt who played in the World Cup final of 1966 while Greaves suffered the greatest disappointment of his career.

Eastham, too, missed out of the ultimate triumph, but there was no denying his quality, and at 35, he scored the winning goal for Stoke City when they beat Chelsea in the 1972 League Cup final. An intelligent, articulate Lancastrian, Eastham said: 'The long through ball lost a lot of its value because it became almost impossible to get someone in on it. Running into forward space has to be perfectly timed but with defences compressing the game into midfield there was an awful long way to run.

'It isn't just a question of sticking the ball in and sending someone after it. That could be called kick and rush. The pass and the run have to be synchronized and the best through passes should leave someone with the immediate opportunity of a shot. If he has to run on, there is always the danger that he will be caught, and the goalkeeper has time in which to assess

the situation. To give a good example, the only real through pass in the 1972 win over Chelsea at Wembley came when our Micky Bernard nearly caught out *our* defence with a back pass.'

But one immaculate move was lost on the majority of the fans who watched Arsenal hanging on to beat Orient in the sixth round of the FA Cup in March 1972. It was not a happy day for Arsenal. Troubled by an uneven surface and Orient's practical football, they survived two efforts which came out off the foot of the same upright and another centre which ran along the face of their crossbar.

But Arsenal managed to produce one telling move which with a little bit of luck would have brought them a vital goal. Alan Ball, pushing up to support Ray Kennedy and Charlie George, sensed that George would run splendidly into an inside-right position and he rapped a perfect sidefoot pass into the channel.

George barely bothered to control the ball as he flashed at it with his right foot when in full flight. It was another example of his talent for the quick strike, the instant kicking action which did not require a back-lift to make it deadly. But an Orient boot was in the way and what might have been a scoring shot merely squirmed through to a grateful goalkeeper.

The through pass is far from obsolete; it simply requires exactness of timing and execution. Nottingham Forest and Arsenal profited from centre-forward Joe Baker's ability to spot when a through pass was on and his acceleration regularly carried him clear of the defence. Midfield players like Johnny Giles of Leeds and Alan Hudson of Chelsea continued to seek out the 'killer' pass, because, if it could be made, a clear chance could be created.

Players performing in top-class football had to work to these fine margins. The days when moves could be created almost in slow motion, when the through pass could be seen coming, had long since gone.

It had become a game of instant decision and immediate use of the ball. As Arsenal proved at the Orient, the best passes, unless they were obviously productive, often went unnoticed.

Coaching: Learn the pass that slits open the opposing defence

A through pass is one of the most effective passes in the game. Its effect can often be measured by the position in which it puts the receiver or the number of opponents it plays out of the game. Opponents will be content whilst the ball is being interpassed in front of them. The longer they can keep the ball in this position, the more time other players have to recover into defensive supporting positions.

A good through ball can beat most defensive systems, but because of its value in attacking play, it has become one of the most difficult to execute. The space into which to play the ball often has to be worked for by the team as a whole, and the direction of the intended pass has to be disguised until the last moment. Accuracy is obviously important, and the pace and timing of the pass must be such that the ball arrives in the intended space at the same time as the player so that he can shoot in his stride.

This need for precision and the fact that opponents will do their utmost to prevent you from getting at the back of them will greatly limit your chances of success unless you aim for perfection. Since through balls mean goals they must be practised with dedication.

Begin by practising the weighting of the pass, working with a couple of team-mates in an area about 25 yards long. Two of you stand at one end with a ball whilst the third member waits at the other end. The object of the practice is for one of the two to make a run across the area whilst the other one plays the ball so that it reaches the other end at the same time as the player. He then turns with the ball and plays it across the area for the third member to reach on the other line. This is now a continuous practice with emphasis on accuracy and timing. The inside of the foot is best used to make this shortish pass; this will help accuracy. Remember in this exercise not to make the player running through check his stride so that he has to wait for the ball.

From this, move on to a practice with a little preliminary movement. Keep the same two lines 25 yards apart as the target lines but have about 15 yards space behind each line. Your team-mate stands on the original line, but you move back 15 yards with the ball. Play it up to your pal and then move forward a couple of yards at an angle so that your pal lays the ball back to you. He then sprints across the 25-yard area to collect a first-time through ball from you. He will then do the same with the third member who in turn will play you through when he comes over to your side.

The same type of exercise can be organized with a finishing movement at goal. Have a small group of players on the half-way line with sufficient balls to ensure continuity. The first player moves about 15–20 yards towards goal—and faces the group. The next member plays a ball up to his feet and advances a few yards at an angle to support. The ball is played back to him by the first player who turns and sprints towards goals for a through ball which must be weighted so that it does not go straight through to the goalkeeper; nor should it be underhit so that the player has to check and wait for the ball. The player who has played the ball through now becomes the advanced man and the next member plays him through so that he gets a shot at goal whilst the first member retrieves his ball and rejoins the group.

Add variety to your practice by using a similar exercise with the use of a third man running. This time the ball is played up to the advanced man, then, as the ball is played back, a third player sprints through for the ball. At this stage, if not before, you will have noticed that the most difficult balls to play through are when the player and the path of the ball are in a straight line. This is because the pace and accuracy of the ball must be perfect. To be really successful, the ball must run alongside the attacking player so that he can shoot first time. He will have difficulty in running and turning his head to watch the ball.

Defenders should now be introduced to the practice. Play three-a-side across the penalty area with small goals. The team without the ball must send back one player to act as a goalkeeper so that the attacking team have a spare player. The attacking team send forward two players who are marked by the remaining two players of the defending team, this leaves the third player spare with the ball and ready to play through balls for the two front men. A few setting-up ploys will have to be made and a great deal of running done, before you are successful in playing one of the players through. The moment possession is gained by the defending team they play it back to the player acting as goalkeeper whilst the other team send one of their players back to defend their goal. This becomes a continuous practice of three against two, going both ways.

You should now have a fair idea of what you are aiming at as you move on to play attack versus defence. Three or four attacking players are marked by the same number of defenders. The attackers are supported by two midfield players and the defending players have a target man to play to when they gain possession. This helps them to move up when in possession and stops them standing around the penalty area. The idea here is for the midfield players to play balls through the defenders so that the front players can get shots in at goal. When possession is lost, the defending players try to play the ball out to their target player, who is said to be successful if he can gain possession of the ball in the centre circle. If this happens the ball is given back to the midfield players to mount another attack; if the attacking players can win possession they play on from there.

Several factors will have an influence on through balls. Ground conditions will have to be taken into consideration. Wet slippery grounds will make the ball pick up pace as it hits the ground; you will have to play more diagonal balls, or the pass will skid on to the keeper, and take some pace off the pass. Heavy, sticky grounds will have to be dealt with by playing firmer balls or passes chipped through. Wind will also dictate how the pass should be weighted. The size of the pitch must be taken into consideration. On long narrow pitches the ball can be played deep into enemy territory; on short wide grounds the diagonal passes are more likely to succeed.

Movement up front is essential to create the opportunity for the through pass. Two or three players willing to run forward should push up and work at the back of opponents. From then on the rest depends on accuracy that can only come from practice.

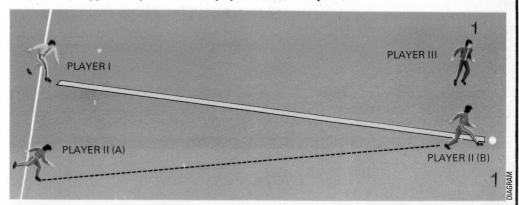

Top A continuous practice for three players designed to develop the accuracy that a through pass requires. Player I passes the ball so that it reaches the other side of an area about 25 yards wide at the same time as Player II who has run across the area. Player II then plays it back into the path of Player III who has sprinted across the area. He then turns and plays Player I through.

Above John O'Hare slides in on a long through pass from Kevin Hector to clinch a vital win for Championship-chasing Derby County over Leeds United in April 1972. The ball rebounded from Gary Sprake's body and went in off Hunter, but the perception of Hector's pass deserved the credit for the goal.

Power in the penalty-area

Liverpool manager Bill Shankly was not slow to rejoice in famous victories. It was inevitable then that he should be seen holding court outside his team's dressing room at Leeds on the last Saturday of September 1972.

'We were great, tremendous,' growled Shankly, his thick Scottish accent wrapped around a string of superlatives. 'We outplayed them where it matters. In both penalty areas. Anyone who wins at Leeds has done something special. And we really turned it on today.'

Leeds had been beaten at home for the first time in eighteen months and the manner of that suggested that they were struggling to maintain the simplicity of purpose which had been basic to their style and success. On the other hand they would dispute Shankly's opinion that they had been reduced to second best and they could claim that Mick Jones had scored the best goal of the match.

Jones' goals were usually products of his enthusiasm and strength. A powerful, willing player, he had a reputation for wearing down defences, for putting players under continuous nagging pressure and for outjumping taller men in the penalty area.

There was little obvious subtlety about his style, but it was significant that of the eight League games Leeds had lost when falling just short of the Championship the previous season, Jones had missed seven of them.

Crowds knew what to expect from Mick Jones. But against Liverpool he was to produce the unexpected when scoring a remarkable goal. Liverpool had weathered heavy pressure when a long cross was driven in from the right touch-line. Had their captain Tommy Smith been fit, the cross might not have carried so much threat.

But when Allan Clarke, the goal-snatching foil to Jones' more muscular play, glanced the cross on, Liverpool were suddenly exposed on the far post.

Jones, after drifting wide, found himself unmarked but perhaps too far in to make simple contact with the chance. Suddenly and quite remarkably he twisted upwards, executing a per-fect overhead kick which sent the ball back beyond Ray Clemence and neatly into the far side of the goal.

It was to be Leeds' only success, Liverpool equalizing with a header from the massive Lloyd and winning with a goal from Boersma. Nevertheless, Jones had made a notable contribution to the game with a goal which was largely out of character.

Athletic skills like the overhead kick were uncommon in British football and yet the more astute managers continually pressed the theory that great players were invariably outstanding athletes.

One of the more graphic pictures taken during the 1966 World Cup in England showed a tearful Pele being led away from a defeat at Liverpool which ended Brazil's bid to retain the World Cup. It was a poignant illustration of football's ups and downs. But the picture also showed the remarkable abdominal development which helped to charge Pele's football with muscular power. Pele had donated his jersey to an opponent. A raincoat was now draped loosely over his fine shoulders, but the rippling abdominals were uncovered.

Athleticism and power appealed to young managers such as Dave Sexton of Chelsea and Malcolm Allison of Manchester City. Both were devoted to skill, its practice and application in terms of team play.

On the other hand, they stressed the need for explosive power and agility especially around the penalty areas. Allison, as a player with West Ham, had experimented with weight training, convinced by then that muscular strength allied to technique was the correct formula.

Some players came by it naturally. Denis Law,

JONES

CLEMENCE

CLARKE

DIAGRAM

Below left Diagram showing the power and agility of Leeds centre-forward Mick Jones as he scores spectacularly against Liverpool in 1972.
Below Jones' athletic strength lifts him into the air to send the ball wide of Ray Clemence.
Right Chelsea needed a moment of supreme agility from Peter Osgood to bring them back into the 1970 FA Cup Final replay against Leeds at Old Trafford. His plunging header levelled the score, and Chelsea went on to win in extra time.
Below right Diagram illustrating how Charlie Cooke's angled cross would have curled harmlessly out of play had not Osgood flung himself into its path and diverted the ball into the net.

unarguably one of the great goalscorers of all time, was an instinctive athlete. When Law returned to sign for Manchester United after a spell with the Italian club Torino, he was not regarded as a great header of the ball. But his natural elasticity enabled him to become one Once Law had convinced himself that there were goals to come by in the air he developed into a threatening and decisive finisher when supplied with centres.

Chelsea's experiments with the athletic prowess of their players revealed that the young Ian Hutchinson was a remarkable all-round performer. Signed from Southern League football, Hutchinson made an immediate impact when first drafted into the Chelsea team. Here was the player they needed to dovetail with the more elegant but less persistent Peter Osgood.

Tall, lean and infinitely brave, he scored 27 times in 62 games before a succession of injuries threatened to end his career. It was Hutchinson's fine build and overall fitness which enabled him to stage a come-back in the autumn of 1972.

John Charles was perhaps the most outstanding figure of his day, when his skills were related to muscular proportion, power and agility. From top to bottom he was all power and many people felt that he was the perfect size and shape for a footballer.

Because he never got involved in unseemly incidents, he was nicknamed the 'Gentle Giant'. But there was nothing gentle about his play when there was a half-chance or when it was necessary to outjump an opponent.

Charles stood six feet two inches, weighed around fourteen stone and could play anywhere. Some felt that he was the finest centre-half in the world. Others said that he had no rivals among the great centre-forwards. But recognition of his supreme athleticism was unanimous. No player has been more beautifully built. Few struck more immediate fear into the opposition.

Athleticism was very much in Dave Sexton's mind at Chelsea. He recalled it in Charles and recognized it in Cliff Jones, whose goalscoring feats for Spurs in the sixties stemmed directly

from the sort of talents which are built into a successful pentathlete.

Jones ran with startling directness and he could outjump men who towered above him. He had bodily strength and immense courage.

Sexton admitted: 'Players like this are exciting because they are athletic. They go beyond football and enter the wider world of all-round games prowess.

'You look at people like Gareth Edwards, the Welsh Rugby Union International. He has tremendous strength which when related to touch and balance makes him an outstanding athletic figure.'

Agility not only enabled players to score outstanding goals but sustain their contribution to the team effort. Those who fell down and stayed down were lost. Those who rebounded back into play could stay in contact even when the initial challenge had proved fruitless.

When beating Leeds in the FA Cup Final of 1970, Chelsea needed an athletic goal from Peter Osgood to get them back into the match, after

COOKE

OSGOOD

HARVEY

Jones had powered through typically to open the scoring.

A diagonal pass from Charlie Cooke pierced the Leeds defence, but the ball might have run harmlessly out of play had not Osgood hurled himself to make contact with a firm, diving header.

Gerd Muller's goal which finally beat England in the quarter-finals of the World Cup in Mexico that same year was taken in mid-air, hooked beyond Peter Bonetti after a mix-up in the England defence. An alert, stocky player, Muller sometimes revealed a strange awkwardness. But his chances were taken with devastating frequency.

Diving headers, overhead kicks, mid-air volleys. These were not common skills. If they were to be executed correctly and punishingly the player had to have confidence in his ability, the suppleness to perform the skill and the courage to attempt it when under pressure.

One of West Ham's goals in a 3-1 win against Sheffield United in October 1972 provided an example of what an agile player could achieve.

When the enthusiastic Billy Bonds dived to head a corner-kick low into the goalmouth, Bryan Robson, with his back to the goal, spun into a volley which was delivered too sharply to be stopped by defenders guarding a post.

This then was the essence of outstanding play in critical situations. Players who could bring off the unexpected as Mick Jones did against Liverpool were exceptional. But by 1972 it was clear that athletic proficiency was a vital feature of individual assessment.

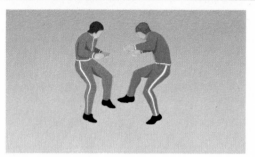

Above Three sets of exercises, performed in pairs, that will help to improve agility and power. Trying to knock away each other's arms in the press-up position, attempting to tread on your partner's toes and trying to run whilst your partner pulls against you constitute amusing as well as useful practice.
Below Scottish international striker Jim Bone scores Norwich City's first ever First Division goal against Everton in August 1972. Bone's foraging forward running epitomizes explosive power.
Right Alan Gilzean, an artist in the air, demonstrates his own brand of agility against Wolves.

Coaching: Add explosive power to your style of play

What we mean by explosive power is the ability to move one's body weight as quickly as possible through variations of movements required for football. Quite obviously the quicker a player can cover ground, the higher he can jump or the sharper he can stop, start, twist and turn, the more likely he is to win the ball from the opposition and have more time on the ball once he has got it.

The faster a player can get to the ball, the more time he will have to use it. This is a mistake often made by young, inexperienced players. They take their time moving after a loose ball and when they finally reach it they are under pressure from opponents; it then becomes extremely difficult to do something useful for their team.

Because football is a sport with bodily contact these movements must be done with power as well as speed. When two players are contesting for a ball it is often the more powerful player that is successful.

Muscle strength is essential for rapid movements and can be developed through weight training or certain gymnastic exercises of which perhaps the most simple is hopping. Whilst doing these, you can execute various leg movements such as scissoring exercises forward and backwards, clicking the heels together, rapidly pulling up the knees and heels of both feet together, and doing full or double turns.

There are many, many other variations. Pick a partner and try to step in each other's feet, a game called 'walking on fire'. Alternatively both of you take up the press-up position and try to slap the other one's hands. This type of exercise can be quite amusing and still sharpens the reflexes whilst developing strength.

Jumping exercises will also breed power. Any type of leap will do; a two-footed jump, a leap forward taking off from one foot from a stationary position, the orthodox hop, step and jump or a double hop-double step, and jump (again from a stationary position), all are excellent exercises of a gymnastic nature. Make the jumps competitive to increase the interest.

As well as using your own body resistance to develop strength you can use a partner's. In 'resistance running' you stand behind your partner and loop your arms round his waist. He then tries to run forward whilst you attempt to resist his movement and hold him back.

Similar principles apply in working in groups of three and competing in a carrying run round a set circuit. One runs carrying another whilst the third trots alongside. After a set distance they change, rider becomes carrier, carrier trots and the trotter is carried. They change again before returning to starting line. A circuit of some 60 yards, each carrying for 20 yards, can be done three times before resting.

There are so many alternative methods. Get the team to sit down on the goal-line within the goal area; on a signal they must get to their feet, sprint to the edge of the six-yard box, sit down again, then return to the goal-line as quickly as possible back to the sitting position.

With your partner again, sit while he bounces a ball; you must leap up and head the ball as it rises. He then moves five or six yards away and bounces the ball higher. You have to get up, spring, and jump to head it again; then return to the starting position as quickly as possible. This type of exercise is excellent for getting players quickly to the ball in an explosive movement, and you will find that extra surge of power invaluable in a competitive game.

In pairs again, stand in front of your partner about 10 yards from a ball. Lean backwards so that your back touches your partner's chest. You push backwards, while he tries to push forward. You must both really put your weight into the shove. On a signal you both race for the ball.

Divide your squad in half—if there are fourteen, into two teams of seven. The two teams should stand facing each other and each player is given a number, so that there are two number ones, two number twos etc. An obstacle is placed eight yards in front of each team. The coach calls a number and the player in each side with that number must race round the obstacle and back to their teams. To keep the players really on their toes, give the players each a colour and place a second obstacle eight yards to the side of each team. If the number is called the two players run round the front marker and if the colour is called then the side marker is used. Players must be encouraged to explode into action the moment their number or colour is called. A team competition will stimulate effort, and keep every player alert on his toes.

Training this way can be great fun as well as being extremely valuable. Really put all your energy into the exercises and you will find yourself a far more powerful player.

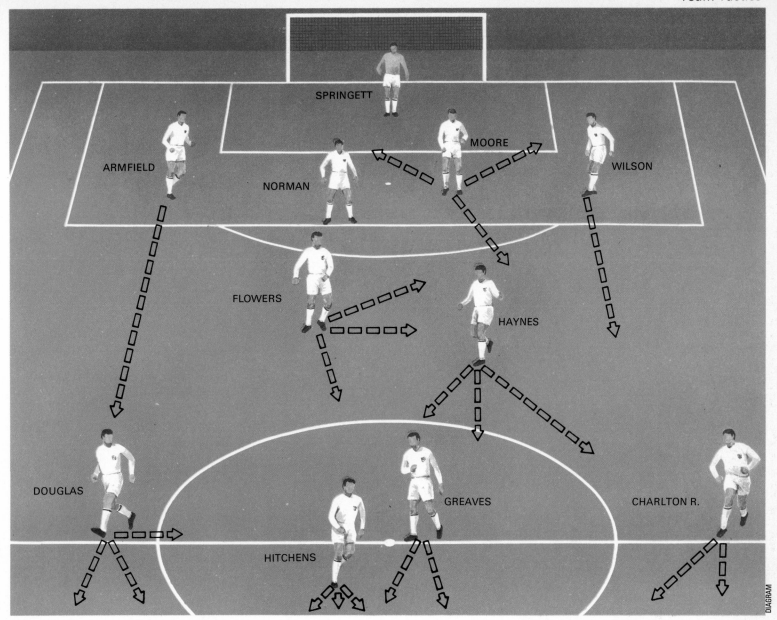

SPRINGETT

ARMFIELD

NORMAN

MOORE

WILSON

FLOWERS

HAYNES

DOUGLAS

GREAVES

CHARLTON R.

HITCHENS

DIAGRAM

Systems of play

It has been said that only three men, Herbert Chapman, Nereo Rocco and Sir Alf Ramsey have been able to claim that they influenced systems of play. Malcolm Allison, Manchester City's successful coach in the late sixties and early seventies, made this claim: 'Chapman, with the introduction of the third back game when with Arsenal in the thirties, hit upon something that lasted for twenty years.

'Rocco perfected the defensive tactics which became the basis of Italian play and of many other countries throughout the world.

'Sir Alf Ramsey won the First Division Championship with Ipswich Town and the World Cup for England by a revolutionary new way of arranging the team.'

Ramsey's 'arrangements' had far reaching effect throughout British football at all levels. Inheriting from Walter Winterbottom a 4-2-4 system, he reluctantly abandoned it because he could not find the players to make it work for him. His compromise, a variety of 4-3-3, won England

their first World Cup, and four years later a further revision of ideas led to the Cup being defended by a team playing 4-4-2.

Ramsey himself was a stylish full-back with Spurs during the 'push and run' era under Arthur Rowe in the fifties. The style of defensive play had remained virtually unchanged since Chapman introduced the third back game twenty years earlier. Cover and depth in defence had been provided by the full-backs swivelling or pivoting on the centre-half who was always positioned to block the middle. If play was on the left then the far full-back—in this case the right-back—would swing around into a position where he could counter a breakthrough.

England were still employing this system in 1953, with Ramsey at right-back, when they met Hungary at Wembley. The Hungarians pulled their two wingers and their centre-forward, Hidegkuti, deep into midfield and sent the two men, who were expected to perform as traditional, deep-lying inside-forwards, upfield to torment

the 'stopper' centre-half. The system of covering full-backs meant that neither of the two men, Kocsis and Puskas, was ever in danger of being caught off-side. England were humiliated, beaten 6-3, and the following summer outplayed 7-1 in the return match in Budapest.

Ramsey never forgot the pain of the Wembley lesson, but by the time he entered management, in 1955 at Ipswich, there were others planning new strategies. In South America, the Brazilians, hurt by their violent failure in the 1954 World Cup, were leading the race.

In winning the World Cup in Sweden in 1958, Brazil demonstrated to the world the basis of what Rocco was doing in Italy—the value of integrating team play and of deploying four defenders in a line across the width of the field.

By the time Brazil triumphed in Sweden other countries' full-backs were beginning to position themselves alongside opposing wingers, so denying them the opportunity of *receiving* the ball in space. The two central defenders provided cover for each other in the middle of the defence, in a way that would have stopped Hungary's barrage in 1953.

Walter Winterbottom, at that time England's team manager and director of coaching, said then: 'Team play must be based on the principle that it is impossible to defend with less than four players and difficult to mount attacks with less than four forwards.'

This left two players to work very hard in

163

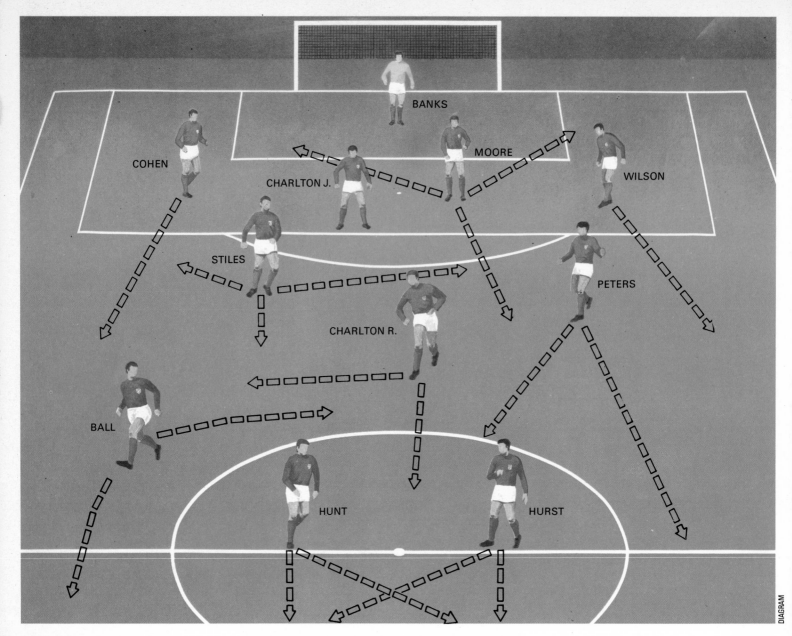

Above By 1966 Ramsey had abandoned the 4-2-4 formation, and he relied upon 4-3-3 for his successful attempt to win the World Cup for England for the first time.

Above England's red-shirted back four in action during the 1966 World Cup final. The defensive midfield player, Stiles, waits in the centre-circle as Wilson passes to Bobby Charlton.

the middle of the field where they were charged with winning the ball and providing a constant service.

They had to have a firm understanding of each other's play and a wide range of passing skills. Brazil, in Sweden, had the splendidly equipped Didi, but were already moving, unknowingly perhaps, towards the more integrated system they were to use four years later when retaining the trophy in Chile.

In the 1958 final against Sweden they found themselves under heavy pressure in the early stages of the match and their left-winger Zagalo, later to manage the successful side of 1970 in Mexico, was forced into a defensive role.

Thus what had been 4-2-4 became for a while 4-3-3—and there was the first clue to a new system.

Whether Ramsey was directly influenced or not is unclear, but he began to experiment at Ipswich on that theme. What he achieved is legendary. With a bunch of average players and one or two of wider gifts, Ipswich won the Second Division Championship in 1960-61. The following season they won the League title although most people in football saw them as relegation probabilities rather than title hopes.

Ramsey dispensed with a recognized winger on one side, and instead used an ageing former half-back Jimmy Leadbetter, wearing a number eleven shirt, to feed the front men.

Two powerful forwards, Ray Crawford and Ted Phillips, were deployed as attacking spearheads and a winger, Roy Stephenson, filled in with speedy runs from a slightly withdrawn position

on the right wing.

Leadbetter's skilled left foot and all-round vision enabled him to make contact with the others by the use of astute forward passes of various range, and it was a while before rival clubs found a way to beat the system.

Spurs found the answer first when, as FA Cup winners, they met Ipswich for the Charity Shield in August 1962.

Bill Nicholson, a former playing colleague of Ramsey's, detailed his half-backs Blanchflower and Mackay to move forward to mark the Ipswich 'wingers' and brought his full-backs Peter Baker and Ron Henry in to play alongside centre-

half Maurice Norman. It was a fascinating tactical duel between teams belonging to two of Spurs' greatest former players.

On this occasion Spurs triumphed 5-1, but Ramsey was soon to be on his way to fashion triumph at a higher level. On 3 December 1962 he was appointed England's team manager.

Winterbottom had been impressed by the Brazilians, and built his teams around their 4-2-4 framework. He might have been more successful if he had been given free choice in selecting his side. But because he had to consult an FA selection committee, every final choice became a compromise.

In defence, he stretched a back line of four across the pitch—two full-backs playing wide, a centre-half on similar lines to the 'stopper' and a defensive wing-half whose duties lay alongside or behind the centre-half. The other wing-half would be a midfield player. Peter Swan of Sheffield Wednesday and Ron Flowers of Wolves held down these two infield back positions during the last years of Winterbottom's reign. But, to illustrate the difficulties the manager faced, he was often forced to field Flowers and the young Bobby Moore as the two wing-halves. Both were naturally defensive players, but one of the two had to play in midfield.

With only two men available to play the specialist midfield role of linking the attack and defence, Winterbottom could ill afford to have one of them playing out of position.

Of the four players selected as forwards, two were orthodox wingers, one was an orthodox centre-forward, and the other was most often

Above To defend the World Cup in 1970, Ramsey felt that he needed extra strength in midfield to combat altitude problems. England played a 4-4-2 system.

Jimmy Greaves. The plan was to feed the wingers, to urge them to evade the full-backs, and to have the centre-forward and Greaves striking for goal from their crosses.

Winterbottom found, however, that the fast attacking wingers he needed to make the system work were rare. He experimented with Alan A'Court, Peter Brabrook, Warren Bradley, John Connelly, Bryan Douglas, Mike Hellawell, Alan Hinton—and Bobby Charlton—among many others.

It was this problem, above all, that led Ramsey to change his system. He gave a hint of what was to follow when he took over the team: 'I am looking for all-purpose players—players who can fill in everywhere as they are required. Players who will work and who are intelligent as well as skilful.'

But he continued to experiment with wingers. In November 1963, England beat Ireland 8-3 at Wembley, and Terry Paine, playing as a right-winger, scored three goals. Peter Thompson made his debut in 1964, and John Connelly was in and out of the side.

Ramsey continued his permutations, but it was not until December 1965—just six months before the start of the World Cup—that he lined up the England team in a 4-3-3 formation. It was in Madrid against Spain, following a run of unimpressive international performances.

It worked splendidly, with England winning a match that was to have a profound effect on the destiny of the World Cup six months later.

A system is useless unless it can be effectively operated by the players available to the manager, and it is the players who must come first in this respect.

Ramsey had an abundance of players. What he wanted was a system which best suited the qualities of the English player. It needed to encompass skill, high morale, fitness and strength. He settled on 4-3-3.

He had an outstanding goalkeeper in Gordon Banks, a world-class central defender in Bobby Moore and a world-class full-back in Ray Wilson. George Cohen was more than adequate at right-back.

The three players deployed in the centre of the field had to have a balance of discipline and flair.

The complement of the team was not decided until fairly late. Nobby Stiles, a fierce competitor, was brought in to act as a 'sweeper' across the front of the back four. The back four itself was completed by the emergence of Jack Charlton of Leeds as a responsible player. Ramsey recalls: 'This was my great stroke of luck. Stiles and Charlton. They came good at just the right time.' Stiles' attitude was infectious, Charlton's lengthy experience and positive headwork invaluable.

In midfield with Stiles, Ramsey chose Martin Peters and Bobby Charlton, although both were given much more scope to attack than Stiles. The subtle skills of Peters were the final adjustment to Ramsey's format, but the master-stroke was the conversion of Bobby Charlton from a dangerous, but inconsistent, winger to a director of operations in the middle of the field. Often, as a winger, Charlton had made spectators catch their breath with majestic cross-field passes to a colleague on the other flank. As a midfield player he was able to use his passing ability to hit more telling balls into the paths of the front players. And retreating defences gave him the space to move forward to exercise his powerful shooting.

For most of the games Ramsey wrestled with the problem of fitting Greaves' unquestionable finishing skills into a system. Greaves played uneasily in the first three games of the finals, but was then injured. Geoff Hurst took his place in the quarter-final against Argentina, scored the only goal of the game, kept his place when Greaves reported fit again, and scored a hat-trick in the final.

Playing alongside Hurst as a forward player, Roger Hunt showed himself a willing runner perfectly fitted to the dictates of the 4-3-3 system. With only three players up front—the third was Alan Ball who played in a withdrawn role, often helping out the midfield men—Ramsey changed the whole concept of forward play. Instead of playing in channels up and down the pitch, forwards had to move sideways—and they had the space to move into.

An essential difference in the attacking formation was the role played by the full-backs. Although the former England captain, Jimmy Armfield, had shown a liking for moving up his touchline to support his forwards, full-back play was still unadventurous. But now he had discarded wingers, Ramsey wanted his full-backs to exploit the space that wingers had previously occupied. Hence George Cohen and Ray Wilson had orders to attack. It was yet another dimension of Ramsey's plea for 'all-purpose players'.

The World Cup won, Ramsey had four years to

plan its defence. In Mexico he would be faced with an entirely different set of circumstances. The altitude of Guadalajara would mean that the pace of the game would be modified. The emphasis would be on accurate passing. In Ramsey's mind the first adjustment to the plan that won him the Cup was simple and obvious. Some of Ball's work in the 1966 series had been in midfield, and it was only a small switch to make him a fourth midfield player. Ramsey was concerned that the arduous job of linking defence and attack in the Mexican conditions would be too much for only three players.

In the four intervening years, he experimented with emergent players, but committed himself to the 4-4-2 system. In Mexico the defensive system was similar to that of 1966, although, apart from Banks, only Moore remained. Cohen had retired and Wilson was in Division IV, but Keith Newton and the ex-winger Terry Cooper were players in similar vein. Jack Charlton and Nobby Stiles were in the squad, but only as reserves. Charlton's place went to Brian Labone, and Stiles' role as the midfield player who won the ball was taken over by Alan Mullery.

Ball, Peters and Bobby Charlton remained, but the altitude went against them. Charlton, particularly, found it harder to move forward to support the attack, and he no longer peppered the goal with shots from 25 yards. Peters rarely showed the form of the previous four years.

Hurst was still there as an isolated, mobile target, but Hunt had given way to the more skilful Francis Lee. But there were still no wingers. Ramsey included wingers, Peter Thompson and Ralph Coates, in his original squad. Yet they showed poor form in the pre-World Cup tour of South America. The irony was that Ramsey had wanted wingers; now he had a system that discouraged them.

Ramsey had wanted wingers—now his system discouraged them

Although there were protracted public inquests after the quarter-final defeat by West Germany, Ramsey remained true to his system of play, and conceded only that the time might have come to try again with three forwards.

Brazil, the winners, were credited with employing two wingers and 4-2-4 in Mexico, but in fact played 4-3-3 as they had done when winning in Chile eight years earlier.

Their manager Zagalo said: 'When Brazil met England in Rio in 1969 it was obvious that we would have problems if we persisted in using only two players in the middle of the field. England only lost that night because they ran out of steam at the end of a punishing tour. Otherwise it would have been different. They outnumbered us in the middle and it was difficult for our players.

'In Mexico we settled on a similar system to England's with Rivelino operating from midfield on the left and Pele playing in the manner of Bobby Charlton. Tostao and Jairzinho were our front men.

'Our advantage was that we had more expressive players and that we were better at altering the rhythm of a game. But England were the best team that we met. I would not have liked to have played them in the final.'

The words provided some vindication of Ramsey although his subsequent use of Francis Lee, Hurst and Allan Clarke of Leeds as a three-pronged attack suggested that he felt he had been over-cautious and that in trying to ease the load he had committed his midfield men to too much effort in Guadalajara.

Controversial Ramsey may have been, but his influence on systems of play is unquestionable. At all levels of English football, his approach made coaches and managers stop and think about team play. But perhaps what Ramsey showed best was that system football required a special relationship between manager and players. Even in defeat in Mexico the England players' respect for him was total.

Coaching: Learn how to attack from full-back in the back four system

Players in schoolboy or junior teams, should not be restricted to a tactical system in the same way as top professional clubs. A team plan should be devised for the side—football is a team game—but the plan should relate to the particular abilities in the side, not copy a favourite professional club.

There are, however, aspects of the game that can be developed by learning from the systems of the top level. For example, Sir Alf Ramsey's England teams pioneered a new role for full-backs, and young full-backs can learn the skills needed to develop their game.

Let us assume that you are a competent defender, and now want to add this new dimension to full-back play by helping in the attack. What you must become is a better all-round player. Instead of being simply destructive, you must become constructive. The secret of this is ball control.

As an attacking full-back, you need control in three phases of your game—receiving the ball, carrying it forward, and putting an accurate cross into the goal mouth. You will also need to beat opponents, but this will come when you have the confidence which goes with mastering the three main skills.

Receiving the ball—This facet of the game you must master whatever position you play. As a full-back you may start your own attacking run from a successful tackle or launch it as a result of an opponent's error, but more likely you will be moving up the touchline into space and you will receive the ball from a colleague.

Practise this with a friend. Get him to play the ball to you from 20 yards. Control it and move off with the ball. Imagine you are receiving the ball on the touchline. If you are a right-back the ball will be coming from your left, and *vice versa*.

Carrying the ball forward—When you are moving forward remember the following principles. Keep the ball within comfortable playing distance. Stay evenly balanced so that you can move easily off either foot if challenged. Try not to concentrate all your attention on the ball. In fact, the less you can look at it and still control it the better. 'Not looking-up' is one of the basic faults in lower-grade football. If you are always staring down at the ball you cannot see what your team-mates are doing.

Practise by dribbling a ball on your own in a confined space, like the penalty area. Do this until you really get the feel of the ball. Repeat the exercise using only one foot—left foot only, then right foot only. All the time concentrate on keeping your head up so that you can see what is going on around you.

Then introduce team-mates into this area—all practising with a ball—and you will see why you have to notice what is going on around you. There will be some painful collisions if you focus all your attention on the ball.

Getting in the cross—As an attacking full-back must help to take the place of an orthodox winger, most of your runs up the touchline will end with your centre. It is enough to get the cross high into the penalty area; it is the forward's responsibility to be there to meet it. Here is a routine which will test this aspect of your game and help improve your ability to cross the ball.

If you are the right-back in your team, line-up on the half-way line by the right touchline. This is the sort of position you might find yourself in during a game. Get your left-back to do the same on his side of the field, and put your goalkeeper in the goal that you are facing. Line up the rest of your team-mates in the centre-circle facing the goal, each with a ball. Team-mate one moves off towards the goal with his ball. After he has gone ten yards or so he passes it out to the right for you to move onto. You must then carry the ball under close control, and as fast as you can without losing control, almost to the goal-line. Then stop, look up, and cross the ball into the penalty area, aiming for your team-mate who has carried on his run into the box. He must try to head the centre into goal.

As you finish the move, team-mate two plays a pass out to the left-back, who repeats the manoeuvre down the left touchline. While he is doing this you are jogging back to the half-way line ready to receive the ball from team-mate three and ready to go through the routine again.

Repeat until the players in the centre-circle have been through the routine twice. When you become more adept you can vary the move by crossing the ball on the run instead of stopping it, and then by introducing a defender whom you must beat before you cross the ball.

Remember in a game to get this cross into areas where your forwards will be looking to meet it. If you make a break from defence on your own, you must be prepared to hold on to the ball until you spot a team-mate—even if it means taking on more defenders. This will require confidence—and confidence only comes from practice.

Once you have mastered these skills, what remains is to learn to 'read' the situation in the game when it is right, and safe, for you to go forward. Obviously your team must be in possession, and the most frequent occasion you will be needed is when the attack is being built on the opposite side of the field. Opponents will be drawn that way, and space will usually open up for you to move forward. A loud call to a colleague in possession will enable him to switch the direction of the attack by playing the ball out to you. Practise moving forward in your training games.

But never forget that as a full-back your primary task is to defend, and only attack when you are sure that there is cover behind you.

Above *George Cohen moves forward down the right touchline. His attacking runs compensated for* *the lack of wingers in the 1966 team. Alf Ramsey watches intently from the trainers' bench.*

NEWTON

TOSTAO (A)

MOORE

TOSTAO (B)

LABONE

BANKS

PETERS

JAIRZINHO (B) JAIRZINHO (A)

MULLERY COOPER PELE

DIAGRAM

Switching the direction of play

Above *Diagram of the goal Brazil scored against England in the 1970 World Cup—by switching the play. Tostao, taking a rebound from Moore's legs, crossed to Pele, who drew Cooper and played the ball into space. Jairzinho, left unmarked, scored.*

Amidst one of the most gripping and absorbing contests in the history of the World Cup, Brazil created a match-winning goal of magical quality. The goal defeated England in a Group game in Guadalajara, and it was made by a rapid switch in the direction of an attack.

Tostao, Brazil's extravagantly talented front man, led the assault down their left touchline. England's disciplined defence moved to their right to cover the threat. As Tostao held the ball, the defenders edged further and further towards him.

Taking advantage of a ricochet off Bobby Moore's legs, he suddenly crossed the ball into the centre of the penalty area, wrong-footing the core of England's rearguard. At that moment, Moore, Newton and Labone were out of the game.

The ball reached Pele, who was confronted by the two remaining defenders, Mullery and Cooper. Drawing these two, he kept up the impetus of the switch of direction, and played the ball into the space on his right.

Alone and unmarked Jairzinho met the ball, and lashed it high past Gordon Banks. The match was won.

The almost carefree execution of the move misled those who argued that football to the Brazilians was all instinct and joy. Don Howe, then assistant manager of Arsenal, had often watched Brazil in training, and he testified to the utter thoroughness of their preparation. He said: 'You watch them score great goals against fine teams,

and you could be kidded into accepting that these goals were entirely the product of natural flair.

'But I watched them practising the most spectacular things, and it was clear that they worked tremendously hard to acquire self-confidence and mutual understanding. It was out of this that they were able to react brilliantly when their opponents were guilty of an error.'

England's one error— Bobby Moore drawn away from his position

England made that one error—in positional play. Because of the sound habits developed in their training, Brazil quickly exploited this by the sharp switch in the direction of the play. With the England defence all drawn to Brazil's left wing, there was space on the right—and Brazil used it to win the game.

The error was that Bobby Moore, England's captain and a model of consistency and application, was for once drawn away from his position on the left side of England's defence and at the left shoulder of centre-half Brian Labone.

England were using a 'zonal' system of marking which required the back four defenders to mark areas of the field rather than particular players. If an attacker moved out of one zone, he immediately became the responsibility of the defender

into whose zone he moved.

It needed great understanding, and no one understood the system better than Moore. Mistakenly regarded as a 'sweeper', his job was to patrol the left flank of England's defence, to provide Labone and left-back Terry Cooper with cover and to offer swift and urgent challenge to those who entered his zone.

A legitimate 'sweeper' would range between both touchlines behind colleagues who marked man to man. But Moore was not asked to go to his right, or Brazil's left, except in an emergency, and it is difficult to recall when he did until that fateful 60th minute against Brazil.

It was then that he found himself confronted by Tostao. Even then the situation seemed innocent enough until Moore was suddenly and unluckily stranded when the ball rebounded to Tostao from the inside of his right leg.

Brazil's move now developed rapidly and with horrible certainty for England's supporters. Labone, sensing that his captain was in trouble, shuttled across to offer himself as a challenger to Tostao leaving Alan Mullery to cover Pele, and Terry Cooper to cover the space on the far side of goal.

The ball was still with Tostao as England's defenders hurriedly rearranged themselves to try and cope with the threat. The little Brazilian, who had been saved for the competition only by the skill of an eye surgeon in Houston, Texas, admitted later that he had nothing definite in mind at that moment.

But there was nothing indecisive about the skill with which he manipulated the ball under pressure, or the trickery which enabled him to steer clear of Labone.

Tostao was then already reacting to those habits developed in training. With England's defence pulled to one side, Tostao struck at the most vulnerable point on the far side of goal.

LONDON EXPRESS

He said later: 'You don't look for specific players in situations like that. You are aware that things have developed in your favour, and try to put the ball where it is likely to do the most damage. The initial victory had been won when we were able to leave Bobby Moore stranded. From that point it was up to others.'

As Pele and Jairzinho were among the 'others', England were in extreme peril as Tostao's pass cut into them.

Mullery's marking of Pele had been convincing enough to deter even the great man from attempting the spectacular, although many of his dynamic contributions to football were accompanied by a willingness to settle for simplicity when it was likely to be most profitable.

Mullery—tuned to the unexpected—but beaten by the obvious

Yet Mullery was tuned in to the unexpected, and so the obvious destroyed him as Pele flipped the ball on into space.

Cooper was faced with the choice of staying with Jairzinho or moving to cover the direct threat of Pele. He settled for the latter, but Pele's quickness of thought caught him half-way. Jairzinho moved smoothly forward into the space on his right flank to shoot past Banks before anyone could get back at him.

It may be too academic to suggest that Brazil deliberately lured Moore out of position. More likely the quality of their reaction to a potential situation caused England's downfall. The England defence had been drawn, and they reacted perceptively to exploit the space that had been created.

Nor was this goal an isolated affair. Similar quickness of thought brought Brazil's fourth goal in the 1970 World Cup against Italy. It was scored as though by decree by their captain and

Above Labone (No 5), Cooper (No 3) and Mullery can only watch as Jairzinho holds off Peters and gives Banks no chance with his right-footed drive.
Above centre Diagram showing how Brazil profited again from switching the direction of their attack in the 1970 World Cup final. Again Pele played the ball to the right, after Rivelino, Clodoaldo, and an off-the-ball run by Jairzinho had drawn the Italian defence. This time Carlos Alberto raced up to score.
Right Carlos Alberto's shot utterly beats Albertosi.
Far right Triumph for Carlos Alberto. His goal ensured that he had led Brazil to a World Cup win.

right-back Carlos Alberto. Again it was a classic example of application in a situation which was developing in favour of Brazil.

Carlos Alberto powered forward to fill in space created for him by intelligent running and a decisive switch in the point of attack.

Unlike England, the Italians employed tight man-to-man marking with the necessary insurance of a 'sweeper', Cera. Left-back Facchetti had to mark right-winger Jairzinho wherever he went.

Jairzinho began the move, running to the left, taking Facchetti vainly with him and opening up space on the right. He rapped a pass at Pele on the right angle of the penalty area.

Cera, unsure of Pele's intent and unsighted, could not see enough of Carlos Alberto's advance to be aware of the threat it presented.

As though determined that the move should be permanently etched on everyone's mind, Pele checked and then sidefooted the ball into Carlos Alberto's path. The excellence of the move was underlined as the Brazilian full-back belted a right-foot shot beyond the bewildered Albertosi.

Examination suggests that while the Brazilians were reacting to a favourable situation against England, they had deliberately set out to savage Italy's marking system.

The vital thing had been to leave the Italians without cover on one side of their defence, and this was achieved by switching the play with

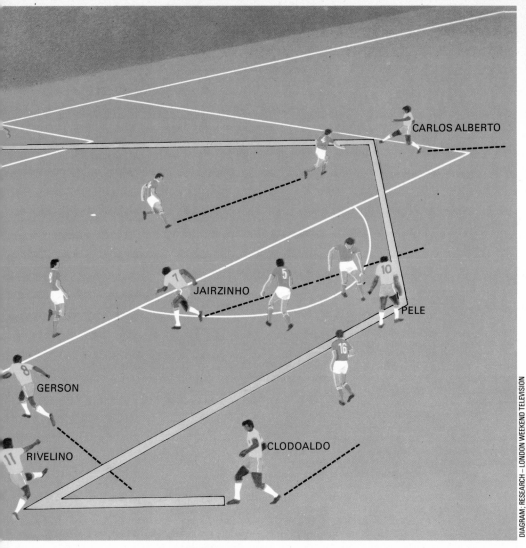

crippling suddenness.

Again, this is not a tactic for which Brazil claim a monopoly. Switching the direction of an attack to destroy regimented defences had been used before. When playing in the European Cup Winners Cup during 1965, West Ham had worked hard at breaking down defences organized around a spare or 'sweeper' defender.

One method was to push forward up on to the 'sweeper' so denying him the comfort of space and time in which to assess the most critical point of attack.

A more sophisticated method was to try and lure the 'sweeper' to one side before switching play to the opposite flank. Much depended on the willingness of attackers to work at taking defenders into false positions and the eagerness and urgency with which players attacked vacant space from midfield.

The switch-play is, in a sense, a replacement for the simple cross-field pass which lost much of its value by the latter part of the 1950s when British football abandoned a balancing defensive system that had the full-backs pivoting fully on the centre-half.

This system meant that the winger on the far side of the field was invariably unmarked and free to receive the ball, if it could be struck accurately over a long distance. Johnny Haynes was a master passer over any distance, and this, allied to tremendous vision, made him one of England's finest midfield forwards until he was seriously injured in a car crash.

Haynes could play the ball first-time with uncanny precision, and full-backs who had taken up extravagant covering positions infield from the touchline found themselves confronted with an immediate threat.

A Scotsman, Alex James, an Englishman, Raich Carter, an Irishman, Peter Doherty, and a Welshman, Bryn Jones, were all master strikers of the cross-field pass in the 1930s.

Bobby Collins had a decisive influence on

Leeds' emergence in the middle 1960s because of his marvellous ability to drive the ball accurately over long distances, and his successor, Johnny Giles, was no less dominating in this respect.

Wolves, too, had a reputation for overpowering directness when they were a force in the 1950s, and made much of the speed and aggression which came from their wingers, Jimmy Mullen and Johnny Hancocks.

These two players switched the play to one another with long, raking passes across the full width of the pitch, often when running at speed, so that defences were stretched into irreparable confusion.

As defences became more organized, with full-backs marking wingers tightly, the pass hit across field became an obvious sign of frustration. Crowds still applauded it, but defences invited it, happy to have the game being played in front of them.

It was the development of attacking full-back play which gave the cross-field pass a new significance. If space could be created on the far flank, if the far full-back could find that space, then the ball had to be sent to him.

Leeds beat Arsenal— by switching the play to catch out McLintock

For Leeds United, Giles' passing and Cooper's eager attacking skills were a relevant feature of the move at that time and, in 1969, Leeds offered a classic example of cunning switch-play.

In a game against Arsenal at Highbury, they set out to expose Frank McLintock, who had just been redeployed as a central defender after years as an attacking midfield player.

They suspected that McLintock could not over-come an habitual eagerness to get at the ball, fatal for a man playing in a role that demanded discipline above all else.

McLintock was lured into trying to win a tackle on the right side of his defence, and then the ball was immediately pushed to Giles lying square with the play. Giles aimed it forward, Arsenal were caught without cover, and Mick Jones ran on to score a memorable goal.

Like Brazil, Leeds had thus gained the rewards for practising hard and often something which could easily be judged at first glance as pure, natural skill.

But moments of true instinct in football are rare. Mostly they are immediate reactions born out of many hours of devoted practice. For Brazil, in 1970, the immediate reactions to situations that required a switch in the direction of play brought them moments of sweet triumph and a permanent hold on the Jules Rimet trophy.

Coaching: Learn when and how to switch the point of an attack

Much of the satisfaction in football is to play in a successful, goalscoring side that is a team rather than a collection of individuals. To score goals there must be organization and team-work in attack, and switching the play or switching the direction of the attack is part of this organization.

The quality that players must have—to be able to switch the play—is vision, or the ability to see what is going on all over the field and to sense the next move before it happens.

You can begin to acquire this awareness by practising in groups of three. Take a ball out on to a park and begin to pass it among yourselves. As always concentrate on hitting the passes crisply so that in a match they would have enough power to reach the intended player.

As soon as you have got the feel of the ball, detach one player from the group and get him to stand about 20 yards away from where you and your friend are passing the ball to each other. His job is now to make a positive run and call loudly for the ball.

When he calls, the player who has the ball must immediately pass the ball accurately and crisply to him. He then returns the ball to the two who begin interpassing again. Another run, another call, another pass and so on—taking it in turns to make the runs.

To do this well, the two players who are interpassing must be aware of what the player who is making the run is doing. They must be aware of where he is positioned. In other words they must have vision. So while you are passing the ball, look up and around you so that you know what is happening. In this practice you have only to watch for one player, but in a match you will have several team-mates and many defenders to keep an eye on.

To make the practice harder, get another friend to join you, and let him mark the player who is making the run. You have now got to time the moment you release your pass. The player who is making the run must help you by trying to get away from the man who is marking him—but you will not make the pass at precisely the right time unless you are totally aware of what both players are doing.

Of course while you are watching these two players you must also focus some attention on the player who is passing the ball to you—or else the simple interpassing will go astray.

At a proper training session you can carry this practice a stage further. 'Keep ball' is a good way to build up vision. Split your group into two equal sides and play in a restricted area—across half a pitch perhaps or, if the numbers are small, across the penalty area. The object of the exercise is to score goals, as usual, but they only count if the move comes from four consecutive passes by the attacking side. Thus if you score from a rebound near the goal it does not count.

As soon as you start to play 'keep ball' you will see how your vision will be put to the test. Unless you notice where your colleagues are running—both the players close to you and those making runs on the far side of the pitch—you will never be able to string together the four passes you need to score a goal.

However, when you do get a goal you will be amazed at how much enjoyment and excitement you feel from it. For to link four passes together and beat a goalkeeper is team-work—and that is the key to football.

As you become better and better at 'keep ball' increase the number of passes for a goal to count. Top players will find 20 very difficult, so if you can manage eight or ten you are doing very well.

You can practise switching the direction of an attack as a team by 'shadow play'. Here you use the whole pitch, and the whole team play against only three or four opponents who allow play to progress unhindered. They are there only to make players release the ball and not carry it too far, and they do not tackle.

Before starting the exercise, discuss with the coach the way you intend to switch the play. It may be that you intend to attack down the left touchline, hoping to make space for the right-back to move into on the right so that he can strike at goal.

The move might run as follows: left-back to the left-winger; he plays the ball inside to a midfield player and races off down the touchline; the centre-forward moves across to a near-post position; other midfield players move close to support the man with the ball; and the outside-right moves into a central position for a pass through the middle.

The midfield player in possession now has several options and the crucial one is the space on the right side of the field. The right-back can move forward into this space and either try to strike at goal or get in a cross to the players on the left of the area.

Play this move through in 'shadow play'. Use your imagination as to what you would be allowed to do by opponents in a match. For example, there will be nothing to stop the left-winger running through to score on his own, but of course in a match there will be two or three defenders. Run through the move until you continually get it right with only the four or so shadow defenders to stop you.

Gradually introduce more 'shadow' defenders and then make them active until you have a full-scale practice match going. Every player will know what is expected of him and what his team-mates are going to do. If the move brings you a goal in the practice match you have done well. If you score several you have done extremely well —because, of course, your defenders will be aware of what you are trying to do.

In a proper match you will now have another weapon to make chances and bring goals, and, just as important, you will get further enjoyment from the game.

Below *Two players interpass—then switch the play with a quick pass to a sprinting, third man.*

Playing to targets

'We don't expect so many goals from our centre-forwards these days, but we expect them to make a hell of a lot for the others,' explained Pat Welton while organizing a Tottenham Hotspur coaching session.

Against the fact that Martin Chivers, Spurs' first choice centre-forward, had scored 28 League and Cup goals in the 1970–71 season, this may have appeared an eccentric statement. But Welton had put his finger on the changing demands on the striker in the seventies. As 'forward lines' dwindled, in the face of defensive football, from five players to sometimes no more than two, so the centre-forward had to become involved in starting attacking moves instead of merely finishing them.

No longer could he loiter upfield waiting for the winger to beat the full-back and lay on the chance, for increasingly there were no wingers. No longer could he take passes, turn to beat his marker, and then exploit the gap, for with a second centre-back in every team, few such gaps existed.

Instead, his first duty was to make himself available to receive passes from his own defenders. To relieve pressure on their own goal or simply to move the ball forward from defensive positions, defenders needed an upfield player whom they could easily spot and reach . . . in fact, a target.

Defenders needed an upfield player to reach – in fact, a target

A fine example of this new breed of 'target men', who had to be prepared to run hard and be hurt often to take a pass and hold it until help arrived, was John O'Hare of Derby County. A strong man with ox-like shoulders, he was ideally suited for the requirements of his role. Within two months of their return to the First Division in 1969–70, Derby were top of the table, and they finished the season in fourth place. O'Hare got vital goals, but his ability to win the ball under extreme pressure made many more.

Derby's most spectacular win in those ecstatic, early months was the 5–0 demolition of Spurs at the Baseball Ground. No goal typified their style of play more than the second of those five.

John McGovern, their talented midfield player, was in possession on the half-way line, but heavily pressed by Tottenham opponents. As he was forced towards the right touchline, he glanced up and saw O'Hare 35 yards ahead. Derby's tactics were always 'when in trouble, try to find O'Hare'–and McGovern did just that. The pass was good. But as O'Hare moved to meet the ball, he was severely challenged from behind by Mike England.

Nevertheless, O'Hare reached the ball first, and instantly played it a little to his right—into the path of Kevin Hector. A fraction of a second later, England flattened O'Hare, but the centre-forward had done his job. Hector was clear of the defence. Taking the ball on the run had given him a couple of yards start on the defenders and he was fast enough to make it count. He rode two despairing tackles, and slipped the ball past Pat Jennings. It hit the far post and was over the line before Phil Beal could hook it out.

Hector's name went on the scorers' list, and he received most of the praise. Yet without O'Hare's contribution, the ball would never have reached him, and without O'Hare, it would never have reached him in such a way that he could take it at top speed, facing the goal he was attacking. All the centre-forward had to do was to lay off a short pass. But he had to control a long pass played to him. He had to place his pass with total accuracy and just the right degree

JOE BANGAY

DIAGRAM (RESEARCH, LONDON WEEKEND TELEVISION)

KNOWLES McGOVERN
COLLINS(A)
HECTOR(A) PRATT
O'HARE
ENGLAND(A)
COLLINS(B) HECTOR(B) ENGLAND(B) MULLERY
JENNINGS HINTON
BEAL

Above left Kevin Hector (far left) watches his shot score for Derby County against Spurs in 1969. The pursuing defender is Philip Beal. *Left* Diagram of the goal, showing how John O'Hare's target man skills created the opening.

of power. And he had to do all this, knowing that he was about to be tackled hard from behind. Goals that came as clear cut as this were rare. More often the target man's initial pass was the first of several before a decisive shot. Yet his pass was the foundation of the move.

O'Hare was the focal point of Derby attacks, and this is the role of the target man. Ideally he should have the height to deal with high balls, and courage and strength so that he can resist continual, belligerent challenges from behind. He should be alert, have a fine touch, and possess the vision to appreciate where colleagues are running.

In the early seventies every First Division club recognized the need for this type of player, though the combination of such power and deftness in one player was rare.

One of the breed, Geoff Hurst, summed up what was required of the target man: 'The main part of my job begins when our own goal is under attack. Then I must "read" the game and judge what my defence is going to do. When we win the ball, the defender with it wants to get rid of it upfield. So I have to find a position where he can spot me at first glance, and where he can "hit" me with a simple pass.

'It is all very different from the job the old-style centre-forwards had to do. Then they were purely and simply finishers. They had inside-forwards to do the fetching, wingers to do the carrying. They just had to keep themselves fresh for the big finish . . . the shots at goal. Today, the striker is often entirely on his own when he runs about to start a move. And has a darn sight too much company when he tries to finish it off.'

Leeds used Mick Jones as their target man, a burly brave forward who would chase anything. Jones would gallop wide to the touchline to turn what often looked like a desperate clearance into a useful pass. This often set Leeds up for a quick counter-attack. In the 1970–71 season, Jones struggled to score goals himself, but his value to his side was never in doubt. Many of the goals that fell to his fellow-strikers Allan Clarke and Peter Lorimer directly stemmed from his bold play.

At Everton Joe Royle was making his name as a determined centre-forward whose headwork could trouble any defence. Yet as his all-round game improved his ability to operate as a target man was making chances for quick colleagues like Alan Ball, Jimmy Husband and Alan Whittle. At Stoke, John Ritchie was doing a similar job, and Terry Conroy and Jimmy Greenhoff were sharp enough to capitalize on it. Derek Dougan, with both Wolves and Northern Ireland, was another big man who had the deftness to operate in this role.

RAY GREEN

Above Geoff Hurst of West Ham shields the ball — the typical target man under pressure.
Below Diagram of a typical Hurst target man move. Moore plays the ball upfield to Hurst. He comes to meet the ball to reach it before his marker. A first-time pass and then he races forward into

space ready to take the return pass. Another lay-off and a scoring chance is made.
Below right Target players should excel in the air. Southampton's Ron Davies (yellow shirt) outjumps the Liverpool defence to meet a clearance and heads the ball to a supporting player.

Geoff Hurst himself has performed outstandingly as a target man for both West Ham and England, his greatest asset an appreciation of space and how it could be found. This, allied to his adroit skill in accepting passes with either his foot or his chest under pressure, became an important feature of England's play. His understanding with his then club-mates Bobby Moore and Martin Peters led to many decisive goals. Hurst will be best remembered for his hat-trick in the 1966 World Cup final, but as a target man his masterpiece was against West Germany in the 1970 World Cup quarter-final. Although England lost, Hurst was superb, and his colleague in that game, Alan Ball, recalled: 'He was magic. He was up there on his own, but wherever you hit the ball, he would put himself in on it.'

Hurst's role as a target player was in fact the third job West Ham had given him. Originally a wing-half, he had become a successful goal-scorer by feeding off one of the most perceptive and skilled of all target men—Johnny Byrne.

In the 1960s, West Ham played some of the most productive and appealing football in Europe, winning first the FA Cup and then the European Cup Winners Cup. Their exceptional standard of attacking play had its roots in early and accurate use of the ball from defensive positions. They could not have managed it without the mobile skills of Byrne.

Physically he was the complete contradiction of a target player. Short, stocky and compact he appeared ill-equipped to cope with high passes. Yet these limitations never hampered him. He had such a wide range of gifts, notably the ability to pull a ball down, however awkwardly it came at him and no matter how heavy the pressure on him.

Byrne made many goals for Hurst, and it was this apprenticeship under the example of the little Cockney that enabled Hurst eventually to take over his role. When Byrne's skills declined, it was nothing short of tragedy for Ron Greenwood, his manager at West Ham. ' "Budgie" Byrne was the greatest player I have ever seen. We shall never see his like again.'

Joe Mercer would insist that the principle of using a target man had roots that went back much further than Byrne. Mercer, a gifted player and subsequently a wise manager, insisted that he was 'hitting' Dixie Dean and, later, Tommy Lawton with long passes when playing for Everton in the thirties. Both centre-forwards were great players in the air, and Mercer said of them: 'They could resist challenge. They were accurate in laying the ball off, and so we hit them with it from long range.'

But although Everton opted to use the talents of Dean and Lawton, the prevailing tactic of that day was to move the ball upfield by means of deep-lying inside-forwards to orthodox wingers.

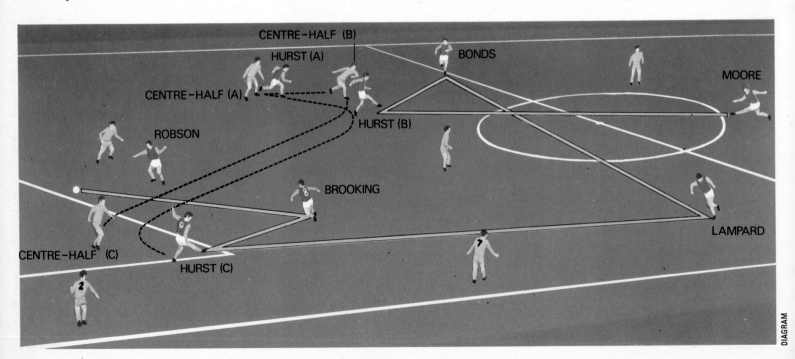

DIAGRAM

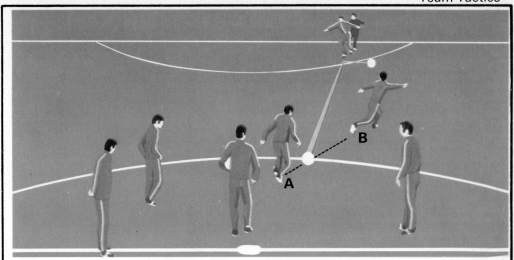

Above Diagram of a training routine designed to develop a forward's skills as a target player.

Perhaps Johnny Byrne's greatest rival to the title of the greatest target man of all time was John Charles, who perfected the role whilst playing for Juventus in Italy. Unlike Byrne, Charles was perfectly built for the job, yet he combined the touch of Byrne with his own tremendous physique. He was also fast, and the possessor of an unshakeable temperament.

Charles left Leeds to go to Italy, where football was plagued by defensive tactics. Juventus were not slow to see what the tall young Welshman could do for them. Although he was an equally capable centre-half, Charles found himself playing up front, where he suffered all the indignities of foul play and gamesmanship. He would often find himself surrounded by five or six defenders, but he had the skill and the strength to lay the ball off to his team-mates. His refusal to be provoked into retaliation was the final frustrating factor for his opponents.

Not all the big men had the grace of a Charles. Vast sums of money were spent by clubs willing to gamble on what they thought they could make of Tony Hateley, a strong forward who played for Notts County, Aston Villa, Chelsea, Liverpool, Coventry City, Birmingham City and again Notts County.

Hateley certainly had all the necessary physical qualities. He was powerful, and an effective header of the ball. But he lacked the deft touches needed when balls were played to his feet, and Liverpool sold him. But doing this meant they had to change their style.

The absence of a tall front player severely restricts the variety of passes which a team can play out of defence, and Liverpool had to accept this until two seasons later, when they bought John Toshack from Cardiff City. Until Toshack arrived they had had to build their attacks with passes played wide to touchline positions, where they deployed small forwards, such as Alun Evans and Bobby Graham, as active, mobile targets. But Liverpool had found that they needed a big front man and they were prepared to gamble again with their money.

As Toshack was learning his trade in the First Division, Martin Chivers was making a fairytale recovery from a tragic knee injury that had the press writing his football obituary. Sir Alf Ramsey congratulated Chivers by making him an England player, and he was one of the outstanding successes of the 1970–71 season. What impressed the fans was undoubtedly the scoring power that brought him 28 goals. But what impressed the professionals—like Pat Welton—was his skill as a target man that led to so many goals from Alan Gilzean and Martin Peters.

For if scoring goals was the hardest thing to do in football in the early seventies, being a success as a target man certainly ran it close.

Coaching: Learn how to play as a target man

If you decide to specialize as a target man, an essential quality is close control of the ball—especially as you will often be left alone upfield. The ball will be played up to you at varying heights, angles and speeds, and you will be expected either to bring it under control or to 'lay it off' first time to a team-mate.

You must develop confidence in your own ability to perform such movements. Begin on your own by playing the ball against a firm surface. As the ball comes back to you, try to control it by cushioning it with the inside of your foot. As you make contact, draw the foot back sharply—if you do this properly the ball should just drop in front of you, ready to be shielded or passed to a colleague.

This movement is just the same as the one you would use when you catch the ball with your hand. Throw the ball up. As you go to catch it, instead of just letting it drop into a flat, stiff palm you draw the hand down and cushion the impact. This is the technique to use with your feet, enabling you to 'kill' the ball.

Continue playing the ball against the firm surface until you have mastered this cushioning technique with both feet. Then introduce movement into the practice. Play the ball, then run in to meet the rebound. As a target man you will continually be required to perform your skills whilst moving at speed.

You can then introduce further variety into the practice. Try the cushioning technique with your thighs, your chest and even the forehead. All the time remember that you are aiming to have the ball instantly ready for your next pass. So far you have been meeting the ball square on—with your back to the imaginary goal you are attacking.

Much of a target man's work is done with his back to the goal and a defender breathing hard down the back of his neck. But sometimes a team-mate will tell you that you have the time and room in which to turn. So now practise taking the ball in a half-turn position so that you are ready to move off at goal with it. Most players naturally turn to one side—either to the left or the right—more easily, but try to practise turning both ways. It will make you a much less predictable player and thus harder to mark.

When you have mastered 'killing' the ball, repeat the exercise but this time lay the ball off first time. Make marks on the surface you are using and as the ball rebounds to you, aim to hit these marks with a first-time pass using the inside of the foot. Practise with both feet and vary the marks, so that you become equipped to lay the ball off at a wide range of angles.

When you have developed your control it is time to introduce challenge into your practice.

Again, this will require perseverance. Put your goalkeeper in one goal and select one defender. Send the rest of the players to the half-way line with a ball each, or as many balls as there are between them. Stand just outside the penalty area, facing the half-way line with the defender, the centre-half, marking you from behind. In turn, each of your team-mates will play the ball up to you. You must get to the ball first, and hold off the challenge from the centre-half until the team-mate has sprinted up from the half-way line to support you. You can do this by 'screening' the ball—in other words, keeping your body between the defender and the ball. Or you can lay off a first-time pass to him. The pass must be hit crisply and accurately.

Whichever you decide to do, the two of you must then go on to beat the centre-half and score a goal. As it is a two-against-one situation, you should always get a shot in, even if you do not beat the keeper. Once one of you has got in the shot—or at worst lost the ball to the defender—you and the centre-half take up your original positions again and wait for the next player to hit the pass from the half-way line. Repeat the move until each of your team-mates has played the ball to you twice.

Since, in this practice routine, you are being marked by only one defender—and he is behind you—it will not have been too difficult for your team-mates to find you with their passes. But in a match it will not be so easy with many other defenders around. The art, then, of the target man is to be able to 'show himself' to the player who is trying to hit the long pass up to him. In other words, your colleague must be able to see you when he makes the pass.

You can introduce practice for 'showing yourself' in the routine outlined above. Simply put in one more defender *between* yourself and the players on the half-way line. His job is to try to intercept the pass before it reaches you. Obviously, if you just stand still or move directly towards the ball, this extra defender will win it every time. But if you begin to move out sideways, your team-mate will be able to see you and find you with the pass. Timing of this movement is very important. If you go too soon, the defence can cover you in time, and if you go too late, your team-mate will not see you early enough and his pass will be badly directed. Be positive and point to where you are going to run.

You have now practised getting into position to receive the ball, and controlling and passing it when you do receive it. All that is left is what to do when you have passed it. This you will have discovered in the training routine. Always be ready to move off into space so that the player with the ball can find you again.

Labels on diagram: JENKINS, FISHER, DAVIES, O'NEIL, CHANNON, PAINE

DIAGRAM

Home and away tactics

After years of patient effort, Southampton finally broke through into the top flight when they won promotion from the Second Division in 1966. But the real toil was only just beginning as they fought to avoid an immediate return to anonymity and to establish themselves as a First Division side.

In their first season, they finished in 19th place, the following season 16th. They were haunted by relegation. But in 1968–69 they finished in seventh place, qualified for Europe and the consolidation had begun.

They were neither a rich club nor blessed with great depths of playing talent, but they did have an astute manager in their former player Ted Bates. And it was his tactical awareness and shrewdness that helped the club survive the toughness of the first two years as a First Division side. By devising two distinct approaches—one for home matches and one for away games—he saw to it that Southampton picked up enough points to survive.

In the cramp surrounds of their home ground, the Dell, they spread their resources, using two orthodox wingers, Terry Paine and John Sydenham, to stretch opposing defences and send over countless crosses to front runners, Ron Davies and Martin Chivers. Only two midfield players were used, and the result was an attacking 4-2-4 system. Davies and Chivers scored a lot of goals, and, though the defence conceded more than its share, the tactic worked.

When playing away from home, Bates made one significant change and occasionally a second. The first involved Paine, a gifted player who was a member of England's 1966 World Cup squad. From his south coast touchline role, Paine was switched to operate in midfield in the away matches. Here his combative nature and his intelligent use of the ball helped support an often pressurized defence.

The second change was the introduction of an extra defender, often the strong tackling David Walker, at the expense of a forward or a more attacking midfield player. These tactics paid such dividends that Bates continued with them even after Southampton's First Division life became less perilous.

In European competition Bill Nicholson, manager of Tottenham Hotspur, was also to learn the value of adopting different tactics for the away leg of a cup-tie. He was to obtain full value from a gamble in buying former player Tony Marchi back from Italy.

Marchi was born at Edmonton in north London, but his surname was a clue to his heritage. He had Italian blood, and Italian clubs, eager to sign British players who could not only play well in a strange atmosphere but also settle down in an unfamiliar climate, were not slow to see his potential for them.

In 1957, just five years after signing as a Spurs professional, Marchi was sold to Lanerossi Vicenza for the then sizeable fee of £35,000. Lanerossi sold him to Torino, a club for whom Denis Law and Joe Baker were to play with such disastrous results.

Then, in July 1959, Bill Nicholson made a typically secretive trip, and returned with Marchi, a player whose true worth was not to be seen for another three years.

Following a season of shattering disappointment during which Spurs had at one time suffered the gruesome prospect of relegation, Nicholson had begun to build a team that was to prove one of the most outstanding and influential in the history of the game.

When the team was assembled, Marchi could not find a regular place in it. Tall, powerful and composed he was essentially a defensive midfield player, and there was no room for him in a system which revolved around the various qualities of two great half-backs, Danny Blanchflower and Dave Mackay.

He came into the team only when defenders were injured, and, in Blanchflower's absence, he captained the side. But it was the deliberate selection of Marchi as a supplementary defender on grounds far from home which confirmed Nicholson's wisdom in bringing him back again to White Hart Lane.

Spurs did not win the European Cup when they competed for it in the 1961-62 season, falling to Benfica of Portugal in the semi-finals. But Marchi's experience of disciplined defensive play while in Italy was confirmed as a valuable asset in the away ties.

It was to be underlined the following season. Spurs, having won the FA Cup for the second year running, went back into Europe. This time the target was the Cup Winners Cup. And this time they succeeded.

Once again Marchi was used as a defensive replacement for a forward in critical away games. It was in the final itself that Marchi was to be rewarded for his loyalty. Dave Mackay was forced

HOLLYWOOD

FISHER

MCGRATH   GABRIEL

O'NEIL

PAINE

KIRKUP

CHANNON

DIAGRAM

COURTESY OF THORN ELECTRICAL

to drop out of the match, and Spurs did not have to look far for his deputy. There was some irony in the fact that Marchi was to win a coveted medal in an orthodox role.

It was strange, too, that Bill Nicholson should make use of a tactic which was deliberately negative. Outwardly a dour Yorkshireman, who had adopted an unsmiling approach to football as a thoroughly competent defender in a brilliant Spurs team during the early fifties, Nicholson's managerial philosophy was based on attack and a style which would be instantly appealing to the public. He was also averse to the principal of changing players for away matches, convinced that a skilful, settled team should be capable of ordering itself to cope with any given situation. He said: 'The same eleven players should be able to conform to any given tactical situation. They must of course have the skill and the experience. But given that skill and experience they should not feel uncomfortable when asked to deploy themselves to meet with special circumstances.'

It was a laudable theory and one which the majority of managers would have been eager to pursue. The advantages were obvious; intrinsic knowledge of each others' strengths and weaknesses, familiarity of a kind which is essential to composed team play.

And yet the best of them conceded the point when confronted with the possibility of failure

away from home in European competition. Leeds, West Ham and Liverpool were among those who made use of different tactics when playing away from home in Europe, and others were seen to extend the policy in domestic competition.

It was often done simply by restricting the activity of certain players. Men who attacked from midfield when playing at home would be seen in more negative roles away.

Leeds, for instance, emerged as a power in the game with a note of caution in their play. They had an outstanding midfield attacker in the fiery Scottish international, Billy Bremner. When playing at Elland Road, Bremner's job was to push forward, to link, and to find spaces among defenders which he could exploit with his alert, neat skills.

But elsewhere and until Leeds had defined the way in which each game was going Bremner would be more restrained and less mobile.

Don Revie, the Leeds manager, recalled: 'At that time we were only really interested in half a loaf away from home. We couldn't afford to lose, and we didn't really have the quality of forward play to be confident of winning. It was all to do with reality.'

Few teams adopted the same policy week by week, and Manchester United suffered a sickening defeat in the Cup Winners Cup of 1964 simply because they allowed themselves to be lulled into a

Opposite left Diagram of the way Southampton played at home, with Terry Paine as a winger.
Top Diagram showing the change for away games. Paine moved to a more defensive, midfield role.
Above Southampton, with their two wingers wide, in attacking action against Stoke at the Dell.

false sense of security.

Drawn against Sporting Club of Lisbon in the quarter-finals of the competition they scored freely at Old Trafford, winning 4-1. Maurice Setters, a tough, intimidating defender whose attitude to football seldom ranged beyond the need to win every match recalls: 'We were so cocky it wasn't true. I pleaded for a defensive policy, because winning was all important. But I was ignored. We just went out and played, with the most minor adjustments to our system. Before we knew where we were, we were out. We attacked them and they took advantage of the gaps we left in defence. It was ridiculous.' United lost the match 0-5, and the tie.

Chelsea, at the time when they played with youthful exuberence under Tommy Docherty, had a similar experience, beating AC Roma 4-1 at Stamford Bridge in the first leg of a Fairs Cup tie.

But Chelsea held onto their lead in the second leg despite the continued abuse of the Italian crowd and in defiance of Docherty's instructions.

P & L PHOTO SERVICES

Docherty had chosen to persist with the normal system of play. The players, on the other hand, were eager to use Marvin Hinton as a 'sweeper' to play behind tight marking defenders.

In the second half, with the pressure really on, Hinton was ordered into the role by his teammates. The Italians were held to a 0-0 draw. There were no recriminations.

Terry Venables, team captain at the time, said: 'Tommy made up his mind how we should set out to play, but a few of us disagreed. We were under a lot of pressure in the first half, but Tommy wasn't keen on altering things. So we took it upon ourselves to do it. It was all forgotten afterwards.'

Venables might have underestimated Docherty's annoyance. Conflicting personalities led to them falling out, and Venables was eventually sold to Spurs.

The introduction of the substitute rule into the Football League during the middle sixties gave greater licence to experiment with tactical changes. Being able to call on a fresh face enabled them to insure against the possibility of being caught out by the flow of fortune of a game.

Some managers chose to play an extra defender when playing away like George Heslop of Manchester City with the forward he replaced waiting on the bench should he be needed to try and save a seemingly lost cause. Adaptability was the key to the reasoning of others. A good all-rounder in reserve like Liverpool's Ian Ross, Arsenal's Eddie Kelly or Leeds' Mick Bates and the ability of other players in the team to switch positions was an obvious advantage.

Above Terry Paine in a typical touchline position during a Southampton home match at the Dell.
Above centre But away at Liverpool, Paine has to defend, here strongly challenging Thompson.
Above far right David Walker, wearing No 10, is sometimes played away as an extra defender.
Right Tony Marchi leaps to clear. Spurs found him invaluable in the away legs of European ties.

All clubs paid urgent attention to the opposition. They accepted that certain individual qualities were suited to particular matches. For instance, if there was a need to contain outstanding individuals in the opposition, it would require a player who could be relied on to mark tightly, someone both disciplined and determined. If this could be established without disturbing the structure of the team, then it could be safely left undisturbed. If there were doubts, then room was made for others who could be relied on to do that particular job.

How to play away from home will always be a problem in football. In everyday League fixtures managers are reluctant to disrupt the structure of their teams much more than the reallocation of roles that Ted Bates has used for Southampton. Cup ties, in which all is won or lost in 90 minutes, leave more scope for changes in the players selected and the way they might play. The decision of Bill Nicholson to use Tony Marchi and the switch of Marvin Hinton urged by Terry Venables showed that such alterations can bring rewards.

In the midst of the tension that accompanies cup games, caution rather than attack was shown to be the best form of defence.

TOPIX

Coaching: Improve your team's performances in away matches

At all levels of football, teams prefer to play at home. Their own pitch, whether it be on the local common, in a park or an enclosed ground, is familiar territory where generally points are easier to gain.

Playing away means a pitch that is strange. It means usually some inconvenient travelling which can distract players before the game, and it means usually the opposition will have more support to encourage them.

It seems clear that a team must therefore approach an away fixture in a different way to a home match. Top clubs will be able to know in advance how their opponents are likely to play on their own ground, and will be able to plan how to counter such tactics down to the smallest detail. At lower levels this fine degree of planning is not possible, but there are certain broad tactics which can help any team overcome some of the problems involved in playing away.

Remember that any tactical plan you propose to adopt for an away match must be geared to both the abilities and standard of fitness of the players in your team. It is no good giving specific tasks to players who have not the particular attributes or stamina to carry them out.

Unless you are certain that you are vastly superior to your opponents, it is always wisest to approach an away match with some caution. A simple example is to adopt the policy of selecting a forward as substitute for a home game—whom you might bring on if you are struggling to score—but selecting a defender for an away game—who can be brought on to defend a lead.

The emphasis away from home is likely to be on defence—at least until the team has adjusted to the conditions and can play its normal game. Playing at home gives confidence. At home a club expects to win, and will attack more.

As an away team, you can counter this by restricting the space available for the home team to play in. Forwards should play a little deeper, players who play as wingers at home should drop back to help out in midfield.

These tactics can be practised at training by simply playing practice matches using the away tactics. This is important because, if players are asked to do a different job on a Saturday afternoon without any previous practice, the team is likely to be in more trouble than if it had not adopted away tactics at all.

Caution rather than pure defence is the best attitude to adopt away from home. A total reliance on defence will give the opposition a lot of possession, and they will be able to apply pressure. Their defenders, who will have little to worry about if they are never forced to defend, will be able to support attacks, and only a supremely organized or fortunate side will survive.

Caution, with the midfield players adopting defensive roles and forwards working back deeper, will give the team a chance to find their feet in strange surroundings. Then, if things are going well, the players can resume their normal roles. If the home team are still exerting a lot of pressure, these cautious tactics should keep you in the game—by restricting the space the opponents have to play in, and by threatening counter-attacks.

Playing away can have its advantages. Forwards will often find that they are given more room to play, as opponents push further and further forwards to support attacks. Here it is important to encourage your front men to accept and exploit the situation. They will probably get less support from the midfield players than usual. They might even go for lengthy periods in the game without receiving the ball. But when they do get possession they could well find that they have this extra space in which to work. They must move quickly at goal to capitalize on this, and they must be prepared to take on defenders themselves to get in at goal. Away games are often won by breakaway goals.

And it is important to take points from away matches. Titles will never be won by teams who cannot win on opponent's grounds.

Calling for the ball

'Leave it Bob,' yelled Spurs' Welsh international winger Cliff Jones as team-mate Bobby Smith shaped up to volley at Norwich City's goal during the crucial, closing minutes of a fifth round FA Cup tie in the spring of 1959.

Norwich were already famous as giant-killers. They had beaten Manchester United and Cardiff City at home and they were now within reach of a major triumph at Tottenham. They had taken the lead in the 25th minute with a goal from Terry Allcock and they looked capable of holding it when Spurs launched one last desperate attack.

Jim Iley sliced a shot wildly away towards the bye-line on the left side of the Norwich goal and the Third Division defence breathed relief. Then Dave Dunmore, his inherent technique contrasting sharply with his powerful build, turned to retrieve the ball. Out of nowhere Norwich were in trouble as Dunmore's instant centre pierced their penalty area.

Smith coiled into an intended volley but Jones' shout strangled the centre-forward's movement. Smith checked. The ball flew on and Jones drove it first time past goalkeeper Ken Nethercott.

Spurs had survived, but in the end it only served to give them temporary respite in time of trouble. They lost the replay at Norwich the following Wednesday and found themselves fighting to avoid relegation to the Second Division.

But Cliff Jones when scoring that goal emphasized an important feature of play—the value of offering an extra pair of eyes to a colleague. Proof of the fact that it was impossible to play top-class football with a closed mouth.

When calling for the ball Jones had complied with the Laws. He had shouted a name, thereby not gaining any unfair advantage.

Ron Ashman, the Norwich captain and later manager of the club, said: 'Cliff Jones was completely aware of the most important point in that situation. He was further from the ball than Bobby Smith. But he was better placed to make contact. He had to make Bobby aware of it too. The only way he could do that was with an intelligent call. The rest was all down to his individual skill.'

This sort of verbal communication was constant in professional football. Yet the public were largely ignorant of the fact simply because the noise they made usually drowned the advice and instructions which passed between players.

It was only in rare moments of lull, when the game had lost some of its immediate arousement that they became conscious of the dialogue. Even then they were unable to accept it. 'Shut up. Get on with it,' screamed supporters when vigorous instruction was heard being issued by players.

Few members of the public were permitted the privilege of attending training sessions in empty stadiums when orders and warnings echoed back from the walls of stands and terraces. It was a world unknown. A part of football which had not registered with most of those who watched it.

And yet managers and coaches spent long hours impressing the need for communication. 'You can't play with your mouth shut,' was a common instruction which often baffled people responsible for developing playing technique at schoolboy level.

One coach recalled: 'I was staffing a course

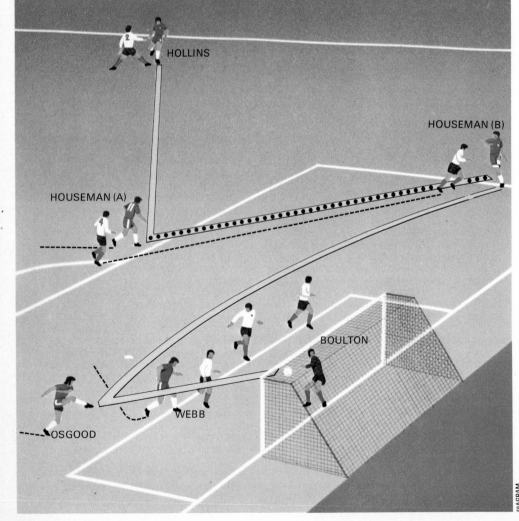

HOLLINS

HOUSEMAN (B)

HOUSEMAN (A)

BOULTON

WEBB

OSGOOD

DIAGRAM

down in Kent which was attended by the best schoolboy players in the area. The one thing we tried to impress upon them was the need to stay in touch with each other.

'To do this they had to call. To shout. To warn each other of things which were happening outside the range of normal vision. I remember spending four days doing this and at last we were getting somewhere. Then on the fifth day I was called away to answer the telephone.

'I left those boys in charge of a master who happened to be there that morning. "Carry on," I said. "Keep it going." I was away for twenty minutes. When I walked back across the playing fields I was suddenly conscious of something different. It was too quiet. The boys had stopped calling to each other.

'So I interrupted the game they were playing. "What's gone wrong?" I asked. "Why have you stopped calling to each other?" They looked at the schoolmaster who in turn looked sheepish.

'"Did you tell them to stop calling?" I asked. He nodded and then muttered something about not agreeing with what I had been teaching. That the game should be played in silence.

'I could see what it was all about. That master had been brought up to accept certain principles about sport. It wasn't his fault. But that was the sort of thing you were up against at that time. Four days' work destroyed in the space of twenty minutes' interference.'

The value of calling was no more clearly emphasized than when Arsenal were forced to play without their English international full-back Bob McNab during the 1971-72 season.

McNab displayed an instinctive professionalism. Quick, alert and an outstanding team player, he was to suffer from a pelvic strain which was the outcome of unrelenting competition.

Arsenal, during a season when they were involved in the European Cup, replaced him with Sammy Nelson, a more than adequate Irish international who was always eager to offer himself as an overlapping auxiliary in attack.

But Nelson lacked McNab's defensive qualities and above all his perceptive appreciation of a communal problem. McNab, although not fully fit, was brought back and a team-mate was to say this: 'He made all the difference to us. Bob is a great "chatter". He takes in the whole area of play and he's always calling, always warning. He's an extra pair of eyes for everyone in our defence.'

When translated in terms of attacking play calling was always critical as Jones proved against Norwich City. Further proof of that came thirteen years later when Peter Osgood scored a dramatic goal against Derby County at Stamford Bridge in a replayed League Cup tie.

Osgood could play. Tall and flexible, he had days when he put it all together, revealing a devastating certainty of touch both on the ground and in the air. When he turned out against Derby at Chelsea in October 1972 he had been passed over by the England team manager Sir Alf Ramsey for the friendly against Yugoslavia at Wembley the following Wednesday.

Osgood had something to prove. And the presence of the entire England squad together with their manager gave him the opportunity to take extravagant advantage of an exciting goal.

Derby were brilliant that night, displaying all the virtues which had become increasingly apparent the previous season when they had won the Football League Championship for the first time in their history.

But it was Osgood's stunning appreciation of opportunity which figured as the most important feature of the match and finally won it.

An impressive move had begun with a characteristic surge of power by John Hollins along the Chelsea left flank. His low centre was collected by the nimble Peter Houseman who picked his way neatly to the bye-line. Houseman looked up and appeared to aim his cross towards the ubiquitous David Webb who was poised at the far post.

But Osgood, loitering beyond Webb, embellished a cunning deployment with a shout which froze his team-mate at the point of contact with the ball.

Webb allowed the centre to run and Osgood, gleefully free of challenge, volleyed a magnificent goal—Chelsea's third in a 3-2 victory. He acclaimed it with a gesture of genuflection towards the stand which housed Ramsey and the England squad. A gesture which was immediately if wrongly interpreted as a defiant rebuke for the man who had not chosen him.

Ramsey's mind might have been elsewhere. Perhaps further north at Newcastle where Malcolm Macdonald was anxious to prove that he was international material. Macdonald had already played for England emphasizing the murderous potential of his left-foot shooting.

Ramsey, on the other hand, cagily aware of the certainty which was necessary in international football, remained unconvinced. But he was not at St James' Park to see the goal which Macdonald scored against efficient Leeds United.

NEWCASTLE CHRONICLE

HARVEY

BARROWCLOUGH

MACDONALD

DIAGRAM

MIKE CORNWELL

Mike Summerbee of Manchester City adds an upraised arm to the strength of his voice to indicate that he is in a position to receive a pass at Highfield Road against Coventry City.

Like Osgood, Macdonald found himself free on the far side of goal as Jim Smith broke free on the right. His cross fell invitingly towards Stuart Barrowclough at the near post, but Macdonald's call gave Barrowclough the chance to let the ball run. Unattended, Macdonald emphatically completed the move, this time with a full swing of his right boot. Sir Alf might well have been influenced. Both Macdonald and Barrowclough were in the next Under-23 squad — and Macdonald responded with a fine hat-trick.

Ill-timed, unintelligent calling could get players into trouble or reduce the effectiveness of a sensible run as Allan Brown stressed to coaches on a course at Lilleshall. 'We are seeking unguarded space. If we can get there without giving ourselves away then we have achieved something important. Think about it.'

A lot of players did. But intelligent calling at the right time was essential to guide the man in possession and could be devastatingly effective as Cliff Jones proved when confronted with defeat and despair in 1959.

Coaching: Learn when to call and how to help your team-mates

For a set of players to operate successfully as a team there must be communication. It is often impossible for the player in possession to know exactly what is going on around him. At this moment an instruction issued by a colleague can help him make the best use of the situation. A clear, concise call, given by somebody in a very good position to judge what is happening, is invaluable help.

The goalkeeper is often in a sound position to see and advise. He is also responsible for most of the play going on in the back third of the pitch and it is from this position that he should take command. But defenders are only willing to receive and carry out instructions from the goalkeeper without hesitation if they are given in a clear and confident manner.

The keeper must work to earn the respect of his fellow defenders if they are to have confidence in his judgement. He should leave no player in any doubt as to what he wishes to take place; instructions given in a firm and definite tone have a strong psychological effect not only on the defenders but on the opposition as well.

Understanding between players will only come through practice and experience. Players become familiar with words used by colleagues and often just one or two words are sufficient to indicate what the situation demands and will act automatically.

The referee can penalize an instruction that might distract opponents so it is safer to call a name or something like 'keeper's ball', when as a keeper you are indicating that you are leaving the goal-line to make contact with the ball. You want a clear passage from defenders and cover should you make an error. Defenders in the immediate playing area should react automatically by getting out of your way and moving towards the goal-line to give the cover.

A hotly pursued defender chasing a ball towards his own goal can be in a tricky position. As you move out you must decide whether you want the defender to play it back or leave it for you to come out and gather. Again, be positive because you are in the best position to read the situation. Call 'touch it', 'play it', 'leave it' or 'keeper's ball' depending on what you want the defender to do.

Free-kicks also require definite instructions from the keeper. First, you must decide whether or not you want a wall and if so how many you want in it and where they should stand. Second

you must make sure that all attackers are marked coming into the penalty area. A shout of 'mark him' or 'cover him', pointing at the opponent concerned, is all that should be required.

Calling players to 'move out' when the ball is cleared or for a full-back to 'cover' are also instructions that a goalkeeper can give because his position gives him such a wide view of the action.

An understanding between the goalkeeper and fellow defenders will not just happen. A lot of work will have to be done during your training and coaching sessions. In games of attack versus defence the goalkeeper can be encouraged to dictate certain situations. Balls can be played into the goal area in the air giving the keeper

the necessary experience and confidence to call and gather or to punch, depending on how he reads the situation. This way an understanding is created and above all the outfield defenders gain a belief in the goalkeeper.

Players out on the field can help one another in exactly the same way. Situations in football change very quickly and a player on the ball or in the act of receiving it can be in trouble from a source he did not expect. Under the circumstances he can be helped by a call from a colleague like 'man on' which would be a clear indication that an opponent was moving in fast.

This in itself is a rather negative call because it does not help him out of the situation. A colleague running into a position to support him can give an instruction like 'play it first time' or just 'first time' or 'play it', more positive calls indicating that an opponent is close and that you are ready to receive the ball from him. Equally a call of 'hold it' or 'get it down' or 'turn' or 'let it run' will indicate that he is on his own, free from a marker.

Inexperienced players can get flustered when they hear more than one call. The player in possession should have more than one passing possibility if his colleagues are working correctly off the ball. Consequently he will receive a number of calls which can be confusing. This happens more in a lower grade of football and the cause is lack of vision on the part of the players off the ball. A player may run into a position where he could receive the ball, at the same time creating space for another player to move into. By looking around him he can tell which is the best ball.

Small-sided games are excellent ways of introducing positive calling. These games of three or four-a-side can be played on the condition that you cannot receive a pass unless you have called for it. This gives the coach ample opportunity to discuss the necessary points.

Calling is a major part of top football. A game may be very even and the calling of both sides equal. One team scores and takes control. You will find that this team will increase their amount of calling whilst the other team's falls away. It has a great psychological effect. Stand close to the touchline and listen, or when watching television look to see if you notice the amount of calling going on.

Remember to keep your calls short and to the point. Be clear, intelligible, loud and positive.

Asa Hartford yells his West Bromwich colleagues into position. Verbal communication, often unheard and unappreciated by spectators, is a vital aspect of successful team play.

RAY GREEN

The rhythm of team play

West Germany's defeat in the 1970 World Cup semi-finals prevented their team manager, Helmut Schoen, from taking what would have been the boldest gamble of his career. He longed for his team to have the chance to play Brazil, to have the opportunity to expose the more serious flaws in their team by first disturbing the rhythm of their football.

To many the rhythm of Brazil meant the samba, the national dance with an infectious pulse that characterized so much of a Brazilian's daily routine. But, like every football team, Brazil had a rhythm about their play—if the side were allowed to settle into it.

Rhythm was established if players were allowed to play the game in their own natural way at their own natural pace. Footballers, like men working in any profession, have their own tempo for going about routine tasks. This style might dictate that usually the goalkeeper prefers to throw his clearances to the full-backs, who choose to play long passes up to target men, who knock the ball down to supporting midfield players. This is their method, and they will certainly have alternatives if opponents interfere with the process. But what they would find harder to change is the rhythm, a much more subtle part of the make-up, if rivals succeed in upsetting the pace with which they prefer to apply their style. Brazil were no exception.

They established their rhythm and confidence by playing the ball about in a series of passes that at times might seem casual and aimless but were all geared to a final sharp thrust at goal. All their players, including their back defenders, enjoyed indulging themselves on the ball; and they possessed sufficient skills to do so, particularly if they were only half-pressed by opposing forwards. This 'slow, slow, quick' rhythm meant much to Brazil, and it was here that Helmut Schoen saw his chance. If there were any doubts about the validity of his thinking, they were removed for him as he sat through the final, three days after Germany had been eliminated.

A tall, impressive figure who always looked as important as he was, Schoen said: 'The Italians threw away a marvellous chance. In the first thirty minutes of the final, the Brazilians were as vulnerable as I felt they would be. If Italy had sustained their attacks after scoring their goal, they might well have emerged as champions. Brazil's play is all about confidence and rhythm. If you can prevent them from settling into a rhythm, then you destroy the confidence. It was even more important to do this in Mexico, because there were obvious flaws in their defence. The thing was to get at that defence. It was this I intended to do. I couldn't wait for our forwards to get at their defenders.'

To put Schoen's plan to the test, the Germans had to overcome Italy and it was not to be. Karl Schnellinger's goal in the early seconds of injury time saved them when defeat seemed inevitable. But it only deferred the ultimate disappointment. Five more goals were scored during extra time when players were seen in grotesque posture unable to co-ordinate mind and muscle in an exhausting parody of a football match played at a killing altitude. Rivera's calm sidefooted goal settled it for Italy and Schoen was left to ponder what might have been.

Rhythm was a critical feature in the play of all outstanding teams. It grew out of self-assurance and collective ability, and once established it was difficult to disturb. Brazil recognized

Below left Brazilian players have been accused of feigning injury to disrupt the rhythm of their opponents' play. The lengthy interventions of their troupe of trainers make it hard for the opposition to settle into a pattern of play.
Below John O'Hare heads Derby into the lead against Leeds at the Baseball Ground in 1972.
Bottom As the diagram shows, the goal came from Derby's deliberate attempt to break the rhythm of Leeds' play. Robson pressured Bremner into a bad pass, and O'Hare converted Durban's cross.

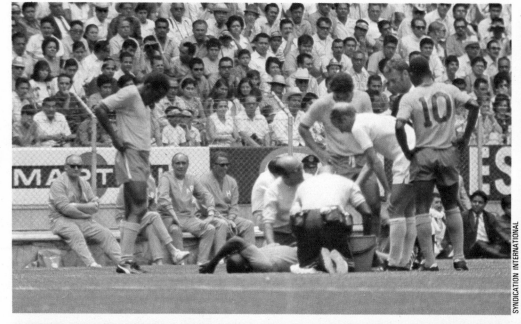

SYNDICATION INTERNATIONAL

RAYMONDS NEWS AGENCY

O'HARE

BREMNER

SPRAKE

DURBAN

ROBSON

DIAGRAM

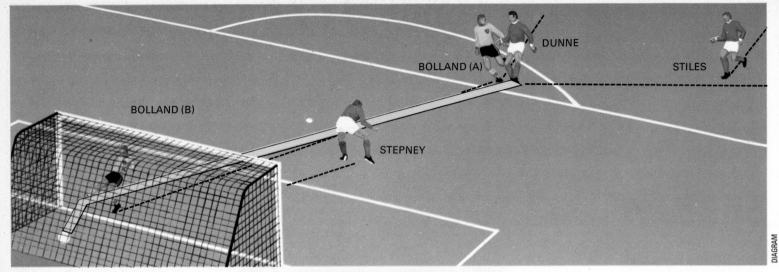

BOLLAND (B)

BOLLAND (A)

DUNNE

STILES

STEPNEY

Above *Diagram showing how Norwich City scored their winning goal when they shocked Manchester United at Old Trafford in 1967. Bolland chased a through ball that he seemed to have no chance of reaching, but his challenge pressured Dunne into turning the ball past his own goalkeeper.*
Left *Bolland follows the ball into the United goal. By challenging for every ball Norwich never let United settle into their normal rhythm, and they won this fourth-round FA Cup tie 2-1.*

this and their gamesmanship when under pressure in Mexico was the least commendable and a largely unnoticed factor in their gathering success. They concentrated on not allowing their opponents to settle.

Careful analysis showed that Pele, their most colourful and popular player, was involved in most of their disrupting tactics when they were in danger of being exposed by sustained assault. Pele, collapsing in pain, was a provocative sight, and it was the signal for mass interference by Brazil's trainers. He rarely took less than three minutes to recover from apparent injury; the result was complete disruption of the pressure which his team had been under.

The Germans, too, employed such tactics and they were widely criticized for them when challenging for the 1966 World Cup. It was evident again when Arsenal, bidding to retain the Fairs Cup while trying to win the League Championship and the FA Cup in 1971, lost to Cologne.

Arsenal had few phases of dominance in that contest, but when they did threaten, the Germans relied on histrionic reaction to the most harmless challenge to upset them. Bertie Mee, Arsenal's manager, said: 'It is time that the Germans looked closely at the reputation they are getting for this sort of thing. Everyone knows about it and it does them little credit.'

There were more subtle and legitimate means of preventing opponents from settling down and they were products of intelligent appraisal. Spurs, for instance, traditionally built their attacks out of defence, putting passes together until they could safely move forward.

By getting forwards to harass aggressively, opponents could force the Spurs defenders to play the ball hurriedly forward and the rhythm was immediately broken up.

A burst of exciting form by Leeds in the spring of 1972 came to an end when they were well beaten at Derby on Easter Saturday. Derby simply refused to let Leeds settle. Whenever

goalkeeper Colin Boulton had possession he drove the ball deep into the Leeds half and persistent midfield play meant that Derby continually won the ball in positions from which Jack Charlton and Norman Hunter could be attacked.

The effect of this industry could be seen in the two goals which Derby scored to go to the top of the First Division. Billy Bremner, an accomplished player in tight situations, was forced into error in the fifteenth minute and Alan Durban's cross was turned into a scoring header by John O'Hare. In the second half John Giles, probably the best midfield man in British football at the time, gave the ball away at a free-kick and Leeds were once again exposed to an attack which led to another goal.

Leeds manager Don Revie said: 'Derby's was a magnificent team effort. They got on top of us from the start and we were never able to get hold of the game. Whenever we looked like creating something, they were in among us.'

Revie's generous praise could not conceal his personal disappointment as he was confronted by the possibility of yet another ultimate failure after a season of outstanding endeavour. Leeds on their day were the most rhythmic of England's teams. They were efficient, good at winning the ball and the best of their players displayed great initiative.

They, too, were accused of using gamesmanship to unsettle opponents who had managed to establish periods of superiority, and they were savagely attacked by West Ham's manager Ron Greenwood for their tactics. Greenwood said: 'Leeds have compared themselves with Real Madrid. There is no comparison. Certainly they have done some great things for English football. But there are other things which they do which should play no part in the make-up of a great side.'

Rhythm in some teams amounted simply to patience. Allied to strength, it made Liverpool one of the most feared teams in Europe. Liverpool concentrated on compressing the game into

their opponents' half of the field and keeping them under incessant pressure. It took great courage and resolution to resist them at Anfield where the fanatical support of a massive congregation on the famous Kop was often enough to unnerve the most composed teams.

Liverpool's play was based on simple principles. They concentrated on moving their passes to feet and relied on the instinctive ability of skilled individuals to make something out of nothing when within range of goal.

It made them less vulnerable than most teams although easier to plan against. They posed few problems of subtlety and their comparative lack of success when appearing in the European competitions was indicative of this.

Manchester United are another side with a reputation for being vulnerable if the pace of their game is upset, and Norwich City won a famous Cup victory at Old Trafford in 1967 by capitalizing on this weakness. Their winning goal typified the success of their tactics of challenging for every ball; United right-back Tony Dunne, under pressure from Gordon Bolland, turned the ball past his own goalkeeper.

One of the weaker points of British play was the inability to alter team style when confronted by alien conditions or a less definitive approach by the opposition. Arsenal, even when winning the League and Cup in 1971, were largely predictable with most of their attacks channelled through to big strikers, John Radford and Ray Kennedy. Unless Radford and Kennedy were willing to spread their runs so that they employed the full width of the pitch, Arsenal found themselves bogged down.

Having achieved success, Arsenal set about establishing more fluency and a greater number of alternatives. But under pressure they reverted to type, and when losing to Ajax in the quarter-finals of the European Cup they relied almost exclusively on aerial attacks.

It was often possible to disrupt team flow simply by pinning down 'feed' players in the middle of the field. Benfica did this when beating Spurs in the European Cup semi-final second leg at White Hart Lane in 1962. Danny Blanchflower was the man who set the mood of Spurs' play with romantic ideal and a high degree of skill.

Benfica, with a 3-1 lead to defend from the first leg in Lisbon, set out to stifle the Irishman's influence. To do this they looked to Coluna, a coloured, perceptive midfield player who could rival Blanchflower's imagination.

Blanchflower liked to receive the ball in space

Coaching: Develop a tempo for your team's play

The pace of the game can be dictated by several factors. Teams not in possession can dictate by applying pressure on the player with the ball and by so doing make him either part with the ball or make quick movements to evade this pressure. If pressure is kept up, then they can make the team in possession move the ball about much quicker than they may want to, thereby forcing them into hurried passes which may go astray.

Try this for yourself. Play three against one in an area about ten yards square. The object here is for the three players to interpass the ball, keeping it away from the one defender and within the ten yard square. If the defender moves about slowly giving the three players plenty of time to work the ball and measure their passes, then he will be in the middle for evermore. If on the other hand he attacks the ball with an aggressive attitude, the three players, in order to keep the ball away from him, will have to move it quickly; they will have to move much quicker to support and will therefore be more liable to make mistakes.

Now increase the area slightly to 12 yards square and bring in another defender making it three against two. Again the same principle will apply, only this time the three players will be under much more pressure; the less experienced the players, the quicker they will lose the ball because they will not have the ability to use the spare player quickly enough in order to slow the game down to a more comfortable pace. The experienced players will adapt themselves to a quick bout of interpassing which will leave the spare man time to put his foot on the ball and slow the pace down. They will also cultivate the ability to hold the ball by screening in tight situations. Working on these principles, the team not in possession will dictate the

pace unless the team with the ball create space and a spare player who must be used at the right time.

It is impossible to play football at sprint pace for the whole 90 minutes. The ability to change the pace of the game is a difficult technique to acquire and the really good teams do this well. The fact that it is difficult should not stop you from practising it because even a slight improvement in this phase of the game will pay dividends.

Start your practices in threes. Many groups can practise at the same time. Interpass the ball between you moving at a jogging pace, keeping in an area about 20 yards square. On a signal, a whistle or a shout, the ball must be interpassed at a much faster rate until another signal when you slow down to a jogging pace. The quick passing for the experienced should follow a pattern—wall passes, through balls, interchange of position, for example—and be played first time if possible.

You can work this same practice and add a finish with a shot at goal. Start this around the half-way line, and move forward slowly as if you were working for an opening. Then suddenly change the pace and after two or three quick passes, using your imagination as to the pattern, finish with a shot at goal.

If you work down one flank, you can jog easily interpassing the ball back to the half-way line on the other flank and then attack the other goal. This means you can have several groups working at once and is a good exercise to cultivate the change of pace.

Build on this exercise by inserting two defenders marking two front players who are supported by the third. Interpass the ball until you feel that you have got the defenders in a poor

position, then go quickly with a change of pace. Interchanging positions with a change of pace is a sure way of beating defenders. As you become experienced, bring in another defender to make it three against three. This is a very hard exercise indeed, highlighting the need for good supporting positions, and your passing and control will be tested here, as well as your ability to hold or screen the ball. It is your own decision as to when to speed it up. Work the ball, passing to feet, make runs and interchange positions and be sure to support the player on the ball.

Look for an opening, try to recognize when the defenders have been deceived, that you have got them moving at a comfortable pace and that you have got sufficient killing space behind them to attack. When you have sensed this, be very positive in your movements. This must be a combined movement because your team-mate may decide that it is not on, in which case you will have to pull out and work for another opening. This can only come with practice and complete understanding between you and your team-mates. It is something like army strategy. Play the ball about, make a few decoy runs looking for a weakness, and when you find one move in fast and furiously.

Five or six-a-side games played across half the pitch are good exercises to cultivate the knowledge of when and how to change the pace. There is a fair amount of space to work in and you will have more of the ball consequently than in eleven-a-side. Success in these matches will not come overnight; you will have to work at it and constant communication between your teammates will help bring about the necessary understanding in the big game.

But remember, space is the essential commodity. Some teams give it to you, other teams will pressure you and make it tight; whatever happens, look for it and use it intelligently, otherwise you will be forced to play at top pace without very much control and little success.

Above *Playing two against three in a confined area is a sound method of learning how to interrupt the natural pace of a team's interpassing.*
Right *In the 1966 World Cup West Germany were often criticized for overacting when they appeared to be hurt. Like Brazil, West Germany found that long pauses for treatment undermined the rhythm of their opponents' play.*

deliberately vacated by John White. From there he could float passes forward, and there were few better at playing the ball through the air. But that night, whenever a great Spurs crowd gathered itself in anticipation of a devastating assault, Coluna appeared to literally stand and stare in Blanchflower's face. The Irishman now had an immediate problem and the opportunity of playing the ball forward early to eager colleagues before the Portuguese could assemble in defence had gone. Blanchflower was skilled enough to find alternative methods, but Spurs' rhythm was disrupted, and they went out of the

competition despite continuous attempts at breaking down Benfica.

Ground conditions could destroy rhythm, and it was clear that they could have a demoralizing effect on play. There was a classic example of this at Stamford Bridge in the autumn of 1970 when Spurs won an astonishing match against Chelsea. It began in a downpour which swamped the pitch and led to the prediction that the game would not finish. But in the opening 30 minutes when the rain had merely slicked the surface Spurs played some of their best football for months. Tuned in to quick, accurate passing,

they were able to move the ball about with such speed that Chelsea could not get near them.

As the ground became heavier Spurs' rhythm disappeared. It could have been Chelsea's game, but it was won by Spurs with two remarkable goals scored in injury time.

Could Brazil's impressive, exciting rhythms have been upset by the Germans in the 1970 World Cup Final? The question remains hypothetical. But certainly Schoen with his massive experience and coaching skill thought so. He would have to wait four years for the opportunity to try again in a competitive fixture.

Breaking quickly from defence

With only seconds remaining of the 1966 World Cup final Geoff Hurst galloped clear of the West German defence to rifle a left-footed shot past goalkeeper Hans Tilkowski.

It was a memorable goal because it clinched England's first World Cup win. It was an unforgettable goal for the rapture it brought the England players and their fans. And it ensured Hurst of instant immortality with a hat-trick unprecedented at that level of the competition.

But the timing of the goal and the importance of the match in which it was scored obscured the quality of the manner in which it was fashioned.

For West Germany had been finally laid to rest by a classic version of a sharp counter-attack —the quick break from defence.

The Germans, trailing through the gradual crescendo of drama in extra time, pushed defenders forward to attack in a desperate late challenge when Bobby Moore struck a crisp thirty-yard pass to Geoff Hurst on the half-way line.

Hurst, taking the ball on his chest, turned and, drawing on the dregs of his energy, ran on, outpacing the remaining defenders, to drive his shot between Tilkowski and the near post.

Most of Tilkowski's team-mates watched this final, killing episode from deep inside the England half, totally isolated by the speed of Moore's clearance and Hurst's determination to capitalize on the chance his captain had given him.

Once West Germany committed the majority of their players to attack, they became immediately vulnerable—once they lost possession and once England used the ball quickly and directly.

It was fitting that such a goal as Hurst's should be taken at a time when British teams were perfecting techniques that were to reaffirm their status in the world game.

Goals were becoming harder to score, defences more difficult to break down. Outstanding goalscorers, like Jimmy Greaves and Denis Law, were beginning to recognize that there might be more opportunity when playing away from home.

Forwards discovered more space playing in matches away from home

Home teams, more likely to attack, would leave exploitable spaces in their defences as they moved more and more players forward.

Liverpool never forgot a lesson taught them by Inter Milan in a European Cup semi-final in 1965, when the Inter full-back, Facchetti, ran through their stretched defence to score.

In the late sixties and early seventies, Bill Shankly instituted an attacking system that relied heavily on players breaking quickly from defensive situations. Tommy Smith and Emlyn Hughes, two defenders, typified not only the value of powerful running from midfield, but the foresight to know when to move forward.

In a First Division game against Southampton at Anfield on 1 May 1971 these two players, with the help of their centre-forward, John Toshack, broke so quickly from defence that they caught Southampton completely flatfooted.

Hughes scored the goal but the real credit belonged to Smith. The Saints were attacking in numbers when the Liverpool captain won the ball for his side in his own penalty area. At that very second he became aware of the possibilities for a rapid counter-attack. Without hesitating, he carried the ball out of danger and up his right touchline, leaving the Southampton forwards and two or three of their defenders struggling behind him.

Over the half-way line he stormed, still bullocking along the touchline. Toshack and Hughes had both understood what their captain was thinking. Toshack, who had been standing in the centre-circle when Smith won the ball, had

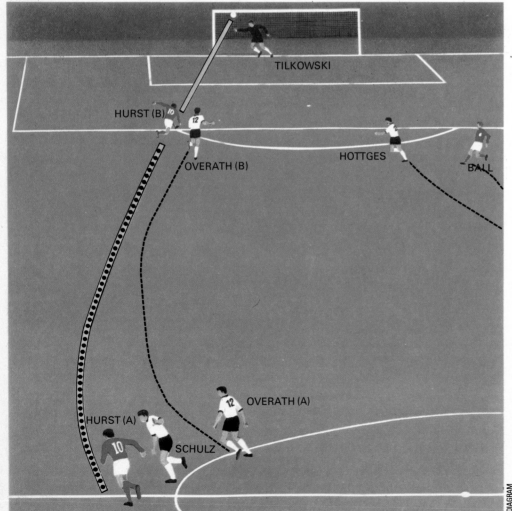

Above left *Geoff Hurst shoots his way into history.*
Left *Diagram of England's most famous quick break, the goal that clinched victory in the 1966 World Cup final and gave Hurst a memorable hat-trick.*

stretched his long legs in a sprint to the far side of the Southampton penalty area. Hughes, even nearer his own goal than Smith had been, was racing upfield in support.

Twenty yards into the Southampton half Smith looked up, spotted Toshack and aimed a cross at the centre-forward's dangerous head. His judgement was perfect; the ball homed on its target. Toshack met it on the far side of the goal, and knocked it down onto the penalty-spot.

At that precise second Hughes, who had outstripped his pursuers, arrived like a runaway tank. He took the ball in full stride, and cuffed it first-time past goalkeeper Eric Martin.

Such was the speed of Smith's run that Southampton had managed to bring back only two defenders to cover the danger. Toshack's jumping power had demolished these two.

Shankly was never slow to project his team and his players. Sometimes outrageous, often extravagant, he could dust the most ordinary incident with world class quality. He had no need to press for effect on this occasion.

Shankly was ecstatic: 'You will never see a greater goal. That, sir, was one of the greatest. Tommy saw the situation and broke so quickly. And Hughes ran 70 yards to take the chance. He wanted to score and that's what it is all about.'

Though the execution was spectacular, the lesson was simple. Southampton were undone because Liverpool had quickly utilized the space that their opponents had only conceded because they were attacking.

At the start of the seventies they introduced Steve Heighway, a southern Irishman with a University background and an untidy style.

Heighway did not look a player, and there were many who doubted that he was. He stumbled through tackles, took opponents on in situations where most players would be happier to lay the

Right *Emlyn Hughes shoots against Southampton.*
Below *Though Hughes scored, the diagram shows that Southampton, who seconds earlier had been attacking, were beaten by a break by Smith.*

ball off, and looked coltish and out of place.

But while he was being dismissed as a freak, Heighway was making things happen. He was blessed with a devastating turn of speed and complete self-confidence. He could turn defences on his own, and designed his own breaks, relying on instinct and speed to take him through.

In a Fairs Cup-tie during the 1970-71 season, Hibernian defenders found themselves trailing ineffectively in Heighway's wake as he exploded from the half-way line with the ball. He raced clear to the by-line. His cross cleared the keeper, and Toshack stood alone as he headed in a winning goal from inches at the far post.

Both Hughes and Toshack scored their goals as a reward for supporting the player who made the initial break.

But in the FA Charity Shield match at the start of the 1971-72 season it was Shankly who had to reflect as Liverpool were continually troubled by Leicester City's use of the quick break. Three times their defence was beaten as astute prompters like Jon Sammels and David Nish played balls into space behind the defence.

Leicester's nippy front men, Fern, Farrington and Brown all broke through on their own, only to be foiled by the vigilance and agility of goalkeeper Ray Clemence. So square were the Liver-

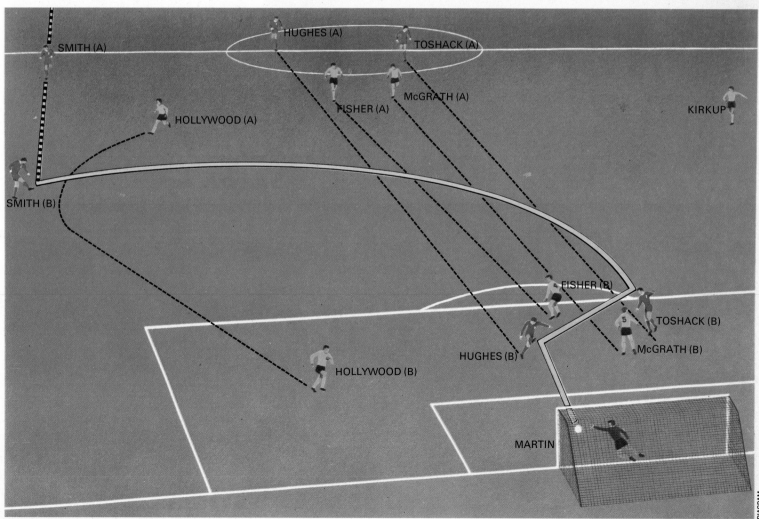

pool back four defenders as they moved up to the half-way line that Clemence was almost forced to act as a sweeper behind them!

Leicester's counter-raids were the product of quick thinking and decisive use of the ball.

Arthur Rowe, who fashioned the 'push and run' football which brought Spurs so much success in the fifties said: 'The great teams are those who are able to recognize and exploit the moments when the initiative changes. Every game has these moments. They could happen as the result of errors by opponents or because of good play by your own team.

'Outstanding players seem to recognize this by instinct. They react to situations where the opposition are suddenly outnumbered or where they have allowed themselves to be lured into false positions.

'Sometimes these moments pass by because no one sees them and the opportunity is lost.'

As the centre-forward—the traditional spearhead of every attacking move—became more and more tightly watched and marked in the seventies, the quick break gave more scope for perceptive midfield players to sneak through defences and score important goals. John Hollins, Howard Kendall, Mike Doyle and Brian O'Neil constantly looked out for opportunities to move forward from their patrols in the middle of the field, and Alan Mullery, John McGovern, Mike Bailey and Billy Bremner all scored match-winning goals for their clubs when the more usual goalscorers were being held in check.

Such players were invaluable. For whatever pressure their team might be under or however deadlocked a game had become they were likely to change everything with a decisive counter-attack. Such was the devastating quality of the quick break.

Coaching: Learn how to switch quickly from defence to attack

Nothing is more exciting in football than to score goals that result from pre-planned strategies. Much of the enjoyment in playing the game stems from seeing a tactic, that has been practised hard in training, bring rewards in proper matches. Switching quickly from defence into a counter-attack—the quick break—is one of the most productive ways of team organization.

Like all team tactics, the quick break is a combination of several distinct skills, which must be practised for the move to work as a whole. High on the list of skills needed in this case is the ability to pass the ball accurately over long distances, and the ability to make a run on to the pass at precisely the right moment.

These skills can be practised anywhere—all you need is a ball, a friend, and room to practise. Begin by standing about thirty yards apart and pass the ball to each other. Concentrate on driving your passes so that they go crisply to your friend—they must not bobble on the ground—and try to be as accurate as you can. When you receive the ball, control it, look up and drive it back again.

When you have become proficient at doing this, get your friend to play the ball to a spot twenty yards or so to one side of you. The point of the exercise is for you and the ball to arrive at this spot at the same time—in other words you are timing your run to reach the pass. If you arrive and have to wait for the ball to reach you, you have gone too soon. In a match you would be quickly marked by defenders if you did this. If you arrive too late, you will miss the ball. It is a matter

Below Practise the quick break—on half a pitch. The keeper on the left throws a ball to the midfield man on his right. He passes across field into the path of the front player on the left-wing, who shoots at goal. The next ball is thrown to the left midfield man, who passes to the right—and so on.

of judging when your friend is going to release his pass.

At the same time he has to be consistent in the strength and weight of his passes and continue to drive them rather than sidefoot them. Practise this, taking it in turns—one playing the passes, one doing the running to meet them.

When you have worked on these skills, you can put them into practice in team training routines designed to encourage the quick break.

Play across half a pitch to start with, making a couple of goals with piles of track-suit tops, and only when you grow in physical strength and confidence should you perform the team practice on the whole pitch.

Put a player in each goal. At one end put your two midfield players in position—one in a right-half position, the other at left-half. Split the rest of your players into two groups. Put half of them on the right touchline and half on the left. Place both groups on an imaginary halfway line running across your half-pitch.

The routine starts with the goalkeeper at the same end as the two midfield players. He throws the ball to the right-half who controls it, and plays a long pass into the space in front of the first player in the group on the left-wing. He sprints on to the pass, and carries on to shoot at the other goal. Having shot, he collects the ball, and returns it up the pitch to the goalkeeper who started the move.

Meanwhile, that goalkeeper again starts the move. He throws the next ball to the left-half who plays his long pass into the path of the first player in the group on the right-wing, who goes on to shoot at goal.

The goalkeeper then throws to the right-half again who plays the ball through to the second player in the left-hand group . . . and so on. Repeat the routine until each player in the groups on the flanks has gone five times.

When the midfield players have shown the ability to place their long passes with a reasonable degree of accuracy, it is time to introduce defenders. Add one defender on each wing, and place him level with, or just behind, the attacker who is going to chase the pass, and about five or ten yards infield from him. As the pass goes through, the defender must turn, chase and try to dispossess the attacker. Of course, it will require more accuracy from the midfield players to get the passes behind the defenders—without them intercepting.

It is not always possible to hit long passes deep into space behind defenders. The defence will often retreat quickly to fill these spaces. But you can still break quickly, if you play the ball up to the feet of a front player. He can either turn and run with the ball at the defenders, or he can play the ball back to a supporting player. The supporting player then plays the ball through for a return pass to the centre-forward or passes to a third player running through.

You can practise this in a similar way to the above routine, using your half-pitch to begin with. Retain the midfield players and the groups on the wings, but add your centre-forward in the centre of the pitch. The goalkeeper now throws the ball to the centre-forward, who plays the ball to the right-half. The move now is as before. The diagonal cross-field pass to the left, and the attacker runs on to shoot at goal. The goalkeeper throws again, the centre-forward plays the ball to the left-half, and he makes his long pass to the attacker on the right.

Again, as you grow in confidence, you can make the practice harder by introducing defenders. As well as adding defenders as you did in the previous routine, you can put the centre-half in to mark the centre-forward, so that he is laying the ball off under pressure.

If you work at these routines, you will be well-equipped to launch counter-attacks whenever your side gains possession after your opponents have attacked in force. Remember, once you have the ball and are breaking forward, the whole team must make every effort to help the player who is making the break.

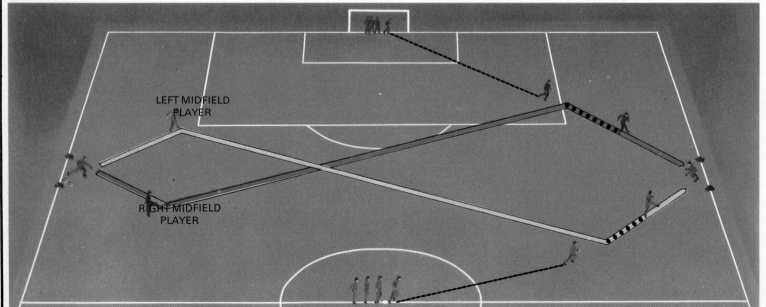

LEFT MIDFIELD PLAYER

RIGHT MIDFIELD PLAYER

DIAGRAM

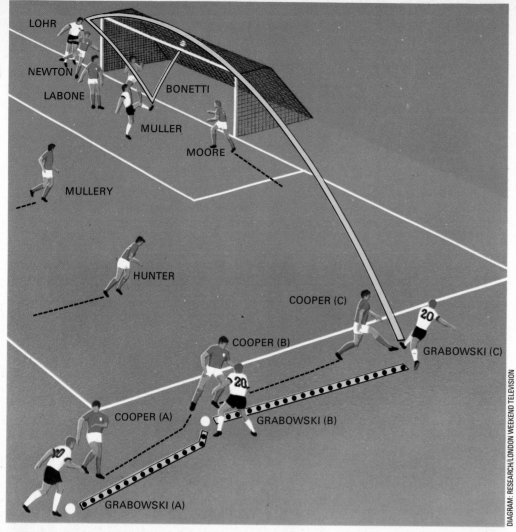

DIAGRAM: RESEARCH/LONDON WEEKEND TELEVISION

FOTOSPORTS

Tactical use of the substitute

Left _Diagram showing the West Germany goal that put England out of the 1970 World Cup. It was a triumph in the tactical use of substitutes for manager Helmut Schoen. He brought on Grabowski, a fast, direct winger, after an hour's play to attack defenders beginning to feel the effect of the heat and the altitude. Grabowski sprinted past Cooper and crossed to the far post. Lohr headed back and Gerd Muller scored._

Below left _Bonetti is beaten and out go England._

games to qualify for the quarter-final.

Grabowski was a hard-running forward whose directness was in sharp contrast to the more elegant Libuda, but Grabowski had not been given one full match. On the other hand Libuda was yet to finish a game and the pattern did not alter in Leon. As the German substitute appeared, Charlton demonstrated expressively, angry with his colleagues for opting for moves designed rather to maintain possession than to increase their lead.

Ramsey might have mistaken Charlton's obvious frustration as a hint of fatigue; in any case he already had his eyes on the semi-final. No England team of his time had failed to defend a two-goal lead. Charlton was into his thirties. It was murderously hot and the semi-finals would be played at an even higher altitude in Mexico City the following Thursday. With only four days in which to rest, the time had come for careful husbandry.

Bobby Charlton trundled off, plastering the sweat drenched strands of his surviving hair across his scalp. Ramsey's arm was around his shoulder, but Charlton could not conceal his annoyance and irritation.

'Bringing off Bobby... was one of Alf Ramsey's few mistakes'

Those sitting near to him at the time recall his muttered admonishment of the way in which England were trying to play and the annoyance he showed at being brought off. His brother Jack watched anxiously from the stands. He was soon to leave the stadium, unable to stand the tension as England's lead was eroded, saying later: 'Bobby seemed to gather everything up for that one game. It turned out to be his last, but I don't think that was ever in his mind. He looked twenty all over again. Full of running. Wanting the ball and doing all the things we knew he was capable of. I'll never understand why Alf brought him off. It was one of the few mistakes he made during my time with the England squad.'

England's defeat was to be dramatically reflected in national gloom. Uwe Seeler's equalizer and Gerd Muller's goal in extra time merely amplified the controversy which grew out of Charlton's withdrawal and a later decision to replace Martin Peters with a more intimidating defender, Norman Hunter.

As the England players sank to the turf at the final whistle, Ramsey turned and offered his hand to his rival manager, Helmut Schoen. He was conceding defeat in more ways than one. The absence of a sick Gordon Banks might have been the most decisive factor in England's collapse. But Schoen was entitled to feel that he had won a crucial battle with his use of an influential substitute.

Ramsey had been faced with the puzzling problem of substitutes from the moment when he first knew that the finals were to be played in Mexico's lofty altitude, and that the competition would allow two substitutes where in 1966 there had been none.

He continually made statements like: 'It has become a 13-a-side game and the England players have got to recognize this without dispute. We must learn how to make the best use of the extra men.' But beneath this public front a doubt, felt by many managers, remained.

The introduction of a fresh player at a late stage of a highly competitive game seemed to suggest an automatic shot in the arm to a flagging

Bobby Charlton had no way of knowing that his glittering international career was over when Sir Alf Ramsey summoned him to the touchline with fifteen minutes left to play in an ultimately disastrous World Cup quarter-final against West Germany in 1970.

Charlton was playing his 106th game for England. It was a new record set in the killing heat of Leon, Mexico. He had gone one better than Billy Wright. But it was to end there and in controversial circumstances, as England's team manager made tactical use of his substitutes.

And that one critical game reflected all the problems faced by managers since the use of an extra player had been legalized.

The decision to replace Charlton with Colin Bell had already been taken when Beckenbauer broke to resurrect a seemingly hopeless German cause with a deceiving shot which carried beneath Peter Bonetti's dive. A few minutes earlier, the Germans had introduced Grabowski, whose reputation as the competition's deadliest substitute had filtered through to Guadalajara, where England had fought out their group

team, but this view ignored the problems facing the substitute. Where the other twenty-one players were loose, he had spent the match cramped and cold on the touchline bench. Whereas they were perfectly tuned to the pace and atmosphere of the game, he was not. And during the substitute's period of acclimatization, the pattern of his team's play was often interrupted as it sought to embrace the newcomer. Often the adjustment could take as long as a quarter of an hour and often this was as much of the game as the substitute had been allowed. Ramsey never rid himself of this doubt, although on the tortuous tour of South America undertaken in 1969 to prepare England for the strain that was to come a year later, he experimented with the use of substitutes to counter the thinness of the air and the dry heat.

In Guadalajara, he took Martin Peters and Alan Ball on one side and instructed them to burn themselves out in the first 45 minutes of play. They both ran themselves silly before being replaced at half-time by Bobby Charlton and Alan Mullery who had both played two days earlier in Mexico City. It meant that Ramsey had used up his quota, and he was to be troubled by second-half injuries. He still was not sure.

In Rio ten days later, England surrendered a 1-0 lead to lose 2-1 to Brazil late in the match, when it was obvious that Peters in particular was labouring. Ramsey elected not to call on fresh players. The uncertainty remained in his mind. Throughout the following winter, he stressed the need for his squad to accept the things which were to come. But he remained a reluctant disciple of the system. He used substitutes more out

of a sense of duty than enthusiasm; Thompson replaced Lee in Amsterdam, Peters came on for Bell against Portugal, Mullery and Hurst substituted for Lee and Jones against Holland at Wembley, but Ramsey, it seemed, was no more than going through the motions.

What finally happened in Leon was an almost logical conclusion to Ramsey's uncertainty; only his firm belief that the match was won led to the departure of Charlton and Peters.

Is a player pulled off being humiliated in front of a big crowd?

It was an uncertainty that enveloped many League managers. Bill Nicholson of Spurs was later to use substitutes as a tactical measure more than most of his contemporaries. Yet he said at the time the rule was introduced: 'I'm far from sure about it. If I pull a player off in front of thousands of people I am humiliating him and admitting to an error of judgement. If he's not good enough to finish the match, then he wasn't good enough to start it.'

The view was nourished by tradition and Nicholson's well-known honesty. But there were others who greeted the innovation as a welcome way of widening the game's scope.

Alan Brown, one of the great thinking coaches and at the time manager of Sheffield Wednesday, said: 'We have got 12-a-side football and we must learn to make use of the extra man. My players have been told that they must all expect to be pulled off if I feel it is necessary. Once they

Top left Diagram of Eddie Kelly scoring for Arsenal against Liverpool in the 1971 FA Cup Final. Kelly's selection as substitute emphasized another tactical use of the No 12—to cover a player who has just recovered from injury. Peter Storey was risked at Wembley after an ankle injury only because his deputy, Kelly, could come on if Storey broke down. Kelly did come on in the second half and scored Arsenal's equalizing goal.
Above Kelly's shot rolls into the Liverpool net.
Top Colin Bell, substitute for Bobby Charlton, in action against West Germany. Unlike Schoen, Ramsey was not convinced about using substitutes, and he brought off Charlton to save him for the semifinal, thinking England had won the game.

are conditioned to this, they will not feel embarrassed. We must also condition the supporters. They too must recognize that it might be necessary to remove a player simply to try to alter the state of the game.'

How to rather than whether to use the extra man became the crucial question for many. British players had learned how to survive when one short and how to take advantage of numerical superiority when the opposition were hit by injury. They had fashioned the technique of possession football to cut down running when outnumbered and the principle of stretching opponents who were outnumbered.

Now it became a question of shrewd management. Substitutes had to be carefully chosen. Which games might need the sudden introduction of an extra defender? Which ones might need the extra impetus a new forward would give?

The answers to these questions varied from

club to club. When Derby County returned to the First Division for season 1969-70, they persistently chose the burly Frank Wignall, a former England centre-forward, as their substitute, and his introduction could transform a 4-3-3 system to the more attacking 4-2-4; others rejected the notion of a regular substitute because of the problems of keeping him match fit.

The allowance of a substitute had an added advantage in that it gave more flexibility in risking the fitness of a key player. Arsenal were prepared to take such a gamble in the 1971 Cup Final when they selected Peter Storey, although he had been fighting an awkward ankle injury for ten days prior to the match and had missed the final Championship-clinching League match at White Hart Lane on the Monday of Cup Final week. Arsenal would have undoubtedly been loath to play him, if they had not been permitted the insurance of Eddie Kelly, an accomplished deputy, waiting on the bench in the Number 12 shirt, should Storey's ankle weaken.

It was a gamble that paid the highest dividend. For over an hour Storey's biting power in the tackle restricted and disheartened the Liverpool attack; then as the effects of the injury took their toll, Kelly was introduced. As the battle continued into extra time, he made his telling contribution, sneaking a half-hit shot past Ray Clemence to put Arsenal back on course to the double.

Other gambles were taken in reverse. In the fourth round of the 1971-72 Cup, First Division Ipswich Town visited Birmingham City, and adopted an ultra-defensive line-up, giving their former England defender, Mick McNeil, his first game of the season as an auxiliary defender, leaving an attacking midfield player, John Miller, as substitute. But their plan came unstuck when Ipswich conceded a goal to Birmingham's young striker, Bob Latchford, in the first minute. McNeil was back in the dressing-room and Miller on well before half-time, but that goal won the game, and many would argue that the change in tactics upset Ipswich's normal rhythm to such an extent that they never really came to terms with the match.

When Spurs took off a player, it was so clumsy it was laughable

But the average spectator found substitution hard to accept, especially when it meant the removal of a man who had become anything like a favourite with them. This was reflected frequently at Spurs, where willing footballers who pleased the crowds with their endeavour were more likely to be called off than the more skilful.

Frank Saul, a hard-working forward, was seen to regularly disappear down the tunnel to a background of cheering disgust. Spurs, like many other clubs, had failed to register the principle of replacement, and when they chose to substitute a player they did it so clumsily it was almost laughable. Terry Venables recalled: 'The trainer, Cecil Poynton, would come to the touchline and whistle, waving his towel. We didn't know who was coming off and it used to get quite funny. No one wanted to go, so we'd all keep clear of that particular touchline. This went on for about ten minutes one day at Coventry. Cecil got into a terrible temper, and the crowd weren't slow to see what was going on. You couldn't help laughing about it.'

Bill Nicholson eventually used the substitute to prove a variety of points, but none more damning than as part of an attempt to shame Martin Chivers back to form. Spurs had dominated Coventry City in a League game at White Hart Lane and led 4-1 when Chivers was summoned to the dressing room. Chivers took the blow on the chin, and his subsequent development into a world-class player proved Nicholson's judgement. But other players found the early bath hard to accept. Roger Hunt, whose physical aggression as a player was equalled by his mildness as a man, tore his shirt from his back and threw it into the trainer's dug-out when he was hauled off by Bill Shankly in a Cup-tie at Anfield. Tony Hateley was another to react in this way.

But football had become a 12 or even 13-a-side game, and by the time Ramsey reached Leon he had no doubts. England would play with more than eleven. The problem was who should be brought off and when?

The choice fell on Bobby Charlton. Had it not rebounded he would have played at least one more game for his country. But when he was called off, he was walking out of international football for the last time.

Coaching: Learn how to make the best use of your substitute

The substitute is just as important as any other member of the team. His selection should be calculated as a major part of the strategy used to win a particular game. The use of a substitute gives the manager or coach a chance to introduce a change in attack, should the game not be going too well, or the opportunity to reinforce his defence if the need arises—apart from the obvious advantage of allowing a replacement for injury. His selection, then, should not be a haphazard affair, but one calculated to cover most eventualities.

A player passing a late fitness test is always liable to break down because it is virtually impossible to create the match atmosphere and tempo in a test of that nature. Under the circumstances, a manager can take a considered risk knowing he has adequate cover.

The venue of a match can also have a bearing on the selection. Playing away in a very important match may mean that a defender as substitute will be more beneficial than an attacker, whereas an attacker might be selected for a home tie when the advantage of familiar surroundings can be taken into consideration. Playing away, a team is apt to be more cautious than when playing at home.

Knowing your opponents' weaknesses may influence your choice of substitute. The opposition may be known to be poor in the air, slow on the turn, weak physically or tactically unsound, in which case another player suited to take advantage of these weaknesses should be selected. Strengths and tactics adopted by opponents can have a bearing on the tactics you employ and consequently the selection of the substitute to give maximum cover.

Most managers select a team which they think is the strongest and best suited for the occasion. They select a substitute, hoping not to have to use him. When a change is forced by circumstances, it should involve as few positional alterations as possible. Some players, because of their versatility, make ideal substitutes. They are able to adapt themselves easily to play a variety of roles. It is a good idea during practices to allow players freedom to express themselves in positions other than the ones they occupy on match days. Experience of

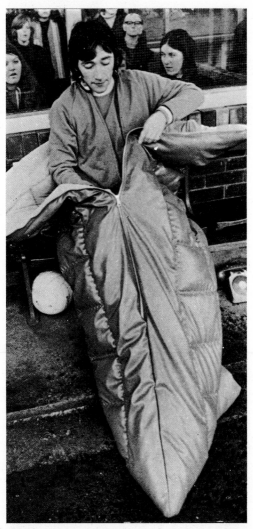

Above *The substitute must always be kept warm on the bench, and a sleeping-bag is ideal for the job as Peter Scott of Everton illustrates.*

this kind can prove invaluable in emergencies.

One of the most difficult positions to cover is that of goalkeeper. This key position must have adequate cover and a considerable amount of time should be spent in finding a replacement from within the team. Throughout the season, the substitute keeper should be kept in practice during your training sessions.

Once selected, the substitute must be looked after on the touchline. Sitting or standing for a long period in all types of weather can affect his efficiency should he be required. He must have the right clothing to keep him warm and dry in mid-winter conditions—plenty of thick sweaters under a warm tracksuit. His boots should not be tied too tight because it can affect the flow of blood, making the feet cold. Some kind of foot muffler can often pay dividends, and a hot foot bath at half-time can also help. He should never be allowed to become cold on the bench.

The substitute should sit with the manager, coach or trainer and discuss the events of the match. He is in a very good position to see what is going on and what is required should he be used. With this in mind, his concentration on the game must be 100 per cent, so that he is fully prepared and in the right attitude of mind to go on at any moment in the game.

Making a tactical substitution is a major decision. Before contemplating such action the manager should satisfy himself that the players he intends to leave on are all fully fit. An early voluntary change is risky because other injuries may occur; to make the substitution during the first 70 minutes, unless something drastic is happening or there is a bad injury is unwise. Yet to leave it until the few remaining minutes is unfair to the substitute who will want as much time as possible to make an impression on the game. One can only generalize about this problem because so many factors have a bearing on the reason and timing of the change.

Finally, the manager should try to give the substitute as much warning as possible that he will be going on, so that he can adjust his footwear, tighten his boot-laces, tie-up his socks, and get his body physically prepared by doing a few stretching exercises.

The manager must make sure that the substitute understands exactly what is required and has instructions to make the necessary positional changes which follow his entry.

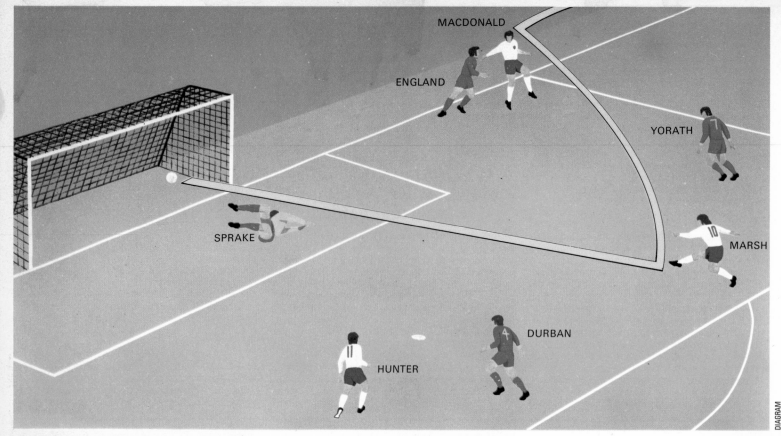

Labels on diagram: MACDONALD, ENGLAND, YORATH, SPRAKE, MARSH, HUNTER, DURBAN

Tactical judgement

Top *Diagram illustrating Rodney Marsh's spectacular first goal for England, a beautifully struck volley against Wales at Ninian Park in May 1972. But although Marsh's skill had the fans chanting superlatives, closer analysis of the move revealed that the goal owed much to the shortcomings of the Welsh defensive play.*
Above left *Peter Storey is unchallenged as he crosses the ball from the England right wing.*
Above centre *Centre-forward Malcolm Macdonald is under no pressure as he leaps to deflect Storey's centre towards the waiting Marsh.*
Above *Marsh has time and room to set himself to volley the dropping ball past Gary Sprake.*

Of all the players tried by Alf Ramsey as he prepared England for the World Cup success of 1966, no one looked more immediately convincing than the Everton striker Fred Pickering.

A powerful, muscular player who had begun his career as full-back, Pickering went on to score 51 goals in 123 games for Blackburn, and by the time he was sold to Everton in 1964 he was clearly ready for examination as a potential international player.

His first chance came in an Under-23 international against Scotland at Newcastle and few have made a more spectacular debut at that level of football. Pickering scored a hat-trick in a 3-2 victory and the first of his three goals had critics searching for superlatives: Ramsey, they claimed, had clearly unearthed a player who would strike fear into the world's defences.

Left unmarked just inside the penalty area when a centre came in from the right, Pickering steadied himself, drew back his right foot and struck an awesome half-volley into Scotland's goal. But had any of Pickering's army of sup-

porters been able to listen in on a conversation which took place in the sleeping compartment of an express train travelling to London they would have heard one, clear, dissenting voice.

Bill Nicholson, highly respected and immensely successful manager of Spurs, had travelled north for the match, maintaining the patrol which kept him in touch with players who might have the qualities he looked for.

A journalist ventured the opinion that Pickering was a bit special, that Spurs with their great purchasing power might have done themselves a favour had they attempted to outbid Everton when Blackburn made Pickering available at £50,000. Wasn't that great half-volley convincing evidence of Pickering's quality?

Nicholson's narrow, cautious eyes drew even tighter as he considered the question. 'That wasn't a great goal,' he said, silencing the debate. 'That was a luxury goal. A really outstanding player would never have attempted a shot like that. There was no one near Pickering. He was so free that he didn't need a shout to confirm that. He

was on his own. He could have pulled the ball down and stuck it away. If he had done that, then we might now be talking about an outstanding prospect. But you can't teach that to someone.

'All the great goalscorers have it. Jimmy Greaves, Denis Law, Puskas. Alright so they score their spectacular goals. But more often than not they get everything going for them. The simple thing, the right thing. Pickering's goal looked marvellous. But it could have gone anywhere. Nine times out of ten that shot would have ended up on the terracing.'

Nicholson's dissatisfaction with imperfect technique was well known, and it was expressed consistently to the Spurs players.

It was also representative of the almost carping analysis that managers and coaches devote to how goals are scored, especially to those goals scored against their teams. For the professionals the vast majority of goals are conceded because at some point in the build up of the move, some player has not done his job; only a small percentage are dismissed with a shrug of the shoulders as unstoppable, as entirely due to the skill of the opposition.

For the spectator the standards of examination need not be so harsh, but it is worth borrowing some of the judgement of the professionals before applying the label of 'great' or 'magnificent'. Many significant goals put under the microscope owe as much, if not more, to shortcomings in defensive play as to brilliant attacking technique or strategy.

Fred Pickering's goal remained a memorable incident on Tyneside. But Nicholson's doubts about him were to be confirmed in startling fashion before two more years were out. The Everton forward travelled with England to South America and on the way collected his first cap and a hat-trick against the United States in New York.

Bill Nicholson had been first to sense Pickering's weakness

Four months later in October 1964, he played and scored against Northern Ireland in Belfast. Three weeks after that he played and scored against Belgium at Wembley. It ended there. Pickering never played again for England. Something had been missing. Few people had sensed it in the beginning. Bill Nicholson had.

A panel of experts set up by London Weekend Television considered the relative merits of defensive follies and attacking skills when debating the quality of goals scored in the 1971-72 season. Six spectacular scores were put in order and some, though highly-praised by the fans, failed the tests applied by the professionals.

A diving header by Martin Chivers for Spurs against Nottingham Forest at White Hart Lane seemed to be well in the running until the poor quality of Forest's defensive play was considered. Jimmy Neighbour's forward pass to Martin Peters, who had run splendidly forward on the blind side, started the move. Peters created an angle for a centre which Chivers gobbled up.

But Jimmy Hill, a former Fulham forward and at one-time manager of Coventry City, who was chairman of the panel, itemized the factors which devalued the effort. He said: 'Forest are a team facing relegation and they lacked most of the ingredients which you expect from players in such a situation. They had no spirit and they were very disorganized. I doubt whether Peters would have been allowed to run as free against a firmer front or whether the movement would have lasted long enough for him to take advantage of the forward pass.'

A cleverly executed chip by West Ham's Trevor Brooking against Spurs also paled under scrutiny. Brooking broke left on to a controlled clearance from Bobby Moore and was confronted by centre-half Peter Collins. Collins backed off his man until the pair reached the edge of the penalty area. Then instead of forcing Brooking wide he allowed him time and space to strike for goal. Brooking's technique was equal to the opportunity and from 18 yards he curled a chip wide of the vast reach of Pat Jennings and into the top corner of the net.

There can be no more famous three goals in English history than the hat-trick struck by Geoff Hurst in the 1966 World Cup final. But if West Germany's Helmut Schoen had been manager of a League club, he would have been quite entitled to hold a serious Monday morning inquest. Hurst had been totally unmarked when he met Bobby Moore's free-kick to score his first goal; for his second, the famous underside-of-the-bar effort, he had been allowed to turn and shoot barely ten yards from goal; and the West Germany defence had been caught hopelessly square as he broke through for his third.

Other goals of note were seen to be similarly deceptive. Allan Clarke's forceful header that won Leeds the 1972 FA Cup Final was acclaimed by the fans, but the professionals would point to Bob McNab's mistimed tackle that allowed Mick Jones to cross the ball.

Johann Cruyff took the headlines throughout

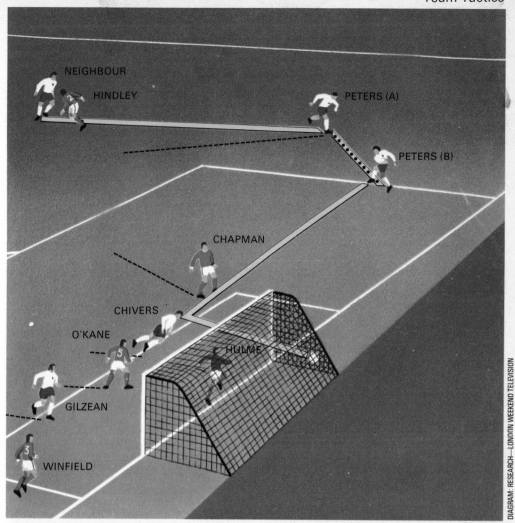

Top Diagram showing Martin Chivers scoring for Spurs against Nottingham Forest in October 1971. The match was televised, and at the end of the season this goal was one of six selected in a competition to decide the season's 'Golden Goal'. Despite the quality of Chivers' header, the effort was placed sixth because it owed so much to the inadequacies of Forest's defence. As Jimmy Neighbour collected the ball on the left touchline, Martin Peters was allowed to run unattended forward of Neighbour. The winger slipped the ball to him and Peters cut in to hit across a centre.

Above Chivers dived in front of a static defence to turn the ball past the exposed Eric Hulme.

Europe with his two goals for Ajax against Inter-Milan in the 1972 European Cup final. But on both occasions his task was simplified by goal-keeping errors from Bordon.

Fritz Kunzli caught the eye when England played Switzerland in 1971 in the European Championship, scoring the second Swiss goal with a perfectly executed near post header. Yet he had dashed in front of a static Bobby Moore to reach the ball.

It was difficult to find fault with the technique of Rodney Marsh's scoring volley when playing for England against Wales in the British Championship at Cardiff in May 1972. England had been unable to impress their supremacy on a poor Welsh side until Malcolm Macdonald, challenging for Peter Storey's centre, nudged the ball back into Marsh's path. Marsh, always willing to attempt the extravagant, drove it

sweetly first time past goalkeeper Gary Sprake. But Sprake had good reason to ask why Storey was virtually unchallenged as he centred and why there was no player within tackling distance of Marsh as Macdonald, who had little alternative, deflected the ball to him.

Television was invaluable in this respect. Action replays enabled managers to trace the build up and their immediate criticisms were often confirmed by the slow-motion camera. For instance, it seemed as though George Best had scored a great goal to end Sheffield United's heady, unbeaten run in the First Division as a newly promoted team in 1971.

Sheffield had just replaced their injured left-back Ted Hemsley, when Best turned on a loose ball just inside Manchester United's half. He chose to run on and there was immediate panic in the Sheffield defence. Instead of shunting Best

across field, defenders flew at him to be destroyed by superb close control at top speed.

Had Hemsley still been on the field the danger might have been avoided. But his deputy, Gil Reece, was a forward and he committed a forward's indiscretion. He sold himself too, and Best was in on goal at the right-hand corner of Sheffield's goal area.

The final mistake was made by goalkeeper John Hope. Instead of giving Best the problem of deciding between a shot or a dribble, he galloped from his line and was still scrambling in search of the ball as the Irishman chipped it across him into the far side of the goal.

It was instantly acclaimed as another indelible moment in Best's colourful career. It was un-doubtedly an example of immense talent. But a repeat showing merely proved that goals were not always what they seemed to be.

Coaching: Learn how to stop conceding 'bad' goals

Generally goals are conceded because of one or a combination of four reasons: lack of pressure applied to the player in possession; lack of support for the player applying the pressure leaving even numbers; failing to track down a player moving forward into a dangerous position; and giving the ball away in your back third of the field.

The first consideration defensively is the goal and this will affect play in every part of the field. Players in the immediate vicinity of the ball must apply pressure and also supply sufficient support so that one-against-one situations are eliminated. Their job is to delay the play in order to give players deeper and further away time to organize themselves so that they can 'balance' the defence; they cover not only the dangerous area some 20 yards in front of goal but are also positioned to apply pressure to attackers should the play be switched.

The second consideration, having lost posses-sion, is to be immediately aware of the space between defending players and, even more important, the space behind them. This supporting position means that the player applying pressure can do so with an aggressive attitude without playing himself out of the game, knowing fully well that a colleague is some little distance away helping him. If he is outnumbered, then he should withdraw from the play and attempt to delay an attacker from getting behind him.

The third consideration is that the nearer the attackers get to your goal the more closely they must be marked. It is generally, then, a violation of one or more of these defensive principles that lead to goals being scored.

The idea, defensively, is to make it as difficult as possible for the team in possession to play. If a player has full possession of the ball, unless an opponent is hustling him, he is able to go and do exactly as he pleases. But if an opponent gets at him aggressively, and puts him under pressure, then he must do things that much more hurriedly; this is likely to make him much more inaccurate with his passing or shooting.

First-class teams find a balance; they attack when the situation is right and they defend when it is necessary, and when that time arrives they do it like a team fighting for its life. These qualities are brought about and developed during their training and coaching sessions with as much importance attached to the defensive as to the

offensive part of the game.

Start with one against one, working across the pitch. One player has the ball and dribbles across whilst the other player concerns himself with jockeying, keeping himself within distance but not allowing the player in possession to go by. Jockeying in this way, you will soon begin to realize that by closing down at an angle you can force your opponent over in the direction that you want him to go and that you can make him play it with his indifferent foot by attacking his good foot.

Having gained some knowledge and experience of jockeying and closing down, ask your friend to attack a target working in an area about 10 yards wide and 20 yards long. This will give you experience of working in close and positioning yourself for the tackle. Pass the ball to your friend from the end you are defending so that he has to make a control before attacking the target. Immediately you have passed the ball, close him down quickly and at an angle, adopting an aggressive attitude in order to stop him getting a run at you. As you come close, approach cautiously so that you are not caught rushing in at him making it easy for him to dribble past you. Approach him so that you force him over towards one of the lines. This is a cat-and-mouse game of hustling your opponent into an error, giving you a chance to tackle or making it very difficult for

Below Trevor Brooking chips an imaginative goal past Pat Jennings at Upton Park. But indecisive defensive play by centre-half Peter Collins had allowed Brooking the chance to get in his shot.
Bottom Tight marking prevents many 'bad' goals. As a defender, practise by playing one-against-one across the pitch, concentrating on not letting your opponent dribble the ball past you.

SOUTHEND EVENING ECHO

him to knock the ball past you. You must present as big a target as possible when you approach: bend your knees slightly keeping your centre of gravity as low to the ground as is comfortably possible, but do not spread your feet too wide in case he 'nutmegs' you (knocks it through your legs); hold your arms slightly to the side and bend them so that you resemble an aggressive, frighten-ing figure of a man determined to stop an opponent from playing. You must be prepared for sudden movements which are aimed at deceiving you. Watch the ball carefully and do not be taken in by body movements. Study your opponent care-fully because most players have a habit of doing the same thing before they pass or attempt to take you on. Try to recognize these movements because they might help you to anticipate.

Working to the same principles, play two-against-two in a slightly larger area, with small goals. Remember here that when the opposing team have the ball you are either applying pressure or supporting your team-mate who is busy closing down on the opponent in possession. The most important lesson you will learn here is that as the attacking team work closer to your goal, the tighter must be the marking. An attacker does not necessarily have to take you on to get a shot in; all he has to do is knock the ball to one side and quickly make a shooting angle for himself or pass it to his team-mate who can take a first-time shot at goal. With this in mind you must be prepared to get a foot in or to block the shot with your body.

This game is very demanding and should only be played for short periods. Stop occasionally and talk about it; try to communicate between one another when you are defending. Another important lesson to be learnt here is that when the opposing team intercepts the ball and your team-mate is out of the game delay is vital and the area behind you is sacred. If you allow opponents in there you are dead. You must with-draw from the play and try to delay as much as possible to give time for your team-mate to recover. If, however, the opponents attack you quickly, you must encourage them to play it wide away from goal or put yourself in a position that makes it necessary for one of them to beat you with the ball, giving you a chance of a tackle. It would be of little value retreating on to your goal-line; you will have to make a stand at a distance from goal that makes it difficult for them to get in a shot.

Too much time cannot be spent at this type of practice. It will help stop your team conceding 'bad' goals.

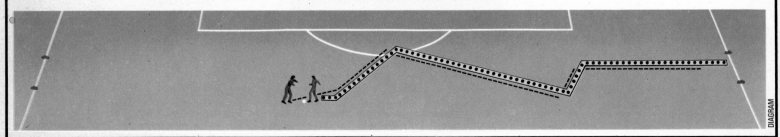

DIAGRAM